F. SCOTT FITZGERALD

in the Twenty-first Century

F. SCOTT FITZGERALD
in the Twenty-first Century

EDITED BY
JACKSON R. BRYER,
RUTH PRIGOZY,
AND MILTON R. STERN

THE UNIVERSITY OF ALABAMA PRESS   *Tuscaloosa and London*

Typeface: Bembo

∞

The paper on which this book is printed meets the minimum requirements of American
National Standard for Information Science–Permanence of Paper for Printed Library
Materials, ANSI Z39.48-1984.

Library of Congress Cataloging-in-Publication Data

International F. Scott Fitzgerald Conference (1996 : Princeton University)
    F. Scott Fitzgerald in the twenty-first century / edited by Jackson R. Bryer, Ruth
Prigozy, and Milton R. Stern.
        p.   cm.
Collected essays of the International F. Scott Fitzgerald Conference held at Princeton
University in 1996.
Includes bibliographical references and index.
    ISBN 0-8173-1216-1 (cloth : alk. paper)
    1. Fitzgerald, F. Scott (Francis Scott), 1896–1940—Criticism and interpretation—
Congresses. I. Bryer, Jackson R. II. Prigozy, Ruth. III. Stern, Milton R. IV. Title.

    PS3511.I9 Z667 1996
    813'.52—dc21

                                                    2002009352

British Library Cataloguing-in-Publication Data available

CONTENTS

ILLUSTRATIONS

ACKNOWLEDGMENTS

Ronald Berman and Scott Donaldson gave us expert advice about revising the essays in this book. Marc Singer helped prepare the manuscript. The staff at The University of Alabama Press expressed confidence and displayed patience throughout the development and production of the manuscript. Jonathan Lawrence provided invaluable copyediting.

Unless otherwise noted, the illustrations in the essay by Anne Margaret Daniel are from the Manuscripts Division or from University Archives, Department of Rare Books and Special Collections, Princeton University Library.

Details from the illustration by Stan Hart and Mort Drucker, "The Great Gasbag," *Mad,* no. 172 (January 1975): 4–10, are used by permission of *MAD Magazine,* copyright © 1974 E. C. Publications, Inc. All rights reserved.

"Fitzgerald: The Authority of Failure" by Morris Dickstein previously appeared in *The American Scholar* (Spring 2000).

F. SCOTT FITZGERALD
in the Twenty-first Century

Introduction

On May 20, 1940, in a plea well known to every scholar of American literature, Fitzgerald wrote to his editor, Maxwell Perkins, to ask about the possibility of a reprint of *The Great Gatsby*. He was desperately unsettled in prospects, family, finances, and even in residence—the return address was in care of the Phil Berg Agency while Fitzgerald was in a West Coast transit from his Amestoy Avenue address in Encino to his new and, sadly, final address on Laurel Avenue in Hollywood.

The desolate quality of his query expressed the bleakness of his situation: "Would the 25-cent press keep *Gatsby* in the public eye—or *is the book unpopular?*" he asked. "Has it *had* its chance? Would a popular reissue in that series with a preface *not* by me but by one of its admirers—I can maybe pick one—make it a favorite with classrooms, profs, lovers of English prose—anybody? But to die, so completely and unjustly after having given so much!" (*Letters* 288). The poor son of a bitch, one wants to say of neglected Scott Fitzgerald, as Owl Eyes said of neglected Jay Gatsby at his funeral. Two wunderkinder, one dying, one dead—and how ironically sad that only posthumously have they been anything but neglected in the immense richness and effect of their radiance and their worldwide reputations.

In the sixty-three years between the letter to Perkins and the publication of this volume, thousands of commentaries—books, essays, articles—have been published in English on Fitzgerald and his works, and other studies as well as translations of his writings have been published in various languages all over the world. Fitzgerald has appeared on a United

States postage stamp. Dick Diver, like Jay Gatsby, has become a widely familiar metaphor for many aspects of "the American." Through cartoons, comic strips, magazine articles, movies, clothing emporia, bars, and restaurants (and even a posh "Fitzgerald" condominium across the road from Fitzgerald's beloved Hotel Belles-Rives in Juan-les-Pins), as well as in seriously comprehensive studies of modern Western literature and American literature and civilization, Fitzgerald's life, wife, works, and characters figure prominently. As for "classrooms, profs, lovers of English prose—anybody," almost every college course in twentieth-century American literature as well as courses in introduction to literature or introduction to fiction include *The Great Gatsby,* and increasing numbers contain *Tender Is the Night.*

As the second millennium of the Common Era drew to a close, one of the many inevitable and foolish (but fun) lists of the hundred "best" or "worst" or "most" or "least" of this or that ranked *The Great Gatsby* second only to James Joyce's *Ulysses* in a Random House decree about the hundred best books of the twentieth century. A "group of mostly female, 20-something future publishers at Radcliffe College," stung by the omission of several female authors, composed a competing list, and for *first* place chose—*The Great Gatsby* (Kruse, "Teaching Fitzgerald's *Tender Is the Night*" 251). Fitzgerald, Zelda, and *Gatsby*'s characters have become not only classroom staples but also household words and popular concepts. Now no presentation of the period between the two world wars neglects F. Scott Fitzgerald, which is a consummation sometimes devoutly to be unwished amidst the silliness and shallowness of the popularization.

In 1996, in centennial commemoration of Fitzgerald's birth, there were celebrations, both academic and popular, of Francis Scott Key Fitzgerald's secure place not merely as a popular icon but as the creator of some of the most compelling short stories, one of the most poignantly promising fragments, and two of the most enthralling novels in American literature, as well as of some of the most just and beautiful passages of English prose. With Fitzgerald, as with Hawthorne, Melville, Twain, Whitman, Dickinson, Faulkner, or any other American author of lasting international stature, there will not be an end to new insights, new appreciations, and new arguments. Because the work of great writers is what it is, there will continue to be fresh responses to it as long as people continue to read and come anew to it through time. And as long as collections of commentary are not stale repetitions of observations too often made, they will not require justification. Like the literature they discuss, they will be, as Emerson said of beauty, their "own excuse for being."

Among the 1996 commemorative festivals, and under the aegis of the F. Scott Fitzgerald Society, the International F. Scott Fitzgerald Conference at Princeton University drew together from various countries a group of widely recognized commentators. Freely engaging in give-and-take, these scholars and teachers participated in the ongoing continuum of Fitzgerald commentary through their several recognitions of Fitzgerald's work and Fitzgerald criticism. This volume offers a selection of those essays, with the one exception of the posthumous publication of Stanley Brodwin's non-conference essay, "F. Scott Fitzgerald and Willa Cather: A New Study," included here because it is a splendid example of studies of the connections between writings by different authors. Brodwin did not live to guide his essay through publication, and it sees the light of day here. The subjects of these essays reflect the conferees' wish to shine new light on less frequently discussed aspects of Fitzgerald's work: there is only one essay here on *The Great Gatsby* and none on *Tender Is the Night*.

The essays are presented here generally in the chronological order of Fitzgerald's works, beginning with *This Side of Paradise* and closing with *The Last Tycoon*. However, the editors have chosen to place essays together with their clearly substantive companions so that discussions of Fitzgerald's Catholicism are grouped together, whatever the work under discussion. Because the editors have favored an organically flexible structure rather than an undeviating one, the placement of essays reveals a clear but not rigid chronological line.

The opening essay is Anne Margaret Daniel's reconstruction, out of the pages of its student newspaper, of the Princeton University in which young F. Scott Fitzgerald, John Peale Bishop, and Edmund Wilson matriculated. *The Prince* indicates a campus in transition to "a community mobilizing for military service." Daniel documents Fitzgerald's undergraduate development as a writer and indicates his future use of materials first touched at Princeton: "When Fitzgerald left Princeton in 1917 for Fort Leavenworth, the emphasis on campus life and the frolic-filled development of the undergraduate had shifted completely toward the outside world, including international affairs, and maturity."

Daniel's materials point toward Fitzgerald's discovery of war as a lasting theme through much of his fiction. Edward Gillin, Walter Raubicheck, Stephen L. Tanner, and Kirk Curnutt discuss other concerns that rise and remain with the young Fitzgerald. In "Princeton, Pragmatism, and Fitzgerald's Sentimental Journey," Gillin suggests that Fitzgerald had a strong sense of time, experience, and discontinuity as defined by William James. James's ideas on pragmatism became an increasing intellectual force in American thought and college curricula during the second decade of the twentieth century and were an established influence by the 1920s.[1] However, "as *This Side of Paradise* reveals, F. Scott Fitzgerald committed himself to no such pragmatist understanding" when it came to his concept of the self. There Fitzgerald's context was much closer to the idealistic concept of a fundamental essence of morality and identity.

Raubicheck and Tanner define that idealism and essence as a persisting Catholicism, despite the secular, agnostic facades adopted by the young Fitzgerald in *This Side of Paradise*. Raubicheck acknowledges that implicit in Amory's final claim of knowing only himself "is a disaffection from all belief systems, from Catholicism to the pseudo-Marxism Amory casually expounds towards the close of the novel." But granting that, Raubicheck presents specifics for the argument that Fitzgerald's Catholic sense of "moral revulsion from sin" becomes "a means to deepen the glow of his romanticism." Tanner examines the contemporary implications of the presence of the devil in Fitzgerald's first novel and concludes that "Fitzgerald, though a lapsed Catholic, nevertheless believed . . . that the territory this side of paradise is territory held largely by the devil. His portrayal of a young man's struggle with a diminishing sense of evil during the beginning years of the twentieth century is instructive as we confront challenging postmodern complications of the problem of evil at the beginning of the twenty-first century."

In "Youth Culture and the Spectacle of Waste: *This Side of Paradise* and *The Beautiful and Damned*," Kirk Curnutt approaches the dark side of Fitzgerald's early books from a perspective in which the defining evil is the flamboyant wastage of youth. Examining the Victorian concept of youth as a temporally determinate training period for success, Curnutt finds that "not only do these novels critique outmoded Victorian ideals of maturation, but they explore the ambiguous power that flagrant displays of youth styles afford young people. Most intriguingly, these works reflect the anxiety of a burgeoning age-consciousness that encouraged the young to maximize their youth before losing it to middle age." Using this as a basis for Fitzgerald's modernist context, Curnutt develops instructive insight into an essential difference between the author's first two novels. Fitzgerald foresaw the ascendance and prevalence of youth culture in America and revealed all the deadly shortcomings underlying its attractions.

Examination of *The Beautiful and Damned* leads into two essays on women in Fitzgerald's work. Michael Nowlin's discussion of H. L. Mencken's *In Defense of Women* and Fitzgerald's second novel brings Mencken's ideas about the sexes to their corollary in Lacan, and from there to a highly original analysis of *The Beautiful and Damned*. That tale suggests "that the continual lure of bourgeois marriage lies in its ironically false promise to repair a sense of fundamental deprivation peculiar to men but affecting both genders, a sense of deprivation that issues in fantasies of possessing and of being possessed by a being who has what one lacks." Gloria's story is that of a loss, through marriage, of her courtly-romantic power as Woman. Similarly revealing the emphasis of literary criticism on class and sex in the last three decades of the twentieth century, Mary McAleer Balkun offers a socioeconomic analysis of dating, petting, vamping, sex, and marriage in the Josephine stories: "Considered from the perspective of the sexual economy . . . a social system that situates women as sexual objects to be possessed and as consumers without independent means or power . . . the Josephine stories represent Fitzgerald's first complete development of the concept of emotional bankruptcy and his earliest actual use of the term."

In "Pastoral Mode and Language in *The Great Gatsby*," Janet Giltrow and David Stouck look at Fitzgerald's most famous novel in a context of literary-historical traditions. They "use, in addition to traditional accounts of English syntax, techniques from discourse analysis and linguistic pragmatics . . . to investigate features of Fitzgerald's style." In so doing, the authors "look at how Nick attends to . . . another order of experience, one beyond his immediate social habitat, an order stable, profound, original," which they "equate with the pastoral mode."

"The typical Fitzgerald manuscript—with its usual amount of rewriting—always constitutes a definite invitation to reconstruct the process of composition and to relate it to the author's immediate biographical situation and circumstances." Thus Horst H. Kruse justifies his scrutiny of "'A Full Life,' a comparatively recent addition to the Fitzgerald canon." In his careful examination, Kruse makes an argument for reconsidering the fantasy as an allegorical version of Fitzgerald's sense of the relationship between his art and his flapper heroine, as well as his sense of how he and that relationship failed each other.

Stanley Brodwin's "F. Scott Fitzgerald and Willa Cather: A New Study" and Veronica Makowsky's "Noxious Nostalgia: Fitzgerald, Faulkner, and the Legacy of Plantation Fiction" widen the view observed from the landscape of individual works. Brodwin focuses not simply on similarities in style, but rather on the two authors' philosophical approaches to a subject both treat memorably: nostalgia and an elegiac commentary on history. Cather "gained control over her art and vision because ultimately she was able to fuse her informed sense of the past with nostalgia for the self's personal history: the longing for youth . . . and the longing for the shared communal past of . . . national history." Fitzgerald's power, on the other hand, "resided in his nostalgia for the history of the self and its quest for the 'ineffably gorgeous' rather than Cather's compulsive need to re-create a place or phase of national history." Makowsky details the complexity of Faulkner's and Fitzgerald's response to southern plantation life as compared to nostalgia in the origins of the plantation-myth tradition, especially in works like "Marse Chan" by Thomas Nelson Page. There is a fundament of bitterness, disillusioned and disillusioning, in the Faulkner and Fitzgerald fictions Makowsky uses for comparison. The two authors share Americans' "love-hate fascination with the South, particularly with the mixture of fact and fantasy known as the plantation South. . . . Our great writers not only present the South *both* as American dream and as American nightmare but also are intensely aware of the artist's ambiguous role in creating, perpetuating, and criticizing these myths," as we see in "The Diamond as Big as the Ritz," and Faulkner's novel *Absalom, Absalom!* (1936).

D. G. Kehl and M. Thomas Inge approach the topic of Fitzgerald and humor from inside and out. From inside Fitzgerald's writings, Kehl has Thalia doing the Charleston in a restorative essay that addresses a quality almost always overlooked in Fitzgerald studies: Fitzgerald was often funny. He had a bright comic sense. Although "humor may not have 'saved' Fitzgerald, as Thurber lamented, it may have saved his art." "Perhaps now," Kehl observes, "nearly six decades after his death, it may be possible to praise Fitzgerald's comic genius without a priori assumptions of patronizing derogation." From outside, in popular culture, seeing Fitzgerald through other people's humor in "F. Scott Fitzgerald in the Funny Papers: The Commentary of Mickey Mouse and Charlie Brown," Inge offers a brief illustrated summary of the extent to which the "various reflections and uses of Fitzgerald in the comics . . . [are] commentaries on his fiction and his importance in American culture. They are comments of praise in that they recognize the integral part Fitzgerald's work plays in our culture and the centrality of a book like *The Great Gatsby* to an understanding of our literary heritage. They are compliments to the reader because they assume . . . knowledge of some of the classic writing to be found in our literature. They are acknowledgments of Fitzgerald, not just as an icon in a period of time in our history, but as a continuing influential force on the products of the American imagination."

The Civil War as a point of reference in several of Fitzgerald's writings has been noted briefly in various studies. In an extended essay dedicated to the subject, Frederick Wegener documents and illuminates its complexity. He finds that there turn out to have been more Civil Wars for Fitzgerald than one: "not only the Civil War of romance and of realism, but also the Civil War in the North and in the South, the Civil War as tragical or farcical, the Civil War in fact and in memory, and the Civil War as actuality and as represented or reconstituted in writing." Fitzgerald's "lifelong engagement with the Civil War . . . came to perform an essential role in the development not only of Fitzgerald's historical awareness but also of his experience of the writer's life and of his aesthetic understanding as a whole."

In our culturally and politically diverse world, of all topics concerning a writer, few are as intriguing as their reputation abroad. Toshifumi Miyawaki presents a charming narrative of Scott Fitzgerald's Japanese afterlife in "The Writer for a Writer: F. Scott Fitzgerald and Haruki Murakami." Formerly "the Japanese public knew . . . [Fitzgerald] in this partial and superficial way until the early 1980s, when a young writer [Haruki Murakami] made his debut and, while writing his own novels, also began to introduce Fitzgerald and his works. This young writer . . . helped change the stereotyped image of Fitzgerald and introduced a truer face." Because of "Murakami, in Japan Fitzgerald is a more familiar name among the universal masters of literature, gaining new and ever wider readership."

These studies of the nature of Fitzgerald's manuscripts, the relationships between Fitzgerald's work and that of other authors, Fitzgerald and humor, Fitzgerald and the Civil War, and Fitzgerald's reputation abroad cut across the range of Fitzgerald's work and form a connection between his early and late writings. Looking at the work Fitzgerald did during the closing months of his life, both Christopher Ames and Tim Prchal focus on the Pat Hobby stories. In "Pat Hobby and the Fictions of the Hollywood Writer," Ames discusses the significance of the stories' plots and structure. This oddly "self-referential" series of stories is one in which "the plots . . . mirror the plots Pat invents within them." And "when we identify the narrative characteristics of these stories—their brevity, their clichéd plots, their predictable structures—we should get the ironic point: they satirize similar conventions in motion pictures and they satirize, by example, the degraded state of Pat Hobby's narrative imagination." Tim Prchal examines the relationship between narrative technique and a market economy in "Tune in Next Month: Fitzgerald's Pat Hobby and the Popular Series." Identifying the need for repetition in serial magazine fiction, Prchal also cautions that "Fitzgerald has not simply created a flat character and placed him within a narrative genre made popular in mass media. Rather, he has cast Hobby in this type of story to portray the incapacity for growth suffered by a character immersed in mass-market fiction."

Two essays round out the collection: Morris Dickstein, in an overview of Fitzgerald's career, muses on the last development of the author's theme; Milton R. Stern, in an examination of Fitzgerald's expressive mode, comments on the last development of the author's style. Beginning where Anne Margaret Daniel's opening essay left off, Dickstein surmises that what "most claims our attention today" actually "may not be the lyrical, romantic Fitzgerald" of "early success, romantic possibility, and nostalgic regret," but the "writing of F. Scott Fitzgerald's last decade, when the lyrical dreamer gave way to the disillusioned realist with his chastened sense of maturity." In parallel with Dickstein's suggestions, Stern traces the vector of Fitzgerald's style, observing that "from the very birth of Fitzgerald's identity as a novelist, the scenarist was beginning to emerge from the lyricist, eventually to become a co-equal and, finally, the senior partner." Fitzgerald managed "to retain his signature power of compelling evocation even as his style moved closer to the *Esquire* aspect of modernism that characterized the circumambient current of his times."

As this collection, continuing commentary, international popularity, and the sales of Fitzgerald's books indicate, the apt last words about Fitzgerald's work were hardly his own despairing "But to die, so completely and unjustly after having given so much!" But, unknowingly, Fitzgerald did write apt last words about his body of work. The last sentence he ever wrote to Maxwell Perkins closed the postscript to a letter of December 13, 1940 (*Letters* 290–91), in which he asked about the sale of the plates of *This Side of Paradise* and discussed his progress on *The Last Tycoon*. Those two works were the perfect reference, for they were to be his alpha and omega, spanning the full output of the "so much" he had given. Fitzgerald's final, inadvertently adumbrative sentence to Perkins understates what he was never to know: the loving admiration and praise the world would come to heap upon the gift of that full output. The close of Fitzgerald's postscript about his work was, "I think it has a chance for a new life."

Jackson R. Bryer
Ruth Prigozy
Milton R. Stern
September 15, 2002

Note

1. The most comprehensive treatment of the subject is Berman, *"The Great Gatsby" and Fitzgerald's World of Ideas.*

I

"Blue as the Sky, Gentlemen"

Fitzgerald's Princeton through *The Prince*

ANNE MARGARET DANIEL

F. Scott Fitzgerald attended Princeton University from the fall of 1913 until the fall of 1917. During these years, an academic setting preparing young men for lives as New York financiers, Philadelphia lawyers, and Washington politicians became a community mobilizing for military service. The concept of a world remade by war recurs in nearly all Fitzgerald's writings, and Princeton's own campus transition is clearly and thoroughly traced through the local coverage in the student newspaper, *The Daily Princetonian*.[1] *The Prince* is an excellent, and arguably the only objectively accurate, contemporary record of Fitzgerald's time at Princeton, detailing the constant and changing interests on campus, what Fitzgerald and his peers found available at the university, and what Fitzgerald himself actually did while in residence there. In those issues of *The Prince* from Fitzgerald's freshman and sophomore years of 1913–15, the most important and impression-forming years for any undergraduate,[2] there is the story of a boy's rise to prominence—literarily, dramatically, and socially—on an elite campus. But by 1916 and 1917 it is clear from *The Prince* that individual and local events were nothing next to the terrible crisis in Europe. Princeton's focus, and the direction in which its privileged students were bound, had changed utterly.

The central role of *The Prince* at Fitzgerald's fictitious Princeton is familiar from *This Side of Paradise*. Amory Blaine's poor academic performance, indicated by that sky-blue grade sheet from the registrar's office, costs him his chance to make the editorial board on *The Prince*. This causes the young egotist to reconsider his Princeton options and

Fitzgerald as a Princeton undergraduate.

Courtesy of Princeton University Library.

future; for after Amory's early disappointment at football, he realizes that "being on the board of the 'Daily Princetonian'" would get him "a good deal." Writing for the humor magazine, the *Princeton Tiger* (as Fitzgerald did), is not something Amory deems a worthy alternative, while "writing for the 'Nassau Literary Magazine'" (as Fitzgerald and his friends John Peale Bishop '17 and Edmund Wilson '16 did) "would get him nothing" (49).

When young Scott Fitzgerald arrived at Princeton in September 1913 to begin his freshman year, the major (though not only) campus publication was *The Daily Princetonian*. Since 1876 *The Prince* had covered international and national news as well as local matters, but its focus, as with most campus dailies, was on Princeton college events. Appropriately, *The Prince*'s editor in chief, James Bruce '14, was selected to introduce all the non-academic and non-athletic organizations to Fitzgerald's class at the Freshman Reception, for *The Prince* would continue to inform students about most of their extracurricular possibilities at Princeton.[3]

Those possibilities were all too plentiful, even for lowly freshmen. At the above-mentioned reception in 1913, "Princeton songs and cheers" were practiced between the speeches (*9/27/13*), as one could not be too ready for football season. The "Freshman's Bible" detailing undergraduate life was just that; it was the young men's immediate responsibility to learn about their new world and their place in it.[4] Freshmen in 1913 were still subject to the quasi-official institution of "horsing," perhaps born of the colloquialism "horsing around" and best translated as a year-long hazing by the sophomores—the formal freshman initiation into Princeton. There was much debate in *The Prince* that year about horsing; the Senior Council voted to abolish the "old custom" in the spring of 1914 (*4/23/14*). Some of the strict campus roles with origins in horsing (and all manner of unofficial hazing) nevertheless continued until after World War II (and, perhaps, up to today). In sartorial matters, freshmen had to wear a black skullcap, the "beanie," until late May (when straw hats were allowed); they could not wear their trousers rolled, "shirts with soft collars," "fancy vests," or the school colors. From 1748, blue, purple, and gold had been associated with Princeton; orange, with a slightly later addition of black, became the school color in the year of Fitzgerald's birth, 1896.

When it came to public behavior on campus, freshmen were subject to a host of prohibitions. They could not walk along Prospect Avenue ("the Street," site of the upperclass eating clubs), had a 9 P.M. curfew until Washington's Birthday, could not sit around the pelican sundial in McCosh courtyard, and could not smoke pipes or cigars outdoors (*12/12/13*). Amory Blaine breaks every one of these rules during the "Spires and Gargoyles" chapter of *This Side of Paradise*. Indoor smoking, though, was downright encouraged. Every week, there were several "smokers" (informal meetings) on varied topics noted in *The Prince;* cigarette and tobacco ads for Bull Durham, Velvet, and Fatimas fill the paper. In a letter to his daughter Scottie, written around 1939, Fitzgerald cautioned her not to start smoking: "I didn't begin to be a heavy smoker until I was a sophomore but it took just one year to send me into tuberculosis and cast a shadow that has been extremely long. . . . I don't want to bury you in your debut dress" (*Letters* 50).

Fitzgerald (*left*) wearing his Princeton freshman beanie.

Courtesy of Princeton University Library.

Rules did not prevent the freshmen, even when confined to campus, from drinking, either. The bars of Princeton were legally closed to minors, and the eating clubs, as a matter of record, insisted that drink was not provided to underage members on the premises. Yet the great number of *Prince* editorials on "Bacchanalian revelry" (e.g., *10/31/13*) and the ease of obtaining liquor on campus—one piece on this cites Edgar Allan Poe and Jack London as rather fatal alcohol authorities (*12/15/13*)—would lead one to believe that such "revelry" was not uncommon. Glenway Westcott would wonder bitterly, in 1941, whether upperclassmen at Princeton taught the young Fitzgerald "a manly technique of drinking" (Wilson, *Crack-up* 329)—the answer is yes. John Peale Bishop and Charles "Sap" Donahoe, another Princeton friend,

Cottage Club.

Courtesy of Garrick Grobler.

both felt upon their first readings of *This Side of Paradise* that the most accurate portions of the book, including Dick Humbird's death, dealt with drinking (Bruccoli and Duggan 35, 49).

Organized on-campus activities included sports, the campus publications, various musical and dramatic organizations (including the mandolin and banjo clubs), and the eating clubs, for which sophomores were (and still are, in the case of the "selective" clubs) chosen during a stressful competition called March "bicker." Fitzgerald would be invited to join the University Cottage Club, or Cottage—as he described it, "where I eat, and where I loaf" (Bruccoli and Duggan 14)—in March 1916. Much public campus entertainment centered around the major sports events, the fall football games. The Harvard game weekend of

1913 featured a long program by the schools' combined musical groups and clubs (headlined in *The Prince* as a "Pretentious Program in Alexander Hall" and boasting popular songs with titles like "Little Sunflower Coon" and "Mr. 'Melican Man," which we would deem politically incorrect today). The annual Senior Dance was that weekend; open to all classes, it went from supper through a breakfast to be brought down by a New York caterer. Additional train service was provided to Princeton from New York (*11/7/13; 11/8/13 [game extra]*), and traffic was completely closed off on Nassau Street, still unpaved at the time—it was paved for $29,000 during the summer of 1914 (*1/12/14; 9/24/15*).

Apart from the football games, always the biggest sports events of the year, professional baseball was popular on campus. The World Series was well reported in *The Prince,* and advertisements featured the likes of Christy Mathewson and Ty Cobb, generally peddling cigarettes. In the spring of 1915, a front-page *Prince* article reminded students to arrive early at the baseball field to see the Princeton varsity hosting the New York Yankees for an afternoon game (the Yankees crushed their hosts, 11–2; *4/12–13/15*).

All this extracurricular work and entertainment could have disastrous effects on an undergraduate's academic performance. The number, though not the names, of young men dropped from the university for failing classes was published each semester in *The Prince.* These unfortunates could work off the failing "conditions" by taking certain exams in the near future and, by passing the exams, be returned to official enrollment. Eleven freshmen from Fitzgerald's class failed out of school after fall semester (*3/13/14*), and in September 1915 *The Prince* ran an advertisement that is quite poignant, if one has Fitzgerald in mind at all: "Special Notice to Students Who Fail / Motion Picture Studio Work opens an almost immediate field for substantial earnings to young men who possess some natural ability" (*9/25/15*). Though Fitzgerald's record at Princeton was, to put it mildly, far from stellar—his mediocre-to-poor transcript survives in the Fitzgerald Papers in Princeton's Firestone Library—he was not officially among those dropped from the college for academic reasons.[5]

Special events of 1913 began with the opening of the Graduate College in October. From the beginning of the month until October 22, the date of the opening exercises, *The Prince* ran several columns about the academic and political personalities who would attend, chief among them former president William Howard Taft, then a Yale law professor. Woodrow Wilson '79 was unable to leave his official duties—being president, that is—and Teddy Roosevelt was in South America. The Philadelphia Orchestra, with "Leopold Stokewski [*sic*]" conducting, was brought up for the occasion, and many of the visiting academics that week at Princeton gave lectures on matters ranging from "The Present Position of Classical Studies in England" to "The Relation of Science and Culture" (*10/21/13*).

Science and culture were among the topics most lectured upon during Fitzgerald's first two years at Princeton. The freshman class of 1913 was the first to be subjected not only to a physical exam but also to something called "psychodetic" recording. While hooked up to the relevant "apparatus," which unhappily is not described in *The Prince,* a student was tested for "standards of speed and accuracy in certain practical things; such as responding to a given signal" (*11/11/13*). Mental health, along with physical coordination, was stressed as important by biology professor Stewart Paton '86, who warned undergraduates in 1914 of the "2,000,000 Maniacs" loose in the nation during the first of a sweepingly named series of lectures on "Human Activities in Relation to Social, Educational and Ethical Problems" (*2/12/14*).

Racial issues were also discussed at Princeton during these times, often under the aegis of science, and in a decidedly opinionated manner. When the sociologist E. A. Ross spoke on "The Comparative Value of Races" in early 1914, he insisted that prejudice "with respect to the backward races"—that is, *all* non-Caucasian ones—was wrong, but that it would still make ultimate sense for American policies to promote the annexing of lands inhabited by such races. In Ross's words, "the Monroe Doctrine enables [a] million and a third persons mostly of Indian blood to possess Ecuador, which could easily sustain fifty millions of people. In the hands of England or Germany Ecuador would provide room for the expansion of the white race" (*3/23/14*). University professor Conklin, speaking on "Heredity and Eugenics" in early 1914, complained that "all the attention . . . that has been fixed on education and environment" should rightly "be given to improvements of heredity and Eugenics," since the latter were far more important in human determination and development than the former (*2/26/14*). In a later lecture on "The Phenomena of Heredity," Conklin concluded that "the growing conflict between racial obligations and the desire for individual freedom is a serious menace to mankind," a question not just of "genetics but also one of ethics" (4/15/14).

Fitzgerald evidently attended, or took note of, these lectures. The ideas they engendered interested him, and they reappear in the debate Burne and Amory have in *This Side of Paradise* over the superior characteristics of blond men (140–41) and in Fitzgerald's own Triangle song, written the next fall for *Fie! Fie! Fi-Fi!* and entitled "Love or Eugenics." In 1921, Fitzgerald sent Zelda's father, Judge Sayre, an inscribed copy of the staggeringly entitled *The Trend of the Race: A Study of Present Tendencies in the Biological Development of Mankind,* by Samuel J. Holmes. Fitzgerald's inscription read, in part, "This is too long a mouthful but it's most interesting to me."[6]

Religion, like race and ethics, was also a "science" at this old Presbyterian school in Fitzgerald's day. Dr. J. M. T. Finney '84 lectured Fitzgerald's freshman class in 1913 on "personal hygiene," or what might once have been called "clean living." Finney's manifesto was that it "is the duty of every man not only to himself but to his God, to civilization, to his children and to the woman that he hopes to marry someday that he should live a clean life" (10/6/13). Students were required to keep and turn in "hygiene notebooks" with their final spring examinations, and could claim them, or permit them to be destroyed, the following fall (10/28/13). Fitzgerald's does not appear to have survived. President John Grier Hibben, at the 1913 opening of the religious Philadelphian Society—whose teachings Amory Blaine terms succinctly "rot"—dipped into science to make an evolutionary argument for man as "the last link in a long chain of development" (10/1/13). Hibben insisted that Princeton boys, as God's emissaries on earth, should learn and teach "the methods of attaining freedom from the lower impulses which permeate men's lives" (10/3/13). Harry Emerson Fosdick, the popular Montclair minister and writer, was welcomed at Princeton in 1913, although, two years later, the hard-hitting evangelical preacher Billy Sunday was not. The Princeton faculty and President Hibben objected to Sunday's "methods" and asked that he not be allowed to appear on campus (2/26/15). Sunday spoke, under the auspices of the Theological Seminary, at First Presbyterian Church on Nassau Street instead (3/8/15).

However, one Clifford G. Roe, attorney and secretary of the National Vigilance Association, spoke in October 1913 "to an audience that packed Alexander Hall to its limit" on "the cause and effect of white slavery." The issue of gender would not become a burning one on campus for decades—though there were several debates and *Prince* editorials during Fitzgerald's time coming out in favor of women's suffrage (*2/3/14; 10/15/15*)—but this particular lecture of Roe's on "fallen women" certainly got the young men's attention. Roe's "stirring address" on prostitution called upon the young men of Princeton to see that debauching an "unfortunate girl who fell because of temptation or circumstances" was that worst of all things, "absolutely unsportsmanlike" (*10/24/13*). Also oversubscribed was a lecture given the following year by an unfortunately named Dr. Ill on "The Sexual Life of Woman in the History of Our Race" (*5/14/14*). No wonder the Mann Act made its way so prominently into *This Side of Paradise;* no wonder something like *Galahad* could emerge from the young Edmund Wilson's brain.

Public lectures on literature were available, too. Early in the fall of 1913, the Irish dramatist George A. Birmingham addressed the subject of "The Irishman in Fiction"—something that might have appealed to the self-described "Celt" Fitzgerald. Birmingham cited Thackeray as the first English writer to "seriously undert[ake] the development of the Irishman's characteristics," but Thackeray could not keep himself from the English tendency to hold "the Irish up to ridicule." While admiring Robert Louis Stevenson's portrayal of something called "Irish highland Jacobite[s]," Birmingham criticized contemporary writers for their complete failure to "impartially represent the Irishman" (*11/4/13*). Alfred Noyes—whom Fitzgerald would refer to, rather aptly, as "Alfred Noisy Highwayman" years later (Bruccoli and Duggan 311)—arrived on campus in December 1913 to deliver the Trask Lectures on "The Future of Poetry." *The Prince* spoke hyperbolically of Noyes's "lyric and epic measures," devoid of "the cockneyism Kipling often descends to," of his rowing prowess at Oxford, and the purported fact (entirely ignoring Alexander Pope, among others) that Noyes was "the first poet who has ever lived and thrived on the mere sale of his writings" (*12/10/13*). Noyes would remain at Princeton in the following years as a visiting professor of English, although he returned to England often to serve as a war correspondent.

In an inverse of the equation generally cited by T. S. Eliot, W. B. Yeats, James Joyce, and other modernists who acknowledged their debt to French writers, André Bellessort informed Princeton students in January 1914 that "France is indebted to America for much that is best in the political and moral content of her literature." He insisted that James Fenimore Cooper, Bret Harte, and Emerson had greatly influenced "Chateaubriand, de Maupassant, Verne, and the French humorists," and that "the freedom, the cordiality, the energy, and the initiative of American character" constituted American literature's greatest contribution to French literature (*1/24/14*). Professor Christian Gauss would turn to this argument the following month to argue for Byron's indebtedness to French literature, despite Byron's inability to speak the language (*2/16/14*). In January 1917, Count Ilya Tolstoy visited Princeton to speak on his father's life and writings. He described *War and Peace* as a "prophecy of what is actually taking place among the nations of Europe at the present time" and recommended his father's ideals of truth and love to his audience (*1/31/17*). Robert Frost was on the campus that same evening, recalling his "experimentations in blank verse" which, according to *The Prince,* had already made him "one of the three or four most prominent American poets of the younger generation" (*1/31/17*). Frost had been brought to campus by a new literary club founded by John Peale Bishop (the original for dreadfully literary Thomas Parke D'Invilliers in *This Side of Paradise*), as were Walter de la Mare and Amy Lowell, the latter referred to by *The Prince* during her campus visit as, first, "a sister of president Lowell of Harvard," and second, as an "Imagiste" poet (*1/15/17; 1/18/17*).

The *Nassau Literary Magazine* was the campus's own promulgator of literature and criticism. Fitzgerald began his reminiscences about his days on the *Lit* staff by noting, if humorously, a basic change in literary concerns: "In my days stories in the Nassau Lit were about the starving writers, dying Poilus, the plague in Florence and the soul of the Great Khan. They took place, chiefly, behind the moon and a thousand years ago. Now they all take place on Nassau Street, no longer back than yesterday."[7] Although they dabbled in the Florentine-plague and dying-

Poilus genres, the *Lit* writers of Fitzgerald's years, chiefly Fitzgerald and Wilson, were really the ones to begin the shift in emphasis from "literary" to "Nassau"—that is to say, from stories of a romanticized or mythical past to the modern here and now.

The monthly *Lit* was regularly reviewed in *The Prince,* a day or two after its appearance, and often by an English professor. Professor Gordon Gerould reviewed the December 1913 *Lit,* commending Edmund Wilson for "imitation of [Henry] James" in his story "Afterwards," and noting with pleasure that one freshman contributor, John Peale Bishop, showed promise of being a good poet (*12/8/13*). "Bunny" Wilson and Bishop were Fitzgerald's closest friends and literary collaborators while the three were on campus. When their relationship of twenty-five years ended with Fitzgerald's death, Wilson and Bishop would elegize him almost exclusively in terms of college memories in their poems bracketing Wilson's careful, compassionate edition of *The Crack-up.*

The performing arts were almost strictly campus-related at Fitzgerald's Princeton, though New York was an easy train ride away, and *The Prince* did carry listings for Broadway theaters. Occasionally, upcoming events closer by would make it into the paper. *The Prince* recommended in 1913 that students travel to Trenton to see Anna Pavlova, "the world's greatest dancer," promising—as an evidently necessary further incentive—that Novikoff, her partner in the company, "would make a slashing halfback" and that ballet "appeals at one and the same time to those who like things classical and to those who ordinarily prefer syncopated tunes and musical comedy choruses" (*10/11/13*). The best entertainments, as far as Princeton undergraduates were concerned, fit just this last description. These were the yearly Triangle Club shows.

Founded in 1882 as the Princeton Dramatic Club, Triangle first performed a play written by undergraduates in 1891; this was the farce *Pocahontas, or the Gentle Savage.* Under the direction of Booth Tarkington '93 the club was renamed Triangle in 1894, and in 1898 it received permission from the faculty to present its comedies off-campus. All roles, including the female ones, were taken by male undergraduates; the chorus and its kickline of dancing, singing "girls"—for which Triangle shows, like Harvard's Hasty Pudding shows, became notorious—was instituted in 1900 (*12/15/13*).

The Pursuit of Priscilla, a two-act Western comedy, was selected as the

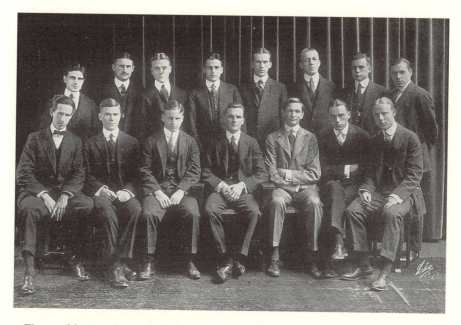

Fitzgerald (*second row, third from left*) as a member of the board of *The Tiger.*
Courtesy of Princeton University Library.

Triangle show Fitzgerald's freshman year. It featured a plot of jewel theft and thwarted love—both situations would of course be happily resolved in the end—and starred the worldly young Priscilla, her rough and rich cowboy suitors, a Chinese cook named Wun Lung (later recast as "Tong, a Celestial dishwasher"), and, in a timely nod, Mexican civil war participants. There was much song and dance. On the company's two-thousand-mile Christmas tour, alumni (including President Wilson, who received the young men at the White House) provided teas, dances, and dinners (*1/6/14*).

National events were writ small in *The Prince,* and when reported they were often framed locally or self-referentially during Fitzgerald's first years. President Wilson was regarded far more as an old boy than the leader of the nation. In November 1913, when Wilson returned to Princeton to vote, more than five hundred cheering undergraduates met him at the campus train, or "Dinky," station. The borough of Princeton itself went Republican that year, and by the next national election year, 1916, campus sentiment on Wilson at first appeared to have changed similarly. Charles Evans Hughes, the Republican presidential candidate, was chosen in an October straw poll by the students (*10/19/16*), and *The Prince* cited New York newspapers in proclaiming on November 8 that Hughes had indeed been elected. When this proved wrong, *The Prince* showed a typically Princetonian deference combined with self-reference, running a large picture, not of President Wilson, but of "Woodrow Wilson '79," on its front page (*11/11/16*).

Fitzgerald himself appeared in *The Prince* during his college years, though not as the future leader, football star, or *Prince* editor in chief he might have liked to have been. Unlike Amory Blaine, "paragraphed in corners of the *Princetonian*" (48) for his quarterbacking before his freshman year was two weeks old, young Scott Fitzgerald was merely listed in the pack of eighty-five who reported for the first freshman football practice, on September 26, 1913 (*9/26/13*). Though he played on the Newman School team in 1912, Fitzgerald did not make the Princeton freshman team, which trounced Yale 30–0 that fall (*11/10/13*). When he was next mentioned in *The Prince,* in the listing of the 430-plus entering class, Fitzgerald's name was set down wrong, as "F.C. Fitzgerald" of 15 University Place (*9/29/13*). This address no longer exists; it would be approximately under the current McCarter Theater. Fitzgerald must have been happier to see himself as "F.S. Fitzgerald," present at the first *Tiger* competition meeting on September 29 (*9/29/13*). Perhaps, just perhaps, he even mentioned the error, and the name by which he preferred to be addressed, to *The Prince,* for two weeks later he is specifically "Scott Fitzgerald" among a host of other young men identified only by their initials as new members of the social and debating society, Whig Hall (*10/15/13*).

The fall 1913 number of *The Tiger* appeared in October; noted by *The Prince* as a *Tiger* "debutante" is "Fitzgerald 1917" (*10/21/13*). For the Junior Prom number of the *Tiger* in early 1914, Fitzgerald was named simply as one who had "contributed to the success of the number" (*2/20/14*). However, the following month, *The Prince* planted tongue firmly in cheek to announce the largest issue ever of *The Tiger,* "by far the most ambitious issue of that paper ever attempted . . . containing gratuitous contributions from practically every well known illustrator and humorist of the present day," including professional journalists

Whig Hall.

Courtesy of Anne Margaret Daniel.

and Booth Tarkington. Particularly Princetonian was the "usual local color . . . supplied by F.S. Fitzgerald 1917" (*3/27/14*).

Fitzgerald was not listed as having made the cuts of any Triangle Club casting calls during his freshman year or any other, nor is he named during the fall or spring competitions for the seven freshman spots available on *The Prince*. He did try out, though, for the Elizabethan Dramatic Association—soon to be renamed, in a nod to more modern drama, the English Dramatic Association—production of Ibsen's *The Pillars of Society* during the spring of his freshman year. Fitzgerald had written and performed in plays in St. Paul, and he also acted at the Newman School, where he appeared in, among other performances, the chorus of a minstrel show.[8] Initially cast as Olaf in *The Pillars of Society*, he was demoted to Mrs. Lynge in the next cast list (*2/28/14; 3/6/14*). *The Prince* printed the director's warning to the cast that, if "any one is loafing on the job, he or 'she' is liable to be dropped immediately" (*3/6/14*). Did Fitzgerald loaf? Whatever befell him, he was not on the final cast list at all, and the role of Mrs. Lynge was taken by John Peale Bishop when the play opened. The production was a critical success, and the Dramatic Association's switch "from the production of Elizabethan to modern drama" was deemed a triumph by *The Prince* (*4/3/14*).

On a sole nonliterary, nondramatic note, Fitzgerald ran in the Freshman Relay Races on Team 6—which didn't win—in the spring of 1914 (*3/6/14*). This is his only recorded athletic attempt in *The Prince* after the football fiasco.

In the fall of 1914, Fitzgerald, a sophomore, finally made a real splash at Princeton. The as-yet-unnamed Triangle show was profiled on the front page of *The Prince,* under the prominent headline "Ellis 1915 and Fitzgerald 1917 Collaborate in Play." Fitzgerald is named as writer of "the plot and lyrics," while Triangle president Walker Ellis reportedly created "the characters . . . and the dialogue" (*10/10/14*). Even at this first mention in *The Prince,* this sounds like a rather odd or tangled division of labor. That Fitzgerald is initially credited here with the "plot" would support his later contention that he had written not only the lyrics but the book itself (*Fitzgerald's St. Paul Plays* 7).

The show was *Fie! Fie! Fi-Fi!* It was cast by November 12, and rehearsals began almost immediately. *The Prince* commended the show even before previews for its "very clever lyrics and dialogue" and for the entertaining plot, explained as follows: "The scene is laid on the cafe terrace of a hotel in Monte Carlo. Most of the characters are Americans, wintering on the Riviera." The "reinstatement of the Prime Minister [of Monaco] and the downfall of the usurper [an American] through the efforts of his deserted wife (Fi-Fi, now a manicurist at the hotel) form the climax of the plot" (*11/14/14*). A song suggesting that Fitzgerald noticed Professor Conklin's lectures the preceding spring, "Love or Eugenics," was performed by two of the "female" leads late in the second act (*11/24/14*). The play's Riviera setting, which entirely shapes the narrative of *Tender Is the Night,* and the star's name, Count Del Monti (the bandit leader and rightful prime minister), would both recur in Fitzgerald's later work. Count del Monti is Amory Blaine's runaway and inadvertently suicidal dog.

Professor Wardlaw Miles, the faculty reviewer of *Fi-Fi!* for *The Prince,* particularly complimented Fitzgerald's lyrics as "very apt and well-turned" (*12/19/14*). During semester break, *Fi-Fi!* traveled by train to ten cities, from Baltimore west to St. Louis, Chicago, and Pittsburgh before concluding in New York. On the eight-day, 3,500-mile trek, the cast, crew, and writers were entertained much as were the fictional boys on Amory's tour with *Ha-Ha Hortense!* in *This Side of Paradise,* with dinners and tea dances thrown by Princeton alumni in every city. Reviews from the *Louisville Post* and, later in his life, of particular interest and doubtless of pride to him, from Fitzgerald's "hometown" *Baltimore Sun* were excerpted in *The Prince.* The *Post* raved that Fitzgerald "could take his place right now with the brightest writers of witty lyrics in America," and the *Sun* stated that much "of the success of the entertainment . . . was due to the clever lyrics of F. S. Fitzgerald, who has written some really excellent 'patter songs'" (*1/8/15*).

Fitzgerald was made a member of the Triangle Club for his lyrics on February 24, 1915, and elected club secretary a couple of days later (*2/25/15; 2/27/15*). He completed his social sweep of sophomore year by accepting on March 20 his spot in the University Cottage Club—"an impressive melange of brilliant adventurers and well-dressed philanderers" (49), as Fitzgerald described them in *This Side of Paradise*—housed in its new location on Prospect Avenue in a magnificent McKim, Mead and White building, its library a replica of that at Merton College Oxford (*3/20/15*). The club elections of 1915 took place in the worst blizzard to hit Princeton for years; much later, in a scribble on a shred of paper, Fitzgerald recalled chasing his friends through the snow on that night after the news came.[9] Fitzgerald was elected to the editorial board of the *Tiger* in May, and in the room draw he was awarded a good single, 32 Little, for his junior year (*5/21/15*). He would, however, occupy 185 Little when he came back to Princeton in the fall of 1916 (Bruccoli and Duggan 13).

Fitzgerald crowned his sophomore year with appearances in the *Nassau Lit.* One reviewer, Professor Miles, liked Fitzgerald's "drama 'Shadow-Laurels' [*sic*] (a piquant title)" for "conveying the intended atmosphere of sordid and suffocating despair"—a despair Miles found entirely, and disappointingly, French rather than honestly Anglo-Saxon (*4/17/15*). This was not the last time Fitzgerald would be accused by critics of a decadent, symbolist, or fin de siècle hangover. The *Prince* review of the June *Lit* criticized Fitzgerald's style, but it nevertheless found his story "The Ordeal" a "noble offering" (*6/9/15*).

Fitzgerald (*second row, second from right*) as a member of the
Triangle Club.

Courtesy of Princeton University Library.

The Prince specifically advised the Princeton sophomore in the spring
of 1915 to "become well enough acquainted with himself to know
what are his tastes and his general likings and to educate himself accordingly" (*5/15/15*). Fitzgerald was doing so. However, both general
likings and education meant for him the Triangle show, and, evidently,
little else during junior year. He and Edmund Wilson wrote the lyrics
and book of *The Evil Eye,* a superstition-ridden and tangled love tale
set in the fishing village of Niaserie, on the Normandy coast, and star-
ring as its villain the philosophically named Count La Rochefoucauld
Boileau (*10/28/15*). Fitzgerald finally got his photograph in *The Prince*
for the first, and most memorable, time as composer of the show's lyrics
and as "F. Scott Fitzgerald '17, one of last year's attractive 'show girls'"
(*12/8/15*). Was Fitzgerald indeed one of the *Fie! Fie! Fi-Fi!* showgirls, or
"ponies"? He is on none of the lists in *The Prince*. And the celebrated
drag photograph is credited in *The Prince* to White's of New York,

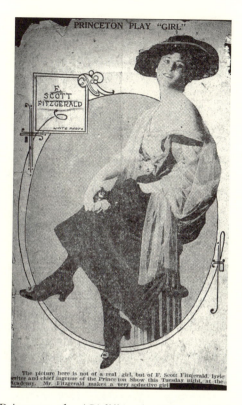

PRINCETON PLAY "GIRL"

E. SCOTT FITZGERALD

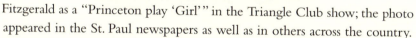
The picture here is not of a real girl, but of F. Scott Fitzgerald, lyric writer and chief ingenue of the Princeton Show this Tuesday night, at the Academy. Mr. Fitzgerald makes a very seductive girl.

Fitzgerald as a "Princeton play 'Girl'" in the Triangle Club show; the photo appeared in the St. Paul newspapers as well as in others across the country.

Courtesy of Princeton University Library.

which had offices in Princeton at 60 Nassau Street and did the school's formal photos, like the senior headshots in the *Nassau Herald*. This photograph is not a candid snapshot but rather a studio job, one for which Fitzgerald prepared, rather than one that might have been taken backstage. Regardless of the circumstances of its genesis, the photograph certainly bears out Fitzgerald's jotting years later, "I look like a femme fatale" (*Notebooks* 71).

The Triangle trip that Christmas of 1915 covered five thousand miles, but Fitzgerald was home in St. Paul when the train full of boys headed out of Princeton for their first tour performance, at the Academy of Music in Brooklyn. He had withdrawn from Princeton in November or early December with an illness he would later refer to as tuberculosis

(Donaldson, *Fool for Love* 20). His grades, though, had been horrendous that fall, and *The Prince* made a not-even-veiled reference to the reasons why some students might have withdrawn before midyear exams in 1915–16: "Fiftynine undergraduates were dropped from their classes, and in addition 11 who would undoubtedly have been dropped from the college withdrew before the examinations" (*3/11/16*). A contemporaneous editorial insisted, harshly, that there is "not much sympathy to be extended to the flunker" (*1/8/16*). John Peale Bishop scolded his friend about his withdrawal in a letter of January 2, 1916, entirely emphasizing academic, and not medical, reasons: "For God's sake and your own get your conditions off and keep them off" (Donaldson, *Fool for Love* 20). Fitzgerald did not remove his conditions in any sort of timely fashion, and during the spring of 1916 he officially became a member of the class of 1918. P. D. Nelson '17 was elected president of Triangle (*3/2/16*). Years later, Fitzgerald would write to Scottie that he had not been allowed to serve in that capacity, though the presidency should rightfully have been his (Wilson, *Crack-up* 292).

When he returned to Princeton in the fall of 1916, Fitzgerald concentrated on writing for the *Nassau Lit,* contributing two pieces to its December parody issue. He wrote the leadoff piece for the December *Lit,* "'Jemima,' by John Phlox, Jr.," described by *The Prince* as "a take-off on the usual 'moonshining story'" of the sort popularized by Virginia writer John Fox, Jr., in *The Little Shepherd of Kingdom Come* and other best-sellers. Fitzgerald's other contribution, "'The Usual Thing,' by Robert W. Shameless," featured the plot that would become Fitzgerald's hallmark, a "love story with its setting among the very rich" (*12/12/16*). Fitzgerald was proud enough of this story to send a copy of the *Lit* to Canadian humorist Stephen Leacock, who responded appreciatively (Bruccoli and Duggan 19). In January 1917, the *Prince* review of the new *Lit* once again located in Fitzgerald's writing elements he would constantly reuse, and of which later critics would also speak approvingly: "Mr. Fitzgerald's devastating skit on the foibles of young femininity ['The Debutante'] is surely mingled enough to please and sate the curious taste of the most catholic of readers" (*1/19/17*). His story "Tarquin of Cheapside" in the April *Lit* was called simply, and aptly, "strikingly well written" (*4/24/17*).

Fitzgerald's Triangle Club collaborator Edmund Wilson had graduated in June 1916 (rating two mentions in the 1916 Senior Statistics: unanimously acclaimed as worst poet, and ironically but quite appropriately receiving eight votes for "most likely bachelor"). Without him, Fitzgerald composed only the lyrics for that fall's Triangle show, *Safety First!* (*12/15/16*). *The Prince* offered a succinct summary: "The action takes place in the Futurist art community of Arden and deals with a counterfeit art school run by a former convict named Howard" (*10/24/16*). Fitzgerald's lyrics contributed the following opinion on modern art that might not have amused Gerald Murphy or Zelda, among others, in the future:

> There are no strict requirements for a cubist,
> You only need a dipper full of paint,
> A little distance bring it
> And at your canvas fling it,
> Then shut your eyes and name it what it ain't. (Fitzgerald
>   et al., *Safety First* 28–29)

Concerning contemporary women and the movies, Fitzgerald also had something to say that he would repeat, rather more eloquently but in the same tenor, later:

> Tell me why are the girls that I meet
> Always simple and slow?
> I want a brunette like those I met
> Back in the seven-reel show. (79)

Booth Tarkington called this "satire on futurism" the best Triangle show ever (*11/25/16*). Doubtless his lyrics earned Fitzgerald his only two mentions in the Senior Stats for his original class of 1917 that spring. He was third in the "thinks he is wittiest" category and got six votes— defeated only by Shakespeare and Shaw!—for best dramatist (*3/1/17; 3/2/17*).

By 1917, though, Fitzgerald's interrupted and often difficult time at Princeton was ending. His closest friends there, including Wilson and Bishop, were gone, already in military service. The war to end all wars had, as Fitzgerald put it, "slowly and inevitably, yet with a sudden surge at the last . . . rolled swiftly up the beach and washed the sands where Princeton played" (*This Side of Paradise* 160).

"War" meant Mexico when Fitzgerald was a freshman. The war in Mexico occupied front-page space in *The Prince* that year, and when the Americans took Vera Cruz in April 1914, *The Prince* covered the incident fully (e.g., *4/23/14*). By the fall of 1914, though, "the war" referred to what was happening in Europe, not Mexico. On June 28 of that summer, Archduke Francis Ferdinand had been assassinated in Sarajevo. During August, the world had gone to war from the Atlantic to the Pacific. Most front pages of *The Prince* in the fall of 1914 carried the latest news of the German march into France and Belgium, with reports from London often quoted at length (*10/3/14*). On October 7, 1914, *The Prince* began as a regular feature a "European War Summary," explaining that "Hereafter . . . instead of presenting the usual motley of war rumors and counter-rumors, [*The Prince*] will each day summarize events at the front, attempting at the same time to trace as it develops the strategy governing the various movements." This column would continue, along with feature stories and other pieces about the war and American involvement, until troops had begun to come home.

Voluntary commitments for Princeton undergraduates included student military summer camps. First organized in 1913 at the Presidio in California and at Gettysburg, Pennsylvania, as elite experiments for college men who wanted to train as officers, the camps grew with the advent of the European war. The War Department held four such camps during the summer of 1914, and students were kept well apprised by *The Prince* as to when and where the camps would be held and how to attend (e.g., *11/15/13; 1/8/14*). The camp for students in the Northeast was held in Burlington, Vermont, in 1914 and on the shores of Lake Champlain in Plattsburg, New York, the following year (*5/28/15*). Just as advertisements ran regularly in *The Prince* to tell the students when Brooks Brothers representatives would be on campus to make looking sharp effortless, so advertisements by 1914 began to tell them what the well-dressed young officer-to-be should take along to camp that summer.

A *Prince* editorial early in the fall of 1914 asked Princeton students to consider aiding the Red Cross, appealing to high ideals and humanity alike: "It is impossible for us—three thousand miles from the scene—to comprehend the stupendous destruction of life which has transformed the plains of Belgium, France and East Prussia into a human shambles; to realize the boundless ruin that follows as the pillars of civilization are tumbled into dust" (*10/6/14*). The school responded immediately; students donated money, books, and old phonograph records intended, said *The Prince,* for "the hospitals and camps . . . where men have had their nervous systems wrecked by the battle strain and the detonations of the big guns. Music is a great factor in the recovery of such patients" (*12/16/15*). An urgent request from the American Ambulance Service for drivers at the front began to run in *The Prince* in early 1916 (*2/17/16*); requirements for such service (a minimum enlistment of six months, one's own costs to be borne) were provided in detail for interested students (*1/29/17*).

Princeton graduates and professors, sometimes observers and sometimes participants (generally as Red Cross volunteers, ambulance drivers, or soldiers in the English or French armies), provided *The Prince* with firsthand accounts from Europe. English professor George Harper, the discoverer of the existence of William Wordsworth's illegitimate daughter, wrote from Cambridge at war. The university town, "not unlike Princeton," was now devoid of students as "the scholastic life" had become "subordinate to another and more urgent mode of existence" (*12/15/15*). Although in early 1915 *The Prince* was still publishing pieces indicating that German food shortages would soon end the war (*2/18/15*), the sinking of the *Lusitania* that May changed everything. *The Prince* adopted the tone of all America in discussing the incident: "to lie in wait and suddenly destroy a merchant vessel carrying a crew of non-combatants and worst of all, an immense number of passengers, is an act that is . . . abhorrent" (*5/10/15*).

Lectures on the war, from sources as disparate as former president Taft and poet-professor Noyes, were regular campus happenings by 1915. Taft advocated neutrality; Noyes insisted on American intervention (*2/3/15; 3/5/15*). This debate would run on at Princeton until the United States actually entered the war, and there were many editorials and articles in *The Prince* on the pros and cons of military training in a still-neutral country (e.g., *3/4/15; 1/28/16*). In early 1917, a group of students, largely attendees of the seminary, formed an antiwar league at Princeton (*3/27/17*). Nearly twenty years later, Fitzgerald would locate himself in such company. Addressing an antiwar meeting at Johns Hopkins around 1935, he related "how he had 'progressed from an enthusiastic first lieutenant, brought up on the American fetish of marching feet and stationary brains' to his present antiwar attitude."[10] There were also mass media events on campus propagandizing the war. In March 1916, *The Battle Cry of Peace,* advertised as a photo-spectacle, was presented in Alexander Hall. It depicted a "realistic invasion of America" beginning at New York, and it made $375 for the Red Cross while showing at Princeton (*3/9/16*). Even *The Prince*'s most basic advertisements had changed by 1916: the polished, black-tie crowd enjoying Bull Durham cigarettes in 1913 had been transformed into polished, uniformed young officers enjoying a smoke while overseeing the digging of trenches.

Major General John O'Ryan, commander of the New York National Guard, had suggested early in 1916 that Princeton students and other college men should be trained as lieutenants. He proposed required lectures on military law, organization, tactics, and sanitation, accompanied by physical training (*2/2/16*). The War Department's summer camp programs provided just such training that year, and by the beginning of 1917 Princeton was preparing a similar on-campus program of its own (*2/2/17*). What *The Prince* dubbed the "Princeton Provisional Battalion" began sign-ups on February 5, 1917. President John Grier Hibben, in approving the training program, reflected that "in case war should be declared and the call should come for volunteers, I think it not a rash prediction that Princeton men as a body would respond" (*2/5/17*). By February 6, during a six-hour period, over five hundred undergraduates had signed up for drill; another hundred would sign up for a proposed Princeton Aero Corps before the end of the week (*2/9/17*). In early April, President Wilson asked Congress to declare war—which, *The Prince* noted, would be the fourth war in Princeton history, personalizing the world conflict for young men at an exclusive school that had suddenly become a training camp (*4/3/17; 4/4/17*).

Fitzgerald was not, initially, on the lists for the Princeton military programs, but on April 27 "F. S. Fitzgerald 1918" entered the official rolls as one of the 204 Princeton students seeking admission to the War Department's military training camps that summer (*4/27/17*). On May 11, he was among the 112 signed up for the third intensive training course,

Bull Durham ads from 1913 (*left*) and 1916 (*right*).

Courtesy of Princeton University Library.

to begin full-time, with little room for classes, on May 14. The course began in Princeton's second-largest lecture hall at the time, McCosh 10, with an 8:10 A.M. lecture on trench warfare, followed by patrol formation drill in Dillon Gym and lectures in the afternoon (5/16/17). In a front-page *Prince* photograph from May 30, unreproduced publicly since, of the "Intensive Men and Companies A,B,C on Brokaw Field," Fitzgerald stands proudly with the intensive men, front and center, blond hair gleaming, in his combat sweater and uniform pants (5/30/17).

Fitzgerald's last fall semester at Princeton was, essentially, that of 1916; by September 1917 he was only waiting for his army commission. In a letter to his mother, on Cottage Club stationery and dated November

Front page of *The Prince* announcing President Wilson's request for a declaration of war.

Courtesy of Princeton University Library.

14, 1917, he said flatly and in a phrase that was one of his strongest condemnations, "Things are stupid here" (*Letters* 451). He couldn't bear stupid. By the end of the month, he was gone. Though Fitzgerald's departing entry in the *Nassau Herald* announced his intention to pursue graduate work in English at Harvard, and then seek a newspaper job, it was never to be. He entered the army as Lieutenant F. Scott Fitzgerald of the Forty-fifth Infantry just after his twenty-first birthday and, while in the army, started drafting and revising the novel about youth at Princeton that would make him too famous a writer to consider graduate school in the future.

Photograph of Princeton men in uniform, including Fitzgerald, from the
May 30, 1917, issue of *The Prince*.

Courtesy of Princeton University Library.

During the years Fitzgerald lived at Princeton, its campus changed
from a quiet place to one where young men who would soon be at war
waited to leave for Europe. Fitzgerald arrived in 1913 at an insular
school of privileged and varied, if self-referential, diversions, where the
glittering figures provided to inspire undergraduates were all campus
ones, from President Wilson to hockey star and football captain Hobart
Amory Hare Baker '14—Wilson, who would soon be embroiled in the
Great War, and Baker, who would die testing a plane over France in
1918, after the Armistice and just before Christmas, with his orders
home in his pocket. When Fitzgerald left Princeton in 1917 for Fort
Leavenworth, the emphasis on campus life and the frolic-filled development of the undergraduate had shifted completely toward the outside
world, including international affairs, and maturity. A *Prince* editorial
of early 1914, entitled "Peter Panism," jokingly warned its readers of
the dire consequences of the possible failure to grow up, and to leave

THE NASSAU HERALD

Fitzgerald prepared at Saint Paul Academy, St. Paul, Minn., and at the Newman School, Hackensack, N. J. He was on the School Papers and in Dramatics at each.

In Princeton, he has been a member of the Triangle Club, (1) (2) (3), Secretary, (3), editor of the *Tiger* and the *Nassau Literary Magazine.* Whig Hall. Cottage Club. Roman Catholic. Progressive.

Freshman Year he roomed at 15 University Place alone; Sophomore Year in 107 Patton alone; Junior Year in 185 Little, with P. B. Dickey.

Fitzgerald was forced to leave college in December 1915 because of illness. He will pursue graduate work in English at Harvard, then he will engage in newspaper work. His permanent address is 593 Summit Ave., St. Paul, Minn.

Fitzgerald's entry in the *Nassau Herald*.

Courtesy of Princeton University Library.

Princeton fit only to "run a male finishing school" (*1/21/14*). By the end of Fitzgerald's time at Princeton, there was no need to remind its students that they would never be so young again.

Notes

1. *The Daily Princetonian* is available on microfilm in the Firestone Library at Princeton University, Princeton, New Jersey. The Seeley G. Mudd Library, which houses Princeton's official university records and manuscripts, also maintains bound and filmed copies of *The Prince.*

2. These were the years Fitzgerald later included in one of his many lists under the "Nostalgia or the Flight of the Heart" category (*Notebooks* 241).

3. *The Daily Princetonian,* September 27, 1913. Hereinafter, references to issues of *The Prince* are parenthetically cited in italics, with the date of the issue of the newspaper in which the information or quotation provided may be found.

4. The "Bible," printed and distributed every year by the religious Philadelphian Society, included such headings as "Senior Council," "Freshman Ath-

letics and How to Go Out for Them," "Princeton Songs and Cheers," and "Hints on General Behavior" (*The Prince, 5/29/14*).

5. Donaldson recaps Fitzgerald's poor Princeton grades; Fitzgerald's continued status in the "fifth group," barely above passing ("fourth group" was a D average), led to disaster in the fall of 1915 (*Fool for Love* 20–21).

6. This book is in a display case at the F. Scott and Zelda Fitzgerald Museum in Montgomery, Alabama, which is in the house on Felder Avenue that he, Zelda, and Scottie occupied in 1931 and 1932.

7. F. Scott Fitzgerald Papers, Firestone Library, Princeton University, Box 26, Folder 13.

8. F. Scott Fitzgerald Papers, Firestone Library, Princeton University, Sheilah Graham Additional Papers, Box 3, Folder 4 (*Newman News* 1912/3).

9. F. Scott Fitzgerald Papers, Firestone Library, Princeton University, Shank Additional Papers, Box 12, Folder 2 ("Notes").

10. F. Scott Fitzgerald Papers, Firestone Library, Princeton University, Box 6, Clippings File.

2

Princeton, Pragmatism, and Fitzgerald's Sentimental Journey

EDWARD GILLIN

"To regard all things and principles of things as inconstant modes or fashions has more and more become the tendency of modern thought," Walter Pater remarked in his famous concluding chapter of *The Renaissance* (233). The temporal conditioning of such a world reduces experience to infinitesimal units, each of which "is limited by time, and . . . as time is infinitely divisible, each of them is infinitely divisible also, all that is actual in it being a single moment, gone while we try to apprehend it" (235).

A Pater-like apprehension of time became one of the key ingredients William James would syncretically blend into the pragmatist philosophy he promulgated in the early twentieth century. James, in *Pragmatism,* proclaimed that the "world we live in exists diffused and distributed, in the form of an indefinitely numerous lot of *eaches*" (*Writings* 602). Temporality determines this variety. According to James, passing moments are the nexus of human experience (Siegfried 68). As the individual apprehends the continual newness of circumstances, he or she discovers the necessity of treating all principles as working hypotheses rather than dogmatic axioms: "A pragmatist," James writes, "turns away from abstraction and insufficiency, from verbal solutions, from bad *a priori* reasons, from fixed principles, closed systems, and pretended absolutes and origins. He turns toward concreteness and . . . facts . . . as against dogma, artificiality, and the pretence of finality in truth" (508–9).

A paradoxically venerable American theme underlies James's dynamic philosophy. Pilgrim and entrepreneur alike had come from Europe, enticed by visions of what might be accomplished in a "New" World. The Jeffersonian notion of the democratic state constantly revolutionizing itself became part of the national political heritage; in the single most famous of all American speeches, Abraham Lincoln would pledge the country to a "new birth of freedom." Meanwhile, Emerson, Thoreau, and Whitman had encoded the experience of the awakening soul into the national literature.

Jamesian pragmatism found a ready place in such traditions. As William Joseph Gavin has noted, James's "emphasis on experience as a process, on becoming as more important than being" (150), offers a special insight into the aesthetics of modern art. Although Gavin concentrates on the applicability of Jamesian principles to visual media (noting, for example, how futurist and cubist paintings underscore the "temporal complexity of life"), literary scholars are well aware that one of James's ardent pupils, Gertrude Stein, found the pragmatist dynamic of cubism readily available for the modern writer as well. Stein sought to capture the "continuous present," as she called it, stylizing now-ness in the insistent present participles and gerunds of her writings. And almost every significant American modernist after Stein addresses, practically or philosophically, some sense of inhabiting a universe where only immediate experience has value. Ernest Hemingway would stress the theme in a story collection significantly entitled *In Our Time.* T. S. Eliot's "Burnt Norton" opens with an observation about this "unredeemable" temporal situation: "What might have been and what has been / Point to one end, which is always present" (*Collected Poems* 175). The quotation might be inscribed on the symbolically broken timepiece featured in William Faulkner's novel *The Sound and the Fury* (1929): in a world whose tolling watchword is "temporary," Quentin Compson's father educates his son in the anti-absolute knowledge "that a love or a sorrow is a bond purchased without design and which matures willynilly and is recalled without warning to be replaced by whatever issue the gods happen to be floating at the time" (178). Less bleakly, in this same period of present-consciousness Ezra Pound cried out to his generation of writers the positive exordium to "make it new," and Marianne Moore celebrated the pangolin-like ability of humans to rise to the "new and new and new" each day (204). If the sense of unrepeatable time has been rightly called modernity's "main constitutive element" (Calinescu 13), living in the continuous present for the modernist writer was, obviously, what one chose to make of it.

The theme of time is especially useful to study in the works of F. Scott Fitzgerald, the writer whom Malcolm Cowley tellingly described as "haunted by time, as if he wrote in a roomful of clocks and calendars" (Kazin 24). Indeed, such clocks have often been discussed in criticisms of *The Great Gatsby*, the novel which, according to Matthew J. Bruccoli, uses some 450 time-words in its 150 or so printed pages (Fitzgerald, *The Great Gatsby* xv). As I will suggest, the temporal concerns of Fitzgerald's mature fiction appear as early as *This Side of Paradise*, a novel in which Jamesian pragmatism and its related time-sense appears to be a significant influence.

Since James was such a successful popularizer of pragmatist intellectual movements at the turn of the century, the question of specific influence may be regarded as relatively minor. Ronald Berman's *"The Great Gatsby" and Fitzgerald's World of Ideas* (1997) presents an excellent summary of James's general influence on American culture during the first decades of the twentieth century, establishing that Jamesian ideas had entered the mainstream of American thought by this period (see especially 29–32). Fitzgerald might have acquired a sense of pragmatism's principles from having read James, C. S. Pierce, John Dewey, or several other contributors to the movement in one of the philosophy courses he enrolled in almost every semester he was at Princeton. Immediately after college, the young author certainly seems to be exploring ramifications of these principles in stories written shortly before and after *This Side of Paradise*. The prototypical heroine of this early fiction derives her notorious shock value by combining the conventional pluck of young womanhood with the new era's philosophy: Fitzgerald's famed flappers routinely possess a kind of Jamesian present-consciousness. Thus Ardita Farnam of "The Offshore Pirate"—who asks, "Don't you know by this time that I can do any darn thing with any darn man I want to?" (*Novels and Stories* 256)—is not merely a spoiled debutante. In a reflective moment she explains her behavior's source in her dissatisfaction with "conventional successes" and an "insistence on the value of life and the worth of transient things": "I wanted things now—now—now!" she exclaims (272, 274). To Fitzgerald, the New Woman's newness seemed to bring its own fascination. While he was capturing these icons of immediacy in many short fictions, he made the pragmatist time-theme a specific narrative foundation for "The Curious Case of Benjamin Button." This story emphasizes living as a process, of course, by reversing its long-established beginning and ending. The "moments" of Button's recorded career must be measured in their own unique settings, absurdly contrasted to the seamless experience of the chronologically conventional human life span. In another story about curiously reordered lives, "Head and Shoulders," Fitzgerald offers his readers some entirely fitting allusions to complement his plotline. Horace Tarbox, the intellectual "head" who eventually becomes the brawny "shoulders" in an acrobatic act, is initially presented as a precocious scholar of modern American philosophy. "Verging more and more toward pragmatism" in his intellectual outlook (*Novels and Stories* 311), Horace specifically acknowledges William James as the great popularizer of the movement he wishes to imitate through his own writings (332). When Horace's career takes its most unexpected turn, it is because he is smitten with an actress who appears in a racy vaudeville show Fitzgerald has slyly entitled "Home James" (311). In the tradition of Jamesian chance, change, and freedom, Horace's future will never look the same; the young pragmatist will not go home again.

The opening pages of *This Side of Paradise* clearly announce time's role in the destiny of its own young male protagonist. Beatrice Blaine, the boy's mother, represents prior human experience; she exemplifies "a culture rich in all arts and heritage," Fitzgerald notes, but "barren of all ideas" (11). Amory Blaine, for all his delicate resemblance to his mother, grows up as if untouched by the past and utterly heedless of a future. Time and a particularly James-like orientation toward process are key elements of his outlook: "It was always the becoming he dreamed of, never the being" (24). Young Blaine exists, in effect, in a pragmatist/modernist "now."

Having chosen a college he regards as "lazy and good-looking and aristocratic" (31), Amory inevitably finds himself the "unadjustable boy" (41) at Princeton. In contrast to the liberating and individualizing tendencies of his process-oriented mind-set, Princeton fixes its Gothic spires on the bedrock of a rich past. The college values and, in various ways, *enforces* tradition, offering a peculiarly refined version of that democratic leveling which Alexis de Tocqueville had once diagnosed as characteristic of all American institutions. "Anything which brought an underclassman into too glaring a light was labelled with the damning brand of 'running it out,'" Fitzgerald relates; "talking of the clubs was running it out; standing for anything very strongly, as, for instance, drinking parties or teetotalling, was running it out; in short, being personally conspicuous was not tolerated" (49). Amory absorbs this austere lesson from the first moment he strolls up University Place and realizes the need to discard a hat that makes him noticeably different (42).

The pressures of personal ambition and social conformity converge in a tense alliance that fascinates Amory as he maneuvers his way through the magnificent game of Princeton life. Almost every significant personal crisis of the college years described in *This Side of Paradise* focuses on a conflict between Amory's willingness to submit to the allure of the Princeton ideal and what can be construed as a Jamesian pragmatist's revolt from the constraints of "closed systems." Amory is intrigued, for instance, by the strange reputation of the *Nassau Lit*'s eccentric poet, Thomas Parke D'Invilliers. But Amory hesitates to approach D'Invilliers in a lunchroom one day, lest a crowd of undergraduate onlookers "might mistake *him* for a bird, too" (54). Such pressures climax in his class's relation to Princeton's fraternal societies, those splendid barometers of social success. Chosen candidates celebrate their acceptance into various clubs "in a weird delusion that snobbishness and strain were all over at last, and that they could do what they pleased for the next two years" (73–74).

For Amory the triumph of delusion is nearly complete. By the end of sophomore year he has worked the system to achieve almost every standard of collegiate success. But his membership in the Cottage Club, his editorship of *The Princetonian,* and other glittering prospects—his "nearest approach to success through conformity"—all are lost when he loses academic eligibility: "The fundamental Amory, idle, imaginative, rebellious, had been nearly snowed under. He had conformed, he had succeeded, but as his imagination was neither satisfied nor grasped by his own success, he had listlessly, half-accidentally chucked the whole thing" (96–97).

The seemingly self-destructive impulse is paralleled in a kindred spirit at Princeton, Amory's friend Burne Holiday. Burne's steadfast opposition to the university's power-wielding social clubs is succeeded by his even lonelier moral stand as a pacifist protesting the popular tide of U.S. involvement in the Great War. Burne's radical departures from convention provoke "the lash of many tongues" (121). Among the iconoclastic writers Amory and Burne discuss together are Walt Whitman, Leo Tolstoy, and, aptly enough, William James (118–19).

What is striking about these particular names (and one could include others such as the somewhat obscure Edward Carpenter and the "sword-like" Renan and Voltaire dropped into the book Fitzgerald would later label "A Romance and a Reading List" [Wilson, *The Crack-up* 176]) is that each one is significantly referenced in James's famed 1902 work *Varieties of Religious Experience.* James cites Whitman as "the supreme contemporary example of . . . an inability to feel evil" in a chapter on "The Religion of Healthy-Mindedness" (*Writings* 82). In one of the conversations recorded in *This Side of Paradise,* Amory rejects Burne's claim that "a healthy man has twice the chance of being good," countering, "I don't believe in 'muscular Christianity'" (122). When Burne asks Amory to ponder a portrait of the Good Gray Poet as an exemplar of superior physiognomy, Amory is insensitive to its attraction, having previously also admitted, "I'm a blank on the subject of Whitman" (123, 118).

Although the last comment may seem the autobiographical admission of an author who considered himself a Keatsian poet during his undergraduate years, it certainly does not therefore reflect an unfamiliarity with Whitman as presented in "The Religion of Healthy-Mindedness." One sign that Fitzgerald read this chapter carefully is that he mimics a considerable portion of it in *This Side of Paradise.* A spiritual catechism included in *Varieties of Religious Experience* features stark exchanges ("Q. *What does Religion mean to you?* A. It means nothing; and it seems, so far as I can observe, useless to others") and penetrating personal questions ("*What things work most strongly on your emotions? . . . What is your temperament?*") (*Writings* 89–90). Opening the last major section of the novel, Amory subjects himself to a remarkably similar self-examination, complete with similarly pointed inquiries ("Where are you drifting?"; "Are you corrupt?") and similarly stark testimonies ("Q—Have you no interests left? A—None. I've no more virtue to lose") (238–39).

Whitman may ultimately be a "blank" for Amory Blaine largely because the "healthy-mindedness" William James associated with the *Leaves of Grass* poet has little correlation to the complexity of human experience recorded in *This Side of Paradise*. Indeed, James himself seems to resist the complacent uniformity of Whitman's sunniest moral outlook. Perhaps this is because such a figure seems uncannily impervious to the erosions of the passing seasons and the ceaseless fluctuations of mortal life. A philosopher who believed that the passing moments of time played an enormous role in perceived experience would predictably find greater authenticity in a literary figure who served as a keener barometer of such vicissitudes. For James this figure was Leo Tolstoy, the dominant literary reference in the chapter of *The Varieties of Religious Experience* entitled "The Sick Soul." James discusses the Russian novelist in terms of his "melancholy" and his "gnawing, carking questioning and effort for philosophic relief" (*Writings* 140). Such attitudes grew out of encounters with what James styles the inevitable human experience: "Failure, then, failure! so the world stamps us at every turn. We strew it with our blunders, our misdeeds, our lost opportunities, with all the memorials to our inadequacy. . . . The subtlest forms of suffering known to man are connected with the poisonous humiliations incidental to these results" (130). *This Side of Paradise* forms a sort of record of such humiliations, of course, from Amory's thwarted football career and failed geometry class to his youthful loss of several loves. James's view of time would only enhance the Ecclesiastes-like despair induced by such events: "Make the human being's sensitiveness a little greater, carry him a little farther over the misery-threshold, and the good quality of the successful moments themselves when they occur is spoiled and vitiated. All natural goods perish. Riches take wings; fame is a breath; love is a cheat; youth and health and pleasure vanish" (131).

From this point James speaks of a spiritual condition called anhedonia, the passive loss of appetite for all life's pleasures. James employs the very allusion that will become recurrent in a novel called *This Side of Paradise:* "When disillusionment has gone as far as this, there is seldom a *restitutio ad integrum*. One has tasted of the fruit of the tree, and the happiness of Eden never comes again" (146). Among the several case studies of anhedonia, most anticipate the general conditions of profound loneliness and spiritual enervation that afflict the protagonist of Fitzgerald's novel, but at least one particular account stands out. A French doctor speaks of a terrifying incident "that fell upon me without any warning" during one period of spiritual melancholia. He mentally conjured up the image of an asylum inmate, "a black-haired youth with greenish skin," who seemingly sat before him "like a sort of sculptured Egyptian cat or Peruvian mummy, moving nothing but his black eyes and looking absolutely non-human":

> There was such a horror of him, and such a perception of my own merely momentary discrepancy from him, that it was as if something hitherto solid within my breast gave way entirely, and I became a mass of quivering fear. After this the universe was changed for me altogether. I awoke morning after morning with a horrible dread at the pit of my stomach, and with a sense of the insecurity of life that I never knew before, and that I have never felt since. It was like a revelation; and although the immediate feelings passed away, the experience has made me sympathetic with the morbid feelings of others ever since. It gradually faded, but for months I was unable to go out into the dark alone. (149–50)

The reader may instantly recognize this account as a close parallel to the odd, mystical encounter Amory Blaine has with a supernatural figure of evil in *This Side of Paradise*. After a fearful night spent fleeing from a man (or devil) with oddly misshapen feet, Amory awakens with "his terror hardened on him like plaster," admitting even many days afterward that his imagination has caused him to hate and fear the dark (113, 123). The lurid supernaturalism of the episode has confounded critics, contemporary and later, juxtaposed as it stands against the realistic incidents of a modern novel. But Fitzgerald evidently thought this manifestation of a "Sick Soul" important enough to rework similar material at a moment of the protagonist's psychological and spiritual crisis in his next novel as well, when the evil Joe Hull makes his uncanny appearance in *The Beautiful and Damned*. Both diabolical figures apparently objectify the decadence that time produces when too much negative experience displaces an individual's clean initiation into life.

When Burne Holiday, the noble classmate with the relish for Whitman, Tolstoy, and James, is finally forced to leave Princeton for his uncertain, ignominious future as a conscientious objector, Amory finds

"primal honesty" in his friend's revolt against state-sanctioned patriotism (141). And at the novel's climax, Amory himself (Fitzgerald's first
spoiled priest?) will repeat the gesture of self-sacrifice, bearing legal
risks and public humiliation in order to conceal classmate Alec Connage's violation of the Mann Act. Thus in one way *This Side of Paradise*
details an individual's journey from the false consciousness of mere
"personality," with all its stamps of upbringing and education and class
convention, to the genuineness of becoming a "personage," one who
pragmatically acts in the freedom from constraints of established creed,
custom, or caste. But if pragmatist escape from "pretended absolutes"
partially liberates the protagonist of *This Side of Paradise,* Fitzgerald's
first novel relentlessly probes another aspect of pragmatic ideology with
much less favor.

As noted earlier, the instants of time provide a framework for many
of James's conceptualizations; "Time itself comes in drops," he once
noted (*Writings* 734). Living within the concentrated space of the current moment forms a temporal basis for the pragmatist's moral decision
making, released as it is from the restrictions and absolute imperatives of
a past moral order. (Dewey spoke of the "constant reconstruction of
experience.") But the freedom gained in a universe where time is measured in instants of "now" is gained at inevitable cost—as the still restless and haunted Amory Blaine has gradually learned to appreciate. The
cost is estimated most evidently in what Amory styles the "woman
problem."

This Side of Paradise achieved best-selling status in part for its depiction of the young century's new morality: "None of the Victorian
mothers—and most of the mothers were Victorian—had any idea how
casually their daughters were accustomed to be kissed," the narrative
voice reminds us (61). From the beginning, Amory (one especially notes
the Latin root in the protagonist's name) actively participates in the
young generation's liberated impulses. In the novel's first dramatized incident, the thirteen-year-old Amory manages to sequester himself with
Myra St. Claire, a schoolmate who "everybody knows" has a crush on
Froggy Parker: "But Amory, being on the spot, leaned over quickly and
kissed Myra's cheek. He had never kissed a girl before, and he tasted his
lips curiously, as if he had munched some new fruit. Then their lips
brushed like young wild flowers in the wind" (21).

As the passage suggests, the boy's "free" and modern morality has been situated in a pragmatist's framing of time. Fresh instants of experience govern. And the reader has only to glance through the serial romances of Amory Blaine—with Isabelle Borgé, Clara Page, Rosalind Connage, and Eleanor Savage—to discover how insistently affairs of the heart are now synchronized to the remorseless, sequential tickings of a pragmatist clock.

In the braver, newer world of modern romance, Fitzgerald's narrator generalizes, "the Popular Daughter becomes engaged every six months between sixteen and twenty-two" (61). As the Myra St. Claire passage indicates, the younger Amory is quite willing to participate in what can only be styled a *process* of the heart. His correspondence with flirtatious Isabelle, for example, is "chiefly enlivened by his attempts to find new words for love" (81). He strives to keep the relationship "infinitely charming, infinitely new" (82). But when his romantic impulses change direction, Clara (the sensible cousin who has "never been in love") describes Amory's feelings as a catalog of emotions he runs through every five seconds (137). Far from abashed, Amory apparently relishes the image of pragmatist freedom this suggests. "I'm romantic," he tells the next young woman to attract his attention: "a sentimental person thinks that things will last—a romantic person hopes against hope that they won't. Sentiment is emotional" (166). Amory's formulation here is repeated one other time, to the fiercely independent young woman he meets in Maryland one summer, Eleanor Savage. But Eleanor rejects his sentimental/romantic distinctions as "epigrams" (212). The shrewd Maryland woman, it seems, correctly sees through their summer idyll. She cannot hope to capture even temporarily a heart that has already been pledged. For Eleanor insightfully inquires, "Was she more beautiful than I am?" (216). She poignantly intuits that her own incidental placement in time happens to follow an unforgotten former love, namely the spectacular Rosalind Connage.

In *This Side of Paradise,* the passing contemporaneity of experience is never more clearly registered than in the depiction of the love affair between Amory and Rosalind. One of Rosalind's failed suitors provides the key thematic exposition just before Amory and Rosalind meet, confessing his notion "that after a girl was kissed she was—was—won." "Those days are over," Rosalind replies. "I have to be won all over again every time you see me" (169). Dating rituals, courtship, and long-term emotional attachments have been subordinated to the pleasures of "that first moment, when he's interested. There is a moment—Oh, just before the first kiss, a whispered word—something that makes it worth while" (170). When this epitome of the New Woman meets up with Amory Blaine, their passion is enacted in such modern moments—"intangibly fleeting, unrememberable hours" (177). Fitzgerald focuses attention on the brilliant and fragile quality of a relationship for such lovers, his prose imagery suggesting how temporal conditions connect to the novel's title: "They were together constantly, for lunch, for dinner, and nearly every evening—always in a sort of breathless hush, as if they feared that any minute the spell would break and drop them out of this paradise of rose and flame" (174).

In paradise, perhaps, such moments are endless, and their exquisite perfections last forever. On the other hand, according to the Rupert Brooke poem "Tiare Tahiti," which gave Fitzgerald his title, "this side of paradise" is the realm of human loves that are by nature always imperiled by time (121). Ironically enough, Rosalind comes nearer to the carpe diem sensibility of Brooke's persona than the poetic Amory Blaine. For Amory is the one who clings to those eternal verities Brooke disdainfully calls "The Good, the Lovely, and the True" (119), and Amory is the one haunted by the memory of Rosalind nearly to the last words of his story. "I love you," he is able to profess softly at the height of his relationship with Rosalind. And in her instinctive honesty as a young woman brought up in the awareness of what James calls "experience's immediate flux," she can only respond in one way: "I love you—now" (173).

The simple adverb carries awful weight in *This Side of Paradise*. For if the exigencies of the present moment permit Amory Blaine a measure of freedom from the straitened orthodoxies of the past and the demanded conformities of Princeton, "now" also circumscribes any action taken, any feeling perceived, any prospective commitment. After losing Rosalind, a fading summer spent with Eleanor Savage, "there on the edge of time while the flower months failed," becomes emblematic of an existence sentenced to unfixity: "Amory resented that life had changed from an even progress along a road stretching ever in sight, with the scenery merging and blending, into a succession of quick, unrelated scenes. . . . He felt that it would take all time, more than he could ever spare, to glue these strange cumbersome pictures into the scrapbook of his life. It was all like a banquet where he sat for this half-hour of his youth and tried to enjoy brilliant epicurean courses" (215–16). The frustration expressed here represents Fitzgerald's own long ambivalence about a condition that offered the allure of "the open air and possibilities of nature," as James styled it in *Pragmatism* (*Writings* 509)— but which was filled with a new kind of woman who, sharing such pragmatic freedom, both attracted and terrified her potential mates. A connection was instinctively made between the Rosalind who entices Amory with the identifying remark "We haven't the same standards of time as other people" (166) and the Rosalind who eventually breaks off their romantic attachment by noting, "I like sunshine and pretty things and cheerfulness—and I dread responsibility" (183). Responsibility is a virtue embedded in time: not pragmatist instants of time, but the time that extends sempiternally backward through memory and forward through everlasting commitment. It was a virtue seemingly excluded from the pragmatist New Woman who lived only in the most current moment of experience.

For all the respect accorded the revolutionary qualities of *The Great Gatsby*, it is worth noting that Fitzgerald's third novel substantially reiterates themes of time that had been introduced in *This Side of Paradise*. Most notably, *Gatsby* will stress the urgency of time experienced in pragmatist instants of consciousness. The action is situated in the fleeting weeks of one summer. Fitzgerald had evoked the aura of this "sad season of life without growth" in *This Side of Paradise* (213) as a metaphor for the ephemeral love affair of Amory and Eleanor. By the time of *The Great Gatsby*, the warm summer's passing becomes all the more terrible for its reminder of ceaseless flux and process:

"What'll we do with ourselves this afternoon," cried Daisy, "and the day after that, and the next thirty years?"

"Don't be morbid," Jordan said. "Life starts all over again when it gets crisp in the fall."

"But it's so hot," insisted Daisy, on the verge of tears. "And everything's so confused. Let's all go to town!"

Her voice struggled on through the heat, beating against it, moulding its senselessness into forms. (118–19)

Ronald Berman cites this passage in remarking that "so much is simultaneous" in the novel that "older and more directly intelligible ways of telling a story no longer apply" (*"The Great Gatsby" and Modern Times* 53). What remains is the acute awareness of the streaming days, each rendered in a "hot" immediacy that seems to have spurred Fitzgerald to echo *The Waste Land* (lines 133–34) in his dialogue.

Amory Blaine's melancholic awareness of "this half-hour of his youth" forecasts the unit that will measure the rapid sequences of pragmatic time in *Gatsby,* where one-half of an hour—time dissected to an effective moment, in novelistic terms—is the time frame specified sufficient for (among other things) extracting the juice of two hundred oranges, or sharing a "wasteful and inappropriate" supper with Jordan Baker, or drunkenly breaking off an engagement to Tom Buchanan and then soberly reconsidering, or reuniting lovers in a bungalow while a rainstorm passes, or transforming from Jimmy Gatz to Jay Gatsby while saving a yacht on Lake Superior, or awaiting a doctor's arrival at a fatal accident scene, or postponing the start of Gatsby's funeral in a futile expectation of mourners (39, 45, 77, 89, 98–99, 142, 175). Alternating such parsed units of time with occasional "hour" references that likewise stress transiency, Fitzgerald created a prose calculus designed to emphasize the fleeting moment, the passing instant. Clearly, the more polished novelist also wished to alloy this temporal element with the ultimate human concern of the novel, the love between Gatsby and Daisy. For Gatsby, impervious to the modern time-sense, it's a simple matter. Daisy ought to have fallen in love forever—as he had fallen in love. During the five years of Daisy's marriage with Tom, despite physical separation, Gatsby maintains that "both of us loved each other all that time" (132). When the incredulous Tom denies this and reminds his wife of their most intimate moments together, Daisy is forced to confront the pragmatist contingency that governs her life, right down to her deepest personal feelings. "Oh, you want too much!" she cries out to Gatsby. Just as Rosalind Connage had done in the earlier novel, Daisy restricts the horizon of her love to a modern moment: "I love you now—isn't that enough?" (133).

For one sort of pragmatist, it should be. For a Platonic son of God, of course, it isn't. On a symbolic level, Daisy's pronouncement of temporal realities in the modern world kills Gatsby as surely as Wilson's bullet does. And on a psychological and spiritual level William James had already described this outcome, for in *The Varieties of Religious Experience* he had noted the phenomena attendant on passionate love: "It transforms the value of the creature loved as utterly as the sunrise transforms Mont Blanc from a corpse-like gray to a rosy enchantment; and it sets the whole world to a new tune for the lovers and gives a new issue to life" (*Writings* 141). Time's passage resists this fancy-work, however; and James is dire about the consequences for the melancholiac who confronts a loss of treasured feeling:

> The world now looks remote, strange, sinister, uncanny. Its color is gone, its breath is cold, there is no speculation in the eyes it glares with. "It is as if I lived in another century," says one asylum patient.—"I see everything through a cloud," says another, "things are not as they were, and I am changed."—"I see," says a third, "I touch, but the things do not come near me, a thick veil alters the hue and look of everything."—"Persons move like shadows, and sounds seem to come from a distant world." (142)

The frightening "new world" of the grotesque rose and raw sunlight is inhabited only by "poor ghosts" as Gatsby perceives it after the foreclosure of his dream. The phrases and references assemble in a brilliant passage conveyed with the poetic concision of a master author. But Gatsby essentially inhabits the same "disillusioning" terrain already defined by the first-time novelist—in his early twenties already an authority of failure—who wrote of a "coarsened" world of "flowers that, when closely inspected, appeared moth-eaten" (258), and where a jilted Amory Blaine had found himself sadly pondering, "What ghosts were people with which to work!" (257). Gatsby's body is last viewed floating on an air mattress in his swimming pool: "The touch of a cluster of leaves revolved it slowly, tracing, like the leg of a transit, a thin red circle in the water" (163). The word "transit" is notorious here as evidence of Fitzgerald's carelessness with words; he had written "transept" on the original manuscript (*Gatsby: A Facsimile* 236). Matthew J. Bruccoli switches the word to "compass" in his re-edited edition of the novel, inserting a more logical visual image into the passage. Yet the original text contains the right word etymologically for describing the floating figure that has become visually a kind of clock—the very clock that had defeated Gatsby in life. *Sic transit gloria mundi.*

The modernist viewpoint had come to accept pragmatism's depiction of human experience as a series of constituent moments. This was the temporal realm of the "microcosmic dimension" Norman Cantor associates with modernism—the fractured source-points of the "immediate understandings" that replace a sense of history and continuity (36). Gertrude Stein and others attempted to capture the essence of the cascading moments of experience in the new literature; "Hugh Selwyn Mauberly" and *The Waste Land* and Quentin Compson's "temporary" world are, so to speak, modernist monuments to the perceptions of time-fragmented consciousness.

As *This Side of Paradise* demonstrates, Fitzgerald began his career as a novelist keenly aware of the urging insistencies of modern time, with the concomitant shrinkage of human experience to the compass of ever-changing units of present time and knowledge. But the awareness was, for him, no merely theoretical discovery, because somewhere between the first and final drafts of *This Side of Paradise,* Fitzgerald found himself in love with a captivating Alabama beauty named Zelda Sayre. For a time they were engaged. And then they weren't. Zelda's decision to break apart had made perfect sense in a temporal condition where, after all, one neither loved nor lived based on pasts and futures. "It was one of those tragic loves doomed for lack of money, and one day the girl closed it out on the basis of common sense," Fitzgerald would write. "During a long summer of despair I wrote a novel instead of letters, so it came out all right, but it came out all right for a different person" (Wilson, *The Crack-up* 77). In Jamesian terms, the concept referred to here would be described as "verifiability." Verifiability is determined in the light of concrete situations, and it changes as situations do. Beliefs verifiable in the experience of one person may not be verifiable in the different experience of another person; beliefs verifiable in one person's experience at one time may be, in later experience, disconfirmed (Suckiel 96). Pragmatically speaking, Fitzgerald's "different person" necessarily married a "different person" from the one he'd first fallen in love with—for time, with all of its discontinuities, had marched on.

As *This Side of Paradise* reveals, Fitzgerald committed himself to no such pragmatist understanding. True, the novel depicts a radically modernized social world, where young lovers may safely intone only the limited conviction that a new age permits—"I love you—now." Perhaps the qualification in such language represents, in the twentieth century and beyond, wisdom. In *Pragmatism,* William James had described the rationalist fallacy as "exactly like the sentimentalist's": "Both extract a quality from the muddy particulars of experience, and find it so pure when extracted that they contrast it with each and all its muddy instances as an opposite and higher nature" (*Writings* 587). Amory Blaine, who believes in a love that exists yesterday, today, and tomorrow, is, by his own definitions, a sentimentalist. Forever "unadjustable," he initiates a line of fictional brothers—Anthony Patch, Jay Gatsby, Dick Diver, and Monroe Stahr—who share their creator's ultimate resistance to that now-ness Eliot styled "unredeemable." The belief "that things will last" may also suggest why young F. Scott Fitzgerald, despite sharing some of the instinctive pragmatism of Amory Blaine, parted from the pathway of high modernism. His own sentimental journey required another route.

3

The Catholic Romanticism of
This Side of Paradise

WALTER RAUBICHECK

In his biography of Fitzgerald, André Le Vot quotes the remarks of the archbishop of Baltimore when, in 1975, the author's remains were moved to St. Mary's Church cemetery in Rockville, Maryland:

> F. Scott Fitzgerald came out of the Maryland Catholic tradition. He was a man touched by the faith of the Catholic Church. There can be perceived in his works a Catholic consciousness of reality. He found in this faith an understanding of the human heart caught in the struggle between grace and death. His characters are involved in this great drama, seeking God and seeking love. As an artist he was able with lucidity and poetic imagination to portray this struggle. He also experienced in his own life the mystery of suffering and, we hope, the power of God's grace. (354)

This insight into the "Catholic consciousness of reality" is certainly a key to the moral center of Fitzgerald's novels and stories. Yet Fitzgerald's Catholicism has not been fully treated in the critical discussion of his work, particularly in relation to *This Side of Paradise*. His own disaffection from Catholic practice after his Princeton years and the lack of specific Catholic references in the four novels that followed *Paradise* surely account in part for this tendency. However, Fitzgerald's first novel cannot be satisfactorily appreciated if the Catholic concerns are underappreciated, and his religious imagination affects all his major work, especially its romantic vision. The nature of Amory's Blaine's romanticism,

as well as Fitzgerald's, differs from that of his nineteenth-century predecessors such as Wordsworth and Emerson precisely in that it is a Catholic
product, not one that is pantheistic or transcendental. The book's published title indicates its Christian concern with a fallen world, while its
original title—"The Romantic Egotist"—reveals both the centrality of
romanticism and its potential threat to one's development of character.

Some critics, of course, have discussed in general terms the moral
sense in Fitzgerald's work as having been influenced by his Catholic upbringing. Thomas J. Stavola observes that "no matter how hard Fitzgerald tried throughout his life to turn his Catholicism into a memory, his
basic feeling for experience remained a religious one. He consistently
viewed life, especially his own, as a dramatic conflict between good and
evil although he occasionally renounced these categories in favor of
what appealed to his own aesthetic imagination" (26). And Kenneth
Eble draws a similar conclusion after reviewing the history of Fitzgerald's Catholic past: "the moral concern and the sense of evil to be found
in all his serious work may be important consequences of his youthful
religious interest" (*F. Scott Fitzgerald* 58). The one specific full-length
treatment of the influence of Catholicism is Joan M. Allen's *Candles and
Carnival Lights* (1978). Allen sees the basic tension in all the major novels
to be derived from Augustine's City of God/City of Man dichotomy:
Fitzgerald's protagonists are caught between the lure of the "carnival lights" of worldly pleasure and success and the "candles" of moral
revulsion from sin. But even Allen does not emphasize that Fitzgerald's
"candles" become a means to deepen the glow of his romanticism. I
would also suggest that Amory is able to resolve this Augustinian tension
through his sacramental view of the world, a view that modern thinkers
such as David Tracy and Andrew Greeley identify as a distinctive feature
of the true Catholic perspective.[1] Underneath Amory's confused search
for values and identity in Fitzgerald's first novel is the constant but only
dimly perceived awareness that life's moments of ecstatic transcendence,
the essence of romanticism, are what his religious tradition would also
define as revelatory moments of the presence of God.

Of course, it is important to realize that the resolution of Amory's
conflicts in the novel is not intended to be an affirmation of faith. The
narrative trajectory of the book is from "egotist" to "personage" (the
key words in the titles of the two subdivisions of the novel), not from

agnostic to believer. It is crucial to Fitzgerald's concerns that the novel end with Amory's certainty about his own character but about nothing else: "'I know myself,' he cried, 'but that is all'" (260). Implicit in this statement is a disaffection from all belief systems, from Catholicism to the pseudo-Marxism Amory casually expounds toward the close of the novel. Joyce's *A Portrait of the Artist as a Young Man* is probably a major influence here, although Stephen Dedalus's rebellion and his rejections of church and state are certainly more dramatic than Amory's ambivalence.

Interestingly, Fitzgerald himself was apparently more inclined to religious practice at Princeton than was his creation. He attended Mass regularly, and it is certainly revealing that he married Zelda in a Catholic ceremony at St. Patrick's Cathedral (Bruccoli, *Some Sort of Epic Grandeur* 131). But Amory returns to Princeton after his brief experience in the army, aware that he is part of a generation that now finds "all Gods dead, all wars fought, all faiths in man shaken" (260). First in his creative life, and eventually in his personal life, Fitzgerald submerged his Catholicism within his growing tragic romanticism, his legacy of the doomed idealist. This mystical impulse surfaces in the idealist's moment of transcendence, such as when Gatsby's imagination soars beyond the limitation of bodily limits—"romp[ing] like the mind of God"—and he knows he can "gulp down the incomparable milk of wonder" (112).

In *This Side of Paradise*, Fitzgerald explicitly traces the course of Catholicism's influence on Amory Blaine's developing romantic temperament. Intellectually, of course, Amory considers Catholicism to be attractive in its medieval, Chestertonian qualities, but it is not an influence that compels him to any active practice: "He was not even a Catholic, yet that was the only ghost of a code he had, the gaudy, paradoxical Catholicism whose prophet was Chesterton, whose claqueurs were such reformed rakes of literature as Huysmans and Bourget, whose American sponsor was Ralph Adams Cram, with his adulation of thirteenth-century cathedrals—a Catholicism which Amory found convenient and ready-made, without priest or sacraments or sacrifice" (119). Yet this "ghost of a code" has impressed itself deeply on his feelings in ways that Amory himself does not fully understand and which emerge in three distinct areas of his life: his relationship with Darcy, his emotional adventures with women, and his repeated encounters with evil. What is particularly interesting is how the Catholic imagery in these episodes is always intertwined with the book's romantic themes.

Amory's romanticism is not made as explicit as Gatsby's "readiness" and his "heightened sensitivity to the promises of life" (2). It consists mainly of Amory's vague awareness that he has the ability to have a positive effect on his world, that his physical and mental attributes must not be wasted but must be used constructively, that he must become a "personage," not a mere "personality," as Thayer Darcy puts it. He is not trying to recapture a golden past or impose an impossible dream on intractable reality, but he is attempting to imagine a future that will be susceptible to his gifts. Herein, of course, lies the danger of pride and self-absorption.

Several times in the book, Amory consciously defines himself as a romantic or an idealist. To Tom, his poet classmate and friend, he claims that he is "a cynical idealist" and then "wondered if that meant any-thing" (84). Later in the novel he tells Rosalind that he is a romantic as opposed to a sentimentalist and then explains that "a sentimental person thinks things will last—a romantic person hopes against hope they won't. Sentiment is emotional" (166). Of course, these self-definitions are part of the pose of the immature egotist, hiding his own confusion behind epigrams and adopting a "carpe diem" perspective toward the transitoriness of romantic intensity. Yet the remark to Rosalind indicates a dim awareness that romanticism is not a panoply of emotions but instead a genuine response of the whole person to reality. It is Monsignor Darcy who prompts Amory to abandon his poses and act from the depths of his being, not from the superficial layer of his charm. Interestingly, the academic tradition of Princeton is presented in the novel as the fruit of the medieval Catholic tradition. The Gothic tower Amory can see from his window induces a rumination on the concept of a university that relates it metaphorically to the church:

> The tower that in view of his window sprang upward, grew into a spire, yearning higher until its uppermost tip was half invisible against the morning skies, gave him the first sense of the transiency and unimportance of the campus figures except as holders of the apostolic succession. He liked knowing that Gothic architecture, with its upward trend, was peculiarly appropriate to universities,

and the idea became personal to him. The silent stretches of green, the quiet halls with an occasional late-burning scholastic light held his imagination in a strong grasp, and the chastity of the spire became a symbol of his perception. (57)

Temporarily, Amory feels that he is part of the "apostolic succession" of both the church and the university, handed down from the unified culture of the Middle Ages. But in both cases Amory cannot maintain his allegiance; he does not actively participate in the church, and he substitutes creative involvement in campus theater and journalism for true academic discipline. Yet these two influences have left a distinct mark on his imagination. Amory takes what he finds useful from the academic and religious traditions and incorporates them into the distinctive characteristics of his own talent and temperament.

Amory's friendship with Thayer Darcy is clearly central to the novel's thematic concerns. Darcy is often described as "worldly" and "ambitious" rather than devout. Typically, Milton R. Stern describes him as a "representative of a resplendent power whose world is more cosmopolitan than theological, whose rich color heightens aphorism rather than pietism, whose machinery is graciousness rather than grace" (*The Golden Moment* 49). However, Darcy's repeated insistence in his letters that Amory is a younger version of himself should indicate to us that he too is essentially romantic. First of all, he had courted Amory's mother when he was a young romantic egotist himself: "When she had first returned to her country there had been a pagan, Swinburnian young man in Asheville, for whose passionate kisses and unsentimental conversation she had taken a decided penchant—they had discussed the matter pro and con with an intellectual romancing quite devoid of soppiness. Eventually she had decided to marry for background, and the young pagan from Asheville had gone through a spiritual crisis, joined the Catholic Church, and was now—Monsignor Darcy" (14). Thus, before his conversion Amory's spiritual father behaved much as Amory does in the novel, and throughout the book he tries to bequeath to Amory his understanding of the world. He impresses on Amory two essential qualities of Catholicism: the intellectual respectability of the faith, something Amory needs to be reassured of, and, more importantly, an awareness that grace can be found through a participation in the world and not only through ascetic isolation from it. This is the essential Catholic sacramental vision, one that is at the heart of the fiction and essays of Chesterton, a writer who is mentioned several times in the novel as an influence on Amory. At the end of the novel it is Darcy's funeral that precipitates an emotional response not unlike Dick Diver's grief over his father's death. Although it does not lead Amory to a conversion, it does point toward the continued influence on Amory of what Darcy represents.

The person/personage distinction that Darcy leads Amory to understand points to Amory's development in the second half of the novel. Personality is a "physical matter," according to the monsignor, whereas a personage "gathers." A personage is "a bar on which a thousand things have been hung—glittering things sometimes, as ours are" (101). The bar for Darcy is formed by the rock of the church, and his glitter is the effect of the dazzling atmosphere he creates as its representative: "When he came into a room clad in his full purple regalia from thatch to toe, he resembled a Turner sunset, and attracted both admiration and attention" (29–30). For Amory the bar is his fear and hatred of evil, his glitter is his talent, and "the cold mentality behind them" that Darcy mentions is clarity of intellect. Rather than vestiges of puritanism, what separates Amory from Dick Humbird and other personalities and "slickers" that he admires at Princeton is essentially the quality Darcy has identified: like the later Charlie Wales in "Babylon Revisited," Amory comes to see that character is superior to personality.

The best examples in the novel of Amory's development are his relationships with Clara and Eleanor. Clara, the Philadelphia widow, has none of Rosalind's overwhelming sensual beauty, but she diffuses a "golden radiance" that completely captivates Amory, a radiance that is inseparable from her essential purity: "she was the first fine woman he ever knew and one of the few good people who ever interested him. She made her goodness such an asset" (133). A practicing Catholic and the mother of two small children, Clara inspires Amory to write a poem about her entitled "St. Cecilia," and he even feels compelled to tell her that he would lose his faith in God if he lost his faith in her. Her influence is explicitly connected to that of Amory's spiritual father: "Clara's was the only advice he ever asked without dictating the answer himself—except, perhaps, in his talks with Monsignor Darcy" (135–36).

Amory is not sure whether he "loves," "adores," or "worships" her (137); implied in this religious diction is that this fascination is his first experience of an erotic attraction that is also infused with the sacred, with the distinct aura of the spirit. If a sacrament is an outward sign of God's providence and grace, then Clara surely serves as a sacrament for Amory, fusing the sensual and the sacred in a radiant image of earthly beauty.

Eleanor, of course, is Clara's opposite. She is a ravishing embodiment of fin de siècle decadence, reveling in her ennui, recklessness, and atheism. Just as Amory was captivated by Clara's "golden hair" in the "stained glass light" (136), he now abandons himself to "the half-sensual, half-neurotic quality of this autumn with Eleanor" (215), the self-proclaimed materialist who, in a fit of romantic impulse, drives her horse to the edge of a precipice and saves her life only by jumping off at the last possible moment. She dares God to strike her just before she commits this folly, repelling Amory: "His materialism, always a thin cloak, was torn to shreds by Eleanor's blasphemy" (221). After her narrow escape from death, she explains to Amory that her mother had gone insane and that she herself has a "crazy streak"; Amory's love dies as he realizes what romanticism can become when it is freed from all moral grounding, from all spiritual yearning and restraint. If Clara is a pre-Raphaelite image, embodying a romantic nostalgia for medieval faith, Eleanor is the representative of a late-nineteenth-century Nietzschean atheism that Amory can never accept.

Of all the women in the novel, it is Rosalind, the epitome of aristocratic beauty and shallowness whose literary descendants will dominate much of Fitzgerald's fiction, who has the greatest impact on him and who causes him genuine suffering. She is foreshadowed in the novel by Isabelle in that the earlier relationship is described through theatrical images—"as an actress even in the fullest flush of her own conscious magnetism gets a deep impression of most of the people in the front row, so Isabelle sized up her protagonist" (66)—and the episode in which Amory first meets Rosalind is presented (form fitting theme) as a one-act play in which the two lovers pose and perform for each other. But whereas the earlier relationship was loveless and served only to elevate and then puncture the egotism of Amory and Isabelle, Rosalind is Amory's first real love, the woman who calls forth from him for the first time "tenderness . . . gentleness and unselfishness" (194). But Rosalind's beauty is the illusory beauty of the world that is untouched by grace. Monsignor Darcy is acutely aware of the danger of this kind of attraction for Amory:

> Your last letter was quite enough to make me worry about you. It was not a bit like yourself. Reading between the lines I should imagine that your engagement to this girl is making you rather unhappy, and I see you have lost all the feeling of romance that you had before the war. You make a great mistake if you think you can be romantic without religion. Sometimes I think that with both of us the secret of success, when we find it, is the mystical element in us: something flows into us that enlarges our personalities, and when it ebbs out our personalities shrink; I should call your last two letters rather shrivelled. Beware of losing yourself in the personality of another being, man or woman. (220)

The mystical element is the touch of grace lacking in Amory's affairs with Rosalind and Eleanor, and without it Amory "shrinks" into the suffering egotist.

"The Romantic Egotist" of the first half of the novel is sometimes merely ridiculously vain, and the distance between Fitzgerald and his protagonist allows him to poke fun at Amory, particularly concerning his repeated posing with women. However, the scene when Amory perceives and is pursued by the devil reveals that Fitzgerald has deeper moral concerns in the novel than the problem of adolescent insincerity. The devil appears to Amory during a drinking party that almost leads him to sleep with a girl he does not love or respect, but this appearance is not a sign that Fitzgerald simplistically associates evil with promiscuous sex. The association of the devil with the recently killed Dick Humbird—when Amory is pursued by this terrifying being he finally sees that it has Humbird's face—connects the episode to both "the supercilious sacrifice" Amory makes for his friend Alec and his lover and Amory's final ruminations in the novel. The devil is associated with personalities who can never become personages (Humbird), characters who lose their souls to gain the world; Humbird has deeply impressed the part of Amory that longs for superficial social triumphs, for Humbird himself is the epitome of the American rich man's son. The devil appears again toward the end of the novel as an aura surrounding Jill, the girl Alec brings to an Atlantic City hotel room to have sex with. (Amory decides to cover for Alec and take the blame when the house detectives suddenly arrive.) Amory is learning that some manifestations of beauty can be evil, those that have "too many associations with license and indulgence" (258). He must learn to transcend his attraction to these insidious temptations if he is to become a personage instead of an egotist. In traditional narrative terms, the internal obstacles that Amory must overcome in order to reach his goal of becoming a personage are his desire to be an exemplar of sophistication and social eminence like Humbird and his susceptibility to beauty in all its forms, no matter how insidious. Unlike Keats, Amory comes to feel that beauty alone is not enough; it must be accompanied by principle and control.

Catholicism appeals to Amory as the best available means to resolve his conflicts, although he has not reached the certainties of faith: "His mind turned a corner suddenly and he found himself thinking of the Catholic Church. . . . Quite conceivably it was an empty ritual, but it was seemingly the only assimilative, traditionary bulwark against the decay of morals. Until the great mobs could be educated into a moral sense one must cry: 'Thou shalt not!' Yet any acceptance was, for the present, impossible" (259). The novel ends, then, with Amory still a skeptic ("There was no God in his heart" [260]), but, I would argue, with a sensibility that has been shaped by Catholic attitudes toward the purpose of human life. Like Stephen Dedalus, Amory will become a priest of art. Also like Stephen, he will attempt to raise the moral level of his people. Life is a "labyrinth" to Amory now, but the death of Monsignor Darcy opens up to him a sense of mission: "of Monsignor's funeral was born the romantic elf who was to enter the labyrinth with him. He found something that he wanted, had always wanted and always would want—not to be admired, as he had feared; not to be loved, as he had made himself believe; but to be necessary to people, to be indispensable. . . . Amory felt an immense desire to give people a sense of security" (246). In other words, he is beginning to overcome his egotism (the crippling desire to be admired and loved) through the continued influence of the central Catholic figure in the novel, Thayer Darcy.

Any discussion of Darcy necessarily brings to mind the other important priest in Fitzgerald's fiction, Father Schwartz in "Absolution." He has been driven into madness by his belief that all the sensual qualities of the world are occasions of sin, exemplified by his fear of "cheap toilet soap" (*The Short Stories* 259) that wafts out of Romberg's Drug Store. Young Rudolph Miller, the Jay Gatsby prototype who is overcome by guilt because he fears he has lied in the confessional, recognizes the priest's terror at the "heat and the sweat and the life" (271) and concludes that God would know he had lied to brighten "the dinginess of his admissions" (271). But the story is not a rejection of Catholicism; it is a rejection of the Jansenism that has infected the theology of the church and undermined its sacramental nature. The "girls with yellow hair" who "walked sensuously along roads that bounded the fields, calling innocent, exciting things to the young men" (272), embody the beauty of life that Fitzgerald responded to more deeply than almost any other American writer and which is always a source of grace if it is not corrupted by the greed and lusts of men. These girls are potential sacraments, but Father Schwartz is blind to this deep Catholic truth, and the result is madness.

These ideas reverberate throughout Fitzgerald's fiction. Jay Gatsby is destroyed by his assumption that the beauty of the world can be contained in tawdry grandeur and purchased with money. In "Babylon Revisited," Fitzgerald's frequently anthologized 1931 story, Charlie Wales develops the need for moral grounding after the excesses of his 1920s hedonism have led to his wife's death and his own alcoholism: "He believed in character; he wanted to jump back a whole generation and trust in character again as the eternally valuable element. Everything wore out" (*The Short Stories* 619). Likewise, Dick Diver in *Tender Is the Night* is destroyed by his need to be loved and admired—to be a "personality"—a need that triumphs over the virtues of "honesty, courtesy, and courage" (271) stressed by his father. Gatsby, Wales, and Diver are older, tragic versions of Amory—romantic egotists who fail to control their susceptibility to the destructive kind of beauty that encourages disdain for self-discipline. On the other hand, several characters from the major novels do learn the difference between a personality and a personage before they self-destruct. Nick Carraway discovers that life cannot be lived among "careless" people who totally lack a moral sense no matter how much beauty they possess. He understands both the power of Gatsby's transcendent vision and the frailty of his character. And Monroe Stahr, the movie producer in *The Last Tycoon,* achieves a balance that is beyond Fitzgerald's tragic heroes; he exemplifies the belief that the promise of beauty can come only through work, through the combination of lavish imagination and rigid self-discipline. Unlike his predecessors in Fitzgerald's fiction, Stahr is destroyed by external forces he cannot control: the money-obsessed moguls who have taken over the industry, and the union movement that undermines his power to create.

It is curious that more critical attention has not been paid to the mutual Catholic influence when Fitzgerald's works are compared and contrasted with Hemingway's. Both writers—Fitzgerald, the lapsed Catholic, and Hemingway, the converted one—repeatedly convey the theme that meaning in life can result only from a sacramental vision, from the moments of transcendence that come from a proper use of the things of this world. And in the case of both writers, their first major novels treat this idea most fully. Obviously, the mature Jake Barnes is a strikingly different character from the young Amory Blaine. However, Jake, like Amory, is struggling to maintain his Catholic allegiance, with its emphasis on discipline. His insistence on "how" things should be done rather than "what" they were all about (148) indicates a need to use the things of this world with attention and respect in order to keep chaos at bay. The understated reverence with which Jake and Bill Gorton approach their fishing trip, as well as Romero's precision and artistry in the bull ring, reflect the importance of transforming human endeavor into a ritual that uncovers the sacred beneath the secular, the eternal values underlying the temporal limits on human life. Again like Amory, in order to maintain his conviction that life can be lived with purpose Jake must finally reject the insidious temptation of a woman, Brett Ashley, who resembles Eleanor in her lack of moral values and her atheism. He must also reject the excessively romantic Robert Cohn because Cohn's idealism is devoid of integrity and an awareness of the importance of meaningful work—the "bar" on which "glittering things" must be hung, according to Monsignor Darcy. And in both novels the protagonists' values find institutional validation only in the standards and traditions of Catholicism.

Thus, far from being an immature work that succeeded only by introducing "flappers" and other flaming youth into the American popular consciousness and of interest now only for its nostalgic look at an earlier, vanished Princeton, *This Side of Paradise* is a worthy introduction to Fitzgerald's thematic concerns and establishes clearly that his investigation of the mores of his time was based on a moral foundation that underlies his romantic idealism, a foundation that is essentially Catholic.

Notes

1. See Tracy, Greeley, and any of Karl Rahner's discussions of grace.

4

The Devil and F. Scott Fitzgerald

STEPHEN L. TANNER

What is the devil doing in a novel like *This Side of Paradise*? This question underlies a good deal of diverse commentary on the novel. Some view "The Devil" section and the other apparently supernatural episodes as the products of an immature writer crowding random and undigested incidents into his first novel. Others explain these aspects as unsuccessful attempts to make artistic use of the grotesque, a device they claim Fitzgerald perfected only in his subsequent fiction. A growing number of others consider the devil episode to be of the greatest significance to the structure and themes of this novel and fraught with implications for Fitzgerald's artistic vision as a whole.[1] I agree with this last perspective and will argue that the supernatural elements in *This Side of Paradise* are part of Fitzgerald's profound concern with the problem of evil, particularly with the diminishing sense of evil. Fitzgerald intended Amory Blaine's struggle with a diminishing instinct for recognizing evil to represent an important phenomenon of modern America on the eve of the 1920s. His examination of the awareness of evil as a vital element in the moral life was shaped both by his American Puritan heritage and by his Catholic upbringing. His use of what might be called the moral supernatural indicates a continuity in his writing with the romances of Hawthorne, the ghost stories of Henry James, and the morally oriented fiction of Catholic writers like the priest-novelist Robert Hugh Benson. I suggest that a large part of the continuing relevance of *This Side of Paradise* lies in its treatment of a vanishing consciousness of evil, for the same phenomenon that Fitzgerald treated as occurring within an individual persists today in American society at large in an even more perplexing postmodern form. In this respect, if in no other, the novel remains relevant to our postmodern culture, in which words like *good* and *evil* are often deemed too judgmental for public discourse.

Fitzgerald's concern with evil is one of the most interesting and complex issues dealt with in Fitzgerald criticism. Leslie Fiedler asserts that "there is in Fitzgerald no profound sense of evil or sin, only of guilt" (Mizener, *F. Scott Fitzgerald* 75). Kenneth Eble, on the other hand, perceives "an immaterial yet powerful evil that has a way of turning up in . . . Fitzgerald's stories" (*F. Scott Fitzgerald* 58). Similarly, Sy Kahn observes that Fitzgerald's concern with evil "is everywhere apparent in his work, and his desire to reveal it prompted him to write in *This Side of Paradise:* 'Every author ought to write every book as if he were going to be beheaded the day he finished it'" (Eble, *Fitzgerald: A Collection of Criticism* 47). Fitzgerald himself acknowledged his moral predisposition when he mentioned to his daughter that he sometimes wished he had devoted himself to musical comedy along with Cole Porter and Rodgers and Hart, and then added, "but I guess I am too much a moralist at heart and really want to preach at people in some acceptable form rather than to entertain them" (*Letters* 63). Certainly the conflict between good and evil is explicit in *This Side of Paradise,* in which the devil himself appears both literally and, as I will demonstrate, in frequent figures of speech.

Let me briefly summarize the supernatural elements in the novel. They range from the explicit to the hinted. Most obvious is Amory's encounter with the man with the peculiar feet, first in a New York City café and then in the apartment where Amory and his friend have taken two showgirls. The title of this section identifies this mysterious apparition as "The Devil." When Amory flees in terror, he hears footsteps following him and then senses that they are ahead of him. Suddenly he glimpses a face, "a face pale and distorted with a sort of infinite evil that twisted it like flame in the wind" (111). He recognizes it as the face of his dead classmate Dick Humbird, who had represented for him tempting but false values. According to the narrator, this is not mere alcoholic hallucination: "He had a sense of reality such as material things could never give him" (111). Later he tells his roommate, Tom, who had dreamed that Amory was in trouble, that he thinks he has seen the devil. The fact that the experience was not simply the result of drink is confirmed when Tom sees something looking in the window at Amory. Robert Sklar suggests that "for all its warnings against the sexual enticements of showgirls like Axia Marlowe, 'The Devil' episode is primarily important for its effort to exorcise the appeal, and the threat, of Dick Humbird's wealth, personality, and charm" (48). I think the temptations represented by Axia and Dick are more insidious than those Sklar lists. They are emblematic of evil in a more profound sense. Clinton Burhans is correct in asserting that, "clearly, Fitzgerald means this figure with the 'unutterably terrible feet' to represent evil as a real force in the universe and in Amory's experience" (616).

Late in the novel, in a hotel room in Atlantic City, Amory encounters this force of evil once again, this time as a gossamer aura hovering over a woman. An opposing force of good is also present, a "featureless and indistinguishable, yet strangely familiar" (228) presence by the window, which Amory later realizes was the spirit of Monsignor Darcy. Even while alive, Darcy has an unrealistic, even fantastic and magical quality. He "really is a wonder," Amory tells Tom (153).[2] As a representative of the forces of good in the morality play at the core of this novel, Darcy appropriately displays a hint of the supernatural in life and makes a supernatural appearance after death.

The Eleanor episode contains a less conspicuous supernatural apparition. In the poem she sends to Amory, she mentions a presence that had leered at them *"out of the dark in the ghostly clover"* (222). Eleanor herself is given supernatural connotations. She is described as "evil," "weird" (206), a "witch" (210), "a grey ghost" (213), "wraith-like" (242), "shadowy and unreal" (216), and "a graceful, facile Manfred" (217). Amory calls her "you little devil" (217), and his "paganism" soars in her presence (213). His relationship with her was "the last time that evil crept close to Amory under the mask of beauty, the last weird mystery that held him with wild fascination and pounded his soul to flakes" (206). Commenting on this passage, Burhans says: "Here, again, a mysterious figure in an apparently sexual situation implies something evil; and again someone else sees it, thereby suggesting once more that such images throughout the novel are symbols of a real force rather than simply of guilt hallucinations in Amory" (617).

The devil also appears in a pattern that, to my knowledge, has gone unmentioned in discussions of the novel. I am referring to repeated and strategic figures of speech involving the devil. Sometimes they appear to be simply trite exclamations such as "what the devil" (50, 127) or "you'll get the devil" (217) or "I'm restless as the devil" (154), but often the word "devil" resonates beyond the trite. For example, one night Amory sits with a young woman in a car outside a country club, reflecting on the moral significance of easy kissing. "Why on earth are we here?" he asks. "I don't know," she replies; "I'm just full of the devil" (62). Both the question and the answer acquire added implications when viewed in the context of the novel's central concern with good and evil and the role played by the devil. The same is true when Amory's shirt stud leaves a mark on Isabelle's neck as they kiss. "It looks like Old Nick," she complains. Afterward they snack on "devil's food" (89, 90). Also a part of this pattern is Tom's calling Amory his "bad angel" and Amory's telling Clara, "what a devil you could have been if the Lord had just bent your soul a little the other way!" (83, 138). The pattern culminates near the end of the novel with two references to the devil that I will discuss later in this essay.

What prompted the young Fitzgerald to employ the supernatural in his first novel? One source, certainly, was a Catholic sensibility acquired in his childhood. His fiction shows the aftereffects of religious concepts and intuitions derived from his origins and from his education at the Newman School in Lakewood, New Jersey. The unpublished early manuscript of the novel, for example, contained even another supernatural scene that was based on a story Fitzgerald heard from his mentor at Newman, Father Fay (Sklar 12; West, *The Making of "This Side of Paradise"* 35). Moreover, Father Fay introduced him to Shane Leslie, an Anglo-Irish Catholic convert and successful writer and lecturer. Leslie, in turn, introduced Fitzgerald to the work of Catholic novelists like Robert Hugh Benson, whose fiction provided precedents for the supernatural episodes. In an unpublished preface to *This Side of Paradise,* Fitzgerald mentions Benson as a source along with Mackenzie, Wells, and "the great undigested butter-ball of *Dorian Gray*" (Sklar 34). And he wrote to Leslie, "you were my first literary sponsor, godfather to this book, and my original intention was to dedicate it to both of you [Father Fay and Leslie]." After the appearance of the novel, Shane

Leslie wrote Fitzgerald, "I think it is a Catholic minded book at heart" (B. A. Moore 239, 240). In her book on Fitzgerald's Catholic sensibility, Benita A. Moore concludes with this observation: "An examination of Fitzgerald's life and work leaves the cumulative impression of an 'old Catholic' fleeing the Hound of Heaven down labyrinthine ways and finding those strong feet following after at every turn" (351). This sentence, besides evoking the "unutterably terrible" feet that pursue Amory down that New York alley, corresponds with Amory's longing to be "delivered from right and wrong and from the hound of heaven" (242), a reference to the poem of that name written by the Catholic mystic Francis Thompson, which fascinated Amory as it did Fitzgerald. According to Joan M. Allen, author of another book on Fitzgerald's Catholic sensibility, what makes *This Side of Paradise* essentially the product of Catholic consciousness "is not so much the character of Monsignor Darcy, Amory's preoccupation with the appearances of Catholicism, and the book's Catholic language, but rather Amory's profound sense of evil and especially his association of evil with sexuality and feminine beauty which had descended to him from Augustine through ages of repressive Church teaching" (73).

This observation suggests a second important source for Fitzgerald's use of the supernatural: his American Puritan heritage. He said of himself that his was a New England conscience raised in Minnesota (Eble, *Fitzgerald: A Collection of Criticism* 34). His appropriation of the supernatural for moral purposes is much like Hawthorne's drawing upon the latitude of romance as a means of exploring "the truth of the human heart," a truth that for him included a vivid sense of the reality of evil. Neither author exploits the supernatural as an end in itself, merely for the titillation of horror; both are governed by moral aims. And those same moral aims determine for both of them their reticent treatment of male-female relationships: the romantic relationships in their fiction generally provide more moral than sexual illumination. James W. Tuttleton's essay on the contrasting female vampires and golden girls in Fitzgerald's fiction suggests another link with Hawthorne: the use of light and dark women (Stern, *Critical Essays* 238–46). Sy Kahn senses the Hawthorne-Fitzgerald connection when he remarks, "No Goodman Brown ever emerged from his bewitched forest more haunted and guilt-ridden than young Amory from the stone jungle of twentieth-century

New York. On the streets of the city he seems caught up in an interior morality play that obliterates his surroundings" (Eble, *Fitzgerald: A Collection of Criticism* 37).

Fitzgerald's use of the supernatural in his first novel was neither trivial nor incidental. Lawrence Buell explains that at a crucial point near the beginning of his career, Fitzgerald saw himself developing into a nonrealistic writer. He called the attention of his editor, Maxwell Perkins, to his "new manner." He considered moving into the field of fantasy and said his next novel "will not be a realistic one." He was dissuaded from this intention, according to Buell, by the lack of commercial success of stories like "The Diamond as Big as the Ritz." But this new manner, says Buell, "continued to lead a thriving sublimated existence . . . in his penchant for injecting destabilizing devices into his later fiction" (Bryer, *The Short Stories* 35–36).[3] "One Trip Abroad," which employs the device of doppelgängers, is a good example of his continued use of what might be called the moral-supernatural. In the omitted preface to *This Side of Paradise,* Fitzgerald says that in his first attempt at a novel he had written "quite above the average" about the things that most interested him, which he lists in capital letters: "THE INFLUENCE OF THE NIGHT, RATHER BAD WOMEN, PERSONALITY, FANATICISM, THE SUPERNATURAL, and VERY GOOD WOMEN" (Sklar 34). Night, good and bad women, and the supernatural obviously—and personality and fanaticism perhaps less obviously—are related to the presence of the devil in the novel. In other words, the devil is in the novel because the author was much interested in his affairs.

The presence of the devil in *This Side of Paradise* must be appreciated within the context of the moral world of 1920. To readers over eighty years later, that presence might appear quaint, melodramatic, or downright baffling. We must recognize that Fitzgerald was not a product of the 1920s, with which he is so indelibly identified. His roots were in an older, prewar America, a world with supernatural sanctions, a world of conscience and guilt—a world probably closer to Hawthorne's than to ours. Part of his temperament involved an almost puritanical impulse toward judgment. Readers of that time knew what the Victorian conscience was in ways that we do not; Fitzgerald's use of the devil should be understood with that perspective in mind. The sexual activity in the novel may seem innocuous by today's standards, scarcely warranting a visit from the devil, but Fitzgerald intended it as an emblem for real and profound evil. The novel is at once dated and timeless. Hailed in its time as a topical portrait of youthful revolt, it is actually a case study of a young soul grappling with the problem of evil. It is too easy, as Burhans points out, "to dismiss Amory's experience with evil as little more than the guilt syndrome of Fitzgerald's Mid-Western Puritan priggishness expressed in pseudo-Gothic ghosts" (618). The priggishness is there, but so is a much deeper awareness of evil. If for Amory this awareness is usually prompted by sex, beauty, wealth, and social position, it is only because such enticements cause him to recognize more frightening and destructive forces within himself. If we can exercise sufficient imagination to bridge the distance of moral attitudes between Amory's time and ours, we might, as John W. Aldridge suggests, be able to rediscover in Fitzgerald "a fresh focus and to see in the important things he wrote that other dimension, always there, but obscured until now by the glitter of his surfaces. The emphasis now is on Fitzgerald's acutely penetrative side, his ability to manipulate the surfaces as if they were mirrors that reflect not only the contents of a room, the splendor of its occupants, but the concealed horrors of its essence—the ghosts hidden just behind the swaying arras, the disenchantment behind the bright masks of faces, the death to which everyone in the room has been spiritually mortgaged" (58). We might, in other words, understand what the devil is doing in this novel.

Let me briefly outline an interpretation of the novel shaped by the recognition that the devil is a major ingredient. This reading assumes that in introspection and in conversation with others, Amory is intensely preoccupied with the problems of good and evil as they are revealed in personal relationships with classmates, in romantic relationships, and in large social issues. He is introduced as a youth "capable of infinite expansion for good or evil," possessing "rather a Puritan conscience. Not that he yielded to it—later in life he almost completely slew it" (24–25). This last phrase foreshadows the principal conflict of the novel as it emerges in Book Two. Book One establishes what Monsignor Darcy describes to Amory as "that half-miraculous sixth sense by which you detect evil, it's the half-realized fear of God in your heart" (102). Amory's intense revulsion at his first kiss signals his initiation into evil and prepares the reader for his encounter with the devil. That revulsion is accordingly described in Adamic terms: he tastes his lips "as if he had munched some new fruit," and he looks at Myrna "as though she were a new animal of whose presence on the earth he had not heretofore been aware" (21).

The devil episode in Book One is pivotal thematically and structurally. Clearly, Fitzgerald intends the devil figure to represent evil as a real force in the universe and in Amory's experience. His purpose is similar to that of Flannery O'Connor—a more orthodox Catholic writer—when she said, "I want to be certain that the Devil gets identified as the Devil and not simply taken for this or that psychological tendency" (360). Readers of *This Side of Paradise,* like readers of O'Connor's stories, will discover that the devil is not just a word; he has legs (in the case of Fitzgerald's novel, "terrible feet")—and those legs are their own. Burhans is correct in saying that Amory "feels a growing sense of evil, not as a moral or theological abstraction but as a real and shocking force which constantly tears the fabric of his experience" (616). In his conversation with Burne, Amory rejects the idea that the dividing line between good and evil is simply will. The superman, he observes, is strong and sane and yet evil—gifted but lacking a moral sense (125). Book One ends with further mention of this superman, the person of strength, talent, and intelligence who is fatally flawed by lacking a sense of evil. This condition prompts Amory to make a statement that encapsulates the thrust of Book One: "If we could only learn to look on evil *as* evil, whether it's clothed in filth or monotony or magnificence" (144). Amory's sense of evil is not simply prudish guilt. It is a profound consciousness that without moral restraints, his emotions, imagination, and intellect will run out of control to the detriment of himself and those he influences.

Book One describes the development of his sense of evil; Book Two describes his struggle to retain it. The interlude separating the two books, consisting of two letters, suggests the transition. In the first, Darcy warns Amory that his generation is "growing hard" (149), losing its sense of evil, and he counsels him to "use heaven as a continual referendum" for his ideas (150). In the second, Amory tells Tom that the war has made him a passionate agnostic and he is "as restless as the devil" (154). The letters together signal the beginnings of Amory's diminishing instinct for recognizing evil.

Book Two traces the course of that diminution. In his relationship with Rosalind he steps "into the sensuous vibrant walks of life" (174–75) and, despite Darcy's warning, experiences a complete reversal of his intense sensitivity to evil and is "hurrying into line with his generation" (174). After the Rosalind experience, he wishes to talk with Darcy but is horrified at the thought of having to tell him the Rosalind story. Instead, he visits Mrs. Lawrence, a very intelligent woman who is a convert to the church and devoted to Darcy. He confesses to her, "I'm rather pagan at present. It's just that religion doesn't seem to have the slightest bearing on life at my age" (196–97). This indifference is violently jarred by his encounter with Eleanor, who denies God and goodness and nearly rides over a cliff in an attempt to escape herself and her tormenting and ineradicable sense of evil. Amory's love for her "waned slowly with the moon" (221) as he realizes that as he "had loved himself [his paganism] in Eleanor, so now what he hated was only a mirror" (222).

Some time later, when he is poor in New York City, his fear of the kind of "moral suicide" suggested by Eleanor's behavior causes him to realize, "I'm not sure about good and evil at all any more" (239). He questions his sense of remorse and concludes, "I don't want to repeat my innocence. I want the pleasure of losing it again" (239). And in this state of mind he wonders "what Humbird's body looked like now" (240). In other words, he is recalling the devil episode. That supernatural episode is echoed ironically when, in wandering the streets and contemplating the evil in his life, he imagines his broodings making a darkness in the tiny soul of a child in a nearby house. He shivers at the thought and wonders, "What if some day the balance was overturned and he became a thing that frightened children and crept into rooms in the dark" (241). To ignore the force of evil is to become a force of evil: "if you doubted the devil it was the devil that made you doubt him" (244). At this low point, Amory feels "an overwhelming desire to let himself go to the devil—not to go violently as a gentleman should, but to sink safely and sensuously out of sight" (242). This sentence culminates the pattern of figures of speech in which the word "devil" appears. At this point in the novel, the banal phrase "go to the devil" has import beyond the trite, and likewise the earlier, apparently casual uses of the word now resonate with meaning beyond the trivial.

This important passage ties together the supernatural scenes and relates them to the evil of a diminishing awareness of evil: "Once he had been miraculously able to scent evil as a horse detects a broken bridge at night, but the man with the queer feet in Phoebe's room had diminished to the aura over Jill. His instinct perceived the fetidness of poverty, but no longer ferreted out the deeper evils in pride and sensuality" (242). The first encounter with the devil had terrified him to the core—made him afraid of the dark, prevented him from praying, caused him to see horrifying evil faces in the crowd and exclaim, "If we could only learn to look on evil *as* evil." The second and parallel encounter in Book Two marks the diminution of his capacity to recognize evil: the terrifying specter of the first devil episode has diminished in the second to a "gossamer aura." Near the end of the novel he says, "I've killed my conscience" (256). The death of conscience, the diminishing awareness of evil—this is the novel's linchpin. At the conclusion, we are left to speculate as to whether Amory will be able to follow Darcy's counsel to "do the next thing" (100) and develop as a "personage" rather than merely as a "personality" (101). He has come a long way on the path of religious doubt, but he nevertheless respects religion as a "traditionary bulwark against the decay of morals. Until the great mobs could be educated into a moral sense someone must cry: 'Thou shalt not!'" (259).

In the light of this reading, *This Side of Paradise* may have an even increased relevance for our time. Consider Andrew Delbanco's recent book *The Death of Satan: How Americans Have Lost the Sense of Evil*. Delbanco, an English professor at Columbia, who identifies himself with "secular liberalism," argues that our society lacks a profound and coherent sense of evil such as our American forefathers experienced when they took the devil seriously. Such a sense of evil, he claims, is requisite to the health of society. According to Delbanco, Satan died in American culture partly because of a preoccupation with personal ambition and wealth, matters which of course were principal concerns for Fitzgerald. There could be no place for the old devil, argues Delbanco, in a modern America whose religion was pride of self. This also is relevant to a consideration of *This Side of Paradise,* the preliminary title of which was "The Romantic Egotist." Delbanco does not advocate a return to a literal belief in the devil, but he insists that we have an obligation to name evil and oppose it in ourselves as well as in others. Such a view runs counter to the moral relativism of our time, which finds words like "evil" and "wicked" quaint and embarrassing, and it also runs afoul of the postmodernist tendency in academic theory and criticism to explain all formulations of good and evil as repressive constructions of the ruling caste.

The postmodern shift toward considering evil as simply an outworn metaphor is reflected in the fact that "ethical" has recently replaced "moral" as the preferred adjective modifying literary criticism interested in conduct as well as beauty. Since the terms are largely synonymous, the shift may seem insignificant, but it is not. "Moral" connotes making judgments between right and wrong, good and evil—an uncongenial practice in a relativistic age that celebrates diversity as an end in itself. On the other hand, "ethical" connotes conformity to the standards of conduct of a given profession, group, or subculture. Unlike "moral," which suggests a universal and unchanging foundation in human nature, "ethical" suggests a constructed code appropriate for certain groups or situations. The shift in terms mirrors the recent shift in literary-intellectual opinion from logocentricism to historicism or social constructionism. Until the last few decades, phrases like "moral criticism," "moral imagination," and "moral nature" were common in literary study. Lionel Trilling used such phrases twenty times in his famous 1948 essay "Huckleberry Finn," an average of nearly twice per page (*The Liberal Imagination* 100–112). But in 1970 he observed in "What Is Criticism?" that "at the present time the idea that literature is to be judged by its moral effect has virtually no place in critical theory" (*Last Decade* 67). Similarly, Wayne Booth used "moral" frequently in *The Rhetoric of Fiction* (1961), titling his concluding chapter "The Morality of Impersonal Narration." More recently, however, he has strategically shifted to "ethical," perhaps because it is more palatable to his audience. The subtitle of *The Company We Keep* (1988) is "*An* Ethics of Fiction" and certainly not "*The* Morality of Fiction."

Delbanco examines what happened to the original Puritan consciousness of the devil and his influence as a way of understanding our own troubled ambivalence in the face of evil. His is the most extensive treatment of the diminishing sense of evil in American literature and society, but he is not alone in commenting on this tendency. Kenneth Woodward observes in a *Newsweek* article titled "Do We Need Satan?" that "among American Catholics, Satan remains a vestigial figure, even among conservatives." As evidence he quotes Lawrence Cunningham, head of the Theology Department at Notre Dame University: "In the last 30 years I've heard only one sermon on Satan. I remember it because it remains a unique experience" (67). Ross Labrie, in his recent study of *The Catholic Imagination in American Literature,* likewise notes "the gradual disappearance of the devil from Catholic rhetoric, if not from Catholic doctrine, in the second half of the twentieth century" (228). But at the same time he observes that the major theme of a writer like Walker Percy is that "the moral norms and behavior of the past, while far from perfect, nevertheless were being replaced by something worse, a technological quagmire in which good and evil cannot be adequately perceived and defined and in which the traditional, though not exclusively Catholic, morality that the end does not justify the means has been virtually ignored by contemporary society" (148). *This Side of Paradise* adumbrates these recent concerns—expressed in both secular and religious quarters—with an evaporating sense of evil and the corresponding loss of significance of "the devil" in our vocabulary.

What is the devil doing in this novel? The answer is: he is there for good reason. Fitzgerald, though a lapsed Catholic, nevertheless believed, much as did Flannery O'Connor, that the territory this side of paradise is territory held largely by the devil. His portrayal of a young man's struggle with a diminishing sense of evil during the beginning years of the twentieth century is instructive as we confront challenging post-modern complications of the problem of evil at the beginning of the twenty-first century.

Notes

1. Lehan, *F. Scott Fitzgerald and the Craft of Fiction,* detects no significance in the devil episode. Ferguson views it as failed grotesque. Burhans, Sklar, Kahn (Eble, *Fitzgerald: A Collection of Criticism*), Hendriksen, and West, *The Making of*

"This Side of Paradise," provide the most extensive and insightful examinations of the novel's supernatural elements. Allen and Benita A. Moore place those elements within the context of the author's Catholic sensibility.

2. West, *The Making of "This Side of Paradise,"* explains that some passages describing Darcy were cut in preparing the final version of the novel (87). These passages reinforced Darcy's uncanny quality.

3. Buell's essay on the significance of fantasy in the short fiction is highly informative; but he divides Fitzgerald's use of fantasy into five categories, only the first of which involves the supernatural as I am concerned with it. This slights the importance of Fitzgerald's concern with good and evil and his in-clination toward the moral-supernatural. In considering the sources of Fitzger-ald's use of fantasy, Buell mentions Samuel Butler, Shaw, Wilde, Twain, Cabell, Anatole France, and even Mencken's "brand of rhapsodic invective" (Bryer, *The Short Stories* 34). But he ignores Catholic writers and Hawthorne.

5

Youth Culture and the Spectacle of Waste

This Side of Paradise and
The Beautiful and Damned

KIRK CURNUTT

I don't want you to see me growing old and ugly. . . .
We'll just *have* to die when we're thirty.
—Zelda Sayre to F. Scott Fitzgerald, Spring 1919 (Milford 49)

"About the Fitzgerald youth," Woodward Boyd wrote in 1922 as she set out to "shoot a few arrows" through the celebrated image of the author as "disillusioned, cynical, and so young": "He is young, certainly, but not so young as to look absurd in long trousers." As she points out, when *This Side of Paradise* was published in 1920, Fitzgerald was Dickens's age when he completed *The Pickwick Papers,* only a little younger than Keats when his final poems were written, and actually older than John Dos Passos when *Three Soldiers* first appeared. "Yet Keats, Dickens, Dos Passos, and hundreds of others who wrote things before they were 25 are not judged as 'infant phenomenons' while Scott Fitzgerald, in spite of the fact that he is only two years younger than Ben Hecht, whom no one ever dreams of calling childish, still suffers under this absurd handicap," Boyd observed (Bruccoli and Bryer 340). She makes what seems an obvious point here: while neither the youngest nor the first writer to chronicle the temperament of his generation, Fitzgerald identified with the theme of youth more intently than his contemporaries did—so much so, in fact, that when Dorothy Parker set out a year after Boyd's essay to skewer the media fascination with the era's flappers and philosophers, she focused her satire on Fitzgerald's reputation as a "special correspondent from the front line of the younger generation" who bravely "broadcasts the grim warning that conditions are getting no better rapidly and that decadence, as those outside the younger generation know of it, is still in its infancy." As the author of such shocking tomes as *Anabelle Takes to Heroin, Gloria's Neckings,* and *Suzanne Sobers Up,* Tommy Clegg, Parker's fictionalized Fitzgerald figure, specializes in exposés of the "scandalous doings of modern youth" that excite parental anxiety while earning their author a pretty penny. While Boyd claims not to understand why Fitzgerald defines himself as an enfant terrible, Parker *does,* for by "cashing in" on the youth craze, "Tommy and his little playmates don't regard being young as just one of those things that are likely to happen to anybody. They make a business of it" (156).

At first glance, Boyd and Parker seem to arrive at disparate conclusions regarding Fitzgerald's relationship with youth. For the former, the popular image of him as "frightfully disillusioned in the younger manner [is] really laughable," since his work glows with an optimism and enthusiasm that suggests "he believes anything and everything and is enchanted and ecstatic because there are so many interesting things to believe" (339).[1] For Parker, by contrast, his "lurid" tales of "debauched doings" evince entrepreneurial opportunism, for this "commercial genius who began the grand work of selling this younger generation to the public" (156) secured an enviable profit by capitalizing upon an erupting fad. Yet in the end, these essays disagree less than an initial reading suggests, for both authors acknowledge that Fitzgerald would never have achieved notoriety had a mass audience not been eager for insight into how the twentieth century's first generation, its "heirs of progress," was shaped by the emergence of modernity.

One would think that Fitzgerald's contribution to the image of the youth of the 1920s as ambassadors of "unchanneled and potentially disruptive energies" (Fass 21) would constitute a central line of scholarly inquiry. Yet, except for the obligatory admission that *This Side of Paradise* inaugurated a brief vogue for novels and films about "bright young things," the question of how his thematic obsession with youth relates to his modernist milieu is largely neglected.[2] The reason can be inferred from Theodore Roethke's comment that Fitzgerald was "born, and died a Princeton sophomore" (249). At worst, his age-consciousness strikes detractors as endemic of the immaturity of his interests; at best, it seems a romantic indulgence whose glitter and gilt distract from the professionalism of his craft. Even ardent admirers like John O'Hara find it necessary to remove Fitzgerald from his era to redeem his artistry. Although he recalled in *The Portable Fitzgerald* (1945) his intense adolescent affection for *Paradise,* O'Hara elsewhere insisted that "one of the worst things that ever happened to Fitzgerald was the simultaneous popularity of John Held's drawings," the cartoons of frolicking flappers that often adorned the covers of Fitzgerald's books: "Who would ever want to take Fitzgerald seriously if all they ever knew about him was that he wrote about those John Held girls?" (18).[3] Scholars are equally anxious about seriousness. As Matthew J. Bruccoli pointedly told an Associated Press reporter during the 1996 Fitzgerald centennial celebrations, the lost-youth legend surrounding Fitzgerald is frivolous and "detracts attention from what's important. . . . And what's important is little black marks on pieces of paper" (Thompson).

Unfortunately, such judgments overlook the deep sociohistorical importance invested in youth in this century. The phrase "youth culture" may bring to mind a never-ending cycle of teen fads, fashions, and fascinations, but its significance transcends the oversimplified images of generational identity that have stereotyped each decade's adolescents, from the 1920s' slicker to today's slacker. As Patricia Meyer Spacks has noted, American culture mythologizes youth as a time of "exploration, becoming, growth, pain," and thus, by implication, dismisses aging as a time of "stodginess, inertia, stasis," and "absence of feeling" (4). As such, the term has become a multivalent measure of everyday life, evoking not just a demographic constituency of adolescents but a standard of psychic well-being achievable by anyone of any age with the correct salutary regard for life. As Lawrence Grossberg puts it, youth is at once a category of "chronology, sociology, ideology, experience, style, [and] attitude" (171). When referring to young people, it most often functions as an index of social change, becoming, in Grossberg's words, a "battlefield" upon which teens and adults fight "for control of its meanings, investments and powers, [as both groups attempt] to articulate and thereby construct its experiences, identities, practices, discourses and social differences" (183). Yet in its broader usage, youth is celebrated as a universal remedy for the encroachments of senescence. As advertisers

incessantly inform us, we can *feel* young even if we can no longer cred-
ibly claim to *be* young—as long as we purchase their particular wares.

Given the prevalence of interest in youth, acknowledging the ways in
which Fitzgerald's early writing reflects its valorization in no way devalues it as Hemingway did when he dismissed his friend's fictional cor-
pus as a "little children's, immature, misunderstood, whining for lost
youth death-dance" (Bruccoli, *Some Sort of Epic Grandeur* 374). Rather,
This Side of Paradise and *The Beautiful and Damned* vividly record evolv-
ing ideas on youth that today are the norm. Not only do these novels
critique outmoded Victorian ideals of maturation, but they explore the
ambiguous power that flagrant displays of youth styles afford young
people. Most intriguingly, these works reflect the anxiety of a burgeoning age-consciousness that encouraged the young to maximize their
youth before losing it to middle age. As Lois tells her brother in the
early short story "Benediction," "Youth shouldn't be sacrificed to age"
(*Flappers and Philosophers* 141). But while Fitzgerald—long before Abbie
Hoffman or Jerry Rubin—insisted that anyone over thirty was corrupt
in morals and imagination, his work acknowledges the impossibility of
staying young forever. The result is a fascinating tension: though these
early novels idealize youth, they also recognize its imminent passing
and thus illustrate the desire throughout American culture to segregate
youth from age.

An obvious way that Fitzgerald's work reflects emerging attitudes toward youth is its rejection of the Victorian myth of adolescence, a critique most apparent in the structure of *This Side of Paradise*. When
Scribner's declined Fitzgerald's first effort at a novel, "The Romantic
Egotist," in August 1918, the austere publishing firm singled out the
story's inconclusiveness as its major flaw: "Neither the hero's career nor
his character are shown to be brought to any stage which justifies an
ending," the rejection letter noted, adding, "This may be intentional on
your part for it is certainly not untrue to life; but it leaves the reader
distinctly disappointed and dissatisfied since he has expected him to arrive somewhere . . . perhaps in a psychological [sense] by 'finding himself' as for instance Pendennis is brought to do" (Bruccoli and Duggan
31).[4] By offering Thackeray's 1848 novel as a model, Scribner's was
encouraging Fitzgerald to subscribe to a bildungsroman formula that
dictated the protagonist's entry into an adulthood governed by genteel

notions of humility, duty, and self-sacrifice. But as Fitzgerald later confessed in a preface to *This Side of Paradise* which he wrote in August 1919 but never published, he was uncertain "how [he] could intrigue the hero into a 'philosophy of life' when [his] own ideas were in much the state of Alice's after the hatter's tea-party" (394).[5] Not yet twenty-two, he knew *he* hadn't yet "arrived" at the vague "somewhere" that signaled the end of his own adolescent uncertainties. As a result, when he repaired to his parents' home in St. Paul, Minnesota, the following summer to redraft the book, eventually reinventing it as *This Side of Paradise,* he again grappled with the conclusion. While "The Romantic Egotist" ended with Stephen Palms declaring his intention to write his autobiography, his new protagonist, Amory Blaine, would finish his education brokenhearted and disillusioned, questioning the value of life's lessons. Alone among the spires and towers of the Princeton campus, Amory stretches his arms to the sky and announces, "I know myself . . . but that is all—" (260).[6] As Fitzgerald decided, "Whether [the] hero really 'gets anywhere'" would be "for the reader to decide" (*This Side of Paradise* 395).

While critics have debated the dramatic merits of the ending of *This Side of Paradise,* Fitzgerald was in fact acknowledging the newfound indeterminacy of the adolescent experience. Victorian pedagogy insisted that maturation was a fixed period in the life cycle in which youth learned "the physical and moral regimen appropriate for success" and the proper "conduct required in the world of affairs" (Kett 167). As in Thackeray's novel, this script formed the plot of dozens of popular young-adult books. According to W. Tasker Witham, "sentimental dramas" like Compton Mackenzie's *Sinister Street,* Owen Johnson's *Stover at Yale,* and Booth Tarkington's *Seventeen* portrayed growing up as a series of moral challenges. Because their heroes inevitably triumph through their character and resolve, their message was that youth's "problems will disappear in time and should not be taken seriously" (10–11).

But while these narratives popularized a teleological view of adolescence, early-twentieth-century social scientists like G. Stanley Hall rejected the determinism of "stages of life" theories of development and questioned instead the cultural prerogative to assume adult roles. In *Adolescence and Its Psychology and Its Relations to Physiology, Anthropology, Sociology, Sex, Crime, Religion, and Education* (1904)—a mammoth study often credited with establishing youth as a viable field of academic study—Hall argued that the "storm and stress" of maturation arose from an effort to reconcile the "hot life of feeling" that "has its prime in youth" with the "prematurely old and too often senile" temper of adulthood (2:59). Unlike other Victorian psychologists, Hall insisted that the young should not capitulate to this process without a fight. Artists and "gifted people," he noted, "seem to conserve their youth and to be all the more children, and perhaps especially all the more intensely adolescent, because of their gifts, and it is certainly one of the marks of genius that the plasticity and spontaneity of adolescence persists into maturity. Sometimes even its passions, reveries and hoydenish freaks continue" (1:547). Growing up, in other words, should not mean growing old. While Victorians insisted that youth was a liability, Hall and other influential social theorists defined it as an important cultural resource that needed to be preserved. The result was an increasing divergence between the idea of adolescence as a set period in the life cycle and the idea of youth as a romantic attitude or instinct symbolizing one's essential humanism. While Fitzgerald was probably unaware of Hall's work, at least one reviewer did make the connection. According to the *San Francisco Chronicle, This Side of Paradise* read like "an additional chapter to G. Stanley Hall's 'Adolescence' or a psychopathological case record" (Bryer, *Fitzgerald: The Critical Reception* 29).

The tension between Victorian and modern definitions of adolescence is prevalent throughout *This Side of Paradise,* lending dramatic coherence to the novel's otherwise episodic structure. At first, Amory's adolescence is guided by a sense of divine purpose. Fueled by the "aristocratic egotism" imparted to him by both his mother, Beatrice, and Monsignor Darcy, he approaches his youth as a series of preparatory adventures for his eventual emergence as a personage able to "see clearer than the great crowd of people . . . [to] decide firmly . . . to influence and follow his own will" (88). For Amory, growing up means disciplining the natural "energy" of youth as he "tr[ies] to orient [it] with progress" (121). Books provide convenient models for achieving this end; not surprisingly, many of the titles cited in this "romance and reading list" (*Notebooks* 158) are Victorian expositions on children's proper moral education. As a preadolescent, Amory reads Alcott's *Little Women,* R. H. Barbour's *For the Honor of the School,* and Annie Fellows Johnston's *Mary*

Ware, among other didactic fictions (23). At eighteen, he devours Tarkington's *The Gentleman from Indiana* and Johnson's *Stover at Yale,* the latter becoming "somewhat of a textbook" (38) for him. Later, during his
junior year at Princeton, he notes his fondness for what he calls "'quest'
books" like Robert Hugh Benson's *None Other Gods* or Mackenzie's *Sinister Street,* in which heroes "set off in life armed with the best weapons
. . . avowedly intending to use them as such weapons are usually used,
to push their possessors ahead as selfishly and blindly as possible" (115).
The books teach Amory what David Bakan calls the "promise of adolescence," the social contract which guarantees that "if a young person
does all the things he is 'supposed to do' during his [maturation], he
will then realize success, status, income, power" (989). By dramatizing
growth as a simple process of applying set moral lessons to ethical quan-
daries, Amory's texts impose upon adolescence a linear structure that
encourages him to think of youth as a time of "going forward in a
direct determined line" (129).

Yet a series of events conspires slowly to erode his belief in the
bildungsroman formula: his romance with Isabelle Borgé goes awry,
he fails a crucial exam that prevents him from assuming the chairman-
ship of *The Princetonian,* and his family's financial setbacks diminish
his privileged sense of noblesse oblige. Most importantly, Amory loses
Rosalind Connage to the wealthy dullard Dawson Ryder, who can
more ably finance her luxurious frivolity. As his "philosophy of success"
tumbles down around him, Amory finds himself haunted suddenly by
a "purposeless[ness]" and a "general uncertainty on every subject" (104).
Stripped of the certainty of its entelechy, the energy of youth threatens
to stagnate into ennui, the "ambitionless normality" of being "très old
and très bored" (197). Continually stimulating himself through drink
and minor forms of debauchery, Amory attempts to simulate the feeling
of motion and purpose, yet he remains painfully aware that "life had
changed from an even progress along a road stretching ever in sight . . .
into a succession of quick, unrelated scenes. . . . It was all like a banquet
where he sat for this half-hour of his youth and tried to enjoy brilliant
epicurean courses" (215–16). Accordingly, the stories that embodied the
ideals of adolescent achievement lose their allure: "Mackenzie, Chesterton, Galsworthy, Bennett, had sunk in his appreciation from sagacious,
life-saturated geniuses to merely diverting contemporaries" (195).

Recognizing the inefficacy of Victorian models of maturation, Amory indulges in various "experiments in convalescence" to assuage his new-found indirection and uncertainty. He gets drunk at the Knickerbocker Bar, hoping to tumble into a "merciful coma" to avoid dealing with his disappointments (185); he quits his job at Bascome and Barlow's advertising agency, telling his employer he couldn't care less "whether Hare-bell's flour was any better than anyone else's" (191); he even manages to get himself pummeled by "some waiters and a couple of sailors and a few stray pedestrians" (192–93). As he tells his Princeton pal and room-mate Tom D'Invilliers, the beating "was bound to come sooner or later and I wouldn't have missed it for anything. . . . It's the strangest feeling. You ought to get beaten up just for the experience of it" (192–93).

Such moments typify the disaffection of youth when the promises of adult culture seem most illusory. As Dick Hebdige writes, young people voice their dissatisfaction with the world they are inheriting "by going 'out of bounds,' by resisting through rituals, dressing strangely, strik-ing bizarre attitudes, breaking rules, breaking bottles, windows, heads, issuing rhetorical challenges to the law." Through such acts, they in-voke "the only power at their disposal: the power to discomfit. The power, that is, to pose—to pose a threat" (17–18). Youth poses this threat by utilizing the power of display; rejecting the obligations of good citizenship and economic productivity before these ideals fail *them,* young people enact what Charles Acland calls the "spectacle of wasted youth"—in effect, a symbolic theater through which they act out their status as "lost" and encourage "the adult world [to crowd] around the accident scene of contemporary youth . . . jostling and stretching to see the carnage" (132). By indulging in an "arabesque nightmare of [a] three weeks' spree," Amory externalizes the "dramatic tragedy" of his failure at Princeton *and* his loss of Rosalind. This intention is realized in the bizarre scene at Shanley's, when Amory announces to a table of casual strangers his decision to commit suicide: "This provoked discus-sion. One man said that he got so depressed, sometimes, that he seriously considered it. Another agreed that there was nothing to live for. . . . Amory's suggestion was that they should each order a Bronx, mix bro-ken glass in it and drink it off" (189–90)—a plan foiled only when Amory passes out.

As he admits to himself when Prohibition "put[s] a sudden stop to the submerging of [his] sorrows," Amory's debauchery is the "most violent, if the weakest, method to shield himself from the stabs of memory, and while it was not a course he would have prescribed for others he found in the end that it had done its business: he was over the first flush of pain" (194). The passage is deceptive, however, for when the Eighteenth Amendment ends his public drunkenness, Amory finds other ways in which to dramatize his dissatisfaction. He assumes blame for the underage girl in his friend Alec's hotel room and flusters the house detective by boasting of his indifference to the corrupt old man's threats of prosecution under the Mann Act (230–33). He shocks Mr. Ferrenby and his supercilious assistant by posing as a socialist when the businessmen insist on lecturing him on the benevolence of capitalism (246–57). Nor is the audience for these supposedly shocking admissions of disdain for adult norms necessarily adults. Even by himself, Amory likes to "congratulat[e] Poe for drinking himself to death in that atmosphere of smiling complacency" (207).

The oft-disparaged "Young Irony" interlude—derided by James L. W. West III as *This Side of Paradise*'s "weakest chapter" for "introduc[ing] new inconsistencies into Amory's character" (*The Making of "This Side of Paradise"* 70)[7]—serves as the novel's most extended examination of the power that self-wastage promises youth. As Hebdige writes, part of the intrigue of ostentatious displays of youth discontent is their ambiguity: while drinking, promiscuity, and other rituals of disaffection constitute a "declaration of independence, of otherness, of alien intent, a refusal of anonymity, of subordinate status," they are also "a confirmation of powerlessness, a celebration of [the] impotence" inflicted by their alienation. "Both a play for attention and a refusal, once attention has been granted, to be read according to the Book" (35), displays like Amory's insist that youth's exile from society's promise locates them outside the norms of comprehension. *If we can't belong,* the message is, *we can't be known.* Throughout "Young Irony," Amory and Eleanor Savage revel in this ambiguity as they try to trump each other's "Bohemian naughtiness." For her, Amory's resemblance to Rupert Brooke is enough to fuel her romantic rebelliousness and prolong her entry into the prescriptive sex roles of wife and mother; for him, Eleanor represents the allure of unconventionality that proved illusory in Rosalind. If his former love needed Dawson Ryder to support her petulant immaturity,

Eleanor seems entirely self-sufficient in "the artificialities of the temperamental teens" (217). That is, Amory knows she will never demand he grow up. Indeed, immaturity for Eleanor is vital because it allows her to avoid boarding "the sinking ship of future matrimony," which she knows is her inevitable future: "If I were born a hundred years from now, well and good, but *now* what's in store for me—I have to marry, that goes without saying" (219).

On a horseback ride during their last night together, Amory and Eleanor test each other's commitment to their nihilism. Infuriated by Amory's insistence that she is not the atheist she pretends to be, Eleanor declares, "If there's a God let him strike me—strike me!" (220), and to authenticate her Byronism, she charges toward a cliff as if to kill herself: "Then some ten feet from the edge . . . she gave a sudden shriek and flung herself sideways—plunged from her horse and, rolling over twice, landed in a pile of brush five feet from the edge" (221). By saving herself at the last minute, Eleanor acknowledges that her disaffection is at least part *affectation;* by extension, Amory must admit that just as he "had loved himself in Eleanor, so now what he hated was only a mirror. Their poses were strewn about the pale dawn like broken glass" (222). By depicting youth's anomie as a facade, a defensive reaction against its ill-defined social integration, such scenes reveal how the young are caught between caring and not wanting to care, how their poses are attempts to avoid the painful uncertainty of the future. In this sense, "Young Irony" is essential to *This Side of Paradise*'s portrayal of the new conditions of youth, for it shows how spectacular or theatrical displays of shocking behavior are forms of both power and powerlessness that dramatize but do not provide an escape from the indeterminacy and liminality of being young.

As Stuart Hall and Tony Jefferson have argued, the strategies by which youths like Amory and Eleanor symbolically respond to their disenfranchisement are not necessarily rejections of "proper" adult behavior; rather, they exaggerate to the point of parody patterns of social behavior otherwise deemed normal. In particular, youth cultures articulate their sense of identity through flagrant pageants of conspicuous consumption that display affluence and prosperity while demonstrating their indifference to the value of frugality and thrift (57). What Acland calls "the spectacle of wasted youth" is in this sense part of a broader consumer attitude that Stewart Ewen describes as the "spectacle of waste," a "live-for-the-moment ideology that . . . avoids the question of the future, except insofar as *future* is defined by *new, improved* items" and experiences promising novel pleasures (245). In a culture that celebrates wastage as a privilege of abundance, the old adage about youth's being wasted on the young takes on a slightly different meaning: while the culture defines it as a quality that is conserved and sheltered, youth is precious to the young not for its fleetingness but for the very ease with which it can be lost. While elders covet the flame of adolescence, the young treat youth as a commodity to be exhausted. Wasting one's youth becomes a quintessential form of youth-culture display, for by utilizing the one quality that is uniquely their own, the young appropriate the central reward of the "promise"—the pleasure of consumption—from which they are otherwise alienated. Intriguingly, Zelda Fitzgerald alludes to this idea in her 1922 essay "Eulogy on the Flapper" when she dismisses the idea that disaffection and disillusion were detriments to her generation. By stripping youth of its innocence, she insists, they have taught young people to "capitalize their natural resources and get their money's worth." The lost generation is not really lost; it is "merely applying business methods to being young" (392–93).

The pleasure of wastage is a central motif in *This Side of Paradise,* for it represents the sensibility that Amory ultimately adopts when his Victorian ideals of adolescence fail him. As youth erodes into that "succession of quick, unrelated scenes," he struggles to acclimate himself to the lingering sense that maturation is a matter of loss rather than growth. At first Amory is demoralized, but gradually he assumes a pose of determined indifference toward the future. When Rosalind accuses him of being sentimental, he insists that he is a romantic, because "a sentimental person thinks things will last, . . . [while] a romantic person hopes against hope that they won't" (166)—a line he later repeats to Eleanor (212). Of course, when Rosalind chooses to marry for security rather than passion, his wish comes true; the experience leaves him aware that "his youth seemed never so vanished as now" (226). The broken affair leaves him with "tireless passion, fierce jealousy, [and a] longing to possess and crush," which he feels are the only "payment for the loss of his youth—bitter calomel under the thin sugar of love's exaltation" (227). Likewise, he comes to understand that through his romance with

Eleanor "he lost a further part of him that nothing could restore; and when he lost it he lost also the power of regretting it" (206). In effect, what Amory must learn here is that he will receive a fair return on his youth only if he transforms the loss ailing him into a proactive principle of self-depletion. No longer believing he possesses the "qualities that made him see clearer than the great crowd of people, that made him decide more firmly and able to influence and follow his own will" (88), Amory must accept that the definitive experience of youth is not moral growth or social achievement but the pleasure afforded by its consumption.

The realization comes to him on a rainy afternoon during which he aimlessly rides atop a bus rattling its way through Manhattan. Interrogating his motives and beliefs, he decides his cynicism is honest if not virtuous. The test of his corruption, he decides, would be "becoming really insincere" by "thinking I regretted my lost youth when I only envy the delights of losing it": "Youth is like having a big plate of candy. Sentimentalists think they want to be in the pure, simple state they were in before they ate the candy. They don't. They just want the fun of eating it all over again. . . . I don't want to repeat my innocence. I want the pleasure of losing it again" (239). In many ways, the passage is even more central to Amory's education than the meditation that ends the novel, in which he declares that his generation has "grown up to find all Gods dead, all wars fought, all faiths in man shaken" (260). The bus-top monologue reveals that Amory has accepted the irrelevance of the bildungsroman in the modern world and that wastage is the lone compensation for one's inability to become "a certain type of artist. . . . a certain sort of man" (259). Youth, he realizes, is not a formative period of promise but a momentary pleasure whose entire raison d'être is defined by its own inevitable passing.

This Side of Paradise proved one of those rare novels that is ultimately remembered more as a part of a fad than as an artistic achievement. The book's initial printing of three thousand copies disappeared from bookstore shelves within a week, while total first-year sales neared fifty thousand, more than ten times the average amount for a debut novel in the 1920s. This unexpected success proved to publishers what other sectors of the commercial marketplace were at the same time discovering: that youth was a lucrative target audience as well as a topic of cultural concern. Savvy media manipulators realized that the prominence of the "rising generation" as a social problem offered unlimited potential for generating interest in their various products and ventures. Fitzgerald was among these skilled press agents. The popularity of *This Side of Paradise* allowed him to establish himself as a spokesman for modern youth. As he wrote his Scribner's editor Maxwell Perkins in May 1922, Amory Blaine's story created his *"own personal public"* composed of "countless flappers and college kids who think I am a sort of oracle" (Kuehl and Bryer 59).[8] And as he declared in interview after interview, he imagined it his duty to limn the attitudes and mores of his peers as accurately as possible. The three-paragraph aesthetic declaration entitled "The Author's Apology," composed in 1920 for the American Booksellers Association, offers Fitzgerald's most succinct statement of this intent: "An author ought to write for the youth of his own generation, the critics of the next, and the schoolmasters of ever afterward" (*F. Scott Fitzgerald on Authorship* 35).[9]

Yet almost immediately, the problem of following up the success of *This Side of Paradise* proved a formidable challenge. Fitzgerald wanted not only to retain his popular appeal but also to strengthen his standing among those literati who dismissed him as precious and pretentious— two seemingly conflicting goals that he intended to realize by reassessing his trademark theme of generational disaffection from the perspective of naturalistic writers whom he admired, including H. L. Mencken and Frank and Charles Norris. Even before *This Side of Paradise* was published, he spoke of at least four prospective projects that never materialized. Part of the reason that "The Demon Lover," "The Diary of a Literary Failure," "The Drunkard's Holiday," and "The Darling Heart" proved false starts may have been a growing need to move beyond the critique of the bildungsroman that had formed the plot of his first novel. "It seems to me that the overworked art-form at present in America is the 'history of the young man,'" Fitzgerald publicly declared in early 1921. "This writing . . . consists chiefly in dumping all your youthful adventures into the readers' lap with a profound air of importance, keeping carefully within the formulas of Wells and James Joyce" (*F. Scott Fitzgerald on Authorship* 43). Fitzgerald was particularly irked by Floyd Dell's *Mooncalf*, which he repeatedly disparaged in 1920–21 for plagiarizing *Paradise* to cash in on its rightful popularity and praise (Bruccoli and Duggan 75). He also dismissed former influences: whereas *Stover at Yale* once served as a "textbook," Owen Johnson's *The Wasted Generation* (1921) struck him as "so obvious as to be painful," a pathetic attempt to palliate his generation's postwar disillusionment with an antiquated sentimentalism (*F. Scott Fitzgerald on Authorship* 50).

By August 1920, Fitzgerald had formulated a plot that freed him from the constraints of the "history of the young man": he would describe "the life of one Anthony Patch between his 25th and 33d years," showing how "he and his beautiful young wife are wrecked on the shoals of dissipation" (*Letters* 145). Ostensibly, in keeping with his ambition to produce naturalistic fiction, Fitzgerald planned to portray the Patches' wreckage as a symbolic testament to the amorality of the era's rampant consumerism. Yet wasted youth and its relationship to the dilemmas of maturation remained an insistent concern over the course of the composition process, albeit in a very different form than in *This Side of Paradise.* Fitzgerald's debut novel can be classified as a coming-of-age story in the sense that it attributes youth's problems to the uncertainty of the *paysage moralisé* into adulthood. But coming of age evokes something far more ominous in *The Beautiful and Damned,* as this second novel was eventually titled. If *This Side of Paradise* focuses on the difficulties of growing up, *The Beautiful and Damned* dramatizes the dread of growing old, for more than wealth or prodigality, it is the fear of aging that compels the wildly self-destructive behavior of the central characters. The result is a more complex and more compelling examination of the causes and consequences of wasted youth than the book's reception history would suggest.[10] In *This Side of Paradise,* displays of disaffection are compensation for Amory's inability to become "a certain type of artist" or "a certain sort of man." By contrast, *The Beautiful and Damned* projects a "use it or lose it" philosophy. Anthony and Gloria Patch so dread the chronological coming of senescence that they decide to squander their youth before its vibrant intensity naturally erodes. Measuring their self-wastage against clock and calendar, the couple ravage themselves prematurely because doing so is for them the only victory possible against the inevitable ravages of time. Their self-destruction is by no means as noble as Amory's; rather than rebel against the false promises of Victorian maturation, *The Beautiful and Damned* depicts wasted youth as a lifestyle adopted by dilettantes and bacchantes as well as romantic egotists. Nevertheless, the book elaborates upon Fitzgerald's belief that, given the temporal fixity of youth, its only practical value is the brief pleasure offered by its consumption.[11]

The novel builds toward a climactic revelation of this point by playing off connotations of youth as a standard of intensity, passion, and joie de vivre. Throughout the first third of the narrative, protagonists in their early twenties insist that they can retain their youthful energy and vigor as they exit their adolescence to assume adult responsibilities. Indeed, they initially believe that their enthusiasms will invigorate and transform stolid adult institutions, marriage in particular. Yet no sooner do Anthony and Gloria feel blessed with this power than an approaching birthday grips them with unrelenting age anxieties, and they are forced to acknowledge their imminent exile from the paradisiacal world of youth. Exploiting the desire to detach youth from time, Fitzgerald promptly insists it cannot be done. In the end, Anthony and Gloria succumb to a deterministic attitude toward age by dating their entry into senescence according to a specific chronological milestone—their thirtieth birthdays. Curiously, the Patches are not alone in dreading this approaching event. Fitzgerald's narrator frequently intrudes into the action with grandiloquent editorials that lament "the inevitable metamorphosis" that this milestone inaugurates. While one's twenties are "a play, most tragic and most divine," life after twenty-nine degenerates into "a succession of speeches, sweated over by the eternal plagiarist in the clammy hours and acted by men subject to cramps, cowardice, and manly sentiment" (170). By its final page, *The Beautiful and Damned* proves so insistent on this point that Fitzgerald might well have subtitled it "Life Ends at Thirty."

The yearning to believe that youth is an eternal quality that can transcend age is dramatized most vividly in the chapters detailing Anthony and Gloria's courtship. Fitzgerald introduces this desire in an atypical supernatural prelude that depicts youth as God's gift to humanity. In a dialogue with the spirit of beauty, the disembodied voice of the Lord announces his intention to reincarnate her as the "susciety gurl" Gloria Patch. "You will be known during your fifteen years as a ragtime kid, a flapper, a jazz-baby, and a baby vamp," the deity declares. "You will dance new dances neither more nor less gracefully than you danced the old ones" (29). However inadvisable, this excursion into the fantastic offers Fitzgerald's most literal representation of juvenescence as a divine blessing. If beauty is youth and youth beauty, the scene implies, that is all we on earth need to know—except, as God assures Beauty, that being young is also a lot of fun. Originally, the novel was to conclude with Beauty's return to paradise, her spirit inexorably diminished by her tenure on earth. "How remote you are," God laments. "You seem to have no heart" (Bruccoli, *Some Sort of Epic Grandeur* 157). Fitzgerald cut this second scene shortly before publication, fearing that its lack of realism would diminish the tragedy of the Patches' dissolution. Had both dialogues remained, they would have served as narrative frames illustrating the point that youth is ephemeral, even in the afterlife. Without the concluding conversation, however, God and Beauty's first exchange serves an ironic function. While the early chapters suggest that youth's spirit is eternal, the rest of the story offers ample evidence of its fleetingness.

As Beauty's earthly incarnation, Gloria embodies the illusory allure of immortal youth in the novel's introductory episodes. On her first date with Anthony, when he tells her that, at twenty-two, she looks eighteen, she insists, "I'm going to start being that. I don't like being twenty-two" (64). She claims the power to reverse the clock; when Anthony asks, "It's your world, isn't it?" she replies, "As long as I'm—young" (66). Paradoxically, her unwillingness to act her age makes her seem wise beyond her years. Anthony is often surprised by how "she seemed to grow gradually older until at the end ruminations too deep for words would be wintering in her eyes" (113). Fitzgerald does not imply here that Gloria suddenly matures; rather, Anthony wants desperately to believe that her melodramatic immaturity embodies the age-old truth of the supremacy of youthful passions over adult contentment. A simple kiss from her convinces him that "he [is] young now," and that status makes him feel "more triumphant than death" (126).

Initially, Gloria resists Anthony's matrimonial advances, claiming incompetence in domestic matters. Once convinced that he shares her youthful fervor, she plots to rejuvenate marriage with juvenescent passion. A diary passage records her pledge not to succumb to "colorless" adult complacencies: "Marriage was created not to be a background but to need one. Mine is going to be outstanding. It can't, shan't be the setting—it's going to be the performance, the live, lovely, glamourous performance, and the world shall be the scenery." Nor will she relin-

quish her immature selfishness in the name of motherhood. Rather than
"grow rotund and unseemly" and "lose [her] self-love" by "think[ing]
in terms of milk, oatmeal, nurse, diapers," she will raise only "dream
children . . . dazzling little creatures who flutter . . . on golden, golden
wings" (147).

Yet this optimism erodes barely six months into the Patches' union
when they realize that marriage is an "extortion of youth" (156). The
revelation first comes during a honeymoon visit to the Virginia home of
Robert E. Lee, where tourists flock to gape at the site's newly restored
antebellum facade. To Gloria, the estate looks like "a blondined, rouged-
up old woman of sixty" (167), an aged thing competing against its lost
youth. The effort to reconstruct and preserve the past violates the natural
tragedy of mutability: "Beautiful things grow to a certain height and
then they fail and fade off, breathing out memories as they decay" (166),
she declares. "I want this house to look back on its glamourous moment of youth. . . . [because] [t]here's no beauty without poignancy
and there's no poignancy without the feeling that it's going, men, names,
books, houses—bound for dust—mortal" (167). Fitzgerald offers little
justification for why Gloria, the reincarnation of eternal beauty, should
suddenly sing the praises of its mortality, yet the scene marks a turning
point in the Patches' attitude toward youth. Oppressed by a sense of
its ephemeralness, the couple begin "extracting poignancy from the
memorable things of life and youth" (169) and pass their entire twenties
measuring its slow disintegration. Certain to be soon dispossessed of
it, Anthony and Gloria commence a countdown to thirty, the age at
which they believe flaming youth gives way to the raked embers of
middle age.

Intriguingly, the Patches' anxieties about aging are so strong that they
date themselves not by their actual age but by the milestones looming
on the horizon. As Fitzgerald implies, age phobias inspire the paradoxical
tendency to soothe that fear by prematurely presuming oneself old.
Anthony at twenty-six initiates this pattern when he bemoans his lack
of accomplishment in life: "Here I am almost twenty-seven—" he declares in an argument with Gloria (211). At twenty-three, Gloria herself
is "in an attractive but sincere panic" over turning twenty-four, because
it means only "six years to thirty!" (192). At twenty-five, she fears turning twenty-six because she realizes that her adolescent narcissism has

decayed into "something that she had hitherto never needed—the skeleton . . . of her ancient abhorrence, a conscience" (278). And by her twenty-ninth birthday, she is reduced to wondering whether "she had not wasted her faintly tired beauty, whether there was such a thing as use for any quality bounded by a harsh and inevitable mortality" (391).[12] These frequent declarations not only insist that the butterfly of youth is broken on the wheel of time but that the most crushing blows come long before they are due.

Controversially, this attitude is reiterated by Fitzgerald's intrusive narrator, who often halts the advancing plot to offer his own ruminations on the significance of chronological milestones: "It is in the twenties that the actual momentum of life begins to slacken, and it is a simple soul indeed to whom as many things are significant and meaningful at thirty as at ten years before" (169). Pessimism about the middle years even leads to the occasional, bizarre reductio ad absurdum: "At thirty an organ-grinder is a more or less moth-eaten man who grinds an organ— and once he was an organ-grinder!" (169). Just when the organ-grinder's image seems to establish a new standard for idiosyncratic symbols, Fitzgerald conveys youth's dissipating energies by referencing another peculiar occupation: "After the sureties of youth there sets in a period of almost intense and intolerable complexity. With the soda-jerker this period is so short as to be almost negligible. Men higher in the scale hold out longer in the attempt to preserve the ultimate niceties of relationship, to retain 'impractical' ideas of integrity. But by the late twenties the business has grown too intricate, and what has hitherto been imminent and confusing has become gradually remote and dim" (283–84). Why an organ-grinder would suffer the loss of these sureties more than a soda jerk is an unresolved ambiguity; yet the interjections complement Anthony and Gloria's attitude by depicting aging as an unceasing erosion of youthful vivacity. Turning thirty, Fitzgerald concludes, marks the point at which "we value safety above romance, [and] we become, quite unconsciously, pragmatic" (284).

For most critics, this editorializing tendency reflects Fitzgerald's unfortunate training in the popular-fiction market of the 1920s, which encouraged authorial intrusions to minimize textual complexity and ensure recognition of a story's point. Matthew J. Bruccoli argues that the aforementioned asides diminish the novel's artistry and that Fitzgerald "would not become a complete novelist until he learned the techniques for controlling point of view and disciplining his habit of obtruding into the narrative" (*Some Sort of Epic Grandeur* 159), a prerogative he would not achieve until *The Great Gatsby* three years later. Yet, however aesthetically flawed, the running commentary on turning thirty in *The Beautiful and Damned* echoes a contemporaneous attitude toward aging popularly known as the "fixed period" theory. This view, disseminated throughout a range of scientific discourse and public policy, held that intellectual, moral, and economic potential decline with age. The early twentieth century witnessed a cottage industry in mathematical formulas and equations claiming to calculate the physiological and psychological effects of aging. Frequently advanced as "natural laws," these theories of senescence held that "a certain number of years mark the limit of human productivity, rationality, and efficiency," and they helped create the cultural presumption that "old age was irrelevant and burdensome" (Cole 169). Fitzgerald's interjections reflect a similar attitude. Not only is the enfeebling that age brings a biological inevitability, but that structure of decline is tied to a specific chronological sequence. Thirty may mark an earlier moment of erosion than most fixed-period advocates argued, but not by much—forty was the average age at which the irrevocable diminishment of capacities was said to begin. As the narrator of *The Beautiful and Damned* insists, age is a "force intangible as air" and "more definite than death" (414).

As if to compensate for their eroding youth, Anthony and Gloria begin to affect a "magnificent attitude of not giving a damn" and hurl themselves headlong into drinking and profligacy. They host endless fetes, wreck cars, and squander their finances, all in an effort "not to be sorry, not to loose one cry of regret, . . . and to seek the moment's happiness as fervently and persistently as possible" (226). The Patches themselves are never quite able to articulate their motives for squandering what youth they still possess; Fitzgerald charges that duty to their close friend Maury Noble, who appears at select moments (much like the novel's narrator) to pontificate on the futility of ambition and effort in the adult world. In one long tirade against maturity, Maury recounts his initiation into the despair of senescence: "I grew up, and the beauty of succulent illusions fell away from me. The fibre of my mind coarsened me and my ears grew miserably keen. Life arose around my island like a sea, and presently I was swimming. . . . I reached maturity under the impression that I was gathering the experience to order my life for happiness. Indeed, I accomplished the not unusual feat of solving each question in my mind long before it presented itself to me in life—and of being beaten and bewildered just the same" (253–54). Growing up, the passage insists, offers little chance of triumphing over life's challenges. Instead, it ensures nothing but a sense of loss and defeat.

For their part, however, Anthony and Gloria fail to appreciate the significance of this dispiriting moral, and they continue their revelries with only slight awareness that both are "vaguely weaker in fibre" and that "things [have] been slipping" (278). But when Anthony's temperance-preaching grandfather happens upon one of their frequent debauches, they are disinherited and must cope suddenly with such adult inconveniences as paying their own bills. To meet expenses, Anthony embarks upon various careers but quits when he finds the work monotonous. Gloria also attempts to economize but grows bitter at her husband's laziness. By the final third of the novel, their marriage weathers adultery, alcoholism, and the humiliation of relocating to a working-class neighborhood. As refuge from this downward spiral, they act out increasingly empty gestures from their glamorous youth. Anthony resorts to drink to renew "those opalescent dreams of future [pleasure]—the mutual heritage of the happy and damned." But intoxication provides only a transitory escape from his fall: "As he grew drunker the dreams faded and he became a confused spectre, moving in odd crannies of his own mind . . . harshly contemptuous at best and reaching sodden and dispiriting depths" (388). Gloria also reverts to her girlhood by dressing dolls and rereading the romantic novels which fuel "that illusion of young romantic love to which women look forever forward and forever back" (371). But whereas being young was once a matter of acting eighteen instead of twenty-two, Gloria can no longer maintain the fantasy. Her most debilitating moment of disillusion occurs when she discovers Anthony scrounging for loose change to buy his morning drink: "For a moment she received the impression that he was suddenly and definitely old" (424).

By their thirties, then, Anthony and Gloria waste their youth and beauty. But if their dissipation is a moral failure, the squandering also realizes perfectly the logic of planned obsolescence, for they consume and exhaust the precious commodity of their twenties and all that the age symbolizes before "harsh mortality" can. Not surprisingly, the toll taken by their wastage is not most visible in their marital discontent or economic misfortunes. The real tragedy of their ruin, Fitzgerald implies, is that they have made themselves old before their time. On her twenty-ninth birthday, Gloria is horrified to discover that she looks too old to star as a silent-film vamp, a part she once effortlessly played in high society. Told she is more suited for "*a small character part supposed to be a very haughty rich widow*" (403), she rushes to the mirror, where she is stunned by the wear and tear of her features. If her beauty once seemed the very essence of vitality, she recognizes now that her eyes are "tired": "Oh, my pretty face," she cries. "Oh, I don't want to live without my pretty face!" The episode concludes with Gloria prostrate on the floor, sobbing, "the first awkward movement she had ever made" (404). As she later explains to Anthony, "I wasn't thirty; and I didn't think I—looked thirty" (428). Gloria's husband must likewise confront the withered youth in the mirror: "He faced his reflection . . . contemplating deject-edly the wan, pasty face, the eyes with their crisscross of lines like shreds of dried blood, the stooped and flabby figure whose very sag was a document in lethargy." The vision leads to the book's strongest evidence of his decline: "He was thirty-three—[but] he looked forty" (444).

As with *This Side of Paradise,* Fitzgerald delivered his protagonists to a final recognition of their wasted youth only to confront his authorial uncertainty over the novel's ending. After discarding the episode in which Beauty, to God's dismay, returns dispirited to heaven, he crafted an orotund coda in which he praised the Patches' faith in the glory of youth: "In the search for happiness . . . these two people were marked as guilty chiefly by the freshness and fullness of their desire. Their dis-illusion was always a comparative thing—they had sought glamor and color through their respective worlds with steadfast loyalty—sought it and it alone in kisses and in wine, sought it with the same ingenuousness in the wanton moonlight as under the cold sun of inviolate chastity. Their fault was not that they had doubted but that they had believed" (Bruccoli, *Some Sort of Epic Grandeur* 157–58). Praising Anthony and Gloria for their romantic idealism satisfied the sentimental dictates of *Metropolitan Magazine,* the high-paying periodical that serialized *The Beautiful and Damned* in the fall of 1921. Yet Fitzgerald eventually rejected this conclusion for violating the tragic tone he desired. Had it ended with this passage, the novel would have implied that the Patches' youth had been lost, not wasted.

At his wife's recommendation, Fitzgerald concluded the novel instead with the Patches sailing for Europe after winning an arduous court battle over his grandfather's thirty-million-dollar estate. Gloating over his replenished wealth and social status, Anthony congratulates himself for "show[ing] them. . . . It was a hard fight, but I didn't give up and I came through!" (448). All around him, passengers gossip about his poor health and the insanity said to accompany his courtroom travails. Their whispering confirms the long-term effects of the emotional breakdown that he suffers in the book's penultimate scene, just before their courtroom victory is announced. When a former mistress appears on his doorstep, Anthony suffers a violent blackout and reverts to his childhood. Gloria discovers him stretched out on his bedroom floor, poring over the stamp collection that he prized as a young boy. "Get out. . . . Or else I'll tell my grandfather," Anthony screams, his voice sounding "like a pert child" (447). Woefully unfit for adult responsibilities, he copes by escaping into a preadolescent world of simple, uncomplicated pleasures. The luxury of remaining childish is, of course, just what his newly refurnished wealth will allow. He can resume believing that youth is a lifestyle best enjoyed by the affluent. Yet the assumption is contradicted by his appearance, for he has been reduced to a "bundled figure seated in a wheel chair" (447). As Fitzgerald makes clear, Anthony and Gloria are neither young nor beautiful anymore, regardless of the fantasies that their fortune can now finance. Instead, they have been damned by the aging process.

The Beautiful and Damned hardly exhausted Fitzgerald's anxieties toward aging and lost youth. Rather, these issues remain a persistent—if unacknowledged—obsession throughout his major work as well as his more commercially minded short stories. In *The Great Gatsby,* Nick Carraway remembers in the midst of the climactic exchange between Gatsby, Daisy, and Tom that he has forgotten his thirtieth birthday: "Thirty—the promise of a decade of loneliness, a thinning list of single men to know, a thinning brief-case of enthusiasm, thinning hair" (106).

And in a later story, "At Your Age" (1929), a fifty-year-old man hopes to revive the "warm sureties of his youth" by romancing a flapper young enough to be his daughter. The tale includes a line that could describe Fitzgerald's attitude toward the subject: "Youth! Youth! Youth!" Tom Squires tells himself. "I want it near me, all around me, just once more before I'm too old to care" (*The Short Stories* 482). Inevitably, however, such characters must admit that they have aged: "I'm thirty," Nick tells Jordan Baker when she accuses him of treating her inconsiderately. "I'm five years too old to lie to myself and call it honor" (*The Great Gatsby* 138). And as Tom Squires realizes that he has "lost the battle against youth and spring," he understands that the affair has stripped him of any illusions he had carried into middle age: "He could not have walked down wasted into the darkness without being used up a little; what he wanted, after all, was only to break his strong old heart" (*The Short Stories* 494). This age-consciousness even works its way into biographical legend. In 1950, Alice B. Toklas described Fitzgerald visiting Gertrude Stein on his thirtieth birthday complaining "that it was unbearable for him to have to face the fact that his youth was over" (1). While its accuracy is questionable—the Fitzgeralds were in Juan-les-Pins, not Paris, in September 1926—the story nevertheless furthers the myth of an artist who memorialized and moralized his generation's wasted youth. But rather than simply mourn the passing of youth, Fitzgerald was the first author to recognize the appeal of youth culture. Intrigued by and yet wary of the freedoms that new rites of passage allowed his peers, Fitzgerald poses in his early work a question that American writing would ask of its teens and twentysomethings for decades to come: Where are you going, and where have you been?

Notes

1. Boyd's desire to rehabilitate Fitzgerald's "disillusioned youth" image may have been an effort to pay him back for recommending her manuscript *The Love Legend* to Scribner's in 1922. Fitzgerald also encouraged Maxwell Perkins to accept Boyd's husband Thomas's novel *Through the Wheat* (Bruccoli and Duggan 94).

2. The major exception is Berman's *"The Great Gatsby" and Modern Times,* which examines how Fitzgerald's most famous novel comments on various cultural phenomena of the 1920s, including the fascination with youth.

3. Held designed the book jackets for *Tales of the Jazz Age* (1922), Fitzgerald's second story collection, and *The Vegetable* (1923), his unsuccessful play. See Bruccoli, *Some Sort of Epic Grandeur* 171 and Le Vot 132.

4. It was long assumed that Fitzgerald's personal editor, Maxwell Perkins, wrote this letter (see Bruccoli and Duggan 32). Recently, however, West and others have suggested that William C. Brownell is the author (see *This Side of Paradise* xix).

5. His first reaction was hasty: before submitting the book again to Scribner's in late 1918, he "dispatched" Stephen Palms "to the war and callously slew him several thousand feet in the air, when he fell . . . down **** down ****" (*This Side of Paradise* 394).

6. As West notes, this final dash turned into a period in the book's first edition. His introduction to the Cambridge edition of *Paradise* makes a convincing case for returning to the original punctuation (xxix–xxx).

7. West's dissatisfaction arises largely from evidence that Fitzgerald spliced a portion of "The Romantic Egotist" into *This Side of Paradise* without revising minor inconsistencies like Stephen Palm's hair color (blond) to match Amory's (auburn) (*The Making of "This Side of Paradise"* 68–71).

8. For a brief but illuminating discussion of Fitzgerald's reputation as a generational spokesman, see Fass, who examines how the same periodical market that rewarded Fitzgerald handsomely for his Jazz Age short stories took up "the theme of youth . . . like a literary leitmotif" as it debated the effects of modernity on the emerging generation: "The central issue was always the failure of modern society; rarely were specific solutions for the youth problem more than an afterthought. The repetition of the catalogue of youth's faults was, in fact, not intended to describe or reform. It was, instead, a form of ritual incantation which, by bringing the problem forward again and again, created a painful consciousness that became a substitute for action, and indeed, even a way of coming to terms with the situation." Like the countless articles sensationally entitled "The Revolt of Youth," "Has Youth Deteriorated?" or "These Wild Young People," both Fitzgerald's early novels and his short fiction employed the "technique of relief by exposure," for by "employing the symbols of his time to tease his readers' curiosity while he exploited their alarm," he "was able to best express the period's aching sense of frustration" (17).

9. Evidence suggests that Fitzgerald later regretted both this statement and his reputation as the voice of the "rising generation." In *The Beautiful and*

Damned he attributes "The Author's Apology" to an unsympathetic character, the novelist Richard Caramel, who complains about how his propensity for "strange pronouncements" pigeonholes him in the literary marketplace. "I believe a lot of it," Caramel admits. "It simply was a mistake to give it out" (189). Later, in what can only be regarded as a bizarre metafictional commentary on his public identity, Fitzgerald has Caramel complain that "Everywhere I go some silly girl asks me if I've read 'This Side of Paradise.' Are our girls really like that? If it's true to life, which I don't believe, the next generation is going to the dogs" (421).

10. With the exception of *The Vegetable, The Beautiful and Damned* has generated less critical interest than any other full-length work in its author's oeuvre. What commentary does exist treats the Patches' story as a critique of capitalist decadence. For a recent representative example of such criticism, see Craig Monk's "The Political F. Scott Fitzgerald."

11. Fitzgerald's age-consciousness surfaces in his stories as well. At times references may seem gratuitous, as in "The Ice Palace" when Sally Carrol Happer is described as "rest[ing] her nineteen-year-old chin on a fifty-two-year-old sill" (*Short Stories* 48). Elsewhere, the theme is more central to the plot. "The Curious Case of Benjamin Button" tells the story of a man born at seventy who grows younger throughout his life; the tale captures the era's belief that vitality and a healthy lifestyle could reverse the aging process. In "'O Russet Witch!'" a young man ages prematurely when he abandons his romantic illusions and settles for a dull but comfortable life whose equanimity is only occasionally interrupted by a woman who symbolizes for him the energy and power of youth. Only at sixty-five does he learn that this woman is not a supernatural being but a former dancer infamous for her role in a sensational divorce trial. The effect on Merlin is immediate: "He was an old man now indeed, so old that it was impossible for him to dream of ever having been young, so old that the glamour was gone out of the world. . . . He was too old now even for memories" (*Six Tales of the Jazz Age* 118–19).

12. In one of the novel's more glaring editorial oversights, Fitzgerald places Gloria's birthday in three different months (August, May, and February). When a reader, one George A. Kuyper, informed him of the inconsistency, Fitzgerald responded with exasperation: "My God! I can never straighten it out without rewriting the whole book. It is really a most embarrassing predicament. God! This bugbear of inconsistency!" (Bruccoli and Duggan 98).

6

Mencken's Defense of Women and the Marriage Plot of *The Beautiful and Damned*

MICHAEL NOWLIN

There is no book on woman by a man that is not a stupendous compendium
of posturings and imbecilities.
—H. L. Mencken, *In Defense of Women*

. . . there is not a woman in all its four hundred and fifty pages who could,
by any stretch of courtesy, be called a lady.
—contemporary review of *The Beautiful and Damned*
(Bryer, *Fitzgerald: The Critical Reception* 105)

One of F. Scott Fitzgerald's working titles for *The Beautiful and
Damned* was "The Beautiful Lady Without Mercy." Fitzgerald obviously
meant this title as an allusion to the work of his favorite poet, the romantic Keats, even as the novel he was writing owed a great deal to the
influence of the ostensibly anti-romantic H. L. Mencken. Fitzgerald acknowledged as much by the end of 1920, in a flattering letter to James
Cabell: "I have just finished an extraordinary novel called *The Beautiful
Lady Without Mercy* which shows touches of your influence, much of
Mencken, and not a little of Frank Norris" (*Letters* 464). Over three
years later, with *The Beautiful and Damned* behind him and the novel he
would eventually call *The Great Gatsby* in progress, Fitzgerald again acknowledged, but now less enthusiastically, the influence of Mencken on
the earlier novel. Sounding like a writer newly confident in the authority

of his own voice and vision, he described *The Beautiful and Damned* as "a false lead . . . a concession to Mencken," and affirmed that "the business of creating illusion is much more to my taste and talent" (Bruccoli and Duggan 139).

Scholars have long recognized Mencken's influence on *The Beautiful and Damned*. That influence has been seen largely in terms of the literary models Mencken set before Fitzgerald—most notably, Frank Norris, with his emphasis on character in decline—and in terms of the iconoclastic attitudes and ideas that permeate the novel, sometimes gratuitously.[1] But little regard has been given to the ways in which Mencken may have helped Fitzgerald articulate the radically unsentimental views of heterosexual relations that we find in *The Beautiful and Damned*. Fitzgerald's superior, later fiction would continue to represent the relations between the sexes unsentimentally, but the unsentimental gaze would be gracefully countered by the romantic's recognition of the power of illusion fundamental to erotic desire. As he stated in the note to Moran Tudury partially quoted above, "my new novel [*Gatsby*] . . . is a new thinking out of the idea of illusion (an idea which I suppose will dominate my more serious stuff)" (Bruccoli and Duggan 139). Central to this "thinking out of the idea of illusion" are romantic configurations of femininity, configurations wherein Woman is the supreme, unattainable object of desire and the embodiment of illusion, "la belle dame sans merci," and the Lamia who presides over an aesthetic, sensual domain. Mencken may have functioned like the philosopher Apollonius in Keats's great poem for the temperamentally romantic Fitzgerald, who in 1920 had married the beautiful and erratic Zelda Sayre, for in no other novel does Fitzgerald so remorselessly deflate the phantasmic, aestheticized ideal of Woman. He does so by deploying a marriage plot that displays a woman in all her "damned" domestic actuality.[2]

Whether he meant it to or not, the title of Fitzgerald's first collection of short stories, *Flappers and Philosophers,* not only distantly recalls the theme of Keats's *Lamia,* but within the context of modernism it evokes the riddle of femininity signifying, in parts of Nietzsche and later in Freud's essays on female sexuality, the limits of masculine rationality. That title arguably originated in a March 1920 inscription to Mencken in a copy of *This Side of Paradise,* in which he professed to have recently "adopted a great many of your views" and in which he described the just published *This Side of Paradise* as "a novel about flappers for Philosophers" (Bruccoli and Duggan 55). Fitzgerald was, of course, drawn to Mencken's ideal of a cultural aristocracy immune to "booboisie" pieties and the tawdry commercialism endemic in American life (this tallying well with the appeal the more genteel Henry Adams had for him). But he was also aware of Mencken's provocative views about the battle of the sexes, as expressed in *The Philosophy of Friedrich Nietzsche* (1908; 1913), *In Defense of Women* (1918; 1922), and the appendix to *Prejudices: Second Series* (1920), the last of which Fitzgerald reviewed (Bruccoli, *Some Sort of Epic Grandeur* 161–62). In that review, Fitzgerald refers to the "Appendix on a Tender Theme" as containing Mencken's "more recent speculations on women, eked out with passages from 'The Smart Set'" (Bruccoli and Bryer 120), a description that implies familiarity. The "Appendix" reiterates and elaborates upon some of the claims made in *In Defense of Women,* itself an elaboration of claims made in *Smart Set* pieces. In a list Fitzgerald compiled in 1922 of "The Ten Books I Have Enjoyed Most," he ranked second Mencken's *The Philosophy of Friedrich Nietzsche,* which assigns a prominent place to the philosopher's musings on women (Sklar 61). In all of his writings on women, Mencken assumes that human beings are inescapably troubled by the "fact" of gender; and if, like those of Nietzsche and Freud, Mencken's views tend toward misogyny, they as frequently subvert the self-aggrandizing pretensions of the masculine ego. They are subversive, at bottom, of a traditional, patriarchal notion of identity, self-sufficiency, or self-presentness, even as they reiterate the notion of woman's Otherness within a discursive framework that grants priority to the question of *man's* selfhood.

Fitzgerald began publishing stories in *The Smart Set* in 1919 and came under Mencken's influence early in 1920, the year the Nineteenth Amendment, guaranteeing women the vote, was finally ratified. Mencken had long shown an interest in women's place in the social and psychic economy of men; an opponent of women's suffrage, he nonetheless penned the book-length *In Defense of Women* in 1918 (revised and expanded in 1922), where he sought to cut through "the vast mass of sentimentalities swathing the whole woman question" (xiv–xv). The book takes radical issue with the institution of bourgeois marriage and the idealization of specifically "feminine" virtues that helped to sustain ideologically an economy divided into public and private spheres. An amalgamation of ostensibly proverbial (and maddeningly contradictory) "truths" rather than a systematic argument, Mencken's *In Defense of Women* ridicules the suffragette movement even as it seems to regard the emergence of the New Woman as a sign of social progress. Whatever support Mencken lends to what we think of today as feminist issues, however, he thought it an inescapable fact that female power is and always will be primarily sexual, a point of dogma to which Fitzgerald's sexually licentious flappers help lend credence. For Mencken, the "eternal romance," or the "agreeable adventurousness which now lies at the bottom of all transactions between the sexes," will always stand in the way of any "transvaluation of values," however desirable. In his summary:

> Women may emancipate themselves, they may borrow the whole bag of masculine tricks, and they may cure themselves of their present desire for the vegetable security of marriage, but they will never cease to be women, and so long as they are women they will remain provocative to men. Their chief charm lies precisely in the fact that they are dangerous, that they threaten masculine liberty and autonomy, that their sharp minds present a menace vastly greater than that of acts of God and the public enemy—and they will be dangerous for ever. Men fear them and are fascinated by them. (*In Defense of Women* 206)

Mencken's "defense of women" is, ultimately, an ironist's defense of the sexual difference women signify: the sexual difference productive of desire. He is in line here with Fitzgerald's Rosalind from *This Side of Paradise,* who, using a line Elizabeth Kaspar Aldrich asserts that Fitzgerald lifted from Zelda (Lee 132), announces her modernity by telling *"a roomful of her mother's friends that the only excuse for women was the necessity for a disturbing element among men"* (160). Fitzgerald in *The Beautiful and Damned* would lend philosophical dignity to this disturbing "feminine" attitude: Gloria Gilbert, the heroine who marries Anthony Patch, is referred to as a "practising Nietzschean" (161), and references to her "Nietzschean" qualities are ubiquitous. While we cannot know how thoroughly Fitzgerald read Mencken's intellectual hero, he did claim retrospectively (on a list that made no mention of *The Philosophy of Friedrich Nietzsche*) that *The Genealogy of Morals* was the book that most influenced him in his twenty-fourth year (the year he met Mencken) (Sklar 61–62). Through even a cursory reading, Fitzgerald could have become aware of Nietzsche's ironic point about Woman being the elusive "Truth" or "Wisdom" being sought by masculine (and nearly emasculated) philosophers. The third essay, on asceticism, from *The Genealogy of Morals* has as its epigraph a passage from *Thus Spake Zarathustra:* "Careless, mocking, forceful—so does wisdom wish us: she is a woman, and never loves any one but a warrior" (*Genealogy of Morals* 94). And Fitzgerald need only have glanced at *Beyond Good and Evil* to take in its provocative introduction: "Supposing that Truth is a woman—what then? Is there not ground for suspecting that all philosophers, in so far as they have been dogmatists, have failed to understand women—that the terrible seriousness and clumsy importunity with which they have usually paid their addresses to Truth, have been unskilled and unseemly methods for winning a woman?" (Nietzsche, *Philosophy of Friedrich Nietzsche* 377).[3] Fitzgerald's first *Saturday Evening Post* story, "Head and Shoulders," about an ascetic philosopher who gets seduced by a chorus girl, might be read as a gloss on this passage.

In *The Philosophy of Friedrich Nietzsche,* Mencken does not cite those passages where Nietzsche entertains a notion of Woman as a kind of trickster figure signifying the desire underlying masculine rationality, but rather emphasizes Nietzsche's less palatable view of woman as man's inferior though complementary physical and economic counterpart (the "shoulders" to his "head"). Mencken drew upon Nietzsche to vindicate his view of bourgeois marriage as primarily a female plot to draw on the economic resources of men and satisfy women's "overpowering maternal instinct" (*Philosophy of Friedrich Nietzsche* 177). In the chapter dedicated to "Women and Marriage," Mencken seems to endorse Nietzsche's analogy between slave nations and women, who, unable to rule because of the physical handicap imposed upon them by childbearing, "cultivate cunning, which commonly takes the form of hypocrisy, cajolery, dissimulation and more or less masked appeals to the masculine sexual instinct" (176). In the later *In Defense of Women,* Mencken judges women's peculiar intelligence more generously, though mainly because he judges American men so harshly. Though he ascribes to masculine intelligence the petty instrumentality governing American public life, he also describes as "masculine" a quality of "divine innocence" (8–9), especially regarding sexual matters. Women, on the other hand, "are the supreme realists of the race" (21). Nothing signals man's intellectual limitations more than his illusions about the fair sex, who have no illusions and whose intelligence works primarily to demolish them.

The section in Mencken's *Defense* on "The Feminine Mind" is especially idiosyncratic, not because he assumes that gender is a function of unevenly distributed attributes rather than of biology, but rather because he assigns conventionally masculine attributes to women, and vice versa: "Find me an obviously intelligent man," he writes, "a man free from sentimentality and illusion, a man hard to deceive, a man of the first class, and I'll show you a man with a wide streak of woman in him" (7). (When Fitzgerald later described himself as "half feminine," he was associating femininity, more conventionally for his day, with a proclivity for sentimentality and illusion.)[4] Still, Mencken looks for no clearer proof of women's superior intelligence than their use of the institution of marriage to establish power over men. "The very fact that marriages occur at all," writes Mencken, "is a proof, indeed, that they are more cool-headed than men, and more adept at employing their intellectual resources, for it is plainly to a man's interest to avoid marriage as long as possible, and as plainly to a woman's interest to make a favourable marriage as soon as she can" (*In Defense of Women* 26). Paradoxically, the "streak of woman" lurking in first-rate men (usually meaning first-rate philosophers) alerts them to the disadvantages of marriage and makes them resist it as long as possible. Thus in his chapter on "Marriage," Mencken attributes the "superiority" of the bachelor to "his relative freedom from the ordinary sentimentalism of his sex—in other words, of his greater approximation to the clearheadedness of the enemy sex. He is able to defeat the enterprise of women because he brings to the business an equipment almost comparable to their own" (84). The superior man's "feminine" clearheadedness allows him to take pleasure in, while recognizing as illusory, the illusion of "femininity" spun by women in order to capture men; it allows him, in effect, to see *the economically and sexually needy woman behind the illusory Woman of men's romantic dreams.*

But what is the source of this "feminine" realism in superior men if not an understanding of (if not outright identification with) women's economic and sexual deprivation? Mencken's *Defense* is especially contradictory, because while he exhibits a clear understanding of the economic motivation behind feminism and of the social and economic conditions governing the mystique of "femininity," he insists on returning the battle of the sexes to the ground of biology, to the "maternal instinct." But this finally will not do, since Mencken recognizes even in the earlier *Philosophy of Friedrich Nietzsche* that women's economic independence, coupled with prospective advancements in reproductive technology, logically threaten to make bourgeois marriage obsolete. There he writes that "the idea of the family, as it exists today, is based entirely upon the idea of feminine helplessness" (189–90). Further, that "so soon as any considerable portion of the women of the world become capable of doing men's work and of thus earning a living for themselves and their children without the aid of men, there will be in full progress a dangerous, if unconscious, war upon the institution of marriage" (190). And finally, without much regard for the damage it does to his otherwise antifeminist stance, "it is plain that the economic handicap of child-bearing is greatly overestimated" (191). Near the end of *In Defense of Women,* Mencken concedes that "nothing could be plainer than the effect that the increasing economic security of women is having upon their whole habit of life and mind" and that "the diminishing marriage rate and even more rapidly diminishing birth rate" are attributable to a "growing disinclination . . . on the female side" (182).

As though intuitively alert to the metaphysical character of the "maternal instinct" he keeps invoking, Mencken falls back on a telling tautology: women "will never cease to be women, and so long as they are women they will remain provocative to men" (*In Defense of Women,* 206). He must finally ground the marriage plot in the mere fact of sexual difference, where women's mystified Otherness creates "a disturbing element among men" (Fitzgerald, *This Side of Paradise* 160). Finally at stake, then, is a masculine sense of a "lack" originating as much in cultural fantasies about difference as in biological exigencies. *The Beautiful and Damned,* as I will demonstrate, goes further in suggesting that the continual lure of bourgeois marriage lies in its ironically false promise to repair a sense of fundamental deprivation peculiar to men but affecting both genders, a sense of deprivation that issues in fantasies of possessing and of being possessed by a being who has what one lacks. This sense of deprivation—metaphorically referred to in Lacanian psychoanalytic discourse as "castration"—underlies the equation Lacan draws between "Woman" and what he calls the Phallus (an imaginary plenitude that signifies desire and is imagined to be its cause), the equation which led to his claim that "the Woman does not exist" (Lacan 74–85, 137–61). The novel's "hero," Anthony Patch, regardless of his economic status, needs a Woman to confirm his phallic power (his knowledge that he *has* the Phallus), and the "heroine," Gloria Gilbert, who could be economically independent, needs to play that Woman to confirm her own phallic power (that she *is* the Phallus Anthony lacks).

Unlike Anthony Patch, Amory Blaine, the hero of Fitzgerald's first novel, finds consolation for having failed to win over his various muses— Isabelle, Clara, Eleanor, and Rosalind—in the ideal of the "spiritually unmarried" man, who, even if literally married, makes no concessions to such conservative institutions as the family or to any maternal/domestic instinct in his quest "for new systems that will control or counteract human nature" (*This Side of Paradise* 251). Amory's sophomoric disillusionment begs to be measured against Anthony's success in marrying his muse, which forms the bitter premise of *The Beautiful and Damned* (cf. Aldrich [Lee 137]). As Anthony tells Dot, the woman with whom he has an illicit affair while in the army: "Things are sweeter when they're lost. I know—because once I wanted something and got it. It was the only thing I ever wanted badly, Dot. And when I got it it turned to dust in my hands." And further: "you can't have *any*thing, you can't have anything at *all*. Because desire just cheats you. It's like a sunbeam skipping here and there about a room. It stops and gilds some inconsequential object, and we poor fools try to grasp it—but when we do the sunbeam moves on to something else, and you've got the inconsequential part, but the glitter that made you want it is gone—" (341). Amory has not really lost anything at the end of *This Side of Paradise,* because the illusory Woman he craves still lies ahead of him and not behind him, and the "spiritually unmarried" man he imagines himself to be is a knightly figure armored against her appeal while unconsciously working in her service: "If living isn't a seeking for the grail," says Amory, "it may be a damned amusing game" (256–57). We find Amory uneasily straddling romance and irony here—like his creator, still under the influence of Henry Adams and, more to the point, still without Zelda. In *The Beautiful and Damned,* having married Zelda and come under the influence of Mencken, Fitzgerald fell more heavily than he ever would again on the side of irony.

If *The Beautiful and Damned* casts a jaded eye on the tradition of courtly love invoked in *This Side of Paradise,* and Fitzgerald was abetted in this by Mencken's cynicism regarding romantic marriage and chivalric idealism, we must ask why Fitzgerald would earnestly reinvoke that tradition in work generally assumed to mark in every way an advance beyond his second novel. I would suggest that he did so, in part, because *The Beautiful and Damned* itself reveals the shortcomings of the naturalist aesthetic favored by Mencken by implying that even the most unsentimental vision of "reality" finally depends on the illusion of "femininity" it pretends to spurn. The later novels would explore with greater imaginative sophistication than we find in Mencken's writings the ways in which the illusion of the feminine Other functions to guarantee the coherence of the masculine subject and thus the very possibility of narrative and "reality." Sexual difference remains the predominant force of inertia, however paradoxically disruptive, in a "reality" marked by bewilderingly rapid change.

Slavoj Žižek has recently claimed that "the logic of courtly love still defines the parameters within which the sexes relate to each other" (89), a claim to which the continual appeal of Fitzgerald's fiction lends considerable support.[5] Žižek's argument in "Courtly Love, or, Woman as Thing" elaborates on the Lacanian equation between the Woman and the Phallus; for like the imaginary Phallus, the Woman instigates desire by prohibiting access to herself. In courtly love, the Lady inhabits the other side of a boundary, recognizes her adorer only through ritualized, theatrical gestures, and remains ever desirable insofar as she forever defers giving the lover satisfaction (she is, to recall Fitzgerald's earlier title, "the beautiful lady without mercy"). Fitzgerald parodically invokes courtly love motifs at two early points in *The Beautiful and Damned:* first, in the campy "Flash-back in Paradise" sequence, where the Idea of Beauty is imagined as awaiting its incarnation in the "jazz-baby" and "flapper" Gloria Gilbert; and second, more subtly, in Anthony's story of the Chevalier O'Keefe. The Chevalier, thoroughly disillusioned with women, takes a vow of chastity and locks himself in a tower. There he takes one last glance out the window and sees a sixteen-year-old peasant girl, who, as she passes him, "with a pretty gesture lift[s] her skirt—as little as possible, be it said to her credit—to adjust her garter" (91). Once he is positioned so that the object of desire is inaccessible, the most ordinary of girls is magically transformed into the Woman. Having sought a romantic's reprieve from what amounts to an ungovernable "reality," the Chevalier ironically finds desire awakened by the very prohibition he laid upon himself, and finds release only by falling from the tower to "the hard earth and eternal damnation" (91).

Fitzgerald's female characters cannot be wholly reduced to ciphers in a masculine fantasy. At the same time, that function is of such crucial symbolic importance in the theater of heterosexual relations that few of his female characters would refuse it. Within that theater, Woman is the consummate masquerader: as the Lack/Plenitude that signifies masculine desire, she gives "femininity" its value and power.[6] If *The Beautiful and Damned* burlesques the Woman figure (however uneasily), it does so partly because the novel is dedicated to divesting Fitzgerald's pseudo-aristocratic "hero" of his romantic illusions and any concomitant romantic qualities of his own. The most significant effect of this is that Gloria Patch gets treated more empathetically as a subject than any other Fitzgerald heroine: *her* story is about her failure to sustain the role of the Woman.[7]

We first meet Gloria Gilbert in a subsection of the chapter "Portrait of a Siren" entitled "The Beautiful Lady": she is the spoiled, willful, and vulgar Fitzgerald debutante of the early short stories and *This Side of Paradise.* But absurd though it may be, she also carries the burden of the transcendental. That Gloria herself is conscious of her crucial *symbolic* function is suggested most pointedly by her refusal to bear children, to identify with those whom Anthony thinks of as "*females,* in the word's most contemptuous sense, breeders and bearers" (104). "I refuse to dedicate my life to posterity," she writes in her diary (147). Whatever illusions she might hold, we are later told, "her ironic soul whispered that motherhood was also the privilege of the female baboon" (393). Gloria chooses rather to embody Beauty and to wield power by making her body the site of an undying mystique: "*She* [Beauty] *was incomprehensible, for, in her, soul and spirit were one—the beauty of her body was the essence of her soul. She was that unity sought for by philosophers through many centuries"* (27).

Gloria's "Nietzschean" quality seems to reside in her defiance of the biological and cultural role that Nietzsche, according to Mencken, consistently assigned to women. For Nietzsche also assigned, as I have suggested, a metaphysical role to Woman, inasmuch as he makes the physical disturbance she causes in man signify "the disturbing element" (Rosalind's phrase again) underlying masculine rationality. On the other hand, Gloria's transcendence of human laws tellingly provokes a return of the repressed "maternal instinct," as when we find her sleeping with a doll in her arms or inexplicably yearning for her dead mother (226, 242). Playing the phallic Woman thus comes with a heavy price: the denial of one's *actual* femininity, insofar as this consists in a heterosexual imperative to breed.[8] Significantly, early in the novel Anthony mistakenly refers to Gloria as "Dora," the name given to Freud's most recalcitrant patient—the woman whose experience, from the standpoint of many feminists, plainly reveals Freud's interpretive audacity and the (patriarchal) will to power informing the psychoanalytic enterprise.[9] Like Gloria, "Dora" both stands for the woman neurotically in denial of her femininity and the enigmatic, elusive Woman that, in Žižek's words, stands for "the self-retracting Real which, in a way, grounds the Ground [of discourse] itself" (98–99), and necessitates the naming of an order devoid of anything radically whimsical, an order set defensively against the possibility that life is, in Amory Blaine's words, "a damned amusing game" (257). Like Freud's case history of Dora and Nietzsche's philosophy of the future, Mencken's *In Defense of Women* and Fitzgerald's *The Beautiful and Damned* testify directly or otherwise to the shortcomings of the man who names, and yet they both ultimately insist on the necessity of those shortcomings.

During the Patches' honeymoon, as Anthony suffers intimations of disillusionment, Gloria is figured sardonically as "the Unfinished Masterpiece" (163), who, presumed to inspire Anthony, has actually displaced his attention from the book he dreams of writing. For by marrying Anthony, she in a sense "finished" herself and took away the power of inspiration predicated upon her ability to be what Anthony lacks. In symbolically becoming his property by giving up her name and taking his, she lost her position as the Woman. Two-thirds of the novel deals with her desperate attempt to perform a role that is no longer legally hers, and Anthony's desperate attempt to accommodate himself to what we might call postcoital "reality," a life without "the Woman" to "be" the grail he pretends to be seeking. Anthony joins the army and has an affair with a woman aptly named Dot. Gloria desperately clings to the illusion that "her beauty" will never fail her: this illusion is rudely shattered, however, when, defying Anthony's wishes, she finally answers the motion picture producer Joseph Bloeckman's invitation to do a screen test. Economic self-sufficiency is not the sole force driving Gloria: anticipating the younger and more successful Rosemary Hoyt of *Tender Is the Night,* Gloria looks to gain masculine economic power by parading her femininity before a mass audience. The cruel blow she receives is not news that there is no work for her (for there is), but the news that, at twenty-nine, she is too old to star in the Woman's part.

In *The Beautiful and Damned,* Fitzgerald exhibits a relatively precocious understanding of the paradox whereby the illusions necessary to sustain heterosexual desire—particularly the illusion that the sexually different Other can ideally complement one—are precisely the illusions that keep lovers apart. Hence the cruel irony he attached to romantic marriage, which, purporting to bring one closer to the Other, actually leaves one more remote than ever from her or him, in the sense that she or he can no longer be the Other one loves. In Mencken's words, "all the mystery of the relation is gone, and they stand in the unsexed position of brother and sister" (*In Defense of Women* 109). Wisdom would seem to consist, then, in eschewing romantic love. As Mencken pointedly puts it in *The Philosophy of Friedrich Nietzsche,* "marriage is most apt to be successful when the qualities imagined in the beloved are all, or nearly all, real: that is to say, when the possibility of disillusion is at an irreducible minimum" (183). But for all the devastation done to romantic illusions in *The Beautiful and Damned,* the novel finally suggests that there is no greater self-delusion than the pretense of having repudiated romance—of having, in effect, no desire to recognize by way of romantic illusion.

"Set for the eternal romance that was to be the synthesis of all romance" (145), Gloria finds that she has written in her journal of their courtship, "I want to marry Anthony because husbands are so often 'husbands' and I must marry a lover" (146). Anthony is particularly attractive in her estimation because he will neither dominate nor worship her; he will be "a temporarily passionate lover with wisdom enough to realize when it has flown and that it must fly" (147). How does the lover relate to his beloved, though, once he is burdened with the wisdom that love, presumably, "has flown"? How does he continue to perform—and live up to the idea of a marriage that Gloria insists will be a "live, lovely, glamourous performance" (147)? When he calls her "my darling wife" on their honeymoon, she responds, "Don't say 'wife.' I'm your mistress. Wife's such an ugly word. Your 'permanent mistress' is so much more tangible and desirable" (158). But subsequent experience will teach Gloria that she can no longer play the "permanent mistress" once her relation to Anthony has been legally sanctioned. What they miss in getting married is the boundary that defined their "love" as "illegitimate," the "artificial barrier" that marked their most poignant prenuptial moments (137). This boundary also highlighted the sadomasochistic basis of their relationship, its basis in a pleasurable experience of the Other's power to bestow recognition or withdraw it. Then, Anthony "was not so much in love with Gloria as mad for her. . . . However much his wild thoughts varied between a passionate desire for her kisses and an equally passionate craving to hurt and mar her, the residue of his mind craved in finer fashion to possess the triumphant soul that had shone through those three minutes [of (her) utter unwavering indifference]. She was beautiful—but especially she was without mercy. He must own that strength that could send him away" (116). We can read "own" here as a particularly clever pun, marking as it does the seeming congruity but in fact radical difference between possession and acknowledgment. Years later, on the verge of having his affair with Dot, Anthony nostalgically remembers when his "authentic devotion to Gloria . . . had been the chief jailer of his insufficiency" (325). He yearns here for a return to the courtly love scenario, in which devotion is characterized not as a strategy for concealing one's castration (issuing in a marriage that signifies fulfillment, a harmonic resolution of differences, a happy "ending") but as a strategy for dramatizing one's castration so that it can be acknowledged and enjoyed—"owned," in the best sense of the term.

The psychological counterpart of nostalgia is anticipation; indeed, nostalgia awakens the memory of anticipation. Jane Gallop reminds us of how, in Lacanian psychoanalysis, "masculine" subjectivity is marked by the anticipation of a threat, "feminine" subjectivity by nostalgia for an irrecoverable loss: these are "the alternative versions of castration" (145–46). This notion helps us articulate the sense that there is something profoundly "effeminate" about the Fitzgerald hero, *who is nostalgic for a condition of masculine subjectivity,* a moment when he is positioned to enjoy what he can never be sure of possessing: the Woman (Phallus) signifying his phallic desire. (Compare Fitzgerald's recollection of his youthful triumph: "I began to bawl because I had everything I wanted and knew I would never be so happy again" [Wilson, *The Crack-up* 29].) Such a moment Anthony enjoys on the eve of his wedding, "a warm night . . . alive with remote anticipation," when he can still imagine "the union of his soul with Gloria's, whose radiant fire and freshness was the living material of which the dead beauty of books was made" (148). The sound of the city, "something the city was tossing up and calling back again, like a child playing with a ball," signifies for Anthony the promise that "life would be beautiful as a story," the promise of happiness, the promise that love can survive (149). The discerning reader might read a different promise into this image, the unfulfillable promise of the *fort/da* game in Freud's *Beyond the Pleasure Principle* (1920), the promise that death can be mastered, that repetition can be overcome *through* repetition. Fitzgerald was most likely unaware of the correspondence, but the sound nonetheless becomes infected with death in the form of "the noise of a woman's laughter" (149). Like the Chevalier O'Keefe, Anthony suddenly yearns to preserve desire by escaping the perils of the body, the most deadly of which is satiation. He wants "to live serene and detached back in the corners of his mind" so as to be out of the range of that "ghastly reiterated female sound" which personifies "Life" (150). Instead, he marries the girl of his dreams—and finds himself "bound for the hard earth and eternal damnation" (91).

That laughing woman should remind Anthony that "the Woman" does not exist, or at least will not survive the marriage plot in which he is about to become enmeshed. *The Beautiful and Damned* is unique among Fitzgerald's novels for the extent to which Fitzgerald seems to be laughing with her, a fact which, as I have been suggesting, may owe as much to Mencken's intellectual authority as to Fitzgerald's experience.

And yet the Woman figure, the Lady of courtly romance, would return to play a central role in Fitzgerald's subsequent novels, in the guise of Daisy Fay, Nicole Warren, and Monroe Stahr's dead wife, Minna. Without her, no tragic dignity could attach itself to his heroes. Without her, Fitzgerald knew himself to be adrift from his aesthetic moorings. When he conceded that *The Beautiful and Damned* was "a false lead . . . a concession to Mencken," he was affirming his commitment to romance or to "the business of creating illusion" (Bruccoli and Duggan 139). He was, in effect, affirming his commitment to "the dead beauty of books" (*The Beautiful and Damned* 148), which in *The Beautiful and Damned* are described as dependent upon the idealized (and yet perishable) feminine Other.[10]

After having precociously adopted the pose of a disillusioned ironist, Fitzgerald happily recognized and embraced the romantic temperament and aesthetic that distinguished him from Mencken. In doing so, he left behind a critique of Mencken's reverence for fact, which was finally not radically opposed to Fitzgerald's cherished illusions inasmuch as both were "founded securely on a fairy's wing" (*Great Gatsby* 105)—namely, the mystique of sexual difference. Fitzgerald's modern reworking of courtly love and romantic quest motifs helps expose "the eternal romance" underlying the iconoclastic "realism" of Mencken, and by extension modernist luminaries like Nietzsche and Freud. Mencken's *In Defense of Women,* we should recall, ends with the tautological assertion that women "will never cease to be women"; at that point it should be clear what sex he is really defending and what sex he is refusing to understand, for upon this most stubborn of "facts," Fitzgerald knew, depends the continuity of man's romance with himself.

Notes

1. See James E. Miller 46–50, Goldhurst 74–104, Sklar 79–107, and, for the most recent discussion of Mencken's influence on *The Beautiful and Damned,* Roulston and Roulston 93–96, 100–102.

2. Throughout this essay, I use the capitalized Woman (sometimes in conjunction with the definite article) to distinguish an imaginary figure, the masculine quester's metaphysical Other, from any actual woman.

3. The Nietzsche translations are most likely those Fitzgerald encountered. The passage from the Horace B. Samuel translation of the *Genealogy* is taken from Fitzgerald's own copy of the Modern Library edition (in the Rare Books Department of the Firestone Library at Princeton University). The passage from *Beyond Good and Evil* is from the widely available Helen Zimmer translation that had also been published in a Modern Library edition.

4. See Kerr's argument (405–11) to the effect that Fitzgerald had good reason to be defensive about his "feminine" attributes in the light of the critical agendas of intellectual mentors like Mencken and Edmund Wilson.

5. There is much validity to Moreland's thesis that Fitzgerald in his novels "explores the cost of a modern allegiance to the courtly model [of love]" (156). She treats *The Beautiful and Damned* too cursorily, however, making more problematic her claim that, except in *The Last Tycoon,* "the validity of the model itself is not seriously called into question" (157).

6. For elaborations of this argument, see Riviere, Lacan 84–85, Montrelay, and Žižek.

7. Gilbert Seldes's review perceptively compared *The Beautiful and Damned* to Edith Wharton's *The House of Mirth* (1905) and *The Custom of the Country* (1913). Oddly, however, while Seldes drew parallels between Gloria and Undine Spragg, he saw no connection between Gloria and Lily Bart (comparing the latter rather to Anthony). Seldes finally criticized Fitzgerald for "seeing [Gloria] as a flapper and not as a woman" (Bryer, *Fitzgerald: The Critical Reception* 108–9). For a sympathetic reading of Gloria's character, though one marred by a dubious methodology, see Fryer 29–41. Fryer draws our attention to some compelling aspects of Gloria's character that are overlooked in critiques of Fitzgerald's representation of women, such as those of Aldrich (Lee), Moreland, and most recently, Dijkstra. Dijkstra's reading is certainly the most hostile in this regard; he reads *The Beautiful and Damned* as an unequivocally sexist and racist diatribe (359–72). Despite its useful insights into the racialist rhetoric peppered throughout the novel, Dijkstra's reading is grossly reductive and oblivious to the novel's ambiguities and contradictions.

8. Contrary to what Sklar argues, then, Gloria's "Nietzscheanism" is not a source of confusion in the novel, when we consider the more playful aspect of Nietzsche's ostensible misogyny. And in the light of Mencken's influence on Fitzgerald, which Sklar discusses at length, it seems odd for Sklar to conclude that "the 'Nietzschean' theme is the least relevant to any other theme of the novel" (103–4).

9. Fryer also suggests that Fitzgerald's use of the name "Dora" is not coincidental (15), as does Dijkstra (365). While Fitzgerald could hardly have read

Freud's case study by 1922 (no English translation was available until 1925), he could certainly have known about it, alert as he was to current intellectual trends.

10. For an excellent general discussion of this motif in Fitzgerald's novels, see Elizabeth Kaspar Aldrich's essay (Lee), especially 133–40.

7

"One Cannot Both Spend and Have"

The Economics of Gender in Fitzgerald's Josephine Stories

MARY McALEER BALKUN

It has long been a given that the idea of emotional bankruptcy is one of F. Scott Fitzgerald's central themes. However, critics have tended to focus upon the "emotional" aspect of the equation, the protagonist's eventual inability to feel and experience fully, rather than to consider the economic implications of the expression.[1] A "bankrupt" is one who no longer has the means for exchange, one who has overextended him- or herself. The language of the marketplace—trade, value, profit, and loss—is also the language of Fitzgerald's sequence known as the Josephine stories. Considered from the perspective of the sexual economy—what Emma Goldman called "the traffic in women"—emotional bankruptcy is the inevitable result of a social system that situates women as sexual objects to be possessed and as consumers without independent means or power. It occurs when a woman attempts to exert her sexuality and/or beauty, the forms of currency she does possess, to satisfy her own desire instead of reserving them for the pursuit of a suitable marriage partner. Recent work in material culture theory and constructions of gender in the early twentieth century provide a unique framework in which to consider the theme of emotional bankruptcy, which is central to the Josephine stories.

Published between 1928 and 1931, the Josephine stories represent Fitzgerald's first complete development of the concept of emotional bankruptcy and his earliest actual use of the term (Fitzgerald, *Basil and Josephine* xix).[2] The five stories in the sequence compose a single narrative unit with a distinct trajectory and denouement: the scapegoating of

Josephine, the "baby vamp" and prototypical New Woman. In them Fitzgerald delineates the process and economics of emotional bankruptcy in elaborate detail. Considering Josephine in terms of material culture, both as an object to be possessed and as a consumer in her own right, reveals the complex work of social criticism in which Fitzgerald was also engaged. Josephine is a paradigm for the sexual-economic relationship embedded as text or subtext in much twentieth-century fiction. Her emotional bankruptcy is merely one result of her condition, which is typical of the luxury-class women about whom Fitzgerald wrote; she is a consumer rather than a producer, economically dependent, and, ultimately, a commodity.

Both the Josephine sequence and its companion series, the Basil stories (published during the same years), trace the coming-of-age of their protagonists, although with far different results. In the Basil series, which was published first, Fitzgerald traces the development of someone who will eventually grow up to become a Nick Carraway—or an F. Scott Fitzgerald—while the Josephine stories explore the roots and emergence of what Jackson R. Bryer and John Kuehl have called "the most important figure Fitzgerald ever drew," the *"femme fatale"* or "vampiric destroyer" (Fitzgerald, *Basil and Josephine* xx). Set between 1914 and 1916, the sequence also records Fitzgerald's response to the changes in American society in the early part of the century and can be read as his attempt to understand and explain the effects of those changes. One of the main transformations occurred in the role and position of women. The growth of industrialism had resulted in an increased number of women who worked outside the home (between one-third and one-quarter of all married women), although at first they worked "primarily in factories or as domestic servants" (Green 57). By 1930, however, the number of women in clerical jobs had also escalated (Green 58). In a time of increasing instability—social, financial, and cultural—women were held "responsible for cushioning the uncertainties of war and economic dislocation" (Green 120). In *The Uncertainty of Everyday Life, 1915–1945,* Harvey Green observes that advertisements of the period "placed women in a position full of responsibility but with little real authority" (24). They were at the mercy of those who advocated scientific and managerial approaches to home care and childrearing, as well as of advertisers who realized that they were the primary consumers in the family.[3] At the same time, they were stereotyped as spendthrifts who could be taken in by any new fad, saved only by the sound judgment of men. As Jackson Lears explains in *Fables of Abundance,* "Mrs. Consumer" had a "ravenous appetite for goods" and was "a stock gag in comic strips and vaudeville humor" (120). The changing roles for women were most apparent in advertisements of the period, in which, for example, "formidable mother figures" were replaced by "giggling teenagers" (Lears 118). "By the 1910s, most commonly, women in advertisements were merely beneficiaries of the largesse generated by the male genius of mass production—new emblematic expressions of old male anxieties. . . . [The] iconic representation of the modern woman was girlish rather than authoritative, and reassuringly dependent on corporate expertise" (120). He also observes that in advertisements, "The positioning of men's bodies vs. women's . . . reaffirmed masculine authority" (184). Men in these ads loom above women and are physically more imposing.

Finally, this period saw the emergence of the so-called New Woman, a term used to describe "successive generations of educated and self-supporting middle-class women who . . . demanded careers and public roles" (Smith-Rosenberg 430). The New Woman was the result of several trends: the changes in sexual relations that occurred between 1880 and 1920 and the "early women's movement [that] had made it possible for women to hold jobs and act autonomously. The developing consumer society promoted sexual pleasure and leisure to sell products and created a culture that separated sex from reproduction and valued the pursuit of sexual interests. . . . In this context women's emotional/sexual lives were transformed" (Kennedy 328–29). In the Josephine stories, Fitzgerald brings together many of these elements—gender, money, power, and class—and explores them within the context of the rapidly changing social and sexual climate in America.

The events of the Josephine sequence exemplify, in a striking way, the theories of sexual economics developed by such writers as Charlotte Perkins Gilman, Emma Goldman, and Gayle Rubin (Reiter). From this perspective, the stories are an examination of a particular female role within capitalist society as well as a critique of what was perceived as a collapsing social and moral order. Josephine's experience is cast in economic terms first and foremost, so that she emerges as a remarkable example of the "sexuo-economic relation" described by Gilman (121), one in which a woman's success and "personal profit" are intrinsically tied to her ability "to win and hold the other sex" (63), and the effects of that relation. According to Gilman, women are forced into the role of consumers, "always to take and never to think of giving anything in return except their womanhood" (118–19). For women, the sex relation counts for everything, even something as simple as having a good time (308), and the outcome is the same as it would be in any creature: "Where one function is carried to unnatural excess, others are weakened, and the organism perishes" (72).

Josephine also typifies the young women of the 1920s described by Paula S. Fass in her landmark study *The Damned and the Beautiful: American Youth in the 1920's.* She is the embodiment of "youthful sexuality," the force that represented "demoralization" and "a continuing threat to the social order" for the older generation (Fass 21). Yet, according to Fass, despite the seeming freedom and rejection of social mores, the youth of the 1920s "had not separated themselves from the roles and responsibilities they would soon assume. They had no reason to doubt that the future held anything but opportunities" (366). That sense of abundant opportunity was also an element of contemporary advertising, which depicted an ideal world of status, wealth, and security. However, ads also reflected the anxiety of the period. On the one hand, they suggested that "failure to achieve the middle-class goals of material success was the individual's alone," while at the same time they alluded to uncontrollable forces that could destroy the ideal at any moment (Green 25). In effect, Josephine's condition at the end of the sequence anticipates that of her female contemporaries who hope to move beyond the confines of gender and discover that woman's role remains circumscribed. Exploiting her newfound sexual power throughout the series, she is eventually brought to the realization that her choices are limited, that she is essentially powerless, and that she no longer wants the ideal mate who is supposed to be her raison d'être.

Josephine Perry is first presented to the reader by way of an episode from her childhood that incorporates the most important elements determining her fate as a woman of her particular time, place, and social class: the connection between gender and the marketplace and the powerlessness of women who are primarily objects of exchange. The title of the initial story, "First Blood," also introduces the vampiric

theme that pervades the sequence and symbolizes Josephine's rebellion
against the economic imperatives that impinge on her even as a young
child. The story opens in the Perry living room, where Mrs. Perry is
entertaining Mrs. Bray. At the sight of Josephine, who sits nearby, Mrs.
Bray is moved to recall an incident from the past: "I remember your
coming to me in despair when Josephine was about three! . . . George
was furious because he couldn't decide what work to go to work at, so
he used to spank little Josephine" (186). She then glances at the young
woman sitting nearby and says, "And so this is Josephine" (186). This
early episode, in which Josephine functions as the object and scapegoat
of male economic concerns, is our introduction to the sixteen-year-old.
She is now "an unconscious pioneer of the generation that was destined
to 'get out of hand,'" according to the narrator (188), a harbinger of
things to come, like the war just over the horizon. But she is also a
product of the past as signified by her mother and Mrs. Bray, a past in
which women existed for the prestige and service of the men they married. Josephine is clearly caught between these conflicting ideals.

The Perry family is part of Chicago society, "almost very rich" (188)
and firmly entrenched in the pecuniary culture (to use an expression
made popular by Thorstein Veblen) of the early twentieth century. The
fact that they are not a "new" family is emphasized from the outset, as
is their relative position in the social hierarchy. All of this underscores
the fact that the family's name and reputation have market value, as
Josephine is reminded whenever her exploits threaten either. The irony
of her position, and her responsibility, is underscored by her name,
which means "she will add; increase." Two generations removed from
the source of the family's wealth (her grandfather produced the family
fortune), she is of the new generation that accepts money and social
position as a given. Josephine has been raised to appreciate the concept
of "value," especially her own, but it is not an understanding born of
experience or supported by anything substantive. It is a value decreed
by her family and social circle, not one substantiated by an awareness of
self or any actual accomplishment. In fact, it is based on something inherent rather than earned, namely her appearance and her family connections. She has no intrinsic value of her own, and even her beauty is
somehow separate and impersonal, something over which she has no
control. It is an asset, one that grows "richer" as she matures (271), but

also one she does not actually "possess." Its worth is based on her ability to utilize it for the greater esteem of her family through marriage. By doing so she will replicate her parents' existence, thereby validating its value as well. If she is successful, the ritual of exchange for profit through marriage will continue for yet another generation.

In actuality, Josephine represents her father's ability to pay, not her own, although she frequently mistakes his power for hers. He is also able to make Josephine pay without her realizing it: taking her out of school when she might have stayed, forcing her to forego an education and experiences she is just beginning to appreciate, as well as compelling her to face the rest of the family's social circle in disgrace. Although he is supportive in some ways, Josephine realizes that her father also feels "a certain annoyance with her *misfortune*" (240; emphasis added). As a result of such regulation (after all, she is a commodity that must be protected at all costs), she is denied those things that might have helped her re-plenish her personal stores or enlarged the scope of her interests.[4] She has no education to speak of, no training or skills, nothing except her beauty with which to bargain, and she instinctively uses it to exert some measure of control over men and her own life.

Both Josephine and the narrator use language associated with the economic sphere—the production and exchange of goods—to describe her condition at crucial moments in the stories. She is established as something "new"—"the newest thing of all"—in the opening pages of the first story, much like an innovative product on the market (188). She also has "the oppressive sense of being wasted" when exiled to Island Farms one summer (214). When she rather melodramatically considers the possibility of her own death after an unsuccessful love affair, she is moved to whisper to herself, "Oh, what a shame" (200), mourning the potential loss of valuable merchandise, not the actuality of death. The narrator also compares Josephine's eventual return to Lake Forest for her sister's wedding "to the moment when the robber bandit evolved through sheer power into the feudal seignior" (219), while later she is likened to "a [s]peculator retired on his profits" (227). Josephine instinc-tively uses the language of exchange and value, whether with regard to herself or other women: she decides that someone must "pay" for her ruined summer on Island Farms, and it is inevitably another woman.[5] Similarly, a chance remark leads her to wonder about Adele Craw, a schoolmate, whether "only those who had known [her] all her life knew her at her true worth" (228). The value of things—of time, of people, of associations, but especially of the female sex—is an essential subtext in these stories, as it is in much of Fitzgerald's fiction.

Yet one of Josephine's "strengths" is her ability to recognize value in others and, conversely, to appreciate their valuation of her. In "A Snobbish Story," she can appreciate that John Bailey, despite his lower social position, has "some particular and special passion for life," just as "she knew that she herself was superior in something to the girls who criticized her—though she often confused her superiority with the homage it inspired—and she was apathetic to the judgments of the crowd" (253). But what might be strengths in a man are fatal flaws in a woman, affecting her pliability and, by extension, her value. Even Bailey recognizes that Josephine's worth is a measure of her father's: when she tells him at their first meeting that her last name is Perry, he immediately asks, "Herbert T. Perry?" (250). While she is able and willing to see the potential in Bailey, to him Josephine is primarily a means for obtaining financial backing for his play. The rest of the story highlights the connections between the marketplace, social class, and marriage in the two subplots: the attempted suicide of Bailey's estranged wife, and Mr. Perry's suspected affair.

Josephine's response to the latter "discovery" indicates that she is beginning to understand the rules of the game into which she is being initiated; she tries to use the information to "blackmail" her father, however innocently, into backing the play. This ploy fails when the truth emerges, and his position as "ideal" is inevitably restored. Gradually she comes to realize that public opinion and the marketplace can be safely ignored only when one has a wealthy male figure to serve as a buffer. Her father may consistently "rescue" her, even when she does not wish to be rescued, but his message is clear when he tells her "Nothing sordid touches you. If it does, then it's your own fault," and in the next breath says to John Bailey, the aspiring playwright Josephine is trying to help, "I understand you need money" (264–65). Anyone in need of money is not a suitable match, and Mr. Perry's job is to safeguard his daughter until he can realize a return on his investment; this will take the form of another man who is financially able to take on that responsibility and produce the next generation of Perrys. Josephine has learned the lesson well by the conclusion of the tale, deciding to "[throw] in her lot with the rich and powerful of this world forever" (269). Her brief interlude among the bohemians in Bailey's circle is enough to convince her that such speculation is not worth the risks. The ideal marriage that she sees in her future is best represented by her parents, regardless of whatever other aspects of their lives she may appear to reject, and not the Bailey marriage with its melodrama, sordidness, and poverty.

Her father remains the yardstick by which Josephine measures all males, and a marriage like her parents' is the final "prize"; but the marriage is clearly one in which Mr. Perry has ultimate control, despite Josephine's romanticizing. His reemergence as loyal husband and supportive father also reaffirms the strength and inherent "rightness" of the economic and social systems he represents. In effect, her father's intrinsic soundness is contrasted with Josephine's apparently increasing corruption. It is beside the point to observe that to get what she wants Josephine has resorted to tactics that are widely used in the business world. However, it is worth noting that had she not been with a man like Bailey in the La Grange Hotel restaurant in the first place, she would never have been exposed to the sight of her father with another woman. Her assumption of an affair is evidence that she already has been overexposed, that she is increasingly in danger of becoming damaged goods.

One effect of these and similar experiences is to reinforce the ultimate power of men in the marketplace and the tenuous position of women. Josephine's very first romantic relationship, with her sister's friend Anthony Harker, underscores this point. Harker may be captivated by Josephine at the outset, but it is he who rejects and then returns to her, the tone of his letter making it very clear, starting with the salutation "Darling *Little* Josephine" (200; emphasis added), that he is asserting his power while seeming to succumb to hers. It is this show of power that frightens Josephine away, as well as the intensity of the emotions he displays, a far cry from the vague and shadowy romance depicted in the novels she reads. For all her maneuvering and manipulating, Josephine continually finds herself at the mercy of men, whether her father, John Bailey, or Dudley Knowleton. Even the man of her dreams, Captain Edward Dicer, must contact her in order for their relationship to continue. It is only when a male "sees" her that the chase can actually begin, so first she must do what she can to attract his attention. Similarly, Josephine realizes at a young age that the dance floor may be "the field of feminine glory," but it is one from which a woman "slip[s] away . . . with a man" (191). Her earliest conscious understanding of the position of women in relation to men comes at her first prom at Yale, described by the narrator in "A Woman with a Past":

> One might have ten men to Adele's two, but Josephine was abruptly aware that here a girl took on the importance of the man who had brought her.
>
> She was discomforted by the unfairness of it. A girl *earned* her popularity by being beautiful and charming. The more beautiful and charming she was, the more she could *afford* to disregard public opinion. (230; emphasis added)

The social whirl, with its dances, proms, and parties, is a marketplace in women where a man like Dudley Knowleton is able to endow a woman with "value" despite the fact that he may not "know anything about girls at all, or be able to judge their attractions" (230). In this case, Josephine understands that Adele has acquired value solely by virtue of Dudley's "possession" of her. It is men who determine value and accord it, both by what they choose and by their association with it, not women.

Josephine's experience with Dudley also leads to what the narrator describes as her "first mature thought" (244): "One mustn't run through people, and, for the sake of a romantic half-hour, trade a possibility that might develop—quite seriously—later, at the proper time" (244).[6] This is also her first, if unconscious, recognition of the economics of social transactions, as signaled by her use of the word "trade." In other words, she is beginning to understand that one must exercise good "business" sense and that one's relationships with others are an investment in the future, with the potential for high returns if handled properly. Thus, what Josephine is engaged in is a form of speculation, a type of economic transaction for which she has neither the means nor the skill for long-term success. More than anything, it is her wanton wastefulness that condemns Josephine; she takes her beauty and social position for granted, and she is even willing to risk public censure (and her future potential for a "good" marriage) by associating with men who are beneath her. And while, as Thorstein Veblen demonstrated, "conspicuous waste" is an element of leisure class life, Josephine is wasting something that does not actually belong to her, namely herself.

Josephine has yet to learn that the laws of supply and demand apply to her as well as to other products in the marketplace, that a woman is valued in direct proportion to the degree to which she withholds herself. Safely reabsorbed into the family circle after her increasingly precarious ventures, she is able to ignore the progressively higher stakes as well. Josephine's failure with Dudley Knowleton is her first realization that payment is coming due. It is even more devastating in view of what he represents: "the little city [New Haven] where men of three centuries had brought their energies and aspirations for winnowing" (233). But by his own admission, Dudley, the man every girl is supposed to want, "[hasn't] any ideas" (233). His value is dictated by his connections and his social position, making him the quintessential eligible bachelor. After Dudley rejects her overtures, Josephine captures the essence of her own dilemma when she tells him "I'm just paying for things" (244). But the statement is about more than kissing a few boys. In addition to paying for her sexual desire and her beauty, Josephine is paying for the inability of her society to deal with the "monster" it has created by consigning women to the position of objects for trade while also restricting their power in the marketplace.

One ramification of Josephine's blatant sexuality is the way she is demonized, even vampirized, by others, including the narrator: the expression on her face when she looks at Anthony Harker is "the very *demon of tender melancholy*" (194); she is referred to as "that little devil" (198); and she is even compared to Mephistopheles in *Faust* (222). And as noted above, the title of the first story in the sequence, "First Blood," establishes her clearly as the "vampiric destroyer" Bryer and Kuehl find so common in Fitzgerald's fiction (Fitzgerald, *Basil and Josephine* xx).[7] The description of Anthony Harker in "First Blood" (whose name brings to mind Jonathan Harker, a victim of the vampire in the original *Dracula*) is a classic account of an encounter with a vampire: he is mesmerized by her gaze, patently unable to resist her. He recognizes that a relationship with her could become "a rather dangerous little mess" (198), but he is only able finally to break it off in a dark anteroom where he is unable to see her face clearly. This repeated demonization suggests that Josephine's desire, and her willingness to act on it, is monstrous and unnatural. By the concluding story in the series, "Emotional Bankruptcy," she has acquired all of the traits necessary for the "vamp" or vampire to which she has been compared throughout: she is without conscience or scruples, she has learned how to manipulate men without getting personally involved, and she recognizes, however unconsciously, the economic basis of gender relations.[8]

It is hard to ignore the connection between Josephine's exertion of "power," limited and short-lived as it is, and her eventual comeuppance. As Gayle Rubin points out in "The Traffic in Women: Notes on the 'Political Economy' of Sex," "the preferred female sexuality would be one which responded to the desire of others, rather than one which actively desired and sought a response" (Reiter 182). Josephine must be brought to the realization that it is only through men that she has any power or authority, and she must agree to lose herself in a man. Even her lack of passion for Edward Dicer, the war hero and supposed Ideal, is not something her mother would have understood; he is the perfect man, one she should marry despite her lack of desire. In fact, by the conclusion of the series Josephine has been brought to the ideal condition for woman-as-product: she has no desire left to distract her.

Ideal types of one sort or another guide Josephine's existence from an early age, including those of the "Ideal Benbower Girl" and the "Ideal Breerly Girl" (191). But the emphasis on the word "girl" suggests the foremost problem with these models: they give no clue as to what form a mature woman might take. Josephine is torn between her desires, which are very real, and the various ideals held up for her to emulate. Her emergence as a "vamp," albeit a "baby vamp," is partly a result of this struggle. The stories trace her movement back and forth between a dream vision of marital bliss and her desire for a more exciting and self-defining existence, her urge to "spend" herself when and how she likes. The alternative is to become like her sister, Constance, whose name aptly describes her most salient feature.

The existence for which Josephine is intended is clearly outlined in the wedding scene that occurs early in the sequence. The bride is described as "unsullied, beloved and holy with a sweet glow," and the plot of her life's story is equally uncomplicated: "an adolescence of uprightness, a host of friends, then the appearance of the perfect lover, the Ideal"

(201). Despite her mother's admonition that "Love isn't like it is in books," Josephine continues to idealize marriage, an attitude that seems to have been increasingly common in the early part of the twentieth century. According to Fass, marriage was perceived by young women of Josephine's type as "the entrance into a fuller and richer life; an opportunity for sharing joys and sorrows, with a mate who [would] not be merely a protector or provider, but an all-around companion. . . . [Marriage was regarded as] the one arena for expression, and the only sphere for personal satisfaction. Within a severely circumscribed sense of life-fulfilling possibilities, marriage was expected to serve every channel, implicitly more for women than for men. In that sense, the very expansion of possibilities now offered to women in marriage implied ultimate frustrations" (80, 82–83). In other words, marriage was perceived as the safest and surest route to self-fulfillment, a way to enlarge upon the freedoms experienced as a daughter of privilege.

The traditional reading of Josephine's dilemma in the last story in the sequence, "Emotional Bankruptcy," is that she has spent herself too freely and wasted her emotional stores through countless meaningless affairs. But what Josephine consumes is men, and she poses a threat to the social order because she attempts to move from the position of product to that of conspicuous consumer in the marriage market. Her string of beaus has much in common with advertisers' emphasis on "multiple consumption" in the 1920s, the pressure to own "two or more radios and even automobiles" (Green 9), which was also a way to publicize one's wealth and power. However, her "romantic conquests," to use James Nagel's expression (Bryer, *The Short Stories* 285), also resonate with another consumer activity: collecting. If, as Nagel observes, Josephine's various men are like "troph[ies] for temporary display" (285), then they can be seen as constituting a collection. Yet, as a woman, Josephine is herself a collectible object, a trophy to be won and displayed. She has therefore upended the traditional system by creating a collection of her own, one for which she has bargained with her sexuality and beauty.[9]

A woman of ever-growing desires and needs, Josephine is more than a match for the men with whom she comes in contact, and their frustration at their inability to possess her is matched by her increasing dissatisfaction with them. Yet it is one of these men whom she is expected one day to marry and spend the rest of her life with. Her only alternative is someone like Dudley, a man without ideas or imagination, and the lesson she learns from him is to be more selective in her consumption. Josephine must eventually pay for what she has done, for the sense of powerlessness that she has left in her wake, and for the danger she has posed to the status quo. As John Bailey so presciently tells her, "We all get what's coming to us" (258). Put in the terms of the marketplace, "ultimately, consumption is about power" (Douglas and Isherwood 89), and Josephine has attempted to claim the power of consumption for herself, with devastating results.

For example, one of Josephine's observations concerning the Yale prom is that it is "a function run by men upon men's standards—an outward projection of the New Haven world from which women were excluded and which went on mysteriously behind the scenes" (230). She attempts to exert her power in this world, but Dudley's reaction to her is telling, especially because he is its chief representative: she frightens him off by her experience with men, her blatant desire for him, and her beauty (just as she is herself frightened off earlier by the intensity of Anthony Harker). She is not afraid to go after what she wants or to acknowledge that she is in turn desirable. But the prom is run on male terms. By the time she attends a prom at Princeton one year later she has learned how to manipulate this world, although it is a shallow "victory" because the men over whom she now exerts her influence no longer appear as "heroes or men of the world or anything. . . . They [are] just easy" (277). The irony of the word "easy" in this context is lost on Josephine, of course, but not on the reader. It is because such conquests are easy for her that Josephine is herself thought to be "easy."

What makes Josephine especially "dangerous" in the early stories is her failure to make conscious decisions. Many of her actions are attributed to instinct rather than to any actual thought process.[10] She represents chaos, a threat to the "natural" order of things where wealth, class, and power give one ascendance over all others. She seems at times to realize the potential risks in her course of action, but whatever inclination she has to be "good" is overwhelmed by her desire to live her life on her own terms. She also does not know what she wants, and so the description of her as an "unconscious pioneer" is not accidental (188). As Josephine dances with Anthony Harker for the first time, the narrator explains that she "did not plan; she merely let herself go, and the over-whelming life in her did the rest" (196). By the last story of the se-quence, however, she is planning every detail, right down to the way she is arranged in Dicer's arms just before he kisses her. She is now vividly aware of the passage of time, of "the seconds passing, each one carrying a load of loveliness toward the future" (285). Instead of living in and for the present, Josephine is anticipating movement into the future.

As Bram Dijkstra points out in *Evil Sisters: The Threat of Female Sexu-ality and the Cult of Manhood,* woman is often figured as "the enemy of time" (35). He observes that in Darwin's *The Descent of Man* women are perceived as having an "instinctive compulsion to re-create, to repro-duce, to repeat themselves, until the end of time" (35). And, in fact, at a key moment in the sequence Josephine decides to forego the future for "the immediate, shimmering present" (269). But the decision is moot; she *must* live in and for the moment because she is unprepared for and not entitled to anything else. Yet, paradoxically, Josephine's entire exis-tence, as understood by her family and society, is predicated on the fu-ture: she is supposed to be "saving" herself for her future husband and hoarding what there is of her "self" to spend on him and her children. Thus, she is the product and prisoner of a social class whose members celebrate living for the moment, who spend freely without thought of future consequences, but who expect delayed gratification from their offspring, in particular their female offspring. The women upon whom Josephine is expected to model herself have no choice but to live in the present, since the future is not theirs to control, either sexually or eco-nomically. In an interesting "slip," Josephine asks one prospective beau, "Don't you want to marry and have children and make some woman a fine wife—I mean, a fine husband?" (213). Of course, that is the very question she must answer; but while men have the option to reply in the negative, Josephine does not. Once she gives herself up to Dicer there will be no future; the search will be over, and the one arena in which she has had some measure of power will be closed to her. She will be in thrall to one man, and that man an actuality rather than an ideal.

It is this that makes the final scene with Dicer so ironic and yet so tragic as well. She has created a scenario that no longer has the power to captivate or hold her; she has had passion, love, and romance. Now she will need more, but there is no indication that anything else awaits her. She turns to Dicer to help her, as she has turned to men all her life, but he is indifferent. She believes he is everything she has always wanted, and she anticipates his arrival at her door with the old thrill, but the present moment is no longer enough. Had he agreed to help her when she pleaded with him to do so this might well have opened a future for them both, one with a plan and a goal. She finds her basket empty because it was filled with only one thing, and she believed there was more.

Josephine has fallen into the sort of trap described so well by Simone de Beauvoir in *The Second Sex:* "It is woman's misfortune to be surrounded by almost irresistible temptations; everything incites her to follow the easy slopes; instead of being invited to fight her own way up, she is told that she is only to let herself slide and she will attain paradises of enchantment. When she perceives that she has been duped by a mirage, it is too late; her strength has been exhausted in a losing venture" (716). Josephine has, in de Beauvoir's words, given "herself completely to her idol in the hopes that he will give her at once possession of herself and of the universe he represents" (717). But what Josephine receives from Dicer is emptiness and apathy. Instead of saving herself, she has dived feetfirst into the shallow world provided for her, growing increasingly dissatisfied with the role she is expected to play. She has had the one "experience" granted to women, the wielding of power in the snaring of a man, and she has squandered it. But the fault is not in Josephine; it is in the society, depicted so precisely by Fitzgerald, that has given her no other options. Without education or experience of the world outside her social circle, she poses little threat to the social order. Straining to understand the limitations that have been established for women, Josephine finds only lack and confusion.

"One cannot both spend and have," Josephine finally realizes (287). Yet a character like Basil Duke Lee, the protagonist of the allied story sequence, is given the means to recoup his "losses," while Josephine is not. Although women have limited emotional capital to spend, Basil's similar romantic experiences lead to maturity and wisdom. Josephine, meanwhile, loses the very "vitality" that Bryer and Kuehl suggest is Basil's greatest strength (Fitzgerald, *Basil and Josephine* xxi). The Josephine stories even cover a much shorter time period; only two years in her life are recounted, while the reader follows Basil from boyhood to young manhood. One effect of such a narrow focus is the suggestion that this is the only part of Josephine's existence of any interest or importance, not how she got to this point or even where she will go afterward. In the final story of the sequence, she is left in a state of limbo. Basil, on the other hand, is described by Bryer and Kuehl as living in "the future, always glowing like a comfortable beacon." But there is good reason for this. Basil *has* a future, one "which holds achievement and power" (Fitzgerald, *Basil and Josephine* xix). Josephine is expected to spend the last of her self in the snaring of a husband, and the rest of her life living off whatever emotional and intellectual reserves he allots to her.

In a letter to his daughter Scottie, Fitzgerald wrote: "Our danger is imagining that we have resources—material and moral—which we haven't got. . . . Do you know what bankruptcy exactly means? It means drawing on resources which one does not possess" (*Letters* 55). Josephine learns early on that she must, as Emma Goldman puts it, "pay for her right to exist . . . with sex favors" (185). Her error is in thinking that her stores are hers to use as she pleases, that they can be replenished, and that she will not be punished for indulging her sexual nature. The blame is not hers alone. She is a product—in both senses of the word—of social, class, and economic forces that turn everything into a transaction, one in which women are unable to participate equitably. It is too late when Josephine finally begins to understand the intractability of the sexual marketplace: how high a price she has unwittingly paid, and must continue to pay, for so small and uncertain a return.

Notes

1. Arthur Mizener (*The Far Side of Paradise*) was the first to recognize the importance of the theme of emotional bankruptcy in Fitzgerald's work. Since then a number of critics have addressed themselves to this idea in the Josephine stories. However, the emphasis has continued to be on Josephine's emotional depletion. Drake, in "Josephine and Emotional Bankruptcy," focuses on Josephine's emotional wastefulness, her having experienced too much too soon. Both Mangum in *A Fortune Yet* and Potts in *The Price of Paradise* refer to Josephine's "reckless emotional spending" (Mangum 114), but they do not pur-

sue this line of analysis, emphasizing instead her eventual "emotional depletion" (Mangum 115). Finally, in "Initiation and Intertextuality in *The Basil and
Josephine Stories,*" James Nagel discusses the Josephine stories as "an abbreviated
feminine bildungsroman," but he also sees the stories primarily as a record of
"Josephine's progressive debasement of emotions" (Bryer, *New Essays* 289).
Nagel is also among the most recent critics to argue for the narrative unity of
the sequences, and he provides an excellent overview of the criticism.

2. The years 1928 to 1931 were marked for Fitzgerald by the collapse of the
economy and the collapse of Zelda. In his ledger for 1929, Fitzgerald wrote,
"*The Crash! Zelda + America*" (*Ledger* 184). The two are inextricably intertwined in his imagination, and this combination is crucial for an understanding
of the Josephine stories. For a complete review of the publishing history of the
sequences, see Jackson R. Bryer and John Kuehl's introduction to *The Basil and
Josephine Stories.*

3. For more about the impact of science and management theories on the
domestic life of women, see Green and Lears.

4. As Gilman notes, "It is among the wealthy classes that the economic dependence of women is carried to its extreme. The daughters and wives of the
rich fail to perform even the domestic service expected of women of poorer
families. They are from birth to death absolutely non-productive in goods or
labor of economic value" (170). It was, of course, this very class that provided
Fitzgerald with the material for his fiction. In addition, while education was
strongly encouraged for elite young men, women of the same class were not
encouraged to attend college. According to Green, "Ninety percent of all
junior and senior high school girls in the United States in the 1930s were directed into home economics classes. . . . Nearly all of those women who went
to college did not do so to pursue a career outside the home" (127).

5. Whenever she believes she has been ill-treated or spoken badly of,
Josephine's reaction is to blame "ugly and jealous girls" (206). This response is
representative of the attitudes and behaviors described by Gerda Lerner in *The
Creation of Patriarchy* as contributing to the position of women in relation to
men, especially with regard to social class: "The system of patriarchy can function only with the cooperation of women. This cooperation is secured by a
variety of means: gender indoctrination; educational deprivation; the denial to
women of knowledge of their history; the dividing of women, one from the
other, by defining 'respectability' and 'deviance' according to women's sexual
activities; by restraints and outright coercion; by discrimination in access to
economic resources and political power; and by awarding class privileges to
conforming women" (217).

6. Fass uses very similar language when describing the mating game among young people in the 1920s: "Since mating was one of the chief aims of both rituals [dating and petting], immediate sexual satisfaction had to be carefully weighed in view of long-term goals" (268).

7. In *Evil Sisters,* Dijkstra explains that in the first two or three decades of this century, the biological sciences in particular were used to confirm the dangers of female sexuality (5). His study focuses on the image of woman as vampire, and his descriptions are strikingly similar to the descriptions of Josephine. I am also indebted to Dijkstra for the expression "baby vamp" (used by Fitzgerald in *The Beautiful and Damned* [29]), which I have used in connection with Josephine.

8. Fass points out that "it was emotional commitment above all that legitimated eroticism, for the young were true romantics who believed strongly in love" (273), so much so that even premarital sex was not condemned in a love relationship, such as that between engaged couples. However, love is the ingredient missing from most of Josephine's affairs. Instead, she is driven by more mundane emotions: curiosity, pride in her physical attractiveness and sexuality, and the joy of acquisition.

9. Jean Baudrillard's observation on the completed collection—"madness begins once a collection is deemed complete and thus ceases to centre around its absent term" (93)—has interesting connotations when considered in the light of Josephine's state at the end of the story.

10. Dijkstra writes of "a growing conviction among physicians, biologists, and other such theologians of the scientific age, that *all* women were, in fact, 'real' vampires, driven by nature to deprecate the male" (46–47).

8

Pastoral Mode and Language in
The Great Gatsby

JANET GILTROW AND DAVID STOUCK

In an account of style in *The Great Gatsby,* George Garrett observes that the created language of the book "allows for the poetry of intense perception to live simultaneously and at ease with a hard-edged, implacable vulgarity" (Bruccoli, *New Essays* 111). He amplifies this observation by stating that "stylistically *Gatsby* is a complicated composite of several distinct kinds of prose, . . . a composite style whose chief demonstrable point appears to be the inadequacy of any single style (a single means of perception, point of view) by itself to do justice to the story" (114). This broad summary accommodates the ways in which *The Great Gatsby* has traditionally been read—as a romantic version of the American dream, as an ironic assessment of American values, and as an elegy for something that has been lost in time.[1] But Garrett's essay, like other studies of Fitzgerald's style, offers little more than general impressions on the subject. Here, and in an earlier essay (Giltrow and Stouck), we respond to Jackson R. Bryer's call for a focus on "small units" of style (Donaldson, *Critical Essays* 127–28) in order to describe the unique voice of Fitzgerald's "composite" prose. In our first essay we examined the endings of Fitzgerald's sentences, where so often the indefinite excitements of ambition and romance are recorded lyrically in syntactically unnecessary appositive structures. We have considered there as well how the materials of romance are undercut by Nick Carraway's ironic representation of other voices around him, the sounds of the age. In this essay we shall look at how Nick attends to yet another order of experience, one beyond his immediate social habitat, an order stable, profound, and original, which we shall here equate with the pastoral mode. To describe the language of pastoral, we use, in addition to traditional accounts of English syntax, techniques from discourse analysis and linguistic pragmatics that will help us to investigate features of Fitzgerald's style that operate beyond the sentence, in the arena of language as socially situated, as utterance addressed and received both within the text and as an exchange between reader and writer.[2]

At the beginning of his story, Nick tells us of his unusually close relationship to his father and conveys a certain pride in the Carraway clan, said to be "descended from the Dukes of Buccleuch" (7). He also turns over in his mind a piece of advice from his father: "Whenever you feel like criticizing anyone . . . remember that all the people in this world haven't had the advantages that you've had" (5). Nick amplifies this counsel in a snobbish generalization, claiming that "a sense of the fundamental decencies is parcelled out unequally at birth" (6). Mr. Carraway's homily, his word of caution, has made a strong impression on his son. And it seems that it is the form as much as the content of the homily that impresses Nick, for although his amplification somewhat distorts his father's intention, his speech habits often exactly preserve the voice of the father. Despite his relative youth and his taste for partying, Nick makes a number of similar generalizations about life: "There is no confusion like the confusion of a simple mind" (131); "No amount of fire or freshness can challenge what a man will store up in his ghostly heart" (101); "there [is] no difference between men, in intelligence or race, so profound as the difference between the sick and the well" (131). In linguistic terms, such statements are maxims, that is, proverbial generalizations about human nature and human experience drawn from long reflection on the order of things. Occasionally they occur in *The Great Gatsby* as independent clauses, as in the second example above, but more frequently they are embedded in longer sentences, sometimes compressed into referring expressions, as when Nick says that he is going to become "that most limited of all specialists, the 'well-rounded' man." Insisting on the wisdom of this paradoxical observation, he continues to generalize, adding: "This isn't just an epigram—life is much more successfully looked at from a single window, after all" (8–9). In a sober mood he reflects on the lack of interest in the deceased Gatsby—

"that intense personal interest to which everyone has some vague right at the end" (172). Such statements and expressions are not only general in reference ("most," "a man," "life," "everyone"), they have no specific time reference, their truth being neither particular nor contingent. They are somehow above, or beside, the narrative order of events, and they establish in the text the speaker's recourse to an order of permanent values beyond the resounding "echolalia" of the present.

Maxims also convey a speaker's claim to knowledge, his or her access to established authority and steady truths; in recognition of this, Aristotle said that while maxims were an effective tool for orators, young speakers should not use them.[3] Aristotle's advice acknowledges an incompatibility between lack of experience and wise sayings, yet Nick is very prone to thinking in maxims, despite his youth and his resolve to stay all judgments. Their incongruence draws our attention to that very divided nature of the novel's narrator, who on the one hand is a heedless partygoer, imagining glamorous encounters with women in darkened doorways, but on the other hand is an apprentice in the banking and bond business and a judicious observer of human behavior. Nick describes this doubleness when he says of himself at the squalid party in Myrtle Wilson's apartment: "I was within and without, simultaneously enchanted and repelled by the inexhaustible variety of life" (40). The voice of the maxim, grounded in paternal authority and wisdom, is a regulating device for Nick—solemn, stable, even magisterial—negotiating the extravagance and moral confusion of West Egg and New York, those "riotous excursions" to which he is so irresistibly drawn. When trying to understand Jordan Baker's behavior early in their relationship, Nick observes that "most affectations conceal something eventually, even though they don't in the beginning" (62). And reflecting on the rumor that she has cheated in a major golf tournament, he makes the sexist claim that "Dishonesty in a woman is a thing you never blame deeply" (63). Nick most often speaks in this voice when under pressure; he says of himself, "I am slow thinking and full of interior rules that act as brakes on my desires" (63–64). The posture of the maxims, distributed in the text beyond particular sentences and situations, signals for the reader something socially conservative in Nick's character—his close relation to his father and his anxieties in terms of class—which in turn has a powerful shaping influence on his narrative. Nick's tie to his personal past, so different from Gatsby's rejection of family and home, is a direct link to another dimension of the novel, a yearning for what is stable and originary but has been lost through time, an aspect of the story that has been described in terms of pastoral elegy.[4]

Nick's story is a lament, a mourning interpreted in terms of gardens and the passing of the seasons, and situated in the history of the imagination in America. We use the term "pastoral" here not to evoke Theocritus's idyllic landscape, Schiller's maturing child, or Empson's social encounter of courtier and rustic,[5] but to suggest another representative anecdote, that of the abject memoirist, and the idea of pastoral not as a rural subject but as a mode of art based on memory. Nick himself says, "That's my middle-west—not the wheat or the prairies or the lost Swede towns but the thrilling, returning trains of my youth" (184). At the center of that memory is the human dream of a harmonious life from which are eliminated the complexities of social ills (greed, poverty, and wars) and natural process (change, decay, and death). What the pastoral imagination seeks to recover (to *re*member) is an existence when there was no conscious division of self from the rest of the world, no separation of subject and object.

   For the study of literary texts, the drama of pastoral is probably best described by language-centered myths of human culture. In Jacques Lacan's rewriting of Freud in terms of language development, infancy is described as an "imaginary" state centered in the mother where no clear distinction yet exists between the self and the external world. The child initially experiences the world as whole or unitary and communicates directly with the mother through the body and through non-representational sounds, what Julia Kristeva calls the semiotic process (124–47). In pastoral writing this state is the "original relationship to the universe" described by Wordsworth and Emerson as prespeech, wherein Wordsworth can describe himself as "a Babe, by intercourse of touch / [holding] mute dialogues with my Mother's heart" (*The Prelude* 267–68). But as the child necessarily grows apart from its mother, becoming aware of its separateness and at the same time acquiring speech, it begins to use language as a means to bridge the gap that has grown between self and other. Consequently, language is haunted by its origins in difference and absence, for to enter the symbolic order of language is, in Lacan's formulation, to be severed from the "real" (*Écrits* 1–7, 281–91) or, as Nick Carraway phrases it, to be convinced of "the unreality of reality" (105). If mode, as Northrop Frye argues, encodes views of human strength relative to the world (33–34), then pastoral is the particular mode that articulates a hero's powerlessness and sense of loss. After his neighbor's death, Nick broods over what has happened, then returns to his home in the Midwest, wanting no more parties, no more "riotous excursions," giving up his bid for power in the world of eastern finance and social advancement. It is from this position that he tells his story.

Nick is acutely sensitive to the evocative power of language, to the overtones of words, and especially to their power to evoke feelings of loss. As he listens to Gatsby rehearsing his past one evening, he reflects: "Through all he said . . . I was reminded of something—an elusive rhythm, a fragment of lost words, that I had heard somewhere a long time ago. For a moment a phrase tried to take shape in my mouth and my lips parted like a dumb man's, as though there was more struggling upon them than a wisp of startled air. But they made no sound and what I had almost remembered was uncommunicable forever" (118). Gatsby has been telling Nick about the autumn night, five years before, when he first kissed Daisy. The scene as Nick recounts it lies at the crux between pastoral and romance, for as Gatsby approaches Daisy he recognizes that he is making an irreversible choice. Before he actually kisses Daisy, he imagines that the blocks of the sidewalk, visible in the moonlight, form a ladder and that if he were to climb it *alone* to a secret place above the trees, like Wordsworth's "Babe," he "could suck on the pap of life, gulp down the incomparable milk of wonder" (117). Gatsby's story, however, is not a pastoral; it is a romance quest, and accordingly he kisses Daisy, realizing "his unutterable visions" in this girl of his dreams. But Gatsby's desire for Daisy is thwarted by his lack of riches, and after she marries Tom Buchanan he is left with the painful memory of his loss and a determination to relive the past and set things right. "You can't repeat the past," Nick cautions Gatsby in one of his frequent maxims, but in fact Nick's counsel probably has more relevance to himself than it does to Gatsby.

This need to repeat the past, we would suggest, is the closest bond between Gatsby and Nick, but it reflects two very different ways of experiencing the past. Gatsby lives in the past, but his dream is still about future prospects; for Nick, on the other hand, the dream is retrospective, linked to some lost, more perfect place and time, some place of origins. Nick's rendering of Gatsby's life at this point, with its intimations of a story that will remain incommunicable forever, tells us much about Nick's imagination and about an elegiac refrain in his narrative. Nick also has set out on an adventure, the path of romance and self-invention; but when the summer of his story is over he can no longer go forward and returns to the "warm center" of his beginnings in the Midwest, where he wants "the world to be in uniform and at a sort of moral attention *forever*" (6; emphasis added).

That powerful undertow in Nick's imagination, which drags him back to his midwestern origins and an ideal of restored innocence, is manifest in the visual surface of his story, wherein the characters and events are repeatedly imagined in terms of summer and childhood and an absence of passion. At the story's opening dinner party, Daisy and Jordan are nostalgic about their "beautiful white girlhood" (24), and Nick continues to see the two women in this abstracted light: seated on a couch, they appear buoyed up in their white dresses as if floating on balloons (12). An ethereal, sexless quality in both women is suggested again when they are described later in the text as lying on an enormous couch, "like silver idols, weighing down their own white dresses against the singing breeze of the fans" (122). Nick refers several times to the complete lack of passion or desire in these women: "Sometimes [Daisy] and Miss Baker talked at once, unobtrusively and with a bantering inconsequence that was never quite chatter, that was as cool as their white dresses and their impersonal eyes in the absence of all desire" (16–17). Jordan says to Nick that perhaps Daisy "never went in for amour at all" (82). Jordan is Nick's potential love interest, but he sees her as even more cool and impersonal than Daisy. Both women are given androgynous qualities: Jordan is described as small-breasted with the hard, tanned, athletic body of a young cadet; and in the city, when Daisy is trying to escape the entanglement of Gatsby's attentions, she says that if they are looking for her, she will be the man on the corner of the street smoking two cigarettes (132). As an observer of women, Nick focuses his attention not on physical sensuality but on what is new and fashionable: "hair shorn in strange new ways," the latest style of dress, the neat, sad little waltz popular that summer.

At Gatsby's parties there is food—buffet tables "with glistening hors d'oeuvre, spiced baked hams crowded against salads of harlequin designs and pastry pigs and turkeys bewitched to a dark gold" (44). But more important in this text is drink, a thirst likely sharpened by Prohibition, but in Nick's pastoral imagination fraught perhaps with the primal pleasures and disappointments of oral gratification: "We drank in long greedy swallows" (124). Drinking is described in almost every major scene in the narrative, and at Gatsby's parties its originary status is evoked: "In the main hall a bar with a real brass rail was set up, and stocked with gins and liquors and cordials so long forgotten that most of his female guests were too young to know one from another" (44). This is linked to Gatsby's desire to "suck on the pap of life, gulp down the incomparable milk of wonder" and anticipates Nick's final revision of Long Island as "a fresh, green breast of the New World" (189).

There is attention to another breast in the novel, that of Myrtle Wilson, torn open in the car accident, letting her life pour away. Myrtle, who "carrie[s] her surplus flesh sensuously" (29), embodies the physical, sexual passion that Nick appears to evade. Her carnal nature is invariably linked to confusion and violence: the party Nick wanted to avoid ends with Myrtle's nose being broken and blood everywhere; her presence in the story concludes with her death on the road, which sets off a chain of events that ends in Gatsby's death as well. Her death takes place on a day that unleashes the passage of time (the enemy in pastoral): it is the last day of summer, Nick observes, humid and hot. For Nick the magic spell of summer is broken: he watches the perspiring passengers on the commuter train and wonders how "anyone should care in this heat whose flushed lips he kissed, whose head made damp the pajama pocket over his heart!" (121). Nick also reflects wryly that it is his birthday, that he has turned thirty, and that he must look forward to both thinning hair and a thinning list of single friends and enthusiasms. Old age and death follow as Gatsby's enfeebled father appears, not to reveal that the hero is of distinguished birth, but to attend his funeral.

In his essays and letters, as well as in his fiction, F. Scott Fitzgerald was obsessed by impermanence. Style was its counterforce, he argued: "material, however closely observed," he wrote, "is as elusive as the moment in which it has its existence unless it is purified by an incorruptible style" (*Afternoon of an Author* 263). Keats's "fine excess" was his model:

Keats's greatest poems, Fitzgerald wrote to his daughter, are "a scale of workmanship for anybody who wants to know truly about words, their most utter value for evocation, persuasion or charm" (*Letters* 88). In a letter to Hemingway, he cites Conrad's preface to *The Nigger of the "Narcissus"* as providing him with a theory of fiction: "the purpose of a work of fiction is to appeal to the lingering after-effects in the reader's mind as differing from, say, the purpose of oratory or philosophy which respectively leave people in a fighting or thoughtful mood" (*Letters* 309). And in a letter to Maxwell Perkins about *The Great Gatsby,* he writes that he "selected the stuff to fit a given mood or 'hauntedness' or whatever you might call it" (*Letters* 551). "Evocation," "lingering after-effects," "hauntedness": at the core of these statements is a poetics of suggestion and allusiveness to describe high quality in writing. Focusing on style per se, Fitzgerald identifies it as this exchange between loss and impermanence on the one hand and abiding persistence on the other—or, we might say, the regret of pastoral elegy on the one hand and its unappeasable longing on the other.

Our thinking so far about pastoral and style in *The Great Gatsby* has been limited to considering patterns of imagery in the text, visual references of a nonlinguistic order. As we ask how Fitzgerald gave his prose this quality of "hauntedness," we will turn to another aspect of language—the nonreferential capacity of words to call to mind other words, thereby making a text both expansive and cohesive.[6] Pastoral art is invariably distinguished by a style that is evocative of loss. In *The Great Gatsby,* style serves this essence by cultivating a feature of language operating through and then beyond syntax: *cohesion,* the quality of sentences' depending on one another for their interpretation, their quality as *text,* or their "texture."[7] Of the various conditions that have been identified as producing *text*—or texture—*lexical cohesion* is the one that works through words' basic materiality, their substance as words rather than as reference items indicating a nonlinguistic entity, or as operators in the syntax of propositions. Of the five types of lexical cohesion, straight *lexical repetition* is the one most open to traditional measures of style. A particular word can recur in a text—in different localities, with different reference—and concordance techniques can calculate these recurrences, which create a network of interdependencies beyond plot, or argument, or image. So a concordance to the novel

lists, for example, 21 occurrences of "road," 16 instances of "dream[ed],"
14 of "flower[s]" (Crosland 272, 93, 121), and, according to Bruccoli's
preface to the authorized text of *The Great Gatsby,* some 450 words
having to do with time (xv). "Flower," reappearing after fifteen pages,
or fifty pages, evokes not only its single instance but its earlier in-
stance(s) as well, however irrelevant at the discursive level. Words acquire a "textual history" (Halliday and Hasan), and the reader's memory
is the archive of this history. To straight repetition—a sort of cohesive
bedrock—the linguistic taxonomy of lexical cohesion adds three types
of *synonymy.*[8] These are less open to traditional concordance techniques,
although their operation may comprise distinctive stylistic features. Finally, measures of *collocation* calculate the ties between words that have
a tendency to appear together, societies of words that have a history of
accompaniment—prior to a specific textual occurrence but activated by
their textual configuration.

The category of collocation registers the potential energies resting in
words themselves, residual from their use. Textual collocations transform that potential to kinetic energy. In Fitzgerald's representation of
Nick's storytelling, such transformation can accompany Nick's surges of
enthusiasm for moments that might leave others untouched. During
Daisy's afternoon visit to Gatsby's mansion, Nick's faithful attention to
time and place—his work as witness and reporter—suddenly expands to
an embracing vision of weather and the time of day:

> Outside the wind was loud and there was a faint flow of thunder
> along the Sound. All the lights were going on in West Egg now; the
> electric trains, men carrying, were plunging home through the rain
> from New York. It was the hour of a profound human change and
> excitement was generating on the air. (101)

At one level this passage is cohesive on basic, practical grounds: a geo-
graphical template develops through the collocation of place-names—
the Sound/West Egg/New York—and a chronological template develops
through the collocation of time words—*now/hour.* These ties serve the
substantive needs of plot, anchoring time and place. But just as *hour* expands to something more than just the time of day, other collocative ties
draw the passage beyond itself. With *electric (trains)* a tie forms with *lights:*

these are words that tend to co-occur. Nick doesn't have to say "electric trains"—"trains" would have done as well—but the choice, reactivating "lights," intensifies a reminder of the technological organization of this epoch. Beyond this immediate tie, another cohesive link connects *electric* with *thunder* in the first sentence, striking a latent association between these words, like a flash of lightning itself, illuminating in a second of exposure the domain these words share. Then, in the third sentence, *generating,* collocative with *thunder/lights/electric,* extends this circuit of sensation. Exploiting the properties of words as words, these collocations seem to make possible the claim about "profound human change and excitement" in a paragraph about commuting on a rainy afternoon. Turning away from the awkward conversation surrounding Mr. Klipspringer's hesitant performance at the piano, Nick finds a thrill of apprehension in the significance of the everyday moment beyond the room. At a level of intensity that could hardly be accounted for by plot, or character, or the social destiny of individuals, Nick, with his finger on some original pulse, expresses a vision of charged simultaneity between humans and their world, sensing even in metropolitan commuting a link between humans and nature. In this passage, the thrill—indefinite or not quite communicable, for, after all, what *is* this expected change?—rises from a dense nest of local collocative links that tie these sentences together beyond their propositional content. But the passage also echoes other parts of the novel, spanning expanses of narrative by reminding us, through "train," of incessant traffic in this book, comings and goings, transportation, even on the most universal level, of human migration itself, the discovery of the New World, or the *re*discovery of an original "fresh green breast" (189).

Other passages in *The Great Gatsby* also exploit this potential for long cohesive spans. Take a sentence describing Daisy's and Gatsby's reactions to each other at the hotel party in New York, where the words seem to draw reverberations from the whole text: "But with every word she was drawing further and further into herself, so he gave that up and only the dead dream fought on as the afternoon slipped away, trying to touch what was no longer tangible, struggling unhappily, undespairingly, toward that lost voice across the room" (142). For the reader who already knows the text and has an ear for language, "fought on" anticipates the novel's last sentence, "beat on . . . against the current" (189), so that we hear "boat" in this sentence even though the word is not there. But we have already been conditioned to hear "boat" because of a textual history of sea words. In the beginning of his story, Nick tells us that at the Buchanans' waterfront home the breeze "rippled over the wine-colored rug, making a shadow on it as wind does on *the sea*" and that Jordan and Daisy on the couch "were *buoyed up* as though upon an *anchored* balloon" (12; emphasis added). And carrying the association of the boat from these crucially situated sentences, "across the room" picks up an echo of across the bay, and Daisy's lost voice becomes one with the green light, one of Gatsby's "enchanted objects." In this context, "trying to touch" recalls Gatsby's hands stretched out across the bay at the end of the first chapter, which in turn recalls Gatsby trying to reconnect with the past "just out of reach of his hand" (117). This elusiveness, not only of object but of language as well, returns with the account of Gatsby's departure from Louisville: "He stretched out his hand desperately as if to snatch only a wisp of air, to save a fragment of the spot that she had made lovely for him" (160). Some of the words of this sentence ("wisp of air," "fragment") echo their own use, although with different reference, from the sentence on page 118; but most powerful is the word "stretch," which gathers up the aspiration of romance and the longing of pastoral and yields their full force in those lines of the resonant penultimate paragraph: "tomorrow we will run faster, stretch out our arms farther" (189).

Words tracings, the imprint they make on a reader's memory, some connection audible but not quite understood—these "lost" but persistent fragments need to be examined as they reach across spans of text. For they create in the attuned reader the sensations we identify as Nick's unique way of speaking; they touch off fleeting and nearly "uncommunicable" recognition of the largest designs in the novel, its mythic dimension, referring us to light and dark, to nourishment, to strange and exotic gardens, to human migrations, to the sea, and to death. It is language deployed in this way that allows the reader of pastoral to hear "an elusive rhythm, a fragment of lost words," from an order of experience before speech and memory, that remains, in Nick's phrasing, "uncommunicable forever" (118). On the whole, sentence endings are the preferred sites for these collocations and haunting echoes. When Nick is first told of Gatsby's dream of reclaiming Daisy, he says: "He came alive

to me, delivered suddenly from the womb of his purposeless splendour"
(83). The word "womb" takes us back to the fourth page of the novel
and a series of beginnings—the rebirth of summer, "new money,"
Nick's quickly acquired status as "pathfinder, an original settler" (8). It
also anticipates the end of the novel and America first seen by Dutch
sailors' eyes—"a fresh, green breast of the new world" (189).

But pastoral innocence evoked in these words is complicated by another account of origins in a sentence describing Dan Cody, which extends by means of appositives to invoke the sweep of American history:
"I remember the portrait of him up in Gatsby's bedroom, a grey, florid
man with a hard, empty face—the pioneer debauchee who during one
phase of American life brought back to the eastern seaboard the savage
violence of the frontier brothel or saloon" (106). Here, original settler, or
pioneer, is redefined in terms of violence and debauchery, and in terms
of hardness and emptiness, implicating by word association Nick's own
family's pioneer beginnings, the Dutch sailors, the very beginnings of
America's European history and its consequences. It also encapsulates all
the elements of the story that are finally Gatsby's undoing. At this point
we are made to recognize that words have lives of their own and that
in a narrative of mixed modes (in this case romance and pastoral) words
can evoke conflicting narrative intentions. "Pioneer" and "frontier"
evoke innocence and origins at one point in the text and then are linked
to crime and the underworld in the next. Fitzgerald's style is "composite" indeed: its language can sound a magisterial voice addressing snobbish concerns of class, then turn and gesture in an evocative phrase to a
timeless order of origins; Gatsby is described in terms of his romance
quest for Daisy, then suddenly in terms of a return to the succor of
infancy. The tensions and complexities of the novel are everywhere
resonant in the language.

Contemporary critical theory demonstrates that a literary text emerges
from the historical conditions of its production and reception, bearing
the imprint of social and historical practice by the users of words. Our
analysis, however, suggests that another way of regarding works of literature may be equally valid, that the language of literary texts is also
deeply tied to essential, radical motives, orders of experience we have
conceptualized as mode. This study of *The Great Gatsby* in the light of

pastoral has been concerned with the intersection of the temporal, "the hour of . . . human change and excitement," and the ahistorical—or, in Nick's words, with the "voice" that was "a deathless song" (101). We would argue finally that *The Great Gatsby* continues to resonate with meaning for readers at the beginning of the twentieth-first century not simply because of its retelling of the oldest story—the fairy-tale romance of the princess and the soldier—but equally and maybe more because of its way of singing to, its murmuring consolations to, our radical nostalgia.

Notes

1. These readings were established in the criticism of the 1950s and remain a point of departure for subsequent studies. R. W. Stallman identifies Gatsby as a mythic hero representing America; Marius Bewley argues that the novel offers a damaging criticism of the American dream; while Arthur Mizener, Fitzgerald's first biographer, refers suggestively but vaguely to the novel as a "tragic pastoral" (*The Far Side of Paradise* 192).

2. Descriptions of style involve controversial issues; these include not only deciding what parts of a writer's work to analyze and how to conduct the analysis, but perhaps more importantly how to interpret the data and what empirical status to claim for the interpretation. One of the major criticisms of stylistics, voiced strongly by Stanley E. Fish, is that observable formal patterns are in themselves without value, or else they are given value in a wholly arbitrary fashion, unless they are situated in a context of reception and reader expectations (Freeman 70). To provide a context for our findings, we describe here and in our earlier essay the different modes in which *The Great Gatsby* is written—naive and ironic romance, pastoral—for it is our claim here that features of style are engendered by mode and consequently they are inseparable from any reading that may be given to the text.

3. Aristotle describes the use of maxims as "suited to speakers of mature years, and to arguments on matters in which one is experienced. In a young man, uttering maxims is—like telling stories—unbecoming; and to use them in a realm where one lacks experience is stupid and boorish" (152). Interestingly, Aristotle's continuation of this advice on maxims also associates their rhetorical efficacy with a certain class sensitivity: "An adequate sign of this is that rustics are especially given to coining maxims, and always ready to vent them" (152).

To us, this observation of Aristotle's relates to Nick's strong sense of identity with his midwestern origins, his tie to his father, and his pastoral longings for the "dark fields of the republic" (189).

4. The idea of pastoral has teased critics since Mizener's description of *The Great Gatsby* as "a kind of tragic pastoral" (*The Far Side of Paradise* 192). Several critics, including Ornstein and Barry Gross, have tried to expand on this observation by focusing generally on the matter of East versus West in the novel. More specific studies of pastoral and *The Great Gatsby* in terms of mode and genre can be found in essays by Kuhnle and Gervais and in Leo Marx's *The Machine in the Garden* (354–65).

5. Paul Alpers provides in *What Is Pastoral?* a comprehensive history of pastoral criticism; he argues, using Kenneth Burke's terminology, that herdsmen and their lives constitute the representative anecdote that most accurately describes the conventions of pastoral that remain stable from Theocritus to the modern novel. Alpers describes at length the poetry of Theocritus (137–53) and Virgil (161–69) and the ideas of Schiller (28–37) and Empson (37–43) about pastoral.

6. Donald Monk, in an essay with interests like our own, has raised the following question: How does F. Scott Fitzgerald make his prose evocative? Monk's answer is to examine the imagery of the text and show how patterns artfully interconnect with each other. Our interest here in the nonreferential dimension of language in *The Great Gatsby* is rejected by Monk as something excessive in Fitzgerald's prose: the "dependence on stylistic effects is . . . responsible for the quasi-hallucinatory sense of words becoming their own substance, their own *raison d'être,* which one can feel when in a mood unsympathetic to [Fitzgerald]" (79).

7. Halliday and Hasan's original and still unassailable work on cohesion identifies five types of cohesion. Three types (reference, substitution, and ellipsis) depend on grammatical systems, and one (conjunction) is semantic. The fifth type, lexical, is the one that concerns us here, although further study of Fitzgerald along these lines could reveal the relevance of the other types to understanding his style in representing Nick's storytelling.

8. These are (a) equivalents (e.g., dream/reverie); (b) hypernyms (e.g., oak/tree); and (c) general terms (e.g., place/city).

9

F. Scott Fitzgerald in 1937

A Manuscript Study of "A Full Life"

HORST H. KRUSE

The typical Fitzgerald manuscript—with its usual amount of rewriting—always constitutes a definite invitation to reconstruct the process of composition and to relate it to the author's immediate biographical situation and circumstances. In the case of "A Full Life," a comparatively recent addition to the Fitzgerald canon of published writings, such an endeavor turns out to be doubly rewarding, leading not only to a better understanding of the meaning of the text but also to a reassessment of its significance as a biographical document.

To begin with, neither "A Full Life" nor the biographical context in which it was written would seem to have much to recommend itself to the critic. The story was never published during the author's lifetime. Its manuscript survived in a batch of papers and documents given to Princeton in 1959 by Martha Marie Shank, who functioned as Fitzgerald's typist and secretary during his stay in the Oak Hall Hotel in Tryon, North Carolina, from January to June 1937. It has drawn practically no attention from critics, although Ruth Prigozy, in her 1974 article on the unpublished stories of Fitzgerald's final phase, does discuss it under the heading "The Unfulfilled Life" ("The Unpublished Stories" 79–80). Even when it did get printed in 1988 in the *Princeton University Library Chronicle,* James L. W. West III, who had pressed for its publication and provided a seven-page introductory essay, considered it an unfinished and discarded item, but nevertheless not without interest as a key to Fitzgerald's state of mind at that period ("Fitzgerald Explodes His Heroine" 165).[1] Despite the story's initial acclaim—and worldwide reverberations even—in 1988 ("The Fitzgerald Flap"), the publication of "A Full Life" does not seem to have given it much literary status. In fact, I know of one critic who persists in calling it a "damn bad story" and a "terrible story."

From the point of view of biography and the author's creative imagination, the time when the story was written also is of little interest. "In the Darkest Hour" is what Bruccoli appropriately calls the chapter that deals with the mid-1930s, and when story and biographical circumstance converge in that chapter—as they do in a mere footnote—the story is cited as one of several of the period that were found to be "not marketable at any price" (*Some Sort of Epic Grandeur* 402, 403n). Citation of the story, however, occurs under its original title, "The Vanished Girl." The fact that Fitzgerald changed the title seems to suggest some significance, and his choice of the resounding phrase "A Full Life" proves to be indicative of major changes in the story itself.

The manuscript of "A Full Life" consists of a total of fifteen pages, three of which (numbered 2, 3, and 4) are the typewritten and heavily revised 8½ × 11 opening pages of the earlier story "The Vanished Girl"; the rest are 8½ × 14 "Corporate Bond" pages written in pencil, also heavily revised by the author himself. The very raggedness of the manuscript may have contributed to the evaluation of it as unfinished and discarded, and such supposition does seem to be supported by the correspondence (between Fitzgerald and his literary agent, Harold Ober, as well as Edwin Balmer, editor of *Redbook* magazine) about the possible publication of the story. It began in early March 1937 with the author sending Ober "The Vanished Girl" and telling him that due to immediate financial pressures he would "rather have a little for it now than a lot in two weeks" (Bruccoli and Atkinson 297).[2] And it ended about a month later with the story still unsold and the author writing that he was now "revamping" it for *Esquire* (Bruccoli and Atkinson 309). This statement has significant implications that actually presage aspects of the transformation that "A Vanished Girl" was to undergo in the process of becoming "A Full Life." In the light of the information and the findings in James L. W. West III's investigation of Fitzgerald's relations with *Esquire,* it meant no less than that the author had given up trying to place his story in the better-paying magazines and had instead decided to settle for the $250 that *Esquire* was prepared to pay him or by which it would reduce his indebtedness to the journal. It also meant that he had decided not to have Ober handle the story, since the latter may have "disapproved of the magazine's racy image" and not considered it "worth his time to handle an *Esquire* story for a ten per cent commission on a $250 fee." This may explain why there is no further reference to "A Full Life" in the Fitzgerald/Ober correspondence. Most of all, the statement indicates the nature and the direction of the revision, for *Esquire,* according to West, was "a more open and sophisticated magazine" and it "placed few restrictions on its authors." In it "Fitzgerald was able to give play to the autobiographical and confessional impulses he felt during the final years" (Bryer, *The Short Stories* 152–53). It is not surprising, therefore, that Fitzgerald should use the term "revamping" even at the beginning of the process. Arnold Gingrich, *Esquire's* editor, has asserted, however, that the story was never actually offered to him (West, "Fitzgerald Explodes His Heroine" 164). This, along with the fact that no typescript has ever turned up, does indeed seem to suggest that Fitzgerald had "decided to put no more effort into the story" (West, "Fitzgerald Explodes His Heroine" 165) and abandoned the project altogether.

A good deal of detective work was required to show that the above suppositions are wrong; that Fitzgerald did, in fact, allow the "revamping" to occupy him for another two months, until the very eve of his departure for California; that when he left Tryon he handed Marie Shank a finished manuscript for her to type; that she did prepare a fair-copy typescript and forward it to him at his Los Angeles address; and that the manuscript itself remained with her in North Carolina, eventually to become part of the papers she gave to Princeton.[3] Important clues to a more precise and a much later dating are that the final episode in the new version takes place "on a June afternoon in 1937" and that the "Corporate Bond" paper of the manuscript matches that of a Fitzgerald letter to Marie Shank postmarked June 10,[4] and most compelling is the fact that there is an earlier but canceled dating of the episode that reads "June 30th 1937."[5] This clearly indicates that "A Full Life" was the very last story and the very last piece of writing Fitzgerald completed before he boarded the Southern Pacific's *Argonaut* only four or five days later to travel west to begin what he felt would be a new life as a scriptwriter in Hollywood.

Conclusive proof for the existence of a now lost typescript made by Marie Shank after Fitzgerald's departure and then mailed to him in California would seem to lie in the fact that long after the author had begun his work on *The Last Tycoon,* he was able to return to the text of "A Full Life" and copy two passages from it for possible use in his novel and eventual insertion in his literary notebooks as typical story strippings. The second of these passages is what appears to be the most felicitous sentence in the whole composition and what becomes the key quotation in support of my argument that the story is no less than a deliberate summing-up and a final self-vindication. From the retrospective vantage point of the Depression era, and at a moment that Fitzgerald felt to be a turning point in his career, "A Full Life" dramatizes, summarizes, and objectifies the involved emotional relationship between himself as an author and the American flapper of the 1920s as his favorite subject. In any case, the sentence, with its truly striking conceit of the flapper, reads as follows: "But he never forgot—he was forever haunted by the picture of the girl floating slowly out over the city at dusk, buoyed up by delicious air, by a quintessence of golden hope, like a soaring and unstable stock issue" ("A Full Life" 168).

The two passages are typed on different sheets along with notes related to *The Last Tycoon* and are filed with further notes for the novel in Box 8, Folder 3 of the F. Scott Fitzgerald Papers in the Firestone Library at Princeton University. The passage quoted follows an entry that reads, "Minna burned in a fire." Although copied by a typist, the sequence of the items was probably determined by the author himself. There is a possibility, therefore, that the later one was called up by—and perhaps intended to be used to suggest—the haunting quality that the image of Minna Davis had never ceased to possess for Monroe Stahr. It should be noted, furthermore, that in both works the woman whose picture continues to haunt the protagonist has been named Davis (emended to Davies in "A Full Life"). Both women, moreover, are based on Zelda, but (in the light of evidence presented below) may also have been inspired by Hollywood actress Marion Davies, which could well explain the Davis-Davies emendation. In the absence of more obvious reasons, "A Full Life" may be adduced to explain the family name Fitzgerald has given to Stahr's deceased wife. A similar if somewhat more tenuous link between story and novel may be seen in the fact that the name of Wilkerson, inserted into an early list of characters for *The Last Tycoon* and later deleted, clearly echoes that of Wilkinson, the male protagonist of "A Full Life."[6]

With the revised chronology and these additional facts in mind, we can begin to look at the recoverable changes between the early and the revised versions and reconsider and reassess the salient points of the final story under four headings—(1) the use of non-mimetic elements, (2) the readjustment of the configuration of characters, (3) the revision of the time scheme, and (4) the introduction of the dynamite motif—all of which combine to transform what was primarily a case history into what now becomes predominantly an allegory that implicitly dramatizes the author's very own situation in 1937, including the rejection of the early version of his story.

(1) *The use of non-mimetic elements.* What both Ober and his assistant, as well as Balmer of *Redbook,* objected to in the early version was the one improbable incident in which the heroine, Cornell Davis, "floated out the window" (Bruccoli and Atkinson 303) in an attempt to demonstrate "inflatable suits for window jumping," as an inadequate summary has it.[7] "Not credible," "improbable," and "too crazy" were their respective responses.[8] Apparently at a loss as to what to make of the incident, Ober told Fitzgerald, "I wish you could work the story out without having the girl a mental case" (Bruccoli and Atkinson 303). Desperately needing the money he would be able to get for the story, Fitzgerald nevertheless declined to take his agent's advice. Instead, Ober's letter must have shown him that as a writer he had failed to prepare his potential readers adequately for what was for him a central non-mimetic element, a crucial conceit.

Rather than sacrifice the conceit in the interest of realism and, more importantly, in the interest of the immediate marketability of his story, he now placed the window-jumping incident at the very beginning and set about to support its startling quality by adding further non-mimetic elements designed to transform the case history of Cornell Davis of "The Vanished Girl" into the more allegorical story of Gwendolyn (or Gwen) Davies. He stressed ideographic rather than realistic presentation and, in the final scene, climaxed his endeavor by having his heroine work in a circus sideshow as "The Human Shell" who is fired into a net from a huge cannon, and then having her prove that she is "not an artificial shell" ("A Full Life" 171): she deliberately explodes herself, "with a tremendous bang" (172), by means of the dynamite that she carries inside her body.

(2) *The readjustment of the configuration of characters.* These non-mimetic and concomitant allegorizing aspects of the story become more meaningful when they are seen in relation to Fitzgerald's revision of the configuration of characters. Quite in line with its "missing person" plot, the early version has a young man who investigates the doings and the whereabouts of the "vanished girl" after she has disappeared from her hometown. In the second version the author comes up with an altogether fortunate substitution by drawing on *Tender Is the Night* and using a young doctor not at all unlike Dick Diver, who is much better suited for Fitzgerald in allegorizing the particular and ultimately destructive relationship that existed between himself as a writer and the flapper as his preferred subject. Curiosity and inquisitiveness as motivation are thus replaced by responsibility and solicitude. Dr. Harvey Wilkinson, an intern, is introduced in the very first scene in the emergency room of a hospital. He is taking care of Gwen Davies, who is "bruised and badly shaken" after her unsuccessful attempt to "sail over fences and street intersections" ("A Full Life" 167). Leaving a permanent mark on her by performing a suture on her forehead (a perfect choice for a symbol of the author's leaving his own indelible mark on the flapper),[9] Wilkinson continues to be fascinated by Gwen as he follows her progress in the many newspapers that celebrate her. Her effect on the doctor seems to express Fitzgerald's own feelings about his flapper heroines: "He felt that he knew her, in some such manner as one might know a composer or a writer one had never seen—he knew her though she had written only on air and there was a mysterious compulsion that made him follow her career with admiration and curiosity" (170).

In fact, when Gwen asks the doctor in the final episode if he is a reporter as well, there is a definite echo of the charge that as an author Fitzgerald had been concerned solely with the exterior and ephemeral aspects of American society and had failed to sound its deeper levels of meaning. But Wilkinson denies the supposition in the strongest terms: "No indeed. My interest is personal" (171). One can hardly help hearing in this the author himself deliberately rejecting the assigned role of journalist capitalizing on the colorful career of the flapper. He asserts instead that she is much more for him than merely a marketable literary commodity that can be dispensed with now that she is no longer in demand. As in Gatsby's attachment to Daisy, the idea of her is immeasurably and allegorically "personal." And by what seems to be another ingenious stroke, Fitzgerald further emphasizes this attitude by stationing the doctor, not with the "crowd of intellectuals . . . inspecting the enormous piece of ordinance" from which "The Human Shell" is to be fired, but all alone and well away from the rest, "beside the net which was to catch the living bullet at the end of its trajectory" (170). The final scene, therefore, in which the heroine dies in the explosion she sets off, and in so doing also kills the doctor, is a perfect allegory of the fact that the attraction the flapper had held for Fitzgerald, and the affection he had felt for her, proved to be fatal to his life as a popularly acclaimed writer. The rejection by Ober and others of "The Vanished Girl" as much as demonstrated to him what the cool reception of non-flapper Nicole Diver had seemed to indicate: as a writer he simply could not survive his heroine's actual demise as a particular type. The popular demise of the flapper was his popular demise as well.

(3) *The revision of the time scheme.* The readjustment of the dates is the most obvious revision that occurs, and the allegorical rationale behind it is readily apparent to anyone familiar with Fitzgerald's writings. By widening the 1927 to 1937 time span of "The Vanished Girl" by twelve years, the author reached back to 1915. The immediate substitution of the titles of the popular music of one year for those of the other—"Babes in the Wood" and "Underneath the Stars" for "My Blue Heaven" and "Among My Souvenirs"—epitomizes the great care expended on the revision as a whole.[10] The new titles, moreover, are perhaps even better suited to strengthen the allegorical implications of the revised version, "Babes in the Wood" having indeed been used in the 1920s, not least by the author himself, as a metaphor for the younger generation.[11] Fitzgerald is brilliant throughout in the technique of relating seemingly insignificant incidents and seemingly individual experience to national history and by doing so making them transcendent and universal. With great care he establishes a close parallel between events and dates in "A Full Life" and events and dates in the history of the 1920s, as he had rendered that decade in his famous essay "Echoes of the Jazz Age" in November 1931.

There are several striking correspondences between "A Full Life" and Fitzgerald's own rendition of the historical span of time. According to "Echoes of the Jazz Age," the new opening year, 1915 instead of 1927, marks the very beginning of the revolution in morals and manners carried forward by the younger generation—at precisely the time that seventeen-year-old Gwen leaves for New York City to begin her glamorous adventure. The manuscript shows the date 1923 to have been inserted with particular care, possibly over an erasure. That was the year that Gwen, after "a little orgy," jumps from the office building, significantly the year that "Echoes of the Jazz Age" describes as the time that "the younger generation was starred no longer," for by now "their elders, tired of watching the carnival with ill-concealed envy, had discovered that young liquor will take the place of young blood, and with a whoop the orgy began" (Wilson, *The Crack-up* 15). In 1927, the year when she married the Compt de Frejus, a Frenchman, Americans had begun to favor the French Riviera. In 1928 (when in a "sudden act" Gwen jumped into the Atlantic and managed to survive in the water for two hours) the American visitors were still able to swim, whereas "by 1929, at the most gorgeous paradise for swimmers on the Mediterranean no one swam any more" (Wilson, *The Crack-up* 19).[12] And while in "Echoes of the Jazz Age" Fitzgerald had had the decade "leap to a spectacular death in October, 1929" (13), he observed in his notebooks that "the flapper never really disappeared in the twenties—she merely dropped her name, put on rubber heels and worked in the dark" (*Notebooks* 204). All he needed to do now to update the history of the younger generation of the 1920s as reflected in the adventures of a representative heroine slightly younger than himself and slightly older than Zelda was to provide a coda in the final scene of the story.

Fitzgerald's care in the dating of the episodes is matched by the success of further revisions to make Gwen appear the typical quintessential girl of the 1920s. Her very attempt in the first episode to jump out the window in her "patented inflatable suit of rubber composition which had just been put on the novelty market for purposes of having fun" and to "sail over fences" (167) is an ingenious and—regarding the origin of the term "flapper"—wholly fitting conceit for the young woman of the 1920s and her reckless striving to emancipate herself from all kinds of custom and all sorts of restrictions. The subsequent episodes are meant to allegorize stages in her later development, and many details invite further interpretation that readily fits the context of the basic allegorical framework. However, attempts by the flapper to get off the ground become increasingly difficult, desperate, and futile. But Dr. Wilkinson, the autobiographical figure, romanticizes her throughout and sees her actually "floating slowly out over the city at dusk" (168). The heavily rewritten page 5 of the manuscript shows Fitzgerald searching his vocabulary for the right words, until eventually, by inserting the phrase "like a soaring and unstable stock issue" (168), he arrives at the very metaphor that is needed to suggest the ephemeral quality of the flapper and the way in which her fate is inextricably linked to and bound up with the economic history of the times.

(4) *The introduction of the dynamite motif.* In terms of the allegorical mode of presentation, Fitzgerald's choice and subsequent weaving in of the dynamite motif proved to be particularly fortunate, for it readily lent itself to illustrating both the special relationship between himself and his heroine on the one hand and the indigenous qualities of the flapper on the other. Ever since its invention in 1866, dynamite has been seen in its dual nature. A product of human ingenuity and a useful tool to achieve progress and to destroy and explode the remnants of an outmoded and oppressive past, it has also come to stand for the dangers inherent in and resulting from an unqualified belief in the perfectibility of man and of human institutions. Because of its particular properties, dynamite has been invoked again and again in literature to dramatize a quixotic quest and to moralize on its outcome.[13] Mark Twain's *A Connecticut Yankee,* Joseph Conrad's *The Secret Agent,* and George Bernard Shaw's *Heartbreak House* are some works in which, in his reading, Fitzgerald may have encountered the motif. But the usefulness of dynamite to characterize the explosive and self-destructive energy of the flapper and to describe the dangers inherent in his own lifelong devotion to her may also have suggested itself quite naturally. The idea clearly exists in some of the metaphors that Fitzgerald exploits throughout to prepare the final scene, from Gwen's not wanting to "raise the roof" (168) of her parental home and her marriage to the son of a powder manufacturer to whom she "had always really belonged" (170) to her statement, "I'm full of dynamite so I always thought I'd go off" (171).

In the catastrophe of the ending, the now forty-year-old Wilkinson

Page 5 of the manuscript of "A Full Life," with Fitzgerald's extensive changes.

Courtesy of the F. Scott Fitzgerald Papers, Manuscript Division, Department of Rare Books and Special Collections, Princeton University Library.

meets his nemesis just as the now forty-year-old Fitzgerald had met his own: the fixation of both on the flapper and her career and the attempt of both to coerce her into responding proves fatal. The heroine, reduced in status to that of a circus performer—dressed, significantly, "in the costume of an aviatrix" (170), still pretending to be able to fly, but dependent now on a cannon to get her off the ground—seems to have spent all her energy and to have become a mere shell of her former self. But Wilkinson, the author-figure, has been unable to see this; his prolonged romantic and foolish pursuit of the heroine in her initial glory, his refusal to accept change and to face reality, is what actually kills him; this is the true significance of the allegory, which by now has turned into the kind of moral fable that is at the bottom of much of Fitzgerald's work. But as the pursuit has also given meaning to Wilkinson's existence and turned the final encounter with Gwen into "the high point of a somewhat humdrum and defeated life" (171), the ending of the story suggests that the title applies to either protagonist: both Gwen and Wilkinson have led a full life, and the lives of both have now come full circle.

It should come as no surprise, in view of the allegorical reading demanded by the text—and the text simply does not make sense unless it is read allegorically—that during his stay in Tryon, Fitzgerald (according to testimony provided by Marie Shank) tried twice to take his own life.[14] He expressed his concern with death in the clearly autobiographical story "Room Nineteen" and in his poem "The Earth Calls";[15] and on June 17, 1937, while in all probability, as I have shown, he was still working on "A Full Life," he had his will executed. This very closeness of the allegory to the facts and anxieties of his own life may have induced him not to send the typescript to *Esquire* after all, nor ever to try to publish it elsewhere. In fact, it is very likely that in its growth "A Full Life" did not merely go through two phases, but actually through three, and that in the third phase it had obviously ceased to interest Fitzgerald as a marketable item altogether. To see him work on the story to within days of his departure for Hollywood, to see him work on it, moreover, with a $1,000-a-week MGM contract in his hands, to see him give the completed manuscript to Marie Shank at the last moment, too late for her, indeed, to produce a typescript before he leaves; but then to see him make no effort whatsoever to have it published—all this gives "A Full Life" a unique status among his work. So does the fact that in writing the story the very same autobiographical and confessional impulses that had produced his "Crack-up" pieces should now result in an outright allegory and actually be controlled by that form. Such uniqueness invites further speculation about circumstances that attended the revision and the forces that helped to give the story its final shape.

Trying to help Fitzgerald solve his financial problems and to overcome the difficulties he had discussed in "The Crack-up," Maxwell

Perkins had suggested in the fall of 1936 that he write an "autobiographical book." Fitzgerald, however, did not like the idea, for he knew that too many people about whose judgment he cared had objected to the confessional nature of his recent *Esquire* contributions. These contributions, he felt in late 1936, "would have to form part of the fabric of a book so projected," but he had become wary of openly exploiting his own life. Such a venture, he believed, "would have a chance at success" only if he "were prepared at this moment to 'tell all'"; otherwise "it would seem to be a measure adopted *in extremis,* a sort of period to my whole career" (*Life in Letters* 312). The same hesitation about further use of autobiographical and confessional material emerges from a letter of April 1937 in which he refers to "those indiscreet *Esquire* articles" (*Life in Letters* 320). But it was also in April 1937 that he wrote his agent that he was now revamping "The Vanished Girl," expressly for the very same magazine. As James L. W. West III points out, all the other items that Fitzgerald published in *Esquire* indicate that such activity actually involved an autobiographical and confessional approach (Bryer, *The Short Stories* 151–53). I suggest that in view of his hesitancy about being autobiographical, he deliberately built on the non-mimetic elements of "The Vanished Girl" and developed and exploited the time-tested strategies of allegory to conceal or to camouflage what would otherwise be seen as indiscreet material.

To a reader familiar with Fitzgerald's life, many details in "A Full Life" still suggest that he is, in fact, dramatizing the complicated, rich, rewarding, and at the same time destructive relationship between himself and Zelda. His revision borrows the doctor-patient relationship from *Tender Is the Night,* a novel "which covers the life we led in Europe," as the author put it in a letter to Dr. Mildred Squires, Zelda's doctor at the Phipps Clinic of Johns Hopkins University (*Life in Letters* 209). It is also true that throughout Fitzgerald's career as a writer Zelda had been the model for his portrait of the flapper. Her disregard for conventional behavior and the obsessions she later developed or cultivated are directly reflected in the behavior of Gwen Davies, as regards swimming as an emancipatory activity, and allegorically, as regards her ballet dancing. And just as his heroine is called a "shell," albeit ambiguously, so Zelda in a letter to Scott of June 1935 had spoken of herself as being "an empty shell" (Bruccoli and Duggan 413).

The list of such details and incidents traceable to Zelda could perhaps be extended, but it is clearly offset by a list of details and incidents that suggest definite avoidance of autobiographical reference along with Fitzgerald's traditional and deliberate procedure of composite characterization.[16] The change of the name of the female protagonist from Cornell Davis to Gwen Davies suggests that in his delineation of the flapper he also drew on actress Marion Davies, whom he seems to have known since at least 1923. He followed her career—as Wilkinson follows that of Gwen Davies—with "admiration and curiosity." Although she was not included in his list of "Cinema Descendants of the Type He Has Made So Well Known" (Bruccoli and Bryer 277–81), and, according to her biographer, "never was a full-blown flapper," she at times "looked and acted the part" (Guiles 137). Unlike that of Zelda, Davies's date of birth exactly fits the time scheme of the story, and so does the sudden end of her career as a popular MGM movie star in 1937. If in preparation for his Hollywood assignment and in anticipation of a renewed meeting with Miss Davies (which did take place when, shortly after his arrival in Hollywood, he paid her a visit at San Simeon), Fitzgerald began to monitor news of the movie world, he could have read in the *New York Times* on June 5 that quite unexpectedly the actress and the Warner brothers were no longer "mutually amicable" ("Screen News") and on June 16 that "no pictures with her as star [had] been included in the Warner production announcement for the new season" ("News of the Screen"). What Zelda Fitzgerald, Marion Davies, and Gwen Davies of "A Full Life" share, then, is their conspicuous daring as well as their unconventional—by standards of the time even immoral— behavior. The sudden end of her spectacular career joins daring and unconventionality among the chief characteristics of the flapper.

There is good reason to add yet another historical personage to the list of possible sources for Fitzgerald's composite picture of the New Woman: none other than Amelia Earhart, the renowned aviatrix. Earhart was born in 1898, a year after Marion Davies, and although her disappearance on a transoceanic flight did not occur until July 1937, her solo crossing of the Atlantic on June 17, 1928, had been the kind of feat that signaled emancipation. In June 1937, her preparations for another (destined to be fatal) venture helped to keep the achievement and its emancipatory implications before the public. It is certain that Fitzgerald was aware of Earhart and her activities, for he had mentioned her as a specialist on "air currents" in a list of acknowledgments in his unused parodic "Preface" to *Tender Is the Night* (Bruccoli and Baughman [ii]). It is quite possible, therefore, that the "costume of an aviatrix" that Gwen Davies wears in the final scene of "A Full Life" hints at Amelia Earhart's contribution to Fitzgerald's composite picture of the flapper.

Another of the features of "A Full Life" that points away from a specific portrait of Zelda and toward the type of the flapper is the information the text provides about the regional origin of the protagonist. In revising "The Vanished Girl," Fitzgerald deliberately retained the fact that she comes from a New England village, but at a later point in the story he added that "there was a vague impression that she was either from the South, North or West, though one paper announced her birthplace as New York City" (170). It is interesting to note that while the author is obviously aiming to suggest a certain universality, historical accuracy has him confine the type to America by deleting the words "though an English or Russian origin was hinted at" from an earlier version of the sentence (MS 8ff.). One also notes that he shrewdly manages to imply that it was New York City, of course, where the flapper had made her first appearance.

Regardless of whether or not Fitzgerald actually drew on the biographies of Marion Davies and Amelia Earhart, however, the manuscript of "A Full Life" shows that in the portrayal of his protagonist he definitely went beyond the facts of Zelda's life. The additional material he incorporated is carefully chosen with a view to concealing outright autobiographical reference as well as with a view to arriving at an even more general and more typical portrait of the flapper. In the course of this procedure, development of the non-mimetic elements of the story served those purposes; they helped to transform the fictive case history of Cornell Davis of "The Vanished Girl" as well as some of the actual facts concerning Zelda Fitzgerald into what is an outright author-allegory about Fitzgerald as a writer and the flapper as his characteristic subject.

In the thoroughly systematic nature of its approach, moreover, the method of composite characterization followed in the portrayal of Gwen Davies epitomizes Fitzgerald's procedure in writing his allegory as a whole. All aspects of "A Full Life"—an occasional loose end notwithstanding—as well as of the course of its writing as it has been reconstructed here testify to the fact that Fitzgerald composited sources for brief, successful flights into allegory fully as much as for his novels. He was willing as well as able to give the requisite attention to his composition over an extended period of time and actually insisted on completing it as his stay in the East was drawing to an end.[17] Achieving the necessary congruity between mimetic level and allegorical level, moreover, always is an analytic exercise that presupposes intellectual detachment and dispassionateness. When its subject is autobiographical, therefore, allegory all but forces a writer to control any confessional impulse and to consider and assess his own situation objectively.[18] The writing of an autobiographical allegory thus may well assume the quality of a ritual and a therapeutic exercise, and I suggest that to some degree this is what happened when Fitzgerald revised "The Vanished Girl" into "A Full Life."

What had begun as a story written to alleviate his financial burden, and what the author then began to revamp "for *Esquire,*" eventually turned into an instrument that in April, May, and June of 1937 must have helped him to analyze and face up to his personal situation as a writer, a situation that had, in fact, been exacerbated through his very failure to sell the story he was now revising. In shaping "A Full Life" he put into perspective both his success and his failure as a writer by recapitulating the history of his involvement with the flapper, by recognizing the mutuality of their lives, and by admitting to himself the end of their engagement. It is wholly adequate, in terms of such realization, that he actually has himself die in the author-figure of Wilkinson. But such death is no longer a sign of the kind of resignation that the metaphors used in the "Crack-up" pieces had suggested. In avoiding what has been termed the exhibitionistic self-indulgence of those pieces, and in objectifying his self-analysis by translating it into a sustained, succinct allegory, Fitzgerald indicated, in fact, that he had overcome his crack-up and was indeed ready to begin a new life—arriving in Los Angeles, as he later wrote, "with the feeling of new worlds to conquer in 1937."[19]

"A Full Life" is likely to continue to be found a flawed piece and a "terrible story" as long as one tries to read it as predominantly realistic short fiction. Fitzgerald's failure to include it in the detailed inventory of works sold, submitted, written, and planned which he sent to Edwin

Knopf of MGM on July 19, 1937 (Bruccoli and Duggan 475n) and the fact that the typescript that he had asked Marie Shank to prepare does not seem to have survived also suggest a negative evaluation. It appears to be a much more creditable achievement, however, as soon as we read it, not as a realistic story, but as what the manuscript revisions help us to see it actually is—an outright allegory and a moral fable. After all the attention the author had given to the revision, the fact that it should practically disappear from view as soon as he had left the East greatly enhances its status as a biographical document. After the reception of the "Crack-up" articles, its significance was something Fitzgerald probably would just as soon have left unpublished. And after all, for him the allegory had served its purpose—and served it well. In his emotional economy he could comfortably afford to let it rest unpublished. But for us, on the other hand, at a distance of sixty-five years, it is a document whose publication enables us to share and to understand Fitzgerald's complex views of himself and his anxieties at a crucial moment in his life.

A Note on Editorial Problems

What I have said about "A Full Life" should give it the status of an important author-allegory, and one would like to see it admitted into the canon of published and readily available Fitzgerald stories. Publication of "A Full Life" does involve serious editorial problems, however.

It is my belief that there was a typescript of "A Full Life," and there is a possibility that it may still be found. It is highly probable that Fitzgerald further revised that typescript, for while one of the quotations used in his notebooks does correspond to the final version arrived at in the manuscript which the author left with Marie Shank and therefore must have been taken from the missing typescript that she prepared for him, the other one differs and therefore would seem to represent a later stage. In the absence of the typescript, an editor is faced with having to resolve significant discrepancies in chronology in the history of the New England town that the protagonist comes from. Such resolution involves actual rewriting of the text: the incidents as given in the copy-text manuscript would literally have to be replaced to match the 1915 rather than 1927 departure of Gwen Davies.

A "clean" version of the manuscript, however, is not likely to result in a typical Fitzgerald short story and, unless heavily annotated, is likely to be misunderstood. Since its importance would seem to lie primarily in its value as a significant biographical document (allegories are meant to be read and "translated," and only secondarily appreciated as mimetic stories), a facsimile of the manuscript or a transcript of the manuscript in its present state would best serve such purposes, the discrepant chronology helping to demonstrate Fitzgerald's revisions and to indicate authorial intent.

While as an outright allegory the item would seem to be all but unique in the Fitzgerald canon, its definite autobiographical implications suggest a grouping with "Echoes of the Jazz Age" and the "Crack-up" pieces as well as the confessional *Esquire* stories of the middle and late 1930s.

Notes

1. All parenthetical references in the text are to the printing of "A Full Life" in the *Princeton University Library Chronicle*. Parenthetical references in the text for quotations from the manuscript of "A Full Life" (F. Scott Fitzgerald Papers, Firestone Library, Princeton University, Fitzgerald Additional Papers, Marie Shank Additions, Box 12, Folder 11) are preceded by "MS" and are published with the permission of the Princeton University Library. © 2003 by Harold Ober Associates, Inc. and the Trustees of the F. Scott Fitzgerald Estate. I gratefully acknowledge the advice of Milton R. Stern, with whom it was a pleasure to argue major and minor points in the preparation of this essay.

2. Fitzgerald goes on to explain why he needs "Four hundred on the 15th and $500 on the 20th" and climaxes his plea with a desperate "for Gods sake raise me something on this story + wire it to Baltimore" (Bruccoli and Atkinson 298).

3. The fact that the manuscript stayed with Marie Shank is of course explained by the compositional history of "A Full Life" as reconstructed here by means of internal and external evidence. The in situ preservation of the manuscript is part of the external evidence and goes to confirm that history.

4. F. Scott Fitzgerald to Martha Marie Shank, n.p., n.d., postmarked Tryon, N.C., June 10, 1937 (F. Scott Fitzgerald Papers, Firestone Library, Princeton University, Marie Shank Additions, Box 12, Folder 18). No other paper in the collection has a "Corporate Bond" watermark.

5. The cancellation of "June 30th 1937" occurs on MS 11. A more detailed study would have to take into account a renumbering of pages as well as numerous insertions, deletions, and corrections, all of which indicate a consistent development of the allegory the story proves to be.

6. See Fitzgerald, *Fitzgerald Manuscripts,* vol. 5, pt. 1, pp. 7, 8, and 9, which, on p. 91, also reproduces the sheet containing the passage from "A Full Life." Both passages salvaged from the story have found their way into the author's notebooks and are listed in Bruccoli's edition as #2046 and #1836—unidentified as to their origin—among the "Loose Notes" of the "Appendix" (*Notebooks* 332n, 311). Minor differences that exist between the opening paragraph of the holograph manuscript and its typewritten version in the above material not only point to a typescript of the story that has been lost but also indicate that Fitzgerald did return to the story and that in his typical manner he used the typescript to revise his text. It is interesting to note, however, that the second passage, which had been perfected through extensive revision in manuscript, remained unchanged.

7. Constance Smith, Ober's assistant, in her synopsis as cited by West ("Fitzgerald Explodes His Heroine" 162).

8. Constance Smith in her summary, Harold Ober, and Edwin Balmer of *Redbook* as quoted by Ober in his letter to Fitzgerald of March 24, 1937 (Bruccoli and Atkinson 303).

9. Less than a year earlier, Fitzgerald had used "suture" as a key term in "An Author's Mother" (*The Price Was High* 736–39), the last of three autobiographical items published in *Esquire* from July to September 1936. Although written while his mother was still living, it actually became an obituary tribute after Mary McQuillan Fitzgerald died in August 1936. The story concerns a halting old lady over eighty who sustains a cut on her forehead but who dies before the intern gets a chance to perform the suture.

10. It should be noted, however, that Fitzgerald (in typical fashion) failed to adjust two minor dates in the history of his heroine's hometown before her departure. Since these dates are of no importance to what his allegory is trying to say, his failure to adjust them still provides evidence for his allegorical intention. As they now stand, however, they pose a serious editorial problem, since both the dates themselves and the incidents they refer to would have to be replaced to match the 1915 rather than the 1927 departure of Gwen Davies.

11. Fitzgerald's wording here, as in "The Love Boat" (1927), is "Babes in the Woods," as it was also in the title of his short story of 1917, which became part of Book One of *This Side of Paradise.*

12. The role of swimming as a significant activity in the emancipated behavior of the American flapper can be seen most clearly in the life of Zelda, always Fitzgerald's model for his portrait of the flapper (see Milford).

13. For an account of the treatment of nitroglycerin and dynamite and their formation into a motif in English and American literature, see chapter 4, "Dynamite," in my *Schlüsselmotive der amerikanischen Literatur.*

14. Martha Marie Shank to Arthur Mizener, October 26, 1949 (F. Scott Fitzgerald Additional Papers, Firestone Library, Princeton University, Marie Shank Additions, Box 12, Folder 19).

15. Both are preserved in the F. Scott Fitzgerald Papers, Firestone Library, Princeton University, Marie Shank Additions, Box 12, Folder 13 and Folder 14. The story was published as "The Guest in Room Nineteen" in *Esquire* (October 1937); the poem is printed in Fitzgerald, *Poems, 1911–1940* (103).

16. "Characterization" may be the wrong term to use in connection with allegory, which depends on types rather than individualized characters. But Fitzgerald's method of composite characterization, defended in his discussion with Hemingway about *Tender Is the Night* (see the 1934 exchange of letters printed in Bruccoli, *Fitzgerald and Hemingway* [170–75]) and explained with reference to "Crazy Sunday" in a letter of February 8, 1936, to Harold Ober (Bruccoli and Atkinson 250), does in fact serve the purposes of allegory well; it helps to transcend the limitations of realism and it presupposes detachment.

17. Even when in April 1937 Fitzgerald told Ober that he had begun to revamp "The Vanished Girl" for *Esquire,* the decision to take his time began to assert itself: "My rate [of finishing stories] is never more than one a month" (Bruccoli and Atkinson 309). Eventually he seems to have reached what as early as May 1930 in a letter to Ober he had found to be an ideal stage: "The only way I can write a decent story is to imagine no one's going to accept it + who cares. Self-consciousness about editors is *ruinous* to me" (*Life in Letters* 183).

18. It is worth noting here that in all of its implications, Fitzgerald's procedure of translating self-analysis into an allegorical story and of using the strategies of allegory for such self-analysis finds a close parallel in "Babylon Revisited" (1931). A much greater achievement than "A Full Life," it likewise relies on an elaborate structure of composite characters to control and to objectify autobiographical and confessional impulses that grew out of a similar crisis. While, as Matthew J. Bruccoli notes, it is indeed "intensely personal, expressing [Fitzgerald's] feelings about his alcoholism, his wife's mental collapse,

and his responsibility to his daughter" (Fitzgerald, *The Short Stories* 616), the story yet enforces a sober assessment of his situation.

19. "Intermediate Notes" for chapter 1 of *The Last Tycoon,* F. Scott Fitzgerald Papers, Firestone Library, Princeton University, Box 8, Folder 2. Published with the permission of the Princeton University Library. © 2003 by Harold Ober Associates, Inc. and the Trustees of the F. Scott Fitzgerald Estate. A similar spirit is evident in a sentence in his autobiographical story "Financing Finnegan," published in *Esquire* in January 1938: "I had just got a thousand dollars advance for a venture in Hollywood and was going to fly out with all the verve of the old days when there was chicken feed in every pot" (*The Short Stories* 745).

10

F. Scott Fitzgerald and Willa Cather

A New Study

STANLEY BRODWIN

On February 2, 1921, Fitzgerald wrote to H. L. Mencken and added a short but exclamatory postscript: "Just finished 'My Antonia'—a great book! Mine is to be called 'The Beautiful and Damned'" (Bruccoli and Duggan 78). In a letter to Cather four years later, Fitzgerald again acknowledged the power of her art and language in a brief apologia disclaiming any "apparent plagiarism" from *A Lost Lady*. He especially referred to the description of Marian Forrester that began with the words, "she seemed to promise a wild delight that he has not found in life," which bore so close a resemblance to his own description of Daisy's voice: "there was an excitement in her voice . . . a singing compulsion, a whispered . . . promise that . . . there were gay, exciting things hovering in the next hour" (Bruccoli and Duggan 155–56; *The Great Gatsby* 11).

Characteristically, Fitzgerald praised Cather's passage as being more "clear" and "beautiful" and "moving" (Bruccoli and Duggan 156) than his own after calling himself one of her greatest "admirers," particularly of *My Ántonia* (1918), *A Lost Lady* (1923), "Paul's Case" (1905), and "Scandal" (1919). Fitzgerald was no doubt heartened when Cather wrote to him on April 28 that she admired *The Great Gatsby* and detected no plagiarism at all. Matthew J. Bruccoli has discussed this literary encounter in full and what it revealed about Fitzgerald's composition of the novel ("An Instance of Apparent Plagiarism"). And yet, as Richard Lehan suggests, there are other resemblances too, as in the striking similarity between Cather's emphasis on Frank Ellinger's powerful (but crude) muscularity and Fitzgerald's initial description of Tom Buchanan (Lehan, *"The Great Gatsby"* 107–10).

Here is part of Cather's trenchant description of Frank Ellinger:

His whole figure seemed very much alive under his clothes, with a restless, muscular energy that had something of the cruelty of wild animals in it. Niel was very much interested in this man, the hero of many ambiguous stories. He didn't know whether he liked him or not. He knew nothing bad about him, but he felt something evil. (*A Lost Lady* 36–37)

And now the look and body of Tom Buchanan:

He had changed since his New Haven years. Now he was a sturdy, straw haired man of thirty with a rather hard mouth and a supercilious manner. Two shining, arrogant eyes had established dominance over his face and gave him the appearance of always leaning aggressively forward. Not even the effeminate swank of his riding clothes could hide the enormous power of that body—he seemed to fill those glistening boots until he strained the top lacing and you could see a great pack of muscle shifting when his shoulder moved under his thin coat. It was a body capable of enormous leverage—a cruel body. (*The Great Gatsby* 9)

It is clear that Cather's description, if given in full, is the more detailed; we even know how tall Frank is—six feet, two inches. Yet, as Lehan has shown, both images center on power—aggressiveness, muscularity—both men have bodies bursting with the power to hurt or crush. Niel Herbert grasps the "evil" in Frank, and Carraway the aggression and arrogance in Tom. But there is one word that leaps out at the reader, a word that makes another "apparent plagiarism" even more likely than the one Fitzgerald so honestly disclaimed concerning *A Lost Lady:* "cruelty" or "cruel." Frank's muscular energy contains "the cruelty of wild animals in it"; Tom's body "is capable of enormous leverage—a cruel body." Coincidental rhetoric? Perhaps. I would like to think that this rhetorical connection reflects a moral affinity between

Cather and Fitzgerald, verbalized in lyric yet unsentimentalized images of a "sin" both writers often dramatized as primal: the cruelty that violates, betrays, smashes up things and people without remorse—the cruelty of Ivy Peters who slits out the eyes of a woodpecker, of Frank's cruel indifference to Marian's feelings when she discovers his marriage, which drives her to drink and insult: "You know, Frank, the truth is that you're a coward; a great hulking coward" (*A Lost Lady* 114). To be sure, there is something in her that needed Frank's sexuality—cruelty and all—and which Niel observes, with what disillusion we know. And, of course, Nick observes the byplay on "hulking" between Tom and Daisy.

In *My Ántonia,* too, and other works, Cather explores the power of cruelty to destroy innocence or social harmony, although Ántonia and Fathers Latour and Vaillant in *Death Comes for the Archbishop* (1927), a novel Fitzgerald owned and read, are somehow able to defeat the cruel and destructive through their power of mind and faith. Even Marian survives her despair over losing Frank, and if, to Niel Herbert, she has gone from bad to worse in taking up with Ivy, she nevertheless manages, in all her emotional and moral contradictions, to survive in her last marriage to Henry Collins, never forgetting to send flowers for Captain Forrester's grave every Decoration Day. Indeed, as we know, Cather is an incisive moralist and treats of cruelty and other "sins" with their ramifications throughout her work. So too Fitzgerald, who constantly sought the poetic justice that should consecrate, or at least justify, the lives of those victimized by the cruelty of the Tom Buchanans and the morally "dead" Tommy Barbans and Nicoles of this world. Nick Carraway's wisely directed sympathetic nostalgia should and does ironically validate Gatsby's dream and character, but nothing can prevent the survival of the Buchanans in their old, destructive ways. On one level at least, the tragedy of *The Great Gatsby* lies precisely in the unresolved tension between the "justice" owed to Gatsby and the absence of a compensating punishment for Daisy and Tom, for they are too spiritually dead to know genuine remorse or the hell of their own relationship. No wonder Nick closes out his interest in the "abortive sorrows and short-winded elations of men" (6). What good would his moral insight and condemnation do for them? His nostalgic re-creation of Gatsby, linked to the Dutch sailors' pristine vision of the New World, is not grounded in his conviction that the tragic pattern of events he has witnessed and recorded can somehow be redeemed from the "foul dust" (6) that preyed on Gatsby.

Fitzgerald's final statement in *The Great Gatsby* is far more disturbing and profound than Cather's in *A Lost Lady*, which essentially affirms Marian's life in spite of the lamentable "passing" of the old frontier values, and her illicit passion (at least in Niel's heart). Hearing of her death, both Niel and Ed Elliot know she was "well-cared for, to the very end" (150), a knowledge that gratifies them—and the reader. But in *Gatsby*, with life ever receding into the past despite our failing effort to beat against the currents, the future will paradoxically be a final entrapment in the past both as refuge and as doom. However much Fitzgerald admired Cather's novel and its hard lyricism, and however much time and history charged both their creative forces, in the end Cather (certainly in her last novels like *Shadows on the Rock* [1931] and *Sapphira and the Slave Girl* [1940]) found a measure of consolation and security in the historical past. Specific eras and events of the historical past, with all their complex patterns and signal personalities, offered settings that Fitzgerald may have yearned for and even at moments achieved. But, unlike Cather, Fitzgerald was not a "historical novelist." No specific era offered him a setting in which he could nourish an optimistic belief about history's constantly renewing powers of redemption.

I have not rehearsed these well-known episodes and their thematic implications simply to establish or even disestablish their literary relationship, a relationship spelled out quite perceptively by James E. Miller, Tom Quirk, Patricia L. Yongue, and Richard Lehan (*"The Great Gatsby"*), among others. Perhaps Cather's theory of the novel *demueblé*, the "unfurnished" novel of "selectivity"—particularly her assertion that "It is the inexplicable presence of the thing not named" (Cather, *Not Under Forty* 50) that is the goal of authentic literary art—did influence Fitzgerald's craft. Yet it seems clear that Fitzgerald's rhetorical grasp of the personal dynamics of illusion, of the disillusioning betrayal of fidelity, and of dream and reality are his by birth and experience. Of course, these antinomies sweep through a good deal of American literature as a whole, and we like to find all kinds of thematic connections from the nineteenth century to the present. Although Cather and Fitzgerald draw from these tensions and contradictions in American culture an occasional but striking similarity of insight and emotional tone (Niel Herbert's disillusion suggesting, but not really duplicating, Nick Carraway's, *Alexander's Bridge* [1912] perhaps being a model for the theme in *The Great Gatsby*), we must recognize that at the very core of their artistic achievements there throbs a radically different perception and emotional confrontation with what is perhaps the most vital creative dialectic of all: the relationship of the past to the present and the prophesied future of hope and desire fulfilled.

The psychological forces of longing and nostalgia need to commemorate and fix, however momentarily, a defining and inexpungible moment of the past from the flux of memory in a living recollection. Of course, these forces emotionally mark many of the artistic challenges in both Cather and Fitzgerald. Indeed, there are some critics and readers who justifiably recognize these tensions as inherent in American literature as a whole, from Washington Irving to the present. The search for a usable past and the dialectic between an elegiac and celebratory apprehension of it—the political-literary party of memory and the party of hope, in Emerson's formulation—has hardly been exhausted by critics, regardless of the plethora of literary theories brought to bear on it. In this context, I would like to suggest that we understand the terms "memory" and "recollection" in the way Kierkegaard analyzed them in *Stages on Life's Way*. In this work, he asserts that "Memory is merely a minimal condition. By means of memory the experience presents itself to receive the consecration of recollection. . . . For recollection is ideality . . . it involves effort and responsibility which the indifferent act of memory does not involve. . . . Hence it is an art to recollect" (27, 28, 30). I don't know whether Cather and Fitzgerald would have affirmed this distinction if they had read it, but it seems to me that in their craft and emotional "selection" they manifest that art of recollection even as they "consecrate" it.

Yet with this Kierkegaardian perspective, we must also reexamine that dominant word, "nostalgia," which has become a critical and descriptive commonplace in our vocabulary of understanding both writers, a kind of critical absolute. But authentic nostalgia is for Kierkegaard the translation of memory into recollection, a recapturing, as the existentialist critic Ralph Harper suggests, of the ontological "presence" of the recollected event or person to provide the spiritual life necessary for either the omniscient author or the first-person narrative recollectors. In this view, nostalgia is the "moral sentiment of the present century," and it must be valued for the way it authentically captures both the "lostness" of spiritual values and love and for how it reminds us of the "good" we have known and then lost (Harper 26–32). Both Kierkegaard and other existentialist philosophers finally recognize that nostalgia can be a morally regenerative force and is not, as Harper insists, a shallow optimism, "illusory" or "unprogressive" (28). Rather, as Kierkegaard believed, nostalgia is a demanding sentiment that resides within us, somewhere between waiting and longing, and it appears amid feelings of unhappiness and failure. At that point, it serves to recall the soul to its inner wholeness—offering to the depressed conscious a psychic experience of its presence. Finally, throughout much of Western literature, I am tempted to assert, it is the soul's natural way of fighting the sickness of despair. Critics have assumed that for Fitzgerald nostalgia is perhaps the salvational principle enabling him to function artistically, as Wright Morris has claimed (157–70). Certainly Morris recognizes, as others have, that *Gatsby* is a novel "recollected in tranquillity," "serene" and "elegiac" (167), although I question whether Fitzgerald was as Wordsworthian as all that.

But Morris also contends that the "depths of nostalgia, the slough of its despair, offered him no key to the facts of the absurd. . . . Having drawn on the resources he no longer possessed . . . he cracked up" (170). Thus for Morris, nostalgia becomes a tragic fate for Fitzgerald because, though it is "inexhaustible," it fails to give him a regenerative vision of life with which to deal with the "absurd." Perhaps. But "The Crack-up" is also nostalgia as a salvational struggle, not found in the novels, where the author tries to get in touch with his authentic self in order to be released from a debilitating despair. Fitzgerald claimed in "My Lost City" that the world may no longer whisper to him of "fantastic success and eternal youth" embodied in New York City, but then, "All is lost save memory." Memory is thus compensation, although Fitzgerald's statement carries the ironic self-awareness that he will return to New York to have experiences he has only read about. But "for the moment I can only cry that I have lost my splendid mirage." And then comes a line Thomas Wolfe could have written: "Come back, come back, O glittering and white!" (Wilson, *The Crack-up* 33). Here then is the homesickness that is only borne by the pain of the memory. This stage must be the consecration of recollection, a nostalgia that *recalls* the presence of a past in its authentic form, providing the reassurance that "being" or past existence is, in fact, never lost, only waiting, as it were, to establish the continuity of "being" in life.

As Harper well says, the task nostalgia sets man again and again is the need and beauty of "presence" (31–32). Surely Fitzgerald's work testifies to the demands of that task, and to his courage. And we are reminded that Wordsworth also spoke of a "presence that disturbs me." Its disturbance is the way we feel fulfilled or redeemed or exalted when we attest the "presence" in our lives (God, love, beauty) that can become the saving grace of hope. Hope is couched in the language of a plea for a recollected presence that is more than a romanticized city or success. It is a cry for the return of reality in the form of ephemeral pastness; it is a longing that will re-create the splendid "mirage" that faded ineluctably into a mere fragmented memory. The whole dynamic and anguished drive of nostalgia in Fitzgerald—and I believe for Cather, too, but in a more concrete historical fashion—is just for that: an ontological, even theological security that was once real and, even though lost, retains its permanence embodied in art. Here now, by way of a brief illustration, is a passage that was not included in the posthumous publication of "My Generation" (1968) and as far as I am aware has not been published to this date:

> Well . . . many are dead, and some I have quarreled with and I don't see any more. But I have never cared for any men as much as for these who felt the first springs when I did, and saw death ahead, and were reprieved . . . and who now walk the long stormy summer. It is a generation staunch by inheritance, sophisticated by fact—and rather deeply wise. More than that, what I feel about them is summed up in a line of Willa Cather's: "We possess together the precious, incommunicable past." ("A Note on My Generation")

Whether Fitzgerald had *My Ántonia* in his hand when he wrote this or simply remembered it almost perfectly doesn't really matter. What this passage reveals is the authentic connection Fitzgerald felt between himself and Cather. Written probably in 1939, this passage reflects the affirmation of the past he found in Cather's novel, which he immediately assigns to his past—his generation. Here there is no cry of "Come back, come back," as in 1932. More important, the past is here seen as precious and not the recessive inevitability Nick voices at his coda. It is a passage about life epitomized, and about his existential relationship to the men who experienced with him the "springs" of love, creativity, beginning, death, reprieve, courage, and the way they became "deeply wise." His possession of the "incommunicable past" is here a form of spiritual life: the past makes them all live; they continue to exist, though many are dead. He feels and experiences their presence as a palpable energy, thus earning the affirmation nostalgia implicitly holds forth as a longed-for gift, the negation of despair through the consecrated recollection. This is certainly the revelation of Jim Burden as he measures his life and failures against Ántonia's life and her regenerative Earth-Goddess spirit. Fitzgerald's "ineffable beauty of my dream girls of 1914" (Wilson, *The Crack-up* 33) may seem to us less substantial than Ántonia's powers, but they are, for all that, his most characteristic and deeply felt image of what he longed for most in his young life.

Now, this kind of existential interpretation of nostalgia—that it comes into being after a primal loss, of paradise, freedom, love, being itself, and exists to "certify" our separation, thus initiating the quest of return to our sources of power and authenticity—also reestablishes history (of the self, community, or nation) as the goal of the return. History is thus not merely the past that can be described and analyzed as a "discipline," however exalted, but an experience waiting to be reinterpreted according to the heart's need in order to release the necessary hope (a theological value, we may insist here) and sense of possibility that validates existence itself no matter how absurd. It is therefore not necessary to relive history as in some costume spectacle or even vicariously through religion and art. It is only necessary to apprehend the sources of what originally nourished us before we "lost it" and *knew* we lost it. Without a sense of history there can be no sense of loss and therefore no nostalgia for renewal, for spiritual integrity, and for authentic self-knowledge. The question then becomes one of both spiritual and critical judgment (the two must surely be one): do our artists reveal an authentic sense of history in their preoccupations with time and the past and the recollections out of which much of their art is shaped?

There may be no absolute answers to this question, but a good deal of modern criticism of Cather and Fitzgerald has offered some very trenchant, if provisional, interpretations of the matter. Morton D. Zabel suggests that Cather, like Dreiser and Fitzgerald, defined a "sense of proportion in American experience," as in her awareness and celebration of "pioneer life and native energy" as well as her experiences of "privation," and the need to escape to the "world beyond" (273). But most important, for Cather, are "what has to be returned to for later nourishment and how little the world appears when its romantic distances . . . are curtailed to the dimensions of individual destiny" (273–74). This sense of enlargement beyond the "tragic limitation" of the individual, Zabel asserts, is also given "superb expression" in the last eight pages of *Gatsby* and in *Tender Is the Night* (274). This is a shrewd and, I believe, accurate assessment, but those things or places or values Cather "returned to for nourishment" are not the places or things (except for the South) that Fitzgerald returned to in order to reexperience the "lost" and a "precious, incommunicable" past.

For Cather, the world may well have split in two around 1922, as she claimed, ultimately leading her back to her youth and the historical experience of the Pueblos and deserts of New Mexico, the Great Divide, the shadows on the impregnable rock of seventeenth-century Quebec, and, finally, the antebellum South. She explored in her story "The Enchanted Bluff" (1909) the pathetic disillusion of a small group of young men who fantasize but never even try to discover a huge red monumental rock in the midst of a desert, an "enchanted bluff" where a tribe once lived before the Spaniards came, and then mysteriously disappeared. But Cather, through Alexanda Bergson, Thea Kronborg, Tom Outland, and Fathers Latour and Vaillant in a profoundly imaginative voyage into the receding past, and finally through Cecile and Sapphira, discovered her rock. And of course, through the complex emotional relationship between Ántonia and Jim Burden, she could affirm the pioneer and immigrant West she had spiritually savaged in such earlier stories as "A Sculptor's Funeral" (1905), "Paul's Case," and "A Wagner Matinee" (1904). Thus, one of the most fertile sources of her nourishment is her sense of *shared* history. This is not merely an imagistic group of the vague frontiers of the past clouded with "longing," but an instrument exploring the social and political realities of a historical moment to which we can respond with both a sense of "enchantment"—an escape into what was once a brave New World—and an objective critical sense of those tragic limitations and horrors we discover in all historical periods.

Did Fitzgerald—for whom, as for Nick Carraway, 1922 was also such a central year of a lost past—possess this kind of historical sensibility? Through his insistent nostalgia—which, according to Morris, sustained him until he rejected it as something destructive to his growth as an artist and man—was Fitzgerald able to create the past as a living entity, a fresh and energizing *presence* that could enable him to find his integrity, his possibilities, his continuity of self against the fragmentations of mere time?

Viewed from this admittedly loose "definition" of an authentic sense of history, I do not think Fitzgerald's genius, like Cather's, was compelled to penetrate and re-create the past, in spite of the fact that his pervasive sense of nostalgia was always attached to it. But Fitzgerald's sense of the past was not, as we know, always "attuned" (to use a favored Fitzgerald verb of power and a full emotional life) to history per se. Rather, that sensibility of time past and present developed, I believe, from a profoundly defining insight recorded in his short story "Absolution" (1924), originally meant to preface *The Great Gatsby*. As Father Schwartz experiences his theological crack-up and loss of faith, he warns Rudolph not to get close to the "heat and the sweat and the life." Rudolph nevertheless spiritually "rises," discovering underneath the surface terror of the event that his own inner convictions are "confirmed," that "there was something ineffably gorgeous somewhere that had nothing to do with God." This discovery occurs in youth and is a secular revelation of a new form of salvation; indeed, the story ends by invoking, against Father Schwartz's hysterical laughter, the calm beauty of the natural world of wheat fields and "girls with yellow hair" calling "innocent, exciting things to the young men working in the lines between the grain." This is a world of "hot fertile life" in the afternoons, ending with the cool of "blonde Northern girls and the tall young men from the farms lying out beside the wheat, under the moon" (*The Short*

Stories 271–72). It is a passage that would not be out of place in *O Pioneers!* (1913) or *My Ántonia,* fusing a pure, sensuous, but fertile sexuality rooted in the earth even as the call of romance springs from the girls' innocent, exciting songs arousing the men to their own sensual but innocent life.

When Fitzgerald connects the "ineffably gorgeous" to a specific historical moment, as he does in *Gatsby* at the instant of enchantment for the Dutch sailors' eyes, that fraction of time is fleeting—but it is a moment of possibilities and beginnings. Fitzgerald thereby achieves his own form of creative nostalgia in which the presence of the New World made manifest reminds us, as nostalgia must, of a paradise lost and, however momentarily, a paradise regained. That moment of loss and fragmentary repossession is accessible to repeated experience in the poetry of Nick's coda. And so too, in his rhapsody over his golden moment with Daisy, indeed in his romantic psychology so perfectly focused by the green light at the end of the dock, Gatsby holds fast to a recollected presence, paradise regained, while the reader suffers, as will Gatsby, the reality of paradise lost.

The tension between living presence and its gift of ontological triumph through a past, lost moment of history on the one hand and ongoing personal experience on the other erupts in "Winter Dreams" (1922), "The Ice Palace" (1920), and, in a slightly transmogrified way, in that curious story "The Swimmers" (1929). In "Winter Dreams," the "ineffably gorgeous" is incarnated in a sexual paradise located in the gardens of wealth, "enchanted" locales of country clubs, beautiful lakes, the magnolia-suffused South or the glittering skylines of Manhattan towers. Presenting it as "dream" in order to internalize the "ineffable" as sensual yet "pure" experience, Fitzgerald traces Dexter's paradise lost through the transformation of Judy Jones, from dream to fallen actuality, victimized by time and change. When Dexter laments, three times over, that the "thing is gone"—the dream made up of fire and loveliness and the magic of nights and the wonder of the varying hours and seasons—he is also testifying to the death of a creative nostalgia within himself. His dream was only made possible by his initial—but very fragile—capacity for a mood of intense appreciation and, like Gatsby, for being magnificently "attune[d] to life" with its "brightness" and "glamour" (*The Short Stories* 223). He laments the death of attunement as well as his capacity for nostalgia, which was his ability to find meaning, if not consolation, in all that was once "ineffably gorgeous." "The glittering things," Fitzgerald tells us, Dexter wanted for "themselves" and not for their associations with "glittering people" (*The Short Stories* 220–21). The story is a powerful and honest indictment of a paradigmatic Fitzgerald type; Dexter's needs are, like Gatsby's, absolute, although, unlike Gatsby, his capacity to re-create a "presence" fades. Either one has the "glittering" objects or not; either one can, like Nick Carraway, recollect or not. There is no room for change or transformation, artistically shaped for a recollection that will preserve the experiences of both triumph and loss.

Yet there is another way Fitzgerald artistically confronted this question, and that is through the process of transmuting memory into recollection. In "The Ice Palace" (1920), he presents identity as a process of easy nostalgia for the Lost Cause of American history. The presentation requires full citation in order to capture the process, appropriately initiated by a stroll through a Confederate graveyard:

"The last row is the saddest—see, way over there. Every cross has just a date on it, and the word 'Unknown.'"

She looked at him and her eyes brimmed with tears.

"I can't tell you how real it is to me, darling—if you don't know."

"How you feel about it is beautiful to me."

"No, no, it's not me, it's them—that old time that I've tried to have live in me. These were just men, unimportant evidently or they wouldn't have been 'unknown'; but they died for the most beautiful thing in the world—the dead South. You see," she continued, her voice still husky, her eyes glistening with tears, "people have these dreams they fasten onto things, and I've always grown up with that dream. It was so easy because it was all dead and there weren't any disillusions comin' to me. I've tried in a way to live up to those past standards of noblesse oblige—there's just the last remnants of it, you know, like the roses of an old garden dying all round us—streaks of strange courtliness and chivalry in some of these boys an' stories I used to hear from a Confederate soldier who lived next door, and a few old darkies. Oh, Harry, there was

something, there was something! I couldn't ever make you understand, but it was there."

"I understand," he assured her again quietly. (*The Short Stories*
53–54)

Here, Sally Carrol indulges in a "safe" dream because it is effectually
"dead" and so protected against disillusion. That is why she can commit
her memory to it and act as if what she fashioned out of stories told
her by "a Confederate soldier" and "a few old darkies" is a coherent
historical recollection. But that is also why she can indulge in the already passionless tropes of conventional romance. It is indeed a beautiful
dream to her, and it partially explains why she cannot live in the North,
the land of the ice palace. Still, it is dream-history and the weakest form
of nostalgia, for the presence of this "past" lacks the tensions and tragic
contradictions that always inhere in defeat and death, courage and fear,
or the traumatic consequences of freedom torn from slavery of which
she has no true sense. And thus her nostalgia defines both her character
and her fate.

And the same problem repeats itself in "The Swimmers." This is a
seriocomic story of Henry Clay Marston, who, with "seven generations
of Virginia ancestors . . . definitely behind him" (*The Short Stories* 496),
works for the Promissory Trust Company's Paris Branch in the era associated with the "lost generation." His story will be of a man prouder of
being a Virginian than of being an American. The story turns on how
Henry divorces his French-Latin wife and manages to retain custody
of his children so that they will grow up Americans, for the "best of
America was the best of the world" (512). The story hovers between a
comic domestic tall tale about marriage and divorce and a pitting of the
values of America against those of France. In the end, after playing a
trick on his wife and her lover, Wiese, that makes them give up their
attempt to hold the children, Marston exults: "France was a land, England was a people, but America, having about it still that quality of the
idea, was harder to utter—it was the graves at Shiloh . . . and the country boys dying in the Argonne for a phrase that was empty before their
bodies withered. It was a willingness of the heart" (512). This is neither
memory nor recollection, but a rhetorical striving to capture the patriotic essence of the past in a brief coda that can stir the hearts of the

living. This passage, however, can almost be read as a satiric comment on Henry's southern pride; yet it is meant as a very sincere evocation of the "ineffably gorgeous" superiority of the idea of America. It is an idea that his children, the Virginian tradition always at their back, will no doubt embrace. But the tonal quality of the coda and the improbability of the plot are at odds with each other, and the story does not resolve the tension between that tone on the one hand and the comedy of the American abroad and the domestic melodrama, which it really is, on the other.

But the evocative success of Fitzgerald's haunting artistry lies in his unerring recognition of tonal qualities. An example of Fitzgerald's power to dramatize the recollected moment containing a coherent, meaningful event that affirms continuity and reality itself experienced as "presence" occurs in *Tender Is the Night,* in the well-studied passage in which Dick Diver emotionally responds to the "gold-star muzzers" (American mothers who have lost sons in the war) sitting in the restaurant:

> Over his wine Dick looked at them again; in their happy faces, the dignity that surrounded and pervaded the party, he perceived the maturity of an older America. For a while the sobered women who had come to mourn for their dead, for something they could not repair, made the room beautiful. Momentarily, he sat again on his father's knee, riding with Moseby while the old loyalties and devotions fought on around him. Almost with an effort he turned back to his two women at the table and faced the whole new world in which he believed. (100)

In this passage Fitzgerald brilliantly condenses two different pasts in the present, fusing the knowledge of death and loss. Dick relives his own lost past for a moment, sitting on his father's knee in his childhood past while regaining events in the even more distant Civil War past. Suspended between two worlds, the adventurous past and the new postwar world in which he felt he had to believe, Dick will live to see the past as nourishing but lost, while in the new world he will collapse in a spiral downward toward his anonymity.

The search for the "ineffably gorgeous" on the one hand and a past morally unpolluted and romantically, adventurously alive on the other broadly represents Fitzgerald's nostalgia-laden artistic vision. Sometimes the two dovetail into one glowing symbol (the green light), but often they remain separate, each explored with fascinating variations. Interestingly enough, in a story like "The Diamond as Big as the Ritz" (1922), Fitzgerald's sharp understanding and artistic use of the American tall tale combines the lure of the "gorgeous" (wealth, fame, women), always susceptible to corruption, with the archetypes of the West and its men who only live for the vastness of enterprise. If there are only "diamonds" and the "shabby gift of disillusion" in the world, as John claims, and he possesses only the latter, then at least the dream could be judged for what it was: *only* a dream, after all (*The Short Stories* 216). Thus, there is no need for nostalgia or a past to be re-created like the western frontier with its moral grotesques and fantasies of wealth and power. Fitzgerald's satiric clarity about the past and his consequent understanding of the *shabby* gift of disillusion, an honest re-romanticizing of an obsessive concern, makes this story so strikingly successful. That the past might not be so precious is a proposition equally trenchant and illuminating as the belief that it is, finally, all we have—the gift of memory transformed into recollection.

The ending of "The Last of the Belles" (1929) bears another one of those suggestive resemblances to Cather's work. At the end of *My Ántonia*, Jim Burden finds the road over which he and Ántonia came to Black Hawk when they were children. His feeling about that experience is so real—so much an existential presence—that he could viscerally touch the children and in touching them come back to himself. Jim's return trip is the final and perhaps only gift of nostalgia and its correlative, a sense of history of the self and the world of which it is a part. In Fitzgerald's story, Andy returns to the now empty field where his army camp once stood. Knee-deep in the underbrush, he is looking for his youth in a "clapboard, or a strip of roofing or a rusty tomato can," crude symbols to authenticate so vital a nostalgic search (*The Short Stories* 462). All he can know is that this was the place once filled with life but which is now as if it had never existed. Fitzgerald's understanding of the uses and abuses of nostalgia was sharp and penetrating. I do not think he simply cast it off as a salvational force and then experienced his crack-up. Surely the psychological dynamics are far more complex than that. Besides, the capacity and need for nostalgia cannot be so abruptly suspended or dismissed; indeed, if nostalgia inheres in us as an existential force, without which we would have no experience of the "being" of the past, it can never really die in us at all.

Nostalgia's most impressive power is to create an ontological dimension of the past, our intimate attachment to it. As Ralph Harper explains, creative nostalgia gives an immediate presentation to our consciousness *of the whole* (of the past experience). In their different ways, such crucial "intimate attachments" shape the inner life of Gatsby and Dick Diver as well as of other protagonists in Fitzgerald's work. "We care for what lasts or should last," Harper concludes, for "what refreshes jaded quests is what promises inexhaustible entertainment and concern" (120). I think Fitzgerald would have recognized and affirmed this description if he had read it; indeed, he could claim with some justification that of all American writers, he lived and dramatized these quests, jaded or vital, for what should "last." All, perhaps, except for Cather. That is why I believe that in 1939, while he was breaking new artistic ground in so contemporary a work as *The Last Tycoon,* Fitzgerald could return to *My Ántonia,* a work that he knew had unforgettably explored what has been called Cather's drama of memory.

I think Cather gained control over her art and vision because ultimately she was able to fuse her informed sense of the past with the nostalgia for the self's personal history: the longing for youth which is the self's history and the longing for the shared communal past of specific places and periods in national history itself. Her settings are in the past. Except for the aborted Philippe stories, Fitzgerald's settings are in the present. His authentic power resided in his nostalgia for the history of the self and its quest for the "ineffably gorgeous" rather than Cather's compulsive need to re-create a place or phase of national history. Rather, the quest for the ineffable became for Fitzgerald a complex and evocative metaphor for the tension between the power of the idea of America and the history of American illusion and disillusion, past and present. His poetic gift was in the masterly way he could link the intimate drama of the self with history through a few dominant symbols that continue to reverberate in our literature. He had, I believe—and I do not quote this judgment facetiously—what T. S. Eliot said of Henry James and his use of Hawthorne. James, said Eliot, only had "a sense of the sense" of the past (Dupee 115). Eliot meant it as a weakness in James's art, certainly as compared to Hawthorne's profound sense of history, but I don't think it necessarily a weakness in James or in Fitzgerald. Fitzgerald's genius lay in his ability to capture in his gorgeous yet trenchant rhetoric and profound symbolism the depth and enchantment of that elusive sense. Perhaps this generalization is true: Fitzgerald believed that a sense of the sense of the past was all that his "lost" generation possessed in order to endure the "New World" with a measure of spiritual meaning.

Noxious Nostalgia

Fitzgerald, Faulkner, and the Legacy of Plantation Fiction

VERONICA MAKOWSKY

"Why do you hate the South?" asks *Absalom, Absalom!*'s Shreve McCannon, a Canadian, of his Mississippi roommate Quentin Compson. "Panting in the cold air" of Harvard, Quentin "immediately" replies, "I dont hate it. . . . *I dont! I dont hate it! I dont hate it!*" (303). For about two hundred years, North Americans, southerners and non-southerners alike, have expressed a similar love-hate fascination with the South, particularly with the mixture of fact and fantasy known as the plantation South. On the one hand there is a nostalgia for a civilization "gone with the wind," a presumably nobler, more gracious, and more cultured life than that of the base, curt, and materialistic modern world. On the other hand there is the plantation as a "platonic conception of the ultimate prison" (Fitzgerald, *Babylon Revisited* 83), where the worst aspects of the national psyche, the materialistic greed that shapes racism and sexism, are perpetually projected and temporarily exorcised. Our great writers not only present the South *both* as American dream and as American nightmare but also are intensely aware of the artist's ambiguous role in creating, perpetuating, and criticizing these myths, as I will later show in Fitzgerald's short story of 1922, "The Diamond as Big as the Ritz," and Faulkner's novel of 1936, *Absalom, Absalom!*[1]

Nostalgia can be defined as a longing for a place, like home, or a time, invariably the past, that cannot be recovered. Nostalgia, then, is intrinsically linked to the pastoral as exemplified in Edenic and Arcadian myths. Critic and historian Lewis P. Simpson argues that "Eden and Arcadia have been symbols of the replacement of the cosmic (the non-conscious or organic) state of human existence with the consciousness of time and history. Simultaneously they have been symbols of an illusory recovery, through pastoral vision and artifice, of the prehistoric state of harmony among God (or gods), man, and nature" (1108). As Simpson suggests, in southern literature the frustrations of nostalgia are exacerbated because nostalgia is manifested as a longing for a state that never existed in the South, that of pastoral innocence. Further, as Simpson notes, "slavery . . . frustrated the desire of the literary mind to project the South as a pastoral homeland" (1109).

For postbellum authors, particularly in the twentieth century, slavery became the fatal temptation that ended the dream of the South as a second Eden, a second chance for mankind. As Walker Percy's protagonist, Dr. Tom More, bitterly muses in *Love in the Ruins* (1971):

> Was it the nigger business from the beginning? What a bad joke: God saying, here it is, the new Eden, and it is yours because you're the apple of my eye; because you the lordly Westerners, the fierce Caucasian-Gentile-Visigoths, believed in me and in the outlandish Jewish event. . . . so I gave it all to you, gave you Israel and Greece and science and art and the lordship of the earth, and finally even gave you the new world that I blessed for you. And all you had to do was pass one little test, which was surely child's play for you because you had already passed the big one. One little test: here's a helpless man in Africa, all you have to do is not violate him. That's all.
>
> One little test: you flunk! (54)

The consequences of that failure are tortuously linked to a hopeless nostalgia for what never was, the plantation as pastoral, in Fitzgerald's "Diamond as Big as the Ritz" and Faulkner's *Absalom, Absalom!*

Before turning to these twentieth-century versions of the plantation myth, though, I would like to present some of the myth's typical features as encapsulated in what is often considered the quintessential plantation nostalgia tale, Thomas Nelson Page's enormously successful "Marse Chan," first published in 1884 and reprinted numerous times.[2] As is characteristic of plantation tales, including those of Fitzgerald and Faulkner, the plot of "Marse Chan" is set in motion by an outsider, like

Fitzgerald's John T. Unger or Faulkner's Shreve McCannon, who is in some sense exploring the postbellum South. As Fitzgerald's and Faulkner's narrators will later, Page's narrator stresses the antebellum South's dreamlike quality as a means of negating the fall into time and history: "Distance was nothing to this people; time was of no consequence to them. . . . [T]he outer world strode by them as they dreamed" (343).

The Edenic atmosphere is enhanced by Page's presentation of a putatively positive South when the outside narrator encounters an elderly former slave called "Uncle Sam" who tells him the tragic tale of the almost incredibly saintly Channing family. As Uncle Sam informs the narrator in the dialect that made these tales so popular with northern audiences, "Dem wuz good ole times, marster" (347). Not only were slaves never whipped on the Channing plantation, but the master blinds himself while saving a slave in a fire. Because of his relatively good situation as a slave, Uncle Sam, as his name suggests, remains patriotic to his cause. That cause is, of course, the Confederacy, but as this tale of reconciliation suggests, this Uncle Sam will turn his allegiance to the national Uncle Sam, despite the nation's racism as demonstrated in Reconstruction politics and in Page's narrator's condescension.

The plantation idyll is what Page and "Marse Chan" are remembered for, but that is an accurate recollection of less than half the story, for Page also shows the evil South in the neighboring Chamberlain plantation. Colonel Chamberlain sells slaves away from their families and feuds with his neighbors over small tracts of land just because his honor is spoiling for a fight. Because he is so preoccupied with pro-secession politics, he neglects his daughter Anne, but then quarrels with her suitor, young Master Channing, over politics and family honor, alienating and dividing the lovers. Anne, a southern belle spoiled by her father and the devotion of young "Marse Chan," clings stubbornly to her family honor and rejects the pleas of her lover until it is too late. Young Master Channing, "Marse Chan" of the title, dies a hero in the war; Anne dies of a broken heart; the Channing and Chamberlain families are extinguished, and so is the Confederacy.

Page, however, is suggesting that the South's fall was not the result of the external machinations of damn Yankees, but rather of its internal failings: the ineffectuality of the southern longing for pastoral of the Channings in the face of crude greed and selfishness, supposedly characteristic of the North, but here embodied in the southern Chamber-lains. Page may have felt nostalgia for the pastoral plantation, but he was too fine an artist not to realize that it never existed and to acknowledge the actual South's affinity with national values. Indeed, that affinity to American values may have contributed greatly to the tremendous popu-larity of "Marse Chan," in that the racism and materialism manifested in the tale were not foreign to the North but could be safely projected onto the supposedly "exotic" South and punished there as part of the Reconstruction drama of penance and purgation that led to the ulti-mate in nostalgia, the Lost Cause, celebrated by both North and South.

F. Scott Fitzgerald had great admiration for Page's work; in fact, in 1922, the same year in which he published "The Diamond as Big as the Ritz," he suggested to Maxwell Perkins that Scribner's republish Page's *In Ole Virginia,* which includes "Marse Chan," as one of eighteen titles that Fitzgerald was proposing for a reprint series (Bruccoli, *Some Sort of Epic Grandeur* 153–54). Faulkner, of course, was highly familiar with the plantation tradition, and his borrowings from and reworkings of other stories from *In Ole Virginia* indicate his familiarity with that collection, a topic too large to be addressed here. Fitzgerald's "The Diamond as Big as the Ritz" and Faulkner's *Absalom, Absalom!* share significant similari-ties with and differences from Page's "Marse Chan" and other planta-tion tales, manifesting their need to participate in and revise the great American cultural melodrama of the fall from the second Eden into a time and history of pain and labor.

Like Page, Fitzgerald and Faulkner depict the fall of the plantation world as a result of inhumane values—not Yankeedom as deus ex ma-china, but Yankee materialism carried to its logical and horrific ex-treme.[3] Fitzgerald's Braddock Washington, significantly named for the father of the whole country who was first a southerner, owns a Montana plantation, suggesting the spread of materialism to the western United States. The plantation is complete with slaves and set atop a "diamond as big as the Ritz." The family leads a life of luxurious pastoral bliss based on a cold, hard rock whose worth is man-made; a diamond won't feed or clothe anyone, making the parody of the southern cotton plan-tation even more extreme. Echoing southern xenophobic defensiveness at Yankee incursions, Mr. Washington thinks nothing of murdering any-one who strays onto his plantation for fear they would betray the secret of his "peculiar institution" for producing wealth. Ironically, he is in effect a land-poor southern aristocrat, for if he tried to sell any of his diamond, the flooded markets would crash from the oversupply, making his treasure trash. In pro-slavery tracts, southern plantation owners would bemoan the fact that they were the real slaves, chained to their patriarchal white man's burden of taking care of the slaves and their acreage. Fitzgerald satirizes this plaint by showing Braddock Washington as enslaved to his materialism, unable to leave his huge, cold rock, bound by his own territorial greed.

In *Absalom, Absalom!* Faulkner similarly depicts the causes of the southern fall from the second Eden as internal yet external, the result of the internalization of American racism and materialism as embodied in southern slavery. Mr. Compson tells his son Quentin about Mr. Coldfield, who starved to death in his attic rather than support the Confederacy and so "would not be present on the day when the South would realize that it was now paying the price for having erected its economic edifice not on the rock of stern morality but on the shifting sands of moral opportunism and brigandage" (209). While Mr. Coldfield is as sanctimonious and ineffectual as Page's Channings, he does recognize the falsity of the southern pastoral ideal. The central character of the novel, Thomas Sutpen, like Braddock Washington, is enslaved by his obsession with maintaining his acreage. Indeed, the name of his plantation, Sutpen's Hundred, suggests that Sutpen has become the plantation, part of a system that can be counted and valued. Immediately after the war, Sutpen frantically and futilely tries to keep every one of his hundred acres from the clutches of carpetbagger tax collectors, but in his monomania he loses most of his family and, ultimately, his life.

Unlike Page, however, Fitzgerald and Faulkner have a much more openly ambiguous view of the ultimate materialism, slavery. From one perspective, their fictive slaves are like Page's eternally devoted Uncle Sam. Sutpen's "wild niggers" work desperately beside their master in his attempt to found his plantation, making no attempt to escape. In Clytie, his daughter by one of the slave women, Sutpen manages to make a slave in his own, if darker, image, and she remains on the Sutpen plantation throughout all of its vicissitudes until she burns to death in defense of Sutpen's son Henry at the end of the novel. The slaves of Fitzgerald's Braddock Washington are even more stereotypically faithful. Like a mammy, the seemingly emasculated Gygsum, the slave designated as body servant to John T. Unger, undresses, bathes, and dresses him. When Washington tells his slaves that Confederate general Nathan B. Forrest, a notorious antebellum slave trader, "had reorganized the shattered southern armies and defeated the North in one pitched battle, . . . they passed a vote declaring it a good thing and held revival services immediately" (87–88). Fitzgerald makes us well aware that they are mindlessly demonstrating their faith in the institutions that have helped brainwash them: a democracy in which they cannot participate and a Christianity that is perverted to stress their obedience, not their worth as souls.

Yet Fitzgerald and Faulkner emphasize one curious detail about the Washington and Sutpen slaves that calls the image of the "happy darky" into question. Sutpen's slaves, who actually speak a version of Caribbean French, a Creole, are suspected by Mississippians of speaking "some dark and fatal tongue of their own" (27). Braddock Washington's slaves have "lived so long apart from the world that their original dialect has become an almost indistinguishable patois" (93). The master class thus tells itself that the slaves are subhuman, as manifested in their incomprehensible sounds, but Faulkner and Fitzgerald are pointing to a justifiable paranoia of slave owners, terrified of slave revolts hatched with secrecy and codes; the slaves, after all, have honed their survival skill of telling the masters only what they want to hear, reinforcing the myth of the plantation pastoral peopled by "happy darkies." Fitzgerald and Faulkner are satirically suggesting that the masters have made themselves subhuman, in that they cannot recognize the slaves as human, cannot speak the same language, and cannot tell truth from falsehood.

Like the slaves and like Page's Anne Chamberlain, Fitzgerald's and Faulkner's women characters are damaged by their allegiance to the ideology that thwarts their human potential. Braddock Washington's youngest daughter, Kismine, is the perfect southern belle.[4] She is the embodiment of the plantation's Edenic ideal: "Just think," she tells John T. Unger, "I'm absolutely fresh ground." Like the marble statues on pedestals to which southern women were often compared, atop her mountain Kismine is "the incarnation of physical perfection" (90) and pure. As she tells John, "I'm very innocent and girlish. I never smoke, or drink, or read anything except poetry. I know scarcely any mathematics or chemistry. I dress *very* simply—in fact, I scarcely dress at all" (91).

Fitzgerald, though, is suggesting that such Edenic near-nudity is artificial, since it is maintained at a tremendous cost of isolation for the belle and the exploitation of others. Kismine's very self-conscious tally of her purity suggests how contrived it really is.

Similarly, Faulkner's women in *Absalom, Absalom!* embody the plantation ideal and lose their humanity. Sutpen's second wife, Ellen Coldfield, comes from family that is respectable, though not rich or aristocratic. When she marries Sutpen, she takes up bellehood with a vengeance, shopping and chattering in a fantasy world that she believed could not end. Like Kismine's need to point out her purity, Ellen's need to work so hard at bellehood also points out its artificial quality in an already-declining and soon-to-be fallen world. When the harsh reality of the Civil War intrudes, Ellen fades and dies rather than confront it. As Mr. Compson tells Quentin, "Apparently Ellen had now served her purpose, completed the bright afternoon of the butterfly's summer and vanished" (61). From her training in southern ideology, Ellen is incapable of saving herself or her children, including her daughter Judith, who will die an impoverished spinster, still loyal to her father's progeny and to his "design." Had Judith rebelled against her father and eloped with Charles Bon, despite the possibilities of incest and miscegenation, much of the tragedy could have been avoided; but like Page's Anne and Fitzgerald's Kismine, Judith is unable to think beyond the law of the fathers. Also like them, she is too loyal to the pastoral ideal to see the menacing reality.

The way the pastoral ideal of the plantation demands a remoteness from real human concerns is suggested by the many references to dreams in *Absalom, Absalom!* and "The Diamond as Big as the Ritz." To some extent, this is reminiscent of Page's dreamlike Virginia, but as in the case of the supposedly "happy darkies" and belles, Fitzgerald and Faulkner add a sinister emphasis. Of Thomas Sutpen's impossible desire to reestablish Sutpen's Hundred after the war, Miss Rosa Coldfield says that "if he was mad, it was only his compelling dream that was insane, not his methods" (134); there was method, but it was madness because his dream consisted of an exclusive dynasty ruling in perpetuity over acres and human beings. Of John T. Unger's temporary seduction into Braddock Washington's dream world, Fitzgerald writes, "Everybody's youth is a dream, a form of chemical madness" (113). The fantasy of the plantation myth is immature, a form of addictive madness when held into maturity by grown men like Washington and Sutpen.

In contrast to the nostalgic tone of Page's story, Fitzgerald's and Faulkner's tales also show that the greatest immaturity, the deepest madness, is the Gatsby-like nostalgia for repeating the past, a past that was never as ideal as the prospective revenant believes. After the war, Thomas Sutpen acts as if "there might not have been any war at all, or it was on another planet" (130) when, at age fifty-nine, he self-destructively attempts a young man's herculean effort of rebuilding an antebellum plantation under Reconstruction conditions. Similarly, after the destruction of the Montana plantation is commenced by men in recently invented "aeroplanes," Braddock Washington desperately tries to bribe God with the world's grandest shrine if "matters should be as they were yesterday at this hour and that they should so remain" (109). The irony of nostalgia is that if the past could be repeated, the consequences would be the same unhappy ones, yet that is what nostalgia so strongly denies.

The isolation of the plantation, also remarked by Page, helps to maintain the owner's pathological immaturity and fixation on the past, according to Faulkner and Fitzgerald. As Thomas Sutpen obsessively worked to establish his plantation before the war, he immured himself at Sutpen's Hundred. When he decided that he needed other people in order to found his dynasty, the townsfolk of Jefferson were so alienated that they refused to attend his wedding and threw trash and garbage as the wedding party emerged from the church. After the war, when Sutpen is asked by local landowners to join the Klan in an attempt to repel cartpetbaggers and scalawags, he replies that "if every man in the South would do as he himself was doing, would see to the restoration of his own land, the general land of the South would save itself" (130). While his refusal to join the Klan may seem praiseworthy, his isolationist reasoning is not, for Sutpen is advocating that southern society be remade in the image of its most perfect exemplar, himself. Braddock Washington also wants to believe that he can remove himself from the larger world, going so far as to murder visitors so that they cannot lead more outsiders into his paradise of narcissism. He, like Sutpen, is a tyrant, not the pastoral plantation's avatar of southern hospitality, and so he refuses guests, telling his son, "This is where the United States ends" (80).

Faulkner and Fitzgerald, of course, do not believe that the United

States ends at the plantation's boundaries, since Sutpen's and Washington's destroyed plantations can also be prophetic of "where the United States" could "end" since nation and plantation share some of the same values. Sutpen has a "design" that he will found a plantation where a poor white boy would not be turned away at the front door as he had been as a poor white boy in his youth (210). His aims of refuge and inclusion recall those of the founders of another plantation, Plymouth Plantation, who were also looking for a chance to redeem history and reclaim purity (Puritans) by founding a "city upon a hill" as an example to those still mired in history. However, as Sutpen's plantation was a refuge only for whites, not blacks, Plymouth Plantation was a refuge only for white Puritans, not other religious sects or other races such as Native Americans; intolerance and ethnocentricity doom the new Eden. Thomas Sutpen does turn a young man away: he rejects his firstborn son, Charles Bon, when he learns that his wife has some "black blood." Charles is killed by his half brother, Sutpen's son Henry, because of the threat of incest and miscegenation in the proposed marriage between Charles and Henry's sister Judith, and Henry himself flees into decades of exile. Because of his inability to accept his first son's racial heritage, Sutpen destroys both sons and his design of a pastoral plantation. Because of the racism that he shares with the plantation South and the antebellum North, his design ends not in a pastoral idyll but in the howls of his black and mentally deficient descendant near the ruins of the plantation house. In one of his characteristic inversions, Faulkner does not suggest "If you can't beat 'em, join 'em," but rather "If you won't let 'em join you, they will beat you."

Braddock Washington shares a similar pastoral vision that thinly masks a lack of true southern hospitality. With devastating irony from Fitzgerald, Washington, like Sutpen, observes that "his one care must be the protection of his secret lest in the possible panic attendant on its discovery he should be reduced with all the property-owners of the world to utter poverty" (89). His secret, like Sutpen's design, appears to be the plantation as Eden, or America's "fresh, green breast of the new world." As it does for Sutpen, it ends for Washington who is, after all, a descendant of the slaveholding Father of Our Country, "among the ruins of a vista that had been a garden spot that morning" (106). The southern Arcadia, the American dream, transforms itself into nightmare because "the United States ends here" unless you belong to the small, exclusive, dominant group.

What, then, is the artist's place in this pastoral dream become nightmare? Page's "Marse Chan" suggests that the artist's role is to preserve, celebrate, and mourn the beneficent aspects of the plantation dream, despite the subliminal doubts that Page expressed through the noble plantation owners' malevolent doubles. "Marse Chan" contains no artists or artist figures who question this cultural imperative, unlike "The Diamond as Big as the Ritz" or *Absalom, Absalom!* For Fitzgerald and Faulkner, such artists do not participate willingly, like Page, but are abducted into cultural servitude. Braddock Washington "had caused to be kidnapped a landscape gardener, an architect, a designer of stage settings, and a French decadent poet left over from the last century. . . . But one by one they had shown their uselessness. . . . [T]hey all went mad . . . and were now confined comfortably in an insane asylum" (98). Washington's chateau is completed by what Fitzgerald and Faulkner regarded as meretricious, but what they both attempted unsuccessfully to become, "a moving-picture fella" (*Babylon Revisited* 98). The true artists are driven to insanity by unappreciative patrons and audiences who may not want to hear the truth about the plantation and much prefer the comforting fantasies of Hollywood's *Gone with the Wind*.[5]

Thomas Sutpen wants a plantation house that sounds remarkably similar to the one Braddock Washington actually built. Sutpen imports a French architect to design it, but as Faulkner's narrator comments, "only an artist could have borne Sutpen's ruthlessness and hurry and still manage to curb the dream of grim and castlelike magnificence at which Sutpen obviously aimed" (29). Despite his success in checking Sutpen's vulgar display, the architect is also effectively kidnapped, since when he attempts to leave Sutpen's Hundred he is hunted like an animal by Sutpen and his "wild niggers." When captured, he "flung" his "hand up in a gesture that [Quentin's] grandfather said you simply could not describe, that seemed to gather all misfortune and defeat that the human race ever suffered into a pinch in his fingers like dust and flung it backward over his head" (207). Although Sutpen's architect does not go mad like Washington's artists, his gesture of resignation and abdication indicates that he too is institutionalized into the particular madness, the "misfortune and defeat," of plantation culture, and of the American culture that likes to buy into that nostalgic myth in the form of fiction and films; yet like Fitzgerald and Faulkner, the architect does not surrender and keeps pursuing art within his captivity.

Perhaps the most chilling aspect of Fitzgerald's and Faulkner's critiques of nostalgia is their depiction of nostalgia's effect on the future as represented by John T. Unger and Quentin Compson, who are too possessed by nostalgia's chimeras to move into the future. For John, all that lingers is the "shabby gift of disillusion" (113). Quentin tells Shreve, "I am older at twenty than a lot of people who have died" (301). While the nostalgia that is so characteristic of plantation fiction might appear to be a harmless if somewhat sentimental indulgence in fantasy, the portraits of John and Quentin indicate that their creators think otherwise. In "The Diamond as Big as the Ritz" and *Absalom, Absalom!* they show how great fiction can convert seductive fantasies about the past into compelling truths about the consequences of belittling and misrepresenting the past. For Fitzgerald and Faulkner, the nostalgia of the plantation myth misrepresents the past, devalues the present, and strangles the future.

Notes

1. In its evocation of an agrarian and uncomplicated idyll in an increasingly urbanized and industrialized America, the plantation myth has been particularly popular with the non-southern audiences who enthusiastically consumed it, from antebellum John Pendleton Kennedy's *Swallow Barn* (1832) through Thomas Nelson Page's postbellum nostalgia tales, and into the twentieth century with Margaret Mitchell's *Gone with the Wind* (1936). For an overview of the genre in Page's era, see MacKethan. For an overview in the twentieth century, see Bargainnier.

2. Like Fitzgerald, Page has been considered a victim of his own early success whose late works were too serious and socially conscious for the expectations of his audience, yet whose artistry can be seen throughout his career, with or without the trappings of the plantation myth; see Cash; Flusche; Theodore Gross; Holman; Simms; and Wilson, *Patriotic Gore*.

3. Critics such as Brooks, Rodewald, Scholes, and Sklar have compared Thomas Sutpen with Jay Gatsby, but they have not explored the comparison with Braddock Washington.

4. Donaldson, "Scott Fitzgerald's Romance," examines Fitzgerald's explicitly southern belles and the history of his fascination with the South.

5. Roulston, "Whistling 'Dixie' in Encino," parallels the southern plantation with the world of the Hollywood studio in *The Last Tycoon*. Way compares Washington's chateau to a Hollywood set (69).

12

Thalia Does the Charleston

Humor in the Fiction of F. Scott Fitzgerald

D. G. KEHL

In "The Crack-up," F. Scott Fitzgerald observed that "the test of a first-rate intelligence is the ability to hold two opposed ideas in the mind at the same time and still retain the ability to function" (Wilson, *The Crack-up* 69). This recognition of disparity perhaps serves less to characterize "a first-rate intelligence" than to provide the basis for Fitzgerald's underrated comic sense. For as Schopenhauer said, "The phenomenon of laughter always signifies the sudden apprehension of an incongruity between such a conception and the real object thought under it" (271). "Show me a hero," Fitzgerald remarked in a notebook entry, "and I will write you a tragedy" (*Notebooks* 51). The corollary would be, "Show me an incongruity and I'll write you a comedy."

Fitzgerald's tragic sense, his service under the aegis of Melpomene, Greek Muse of tragedy, has been well documented, early by Mark Schorer (Kazin 170–72), later by Henry Dan Piper (287–300) and others. Generally overlooked, except for isolated references, has been Fitzgerald's comic sense, his service under the aegis of Thalia, Muse of comedy. Richard Chase noted that "*Gatsby* is one of those serious comedies that are finally indistinguishable from tragedy" (161). Similarly, F. H. Langman has noted that *The Great Gatsby* is clearly intended to be "a very funny book" but that "one can read quite widely in critical discussions . . . without finding reference to the presence—let alone the preponderance—in it of comedy" (Donaldson, *Critical Essays* 53–56). More recently, Brian Way has stated, but not developed and supported the conclusion that, "in his mature fiction, Fitzgerald is the wittiest

American writer since Henry James, and possesses an exquisite comic sense" (65). In his essay "Style as Meaning in *The Great Gatsby:* Notes Toward a New Approach," Jackson R. Bryer has pointed out the wit and humor of small stylistic units (Donaldson, *Critical Essays* 127). As for the surprising lack of attention to Fitzgerald's humor, perhaps Linda Wagner-Martin is correct in her speculation that because "there had been little [humor] in modernist writing . . . when it did appear, readers usually overlooked it" (6). Even such a comic master as James Thurber, who acknowledged *The Great Gatsby* as his favorite book, seems to have missed the humor in Fitzgerald. "I can't remember any humor in old Scott Fitzgerald," Thurber said in a 1952 interview. "Humor would have saved him" (Breit).

Evidence indicates not only a great deal of humor in Fitzgerald's work but also its significant function in his art. Henry Dan Piper concluded that the publication of "The Crack-up" in 1936 marked Fitzgerald's "recovery of his sense of humor" because now he saw himself not as "the victim of a tragic destiny, but as a slightly absurd and very human being" (238). To be sure, humor is more pervasive in Fitzgerald's earlier work like *Flappers and Philosophers* (1920), *Tales of the Jazz Age* (1922), and *The Beautiful and Damned* (1922). By 1926, with the publication of *All the Sad Young Men,* humor is less obvious. Even the three domestic comedies in that collection tend toward the bitter sadness of the title. Similarly, *Tender Is the Night* (1934) has humor, but almost exclusively of the darker variety. The same is true of *Taps at Reveille* (1935), Fitzgerald's fourth and last collection (exclusive of posthumously published collections, such as *The Pat Hobby Stories* (1962), with their "funnier aspects of failure," as K. G. W. Cross has noted [99]). In fact, however, there is no evidence that Fitzgerald ever lost either a sense of his tragic destiny—progressing "from despair and self-pity to a confident detachment," as Piper argues (238)—or his exquisite sense of humor. Such late works as *The Last Tycoon* (1941), *The Pat Hobby Stories,* and the uncollected "Financing Finnegan" (1938), one of the funniest pieces Fitzgerald ever wrote, all convey a sense of tragic destiny with, at the same time, flashes of humor grown increasingly dark.

Ironically, the basis of Fitzgerald's widely recognized tragic sense is also the basis of his comic sense: recognition of incongruity. Piper correctly notes that Fitzgerald made "the American myth of success the basis for high tragedy" and "transformed the self-made man into a tragic hero" (300). It is also true, however, that the incongruity between the American dream of success and the harsh reality of circumstance, between heroic ideal and mundane reality, constitutes what Louis D. Rubin, Jr., has called "the great American joke." Indeed, "a central motif of American humor [is this] contrast, the incongruity between the ideal and the real" (Rubin 5). The Declaration of Independence, with its huge promise of equality and opportunity, has put a "burr under the metaphysical saddle of America," to use Robert Penn Warren's graphic metaphor (Rubin 5)—or a green light across the bay. The pricking of that burr—or the gleam of that elusive green light—leads in Fitzgerald's fiction to tragedy or comedy, or to both, since the two are not antithetical but contrapuntal and often complementary. Accordingly, the primary target of Fitzgerald's social satire is the American preoccupation with mammon, "a system where the richest man gets the most beautiful girl if he wants her, where the artist without an income has to sell his talents to a button manufacturer" (*This Side of Paradise* 256).

Fitzgerald's humor was shaped by such influences as vaudeville—with its mixture of convivial songs, dances, and comic farce—and musical comedy, his métier at Princeton. One might get the impression that Fitzgerald, like Basil Duke Lee in "The Captured Shadow," "had recourse to a collection of joke books and to an old Treasury of Wit and Humor which embalmed the faded Victorian cracks" (*Basil and Josephine* 103).

The influence of Mark Twain, whom Fitzgerald much admired, seems evident. Robert Sklar has pointed out the possible influence of Van Wyck Brooks's *The Ordeal of Mark Twain* on "The Diamond as Big as the Ritz" (141–46) and, at the story's conclusion, "a sudden touch of Mark Twain pessimism, in which wealth becomes an illusion of youth, and youth itself a dream" (146). Unlike the motto of Twain's Hadleyburg, which changed from the negative "Lead us not into temptation" to the positive, the "depressing . . . old-fashioned Victorian motto" over the gate of Hades has not changed, though John T. Unger's father "had tried time and time again to have it changed to something with a little more push and verve about it" (*The Short Stories* 183). We are never told what the motto is—perhaps "Abandon hope all ye who exit here."

Kenneth Eble has noted that the plot of "The Curious Case of Benjamin Button" was "created from a remark of Mark Twain that it was a pity that the best part of life came at the beginning and the worst at the end" (*F. Scott Fitzgerald* 79). Accordingly, Benjamin Button is born at the age of seventy and dies as an infant. At least two other stories bear the mark of Twain. In "The Scandal Detectives," fourteen-year-old Riply Buckner, with his "breathless practicality," plays Huck Finn to Basil Lee's Tom Sawyer–like "fantastic" "imagination" (*Basil and Josephine* 18). Similarly, in "The Jelly-Bean" the southern girl's preoccupation with "style" ("People over there have style. . . . I'm really the only girl in town that has style" [*The Short Stories* 151]) is reminiscent of the similar obsession with "style" shown by Tom Sawyer, the Grangerfords, and the South in general. Just as Twain, who noted that Sir Walter Scott was the cause of the Civil War, showed how adolescent obsession with "style"—facile appearances and abstract "honor"—can lead to manipulation, violent death, and full-scale war, so Fitzgerald showed how adolescent obsession with wealth and materialism, as demonstrated particularly by Ginevra King and all the characters modeled after her, can lead to deep personal hurt and national disgrace.

Another major influence on Fitzgerald's humor were popular comedians of his day, including his neighbors in Great Neck: Groucho Marx and caricaturist Rube Goldberg. Monroe Stahr, in *The Last Tycoon,* refers to routines in "the Keystone days" and how "Georgie Jessel talks about 'Lincoln's Gettysburg routine'" (*Love of the Last Tycoon* 33). (Probably few people know that Fitzgerald wrote an 8,000-word radio script for Gracie Allen [Piper 229].) Fitzgerald considered Charlie Chaplin more of a poet than Carl Sandburg (Turnbull 126). In his story "Pat Hobby and Orson Welles," he alludes to the "old Chaplin picture about a crowded street car where the entrance of one man at the rear forces another out in front" (*Pat Hobby Stories* 44).

Perhaps the writer who had the most immediate effect on Fitzgerald's humor was his friend and neighbor in Great Neck—his confidant, his "double" (Le Vot 122), his "secret sharer" (Mizener, *The Far Side of Paradise* 176) in the "brotherhood of the intemperate" (Turnbull 137)—Ring Lardner. In a letter to Edmund Wilson, Fitzgerald nominated Lardner as "America's most popular humorist" (Bruccoli and Duggan 125) "because with a rare, true ear he has set down for the enlightenment of posterity the American language as it is talked today." Much of what he said of Lardner in his moving encomium "Ring," collected in *The Crack-up,* applies equally as well to Fitzgerald himself: "He was a disillusioned idealist . . . he had been formed by the very world on which his hilarious irony had released itself" (Wilson, *The Crack-up* 37, 36). Significantly, both of Fitzgerald's characters putatively modeled on Lardner—Miles Calman in "Crazy Sunday" ("shades of Ring Lardner," according to Turnbull [203], though the consensus, of course, is that Irving Thalberg was the primary model, with King Vidor perhaps a secondary, partial model) and Abe North in *Tender Is the Night* (Mizener, *The Far Side of Paradise* 68; Le Vot 123)—demonstrate what Fitzgerald attributes to both and sometimes manifests himself, "a desperate humor" (*The Short Stories* 704; *Tender Is the Night* 19), echoing the similarly oxymoronic phrases "tragic humor" in "Tarquin of Cheapside" and "despairing humor" in "The Adjuster" (*Six Tales of the Jazz Age* 88, 154).

    In a broad perspective, Fitzgerald's is a genre of deflation, of social satire inclining as much toward the Juvenalian as toward the Horatian variety. The main target is American preoccupation with wealth, the American dream turned nightmare, values sacrificed for mammon. Fitzgerald's social satire runs the gamut of issues. He satirizes higher education: "In spite of going to college I've managed to pick up a good education" (*This Side of Paradise* 255). He caustically stresses the affinity between uncouth, rich Americans and Hollywood producers, both motivated by a "vast, vulgar and meretricious beauty" (*The Great Gatsby* 77): the man who designed the Braddock Washington chateau in "The Diamond as Big as the Ritz" was a motion picture producer, "the only man we found who was used to playing with an unlimited amount of money, though he did tuck his napkin in his collar and couldn't read or write" (*The Short Stories* 203). No less caustic is his satire of American kitsch and religiosity: "The righteous of the land decorate the railroads with bill-boards asserting in red and yellow that 'Jesus Christ is God,' placing them, appropriately enough, next to announcements that 'Gunter's Whiskey is Good'" (*The Beautiful and Damned* 251). The humor here derives from the ironic incongruity, communicated especially by the adverbial phrase "appropriately enough," which intensifies the comic possibilities. The timeless relevance of Fitzgerald's humor can further be seen in his description of the misplaced values that result in the protagonist of "Dalyrimple Goes Wrong" being put forth as a political candidate because he has learned to "cut corners" by committing burglary (*Flappers and Philosophers* 158–59).

Malcolm Cowley pointed out that "The Baby Party," collected in *All the Sad Young Men,* was "Fitzgerald's one expedition into the field of domestic comedy" (Fitzgerald, *The Stories* 176). The story satirizes parents who seek to live vicariously through their children and who, in idolizing their offspring and failing to see their own flaws perpetuated in them, are more childish than their children. The popular notion that "children can't have children" is patently false, according to Fitzgerald. The "expeditionary force of mothers" was "each one looking at nothing but her own child. All the babies breaking things and grabbing at the cake, and each mama going home thinking about the subtle superiority of her own child to every other child there" (*The Stories* 210).

This story, reportedly written in a single all-night session for money to pay debts, may be the clearest example of domestic comedy written by Fitzgerald, but it is neither the first nor the only example. Several other domestic comedies or tragicomedies, originally published between 1920 and 1923, tend toward bitter tragedy. Each contains humor, most significantly a humorous scene that effectively epitomizes the domestic conflicts. The earliest, "The Lees of Happiness" (*Chicago Tribune* [December 12, 1920]; *Tales of the Jazz Age* [1922]), depicts the lees (the dregs, the insoluble, valueless matter that settles from a liquid) of a marriage. The narrator ironically calls it "a marriage of love": "[Jeffrey] was sufficiently spoiled to be charming; [Roxanne] was ingenuous enough to be irresistible. Like two floating logs they met in a head-on rush, caught, and sped along together" (*Six Tales of the Jazz Age* 121). The central image, however, is neither logs nor liquid (cocktails, mint juleps) but biscuits (*bis coctus,* "twice-baked" bread), and the story recounts the problems of not one marriage but two. Jeffrey's friend Harry is married to Kitty—"nervous without being sensitive, temperamental without temperament, a woman who seemed to flit and never light" (124). When, on the occasion of Harry's visit, Roxanne bakes a pan of unpalatable biscuits, Jeffrey pronounces them "decorative," "masterpieces"— and nails them to the wall: "'We'll make a frieze out of them' . . . Bang! The first biscuit was impaled to the wall, where it quivered for a moment like a live thing. . . . When Roxanne returned with a second round of cocktails the biscuits were in a perpendicular row, twelve of them, like a collection of primitive spear-heads" (123–24). A short time later, after Jeffrey suffers a debilitating stroke and Kitty goes back to her mother, Harry visits the country house again and, in a moment of ravenous hunger, begins to eat the impaled biscuits. It is the story of two marriages "on the rocks" for different reasons, and crumbling like biscuits—at various points half-baked, overbaked, and twice-baked.

Another domestic comedy of the same period is "Hot and Cold Blood" (1923), which depicts the conflicts developing between Jim and Jaqueline Mather in the first year of their marriage. Jaqueline comes to resent the charitable goodwill of Jim, who "was essentially and enormously romantic," whereas she, whose "voice was of the texture of Bessemer cooled" (*Six Tales of the Jazz Age* 168, 162), possessed "a harder, feminine intelligence" (168). She sees him as "a professional nice fellow" (164), "a professional Samaritan who's going to fetch and carry for the world!" (166). A humorous scene that epitomizes their troubled relationship occurs when Jim incurs Jaqueline's anger by offering his seat on the trolley to a woman of "about fifty and enormous," who sits "without so much as a grunt": "When she first sat down she was content merely to fill the unoccupied part of the seat, but after a moment she began to expand and to spread her great rolls of fat over a larger and larger area until the process took on the aspect of violent trespassing. When the car rocked in Jaqueline's direction the woman slid with it, but when it rocked back she managed by some exercise of ingenuity to dig in and hold the ground won" (163). This humorous, microcosmic scene effectively demonstrates conflict between a romantic but gullible idealist and a pragmatic but self-centered realist, a domestic conflict that is sure to worsen when Jim, at the end of the story, decides to make yet another loan he cannot afford to a needy acquaintance.

The Beautiful and Damned, also from this period (1922), is a satiric comedy of manners, with the domestic conflicts of Anthony and Gloria resembling those of Jim and Jaqueline, Jeffrey and Roxanne, and Harry and Kitty. It is the story, Fitzgerald told Charles Scribner, of "how [Anthony Patch] and his beautiful young wife are wrecked on the shoals of dissipation" (Mizener, *The Far Side of Paradise* 136). This work, perhaps more than any other, demonstrates Fitzgerald's attention to the wide varieties of risible experience, ranging from titter and snicker through the gradations of the gamut all the way to howl.[1] In a key symbolic passage, anticipating the range of Harry Greener's laugh in Nathanael West's *The Day of the Locust,* Fitzgerald describes "the noise of a woman's laughter" that Anthony hears from his rear window after the bridal dinner:

> It began low, incessant and whining . . . and then it grew in volume and became hysterical, until it reminded him of a girl he had seen overcome with nervous laughter at a vaudeville performance. Then it sank, receded, only to rise again and include words—a coarse joke, some bit of obscure horseplay he could not distinguish. It would break off for a moment . . . then begin again— interminably; at first annoying, then strangely terrible. . . . It had reached a high point, tensed and stifled, almost the quality of a scream—then it ceased and left behind it a silence empty and menacing as the greater silence overhead. (149)

"Some animal quality in that unrestrained laughter" left Anthony "upset and shaken" as it "aroused his old aversion and horror toward all the business of life," for "life was that sound out there, that ghastly reiterated female sound" (149–50). Given Fitzgerald's ironic use of alluring female beauty as the illusory identification of everything for which the young man yearns, it is fitting that Fitzgerald's choice of a sound to epitomize Anthony's horrified sense of life's ghastliness is female laughter.

Henry Dan Piper is correct in calling "Financing Finnegan" "one of the funniest pieces" (243) Fitzgerald ever wrote, though "The Curious Case of Benjamin Button" and "The Camel's Back" are arguably even funnier. "Financing Finnegan" is about a down-on-his-luck writer who has the upper hand over his agent and publisher because they have invested so much money in him that they dare not disown "a name with ingots in it" (*The Stories* 449). When Finnegan breaks his shoulder while diving from a fifteen-foot board, he has a device suspended from the ceiling so he can lie on his back and write in midair. Later, he is reported missing on an arctic expedition. With Finnegan "scarcely cold" (453), his agent and publisher are about to collect on his insurance when a cable arrives from Norway informing them of his safety and requesting still more financing.

Arguably Fitzgerald's most humorous piece, "The Camel's Back" (1920) is almost pure farce and slapstick. Perry Parkhurst's dilemma is that he cannot win the hand of Betty Medill: "Their secret engagement had got so long that it seemed as if any day it might break off of its own weight" (*Six Tales of the Jazz Age* 36). Goaded by friends to attend a costume party, Perry goes as a camel, having recruited a run-down taxi driver as the animal's posterior: "The beast walked with a peculiar gait which varied between an uncertain lockstep and a stampede—but can best be described by the word 'halting'. . . . As he walked he alternately elongated and contracted like a gigantic concertina" (45). At the party, the camel, purported to contain a highly desirable architect from New York, attracts the attention of an Egyptian snake charmer, Betty Medill, who flirts with the camel "violently" (51). When the snake charmer and camel win prizes for most original and amusing costumes, Folly and Mirth are united in what is thought to be a mock wedding but which moments later is realized to be genuine because the black man who presided is a minister and the pseudo-license is the real one Perry has carried with him for years. Only when the back of the camel argues that it/he is as much Betty's husband as the front is Betty persuaded to leave with Perry: "Over her shoulder the front part of the camel looked at the back part of the camel—and they exchanged a particularly subtle, esoteric sort of wink that only true camels can understand" (59).

In addition to sustained humorous pieces, Fitzgerald wrote humorous vignettes, episodes, and scenes in longer works. *This Side of Paradise* includes a highly amusing scene describing Mr. Rooney tutoring dull jocks to eligibility:

> "Now, Langueduc, if I used that formula, where would my A point be?"
> Langueduc lazily shifts his six-foot-three of football material and tries to concentrate.
> "Oh—ah—I'm damned if I know, Mr. Rooney."
> "Oh, why of course, of *course* you can't *use* that formula. *That's* what I wanted you to say."
> "Why, sure . . . of course." (93)

In *The Beautiful and Damned,* when a progressively more drunken Anthony Patch attempts to sell bonds in six Manhattan businesses, the result is hilarious farce and slapstick. Desperate, he answers a newspaper ad and attends a series of hackneyed lectures, "Heart Talks," on "principles of success" in selling. On the fifth day, sallying forth "with all the sensations of a man wanted by the police" (383), he attempts to sell bonds, first in an architect's office, where "his confidence oozed from him in great retching emanations that seemed to be sections of his own body" (384). "After an hour and with the help of two strong whiskies" (385), he tries a plumber's office, then a grocery store. After several more drinks he tries a real estate office, and yet another drink later "he conceived the brilliant plan of selling the stock to the bartenders along Lexington Avenue. This occupied several hours, for it was necessary to take a few drinks in each place in order to get the proprietor in the proper frame of mind to talk business" (385–86). Finally, approaching "a dark and soggy five o'clock," he selects "a medium-sized delicatessen" (386):

> "Af'ernoon," he began in a loud voice. "Ga l'il prop'sition." . . .
> "Buy a bon'," he suggested, "good as liberty bon'!" . . . His mind made a hiatus and skipped to his peroration, which he delivered with appropriate gestures, these being somewhat marred by the necessity of clinging to the counter with one or both hands. "Now see here. You taken up my time. I don't want know *why* you won't buy. I just want you say *why*. Want you say *how many*!"

When the proprietor threatens to call a policeman, Anthony again asks, "How many?" "The whole force if necessary!" the proprietor thunders, "his yellow mustache trembling fiercely." "Sell 'em all a bon'," Anthony vows, but he merely turns and "wabble[s]" from the store (387).[2]

Fitzgerald's ability to incorporate pure farce into stories of high tragedy is further illustrated in such works as "'O Russet Witch!'" (1921). In this story, the alluring femme fatale, Caroline (aka Alicia) Dare, prompts Merlin Grainger to join her in "a perfect orgy" (*Six Tales of the Jazz Age* 96) of tossing books in all directions, making a shambles of the Moonlight Quill Bookshop where he works. Even more darkly ironic is the slapstick in "May Day" (1920) in which Gordon Sterrett, down on his luck and unable to get a job or a handout, commits suicide in the final sentence, an event made more poignant by two farcical passages. In a restaurant on Columbus Circle, drunken friends, Dean and

Peter, taunt the waiters: "Four waiters were sent around one way and four another. Dean caught hold of two of them by the coat, and another struggle took place before the pursuit of Peter could be resumed; he was finally pinioned after overturning a sugar-bowl and several cups of coffee. A fresh argument ensued at the cashier's desk, where Peter attempted to buy another dish of hash to take with him and throw at policemen" (*The Short Stories* 135). Later, at Delmonico's, Dean and Peter remove "In" and "Out" signs on the coatroom doors and perform what is surely one of the most effective farcical scenes in modern literature—"Mr. In and Mr. Out"—appearing just before Gordon, lacking an "in" with anyone and having no way "out," fires a "cartridge into his head just behind the temple" (141).

Fitzgerald's success in juxtaposing farce and tragedy in these scenes prepared him for farcical scenes in *The Great Gatsby*. The first is the familiar description of drunken revelers leaving one of Gatsby's parties. A new coupe has run into a ditch, shearing a wheel; the driver, too drunk to realize what has happened, thinks he has run out of gas:

> "Wonder'ff tell me where there's a gas'line station?"
> At least a dozen men, some of them little better off than he was, explained to him that wheel and car were no longer joined by any physical bond.
> "Back out," he suggested after a moment. "Put her in reverse."
> "But the *wheel's* off!"
> He hesitated.
> "No harm in trying," he said. (60)

As the appropriately "caterwauling horns" reach a crescendo, "[a] wafer of a moon . . . shin[es] over Gatsby's house" (60). The tragedy of Gatsby's unrealized dream is rendered more poignant by the farce of its wasteland surroundings.

The departure scene is counterpointed in the next chapter by an arrival scene: a burlesque catalog of guest names, each an animal, fish, plant, or pejorative-sounding name.[3] This catalog, which cries to be read aloud, is effective on one level simply as a humorous spoof. One whole section of Fitzgerald's *Notebooks,* part of the 40 percent omitted in Edmund Wilson's edition of *The Crack-up,* is labeled "Proper Names" and consists simply of lists of highly connotative names, such as "Nuts Vandernut," "Darky Dolittle," "Harry Fantrum," "Tookey Ledoux," "Megalomania McCarthy," "Byron Appledeck," "Howya Bartlett" (*Notebooks* 209), and "Henry Haukinspit" (*Notebooks* 335). Another section of the *Notebooks* includes this entry:

> Shy beaten man named Victor.
> Clumsy girl named Grace.
> Great truck drivers named Earl and Cecil. (54)

Robert Sklar has referred to the scene in which Gatsby is reunited with Daisy in Nick's cottage as "a comic scene that marks the death of time" (184). In the scene, a distraught Gatsby reclines against the mantelpiece, his head leaning back so far that it rests against the face of a defunct clock. At that instant Gatsby makes perhaps the understatement of the century, "We've met before," and makes "an abortive attempt at a laugh," the clock tilts "dangerously at the pressure of his head, whereupon he turned and caught it with trembling fingers and set it back in place." Nick adds, "I think we all believed for a moment that it had smashed in pieces on the floor" (91–92). The real crash—of Gatsby's dream—does not come until later, however, and the reader, sensing its inevitability, anticipates it, waiting for the other shoe to fall. The scene with the tilting clock, like the one in which Gatsby shows Nick and Daisy his piles of beautiful imported shirts, hovers between tragedy and comedy.

In addition to entire pieces devoted to humor and humorous scenes within stories and novels, Fitzgerald's canon is replete with a wide variety of humorous elements, each based on some form of incongruity, constituting circumstantial humor, rhetorical humor, and linguistic humor.

Perhaps the most pervasive form of circumstantial humor in Fitzgerald's fiction is irony—to Anthony Patch "the final polish of the shoe, the ultimate dab of the clothes-brush, a sort of intellectual 'There!'" (*The Beautiful and Damned* 3). Situational irony, based on incongruity between expectation and reality, is ubiquitous in Fitzgerald's work. Perhaps the best example from his *Notebooks* is this entry: "Gave up spinach for Lent" (288). One of the most cogent examples in his fiction appears in *The Last Tycoon* when Prince Agge, a foreign visitor to a Hollywood movie set, sees his long-admired Abraham Lincoln in the commissary: "This, then, was Lincoln. . . . This, then, he thought, was what they all meant to be." But when "Lincoln suddenly raised a triangle of pie and jammed it in his mouth," the adulatory prince hurries on, disillusioned and "a little frightened" (49). Later in the novel, producer Monroe Stahr receives a long-distance call asking him to speak to the president—who turns out to be an orangutan who talks like and is a "dead ringer for McKinley" (83).

Dramatic irony, based on incongruity between what a character says and what the reader realizes, is best illustrated by a character in *Tender Is the Night* who tells Dick Diver in early 1929, "I have good stocks in the hands of friends who are holding it for me. All goes well" (274). Verbal irony, involving incongruity between word and referent or between denotations and connotations, between denotations, or between connotations, is exemplified in the title "The Baby Party," in which adults are depicted as the real "babies."

The element of surprise, the incongruity between propriety and impropriety, is illustrated in the lowest form of circumstantial humor: practical jokes, japes, or "didoes" (after the mythological Dido, who, having been offered as much land as could be covered with the hide of a bull, ordered the hide cut into strips with which she surrounded a large area). In *This Side of Paradise,* Amory Blaine and friends at Princeton fill a roommate's bed with lemon pie (51). Later they buy a taxicab, disassemble it, and then reassemble it in the office of a dean who had been heard arguing with a taxi driver, "[I] might as well buy the taxi-cab" (119). In "The Bridal Party" (1930), a French girl is hired to appear at a bachelor party holding a baby in her arms and crying, "Hamilton, you can't desert me now!" (*The Stories* 275); later the joke becomes reality when "an American girl a little the worse for liquor" (279) does show up with blackmail in her eye.

Black humor, another form of circumstantial humor based on incongruity between the sacrosanctity of topics like death and the irreverent spoof thereof, becomes increasingly pervasive in Fitzgerald's work. In *The Beautiful and Damned,* Fitzgerald satirically describes the death of Gloria's mother as follows: "The Bilphistic demiurge decided suddenly in mid-December that Mrs. Gilbert's soul had aged sufficiently in its present incarnation" (189). Just before the farcical duel in *Tender Is the*

Night, Abe North remarks, "There's a wonderful duel in a novel of Pushkin's. . . . Each man stood on the edge of a precipice, so if he was hit at all he was done for" (46).[4]

Surely no Fitzgerald work illustrates black humor so dark and so pervasive as the tall tale "The Diamond as Big as the Ritz" (1922). Having inherited a mountain-size diamond in Montana, Braddock Washington (a descendant of George) manipulates and murders anyone who finds out about his treasure. Two dozen men imprisoned in a pit try to reason with him as "a fair-minded man." "You might as well speak of a Spaniard being fair-minded toward a piece of steak," Washington responds, and "at this harsh observation the faces of the two dozen steaks fell" (*The Short Stories* 200). When the subject of an Italian who tried to escape is broached, Washington remarks, "'The man—what was his name? Critchtichiello?—was shot by some of my agents in fourteen different places.' Not guessing that the places referred to were cities, the tumult of rejoicing subsided immediately" (201). In what is arguably one of the most poignant black humor scenes in modern literature, a scene anticipating the humor of Monty Python, Washington offers a bribe to God when his diamond mountain is threatened. "'Oh, you above there!' The voice was become strong and confident. There was no forlorn supplication. If anything, there was in it a quality of monstrous condescension. 'You there—'" (211).

A second major division of humor in Fitzgerald's work is rhetorical, based on incongruity of rhetorical constructions. Fitzgerald was a master of humorous description, even devoting three whole sections of his *Notebooks* to "Description." He was especially aware of incongruous tropes, such as this example from *Tender Is the Night:* it was "a definite nervous experience perverted as a breakfast of oatmeal and hashish" (71); and this one from *The Beautiful and Damned:* "With much difficulty Anthony retained a scanty breech-clout of dignity" (212). Fitzgerald's metaphors and similes are especially effective because they render the abstract so vividly concrete through sensory appeal: "Of late their income had lost elasticity; no longer did it stretch to cover gay whims and pleasant extravagances" (*The Beautiful and Damned* 221). Note the humor through sensory appeal in these examples from the stories: "From the age of twelve Kay Tompkins had worn men like rings on every finger" ("Magnetism" [*The Stories* 226]); "her voice was flip as a whip and cold as automatic refrigeration" ("Two Wrongs" [*The Stories* 296]); "he looked like a rough draft for a riotous cartoon" ("The Camel's Back" [*Six Tales of the Jazz Age* 38]); "how wearily Ethel regarded Jim sometimes, as if she wondered why she had trained the vines of her affection on such a wind-shaken poplar" ("Bernice Bobs Her Hair" [*The Stories* 40]); "The tingliness of Miss Masters . . . increased until it seemed that she would shortly be electrocuted by her own nervous reactions" ("'O Russet Witch!'" [*Six Tales of the Jazz Age* 99–100]). Each of these descriptions has just the right amount of freshness and surprise (which Pascal considered to be the essence of humor).

Sometimes the humor of description comes from the absurdity of excess or want, as in this description of the prototypical nerd: "He was twenty-one, his trousers were too short and too tight. His buttoned shoes were long and narrow. His tie was an alarming conspiracy of purple and pink marvellously scrolled, and over it were two blue eyes faded like a piece of very good old cloth long exposed to the sun" ("The Jelly-Bean" [*Six Tales of the Jazz Age* 18]).

In other descriptions the surprise comes when one part of a statement undercuts another, as in this example: "She clapped her hands happily, and he thought how pretty she was really, that is, the upper part of her face—from the bridge of the nose down she was somewhat out of true" ("'O Russet Witch!'" [*Six Tales of the Jazz Age* 100]). With this rhetorical technique, the pinprick of reality deflates the balloon of idealism; the beginning expectation of consummate female beauty is undercut by the intrusion of reality: except for her eyes and forehead, she was quite plain. Sometimes the humorous effect of the description comes from a rhetorical device like chiasmus: "He wondered idly whether she was a poor conversationalist because she got no attention or got no attention because she was a poor conversationalist" ("Bernice Bobs Her Hair" [*The Stories* 42]).

Another rhetorical device used to achieve humor is anticlimax, as in this example: "He was critical about women. A single defect—a thick ankle, a hoarse voice, a glass eye—was enough to make him utterly indifferent" ("Diamond as Big as the Ritz" [*The Short Stories* 196]). Similarly, "Terrence R. Tipton [is], by occupation, actor, athlete, scholar, philatelist and collector of cigar bands" ("That Kind of Party" [*Basil and Josephine* 1]). In *The Beautiful and Damned,* Fitzgerald achieves effective

humor with a metaphor followed by a triple simile in anticlimactic order: "From the tenement windows leaned rotund, moon-shaped mothers, as constellations of this sordid heaven; women like dark imperfect
jewels, women like vegetables, women like great bags of abominably
dirty laundry" (283). At other times the humor comes from paradox:
"He wondered that people invariably chose inimitable people to imitate" (*The Beautiful and Damned* 84); "There's only one lesson to be
learned from life. . . . That there's no lesson to be learned from life"
(*The Beautiful and Damned* 255).

A form of rhetorical humor based on surprise is what Peter De Vries
called the "snapper," that is, a familiar statement altered with an ironic,
surprising "snap." It seems clear that Fitzgerald was intrigued with this
form, as illustrated by this entry from his *Notebooks:* "All things come
to him who mates" (56). Examples appear in early work, such as this one
from *This Side of Paradise:* "Blood being thicker than broth, he was
pulled through" (13); and this one from "The Offshore Pirate," which
appeared in the same year (1920): "blessed are the simple rich, for they
inherit the earth!" (*Flappers and Philosophers* 29). An example from *The
Beautiful and Damned*—"She lapsed into silence, giving him rope. And if
he had not hanged himself he had certainly come to the end of it"
(212)—plays on at least two common sayings, thus providing a double
"snap." In the same novel, this version of the "snapper" appears: "[Mrs.
Gilbert] had expected an announcement [of her daughter's engagement]
in a few weeks. But the announcement never came; instead, a new man
came" (80). The form also appears in later work, such as this example
from "Financing Finnegan": "[In] the old days . . . there was chicken
feed in every pot" (*The Stories* 454).

Closely related to the "snapper" is the humorous aphorism or epigram. Fitzgerald's interest in this form is suggested by his devoting an
entire section in his *Notebooks* to "Epigrams, Wisecracks, and Jokes"; included among those are "Death in most countries is considered practically fatal" and "Thank gravity for working your bowels" (53). Examples
in Fitzgerald's fiction include "like all men who are preoccupied with
their own broadness, he was exceptionally narrow" ("The Cut-Glass
Bowl" [*Flappers and Philosophers* 90]); "At eighteen our convictions are
ills from which we look; at forty-five they are caves in which we hide"
("Bernice Bobs Her Hair" [*The Stories* 45]); and "when you're sober

you don't want to see anybody, and when you're tight nobody wants to see you" (*Tender Is the Night* 82). These aphorisms, and others like them, have the same rhetorical construction, with the first clause counterpointed by the second. Most of such epigrams appear in early works of the 1920s, perhaps indicating the influence of Oscar Wilde's epigrammatic style, which Fitzgerald later virtually abandoned, perhaps because it seemed too labored, too contrived.

Still another rhetorical strategy Fitzgerald used effectively for humor is stichomythia, an interchange in which a second statement undercuts the first, made by a "fall guy/girl," as in these examples:

Rosalind: Mother, I never *think* about money.
Mrs. Connage: You never keep it long enough to think about it. (*This Side of Paradise* 167)

Rosalind: . . . if I were poor, I'd go on the stage.
Cecelia: Yes, you might as well get paid for the amount of acting you do.
Rosalind: Sometimes when I've felt particularly radiant I've thought—why should this be wasted on one man—?
Cecelia: Often when you're particularly sulky, I've wondered why it should all be wasted on just one family. (*This Side of Paradise* 162)

Miss Saunders: Then you believe in spirits, Mr. Rudd.
Chinaman Rudd: Yes, ma'am, I certainly do believe in spirits. Have you got any? ("The Captured Shadow" [*Basil and Josephine* 117])

A third major category of humor in Fitzgerald's fiction is the linguistic, ranging from the lowly pun to more formal but nonetheless humorous definitions. Fitzgerald was fond of paronomasia, in which humor comes from the incongruity between the two definitions or between denotation and connotation. Examples recur in his work from *The Beautiful and Damned* to *The Last Tycoon*. In the former, Richard Caramel, Anthony Patch's writer friend, "made some sad pun about Bounds doing patchwork, but if there was one thing worse than a pun [Gloria says], it was a person who, as the inevitable come-back to a pun, gave the perpetrator a mock-reproachful look" (59). Later, Gloria herself puns relentlessly on "Bloeckman," the name of a movie producer: "First it had been 'Block-house,' lately, the more invidious 'Blockhead'" (99). Still later, the protagonist recalls "a hoary jest about the elevator man's career being a matter of ups and downs" (299–300).

In *Tender Is the Night,* Fitzgerald refers to "an arriviste who had not arrived" (33). Later in the same novel, Rosemary whispers to an astonished Dick Diver, "Take me." "Take you where?" he responds (64). Similarly, in *The Last Tycoon,* when Monroe Stahr remarks to Cecelia, "I'm lonesome as hell. But I'm too old and tired to undertake anything," Cecelia says, "Undertake me" (70–71). Later Cecelia assures Stahr that at Bennington "there was the usual proportion of natural born skivies and biddies tastefully concealed by throw overs from Sex, Fifth Avenue" (103).

A related form is the *malentendu* expression, or verbal confusion. In *Tender Is the Night,* a character says, "Mac thinks a Marxian is somebody who went to St. Mark's school" (198). Later in the same novel, during a grave talk between Dr. Franz Gregorovius and Dick Diver concerning Dick's alcoholism, Franz says, "Why not try another leave of abstinence?" "'Absence,' Dick corrected him automatically. 'It's no solution for me to go away'" (256).

Another example of such humorous wordplay appears in "The Curious Case of Benjamin Button" when the protagonist, born as a seventy-year-old and growing younger, has a conversation with his father, who is in the wholesale hardware business:

> " . . . And what do you think should merit our biggest attention after hammers and nails?" the elder Button was saying.
> "Love," replied Benjamin absent-mindedly.
> "Lugs?" exclaimed Roger Button. "Why, I've just covered the question of lugs." (*Six Tales of the Jazz Age* 73)

The reader, from a safe aesthetic distance, smiles at the incongruity between "love" and "lugs," but even more significantly, the verbal confusion serves to illuminate the disparity between the mundane, materialistic father and his anomalous but romantic son. A similar contrast between characters is illustrated in this interchange between Horace and Marcia in "Head and Shoulders": "'*Mens sana in corpore sano,*' he said.

'Don't believe in it,' replied Marcia. 'I tried one of those patent medicines once and they're all bunk'" (*Flappers and Philosophers* 78).

Fitzgerald also achieves linguistic humor with the whimsical definition: "Jelly-Bean," in the story with that title, is defined as "the name throughout the undissolved Confederacy for one who spends his life conjugating the verb to idle in the first person singular—I am idling, I have idled, I will idle" (*Six Tales of the Jazz Age* 17). Political satire is the basis of this definition: "An alderman is halfway between a politician and a pirate" ("The Captured Shadow" [*Basil and Josephine* 117]). Social satire is the basis of this one in Fitzgerald's *Notebooks:* "Debut—the first time a young girl is seen drunk in public" (55). Two other humorous, satirical definitions in the *Notebooks* are "Optimism is the content of small men in high places" (51) and "Great art is the contempt of a great man for small art" (162). In *This Side of Paradise*—a novel that makes extensive use of definition (*personality* vs. *personage, medievalist, egotist,* et al.)—a *romantic* and a *sentimentalist* are distinguished: "[A] sentimental person thinks things will last—a romantic person hopes against hope that they won't" (166).

Fitzgerald left no definition of humor, either whimsical or formal, but it is possible to deduce one from the extensive humor in his fiction and to draw conclusions about its function. Humor in Fitzgerald serves at least six functions, each grounded in the perception of incongruity.

On a basic level, humor provides entertainment, for Fitzgerald a significant criterion of fiction. Second, humor often functions as an objective correlative, the means by which Fitzgerald objectifies a particular emotion or mood, correlating it with a form of humor, often with a specified variety of laughter. According to T. S. Eliot, an objective correlative is "a situation, a chain of events which shall be the formula of that particular emotion, such that when the external facts, which must terminate in sensory experience, are given, the emotion is immediately evoked" (*The Sacred Wood* 100). Third, rather than reflecting the stereotypical view of humor as an escape from reality, Fitzgerald's humor tends to be an escape from unreality. Jesse Bier's comment in *The Rise and Fall of American Humor* could have been fashioned particularly for Fitzgerald's humor: "It drives for truth behind the big and little stultifying lies of our national life. Its blasphemy has been a counteractive both to our made-up myths and to all the forces of obvious and subtle conformism" (123). Fourth, humor often provides Fitzgerald with an effective means of artistic balance. As F. H. Langman has noted about *The Great Gatsby,* humor "is the source of the balance which can give full measure of sympathy to the characters without glossing over their folly, vanity and self-deceit" (Donaldson, *Critical Essays* 53). Or, as Jackson R. Bryer has noted, "humor contributes in a major way to the presence in *Gatsby* of what Malcolm Cowley has called Fitzgerald's 'double vision'" (Donaldson, *Critical Essays* 127). Fifth, humor juxtaposed variously with the serious and tragic results in both being enhanced, humor sometimes functioning structurally, as when a key humorous scene epitomizes the central idea and serves as microcosm of the story. Finally, though humor may not have "saved" Fitzgerald, as Thurber lamented, it may have saved his art, for as E. B. White observed, "humorists fatten on trouble. They have always made trouble pay. . . . There is often a rather fine line between laughing and crying, and if a humorous piece of writing brings a person to the point where his emotional responses are untrustworthy and seem likely to break over into the opposite realm, it is because humor, like poetry, has an extra content. It plays close to the big hot fire which is Truth, and sometimes the reader feels the heat" (244). It could be argued that Fitzgerald often "made trouble pay," transforming it into significant art, often through humor.

Perhaps now, more than six decades after his death, it may be possible to praise Fitzgerald's comic genius without a priori assumptions of patronizing derogation. Fitzgerald has long been the deserving recipient of numerous laurels as a "serious" artist. E. B. White correctly stated that "the world likes humor, but it treats it patronizingly. It decorates its serious artists with laurel, and its wags with Brussels sprouts" (244). Surely it is time now, as a further tribute to Fitzgerald's genius, to remove the Brussels sprouts and to replace them with the sweet bay (*Laurus nobilis*) of Thalia.

Notes

1. For further consideration of grades of laughter and their significance, see my article "Varieties of Risible Experience: Grades of Laughter in Modern American Literature."

2. Fitzgerald's use of this less common, variant spelling of *wobble* may be nothing more than another example of his well-known orthographic difficulties not caught by a copy editor.

3. Because Gatsby's guest list, including its satiric nature, has been widely discussed, there seems little point in doing so here. Note especially Crim and Houston; Prigozy, "Gatsby's Guest List"; Stone; Long, "The Vogue."

4. Fitzgerald apparently got the idea from Mikhail Lermontov's *A Hero for Our Time* rather than from Pushkin.

13

F. Scott Fitzgerald in the Funny Papers

The Commentary of Mickey Mouse and Charlie Brown

M. THOMAS INGE

Few major American writers have figured so prominently in our popular culture as has F. Scott Fitzgerald. Placing himself and his wife, Zelda, in the public view seems to have been a preoccupation during the early years of his success, perhaps with a conscious eye on the relationship between media exposure and the sale of books, but also for the sheer pleasure of conspicuous consumption of his hard-earned money. He was so successful that any effort since then to invoke the Jazz Age or the Roaring Twenties is inevitably accompanied by a photograph or a reference to Fitzgerald. Motion pictures, television commercials, magazine advertisements, record covers, art prints, and mail-order catalogs are places his face or image has appeared, and one can purchase articles of clothing and products designed in the spirit of Fitzgerald, Zelda, or his fictional characters, such as Gatsby shirts and sport coats or Daisy dresses and cosmetics.[1]

His name seems to wend its way through newspaper gossip columns and news reports. When Earl Wilson interviewed actress Sarah Miles about the suicide of her companion and manager in 1973, she noted, "David was not in love with me. He was in love with F. Scott Fitzgerald. He always carried a copy of 'The Great Gatsby.'" When political columnist Jeffrey Hart wanted to explain Richard Nixon's involvement in Watergate, he read the event against the same novel and discovered a streak of Gatsbyism in the president, "the self-made man, combining undoubted idealism with ruthlessness." Because Fitzgerald's name has had such common coin, some have doubted the lasting importance of his fiction. As recently as 1973, Walter Scott could say without equivocation in *Parade* magazine that Fitzgerald "was a man of shallow Princeton education. There was no appreciable depth in any of his novels."

It is little wonder, then, that the comic strip, that reflector of American values and social mores, the literature of the common and the uncommon man, whose primary mission seems to be to lend a laugh or two to daily life, also has used references to Fitzgerald and his fiction. This is especially true of *The Great Gatsby* ever since it achieved canonical status as a classic of American literature. There has always been a clear relationship between comics and literature, in that most people have their first reading experiences as children with the funny papers before they go on to novels and specialized reading matter.

As I have argued in full in *Comics as Culture,* the comics clearly belong to the great body of humor which Americans cherish in their oral traditions, literature, stage entertainments, film, radio, and television. They soften the impact of reality by providing a comic distance from life's dangers, frustrations, and tragedies and by enabling us to laugh at ourselves as the pretentious creatures we happen to be. They please our visual sensibilities by bringing to life the kinds of dramatic conflicts and absurd situations that allow us vicariously to work out our own internal neuroses. They have long served sociologists and historians as revealing reflectors of popular attitudes, tastes, and beliefs, but they can do more than that and very often are used as creative ways of commenting on contemporary culture.

There has always been, for example, a satirical tension between the comics and highbrow or elite culture. As a part of American humor and its spirit of subversion, the comics satirize the institutions and established opinions of authority. Thus everything from the Bible and *War and Peace* to *Moby-Dick* and *The Adventures of Huckleberry Finn* is likely to be made sport of by cartoonists, the more "classic" the better. Even James Joyce's *Ulysses* has been adapted as a ten-page "Minit Classics" comic book by David Lasky, an act of comic arrogance that brilliantly captures the essence of Joycean humor. If it takes Joyce more than 760 pages to record one day in the life of Leopold Bloom, imagine the challenge of reducing it to 36 small comic strip panels. This is the other extreme of creative expression.

A 1951 series of *Li'l Abner* sequences shows how the references to

Al Capp, *Li'l Abner,* March 31 and April 2, 1951.

Fitzgerald sometimes work. Given their frequency, comic artist Al Capp must have been reading *The Great Gatsby* that year. On March 31, 1951, a highly prolific Dogpatch father, who has sired so many children he has lost count, is introduced as "The Great Begatsby." When Abner sees the entire family at the carnival, he comments, "Now—thar's a purty sight!! Th' Great Begatsby an' his fambly!! Hain't seen 'em fo' weeks, now, so natcherly thar's quite a few new kids!!" In the strip two days later, two gangsters from New York have infiltrated the family to assassinate Abner, so a degree of irony is introduced, for the situation as well as for those who know the novel, when Abner adds, "But, one thing 'bout thet fambly—yo' kin trust anyone of 'em!!" (41–42).

Just six months later, on September 22, Capp introduces a murderous and cold-blooded hobo named "Blood an' Guts" Gatsby, so cruel he can carve up the sacred and personable Dogpatch ham without compunction (116). Then, four months later, on January 29, 1952, a more subtle reference appears. Fooling around with an amateur chemistry set, Abner accidentally concocts a perfume that fatally attracts anyone who comes near him. An unscrupulous businessman, who has wrecked his car over the fragrance, recognizes its appeal: "You've discovered a perfume that'll

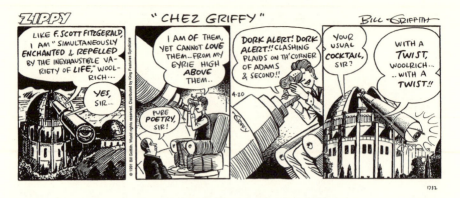

Bill Griffith, *Zippy,* April 20, 1990.

make men irresistible to women!! *It smells like money!!"* (18). This is an echo, of course, of Gatsby's famous line about Daisy, that "Her voice is full of money" (94). One needs to have read the novel to catch that one.

This is equally true of a 1991 *Zippy* comic strip by Bill Griffith. *Zippy* is one of the most sophisticated and culturally allusive of the current comic strips, by turns surrealistic and self-reflexive, but always postmodern in its wit and attitude. The character named Griffy (a stand-in for the artist himself), peering through a large telescope located on Mount Palomar, notes, "Like F. Scott Fitzgerald, I am 'simultaneously enchanted & repelled by the inexhaustible variety of life.'" The attentive reader knows that this is a quotation from Nick Carraway (30), not Fitzgerald, but it suggests the extent to which the author and his characters have become one and the same in the popular mind. Critics have had the same problem, since it is very easy to identify Nick as narrator with the author of *The Great Gatsby.* In the same manner, in the case of *Zippy,* it is fair to say that the character Griffy does indeed reflect, in the comic strip, the stance of the cartoonist, who remains "enchanted and repelled" with the variety and banality of American culture. In this particular strip, the eye of Dr. Eckleburg located at the end of Griffy's telescope is a visual quotation from the novel which reminds us that Griffith's satiric gaze is directed at all of us.

The one cartoonist who most frequently mentioned Fitzgerald and counted himself among the writer's greatest admirers was Charles M.

PEANUTS

Charles Schulz, *Peanuts,* May 31, 1991.

Schulz, creator of *Peanuts.* In the summer of 1991, *The Great Gatsby* was referred to several times. Sally, Charlie Brown's little sister, is teaching a Sunday school class on May 31, 1991. "Today we're going to talk a little about the Sea of Galilee," she begins, when a new child in the class named Larry, a scholarly looking little boy with glasses, speaks up, "Gatsby stood by the Sea of Galilee, and picked out the green light at the end of Daisy's dock." Sally's nonplussed response is, "Do you live around here, kid?" A few days later, on June 3, he again interrupts Sally, who is discussing the parting of the Red Sea, with "The Great Gatsby did that!" This time she banishes him from class, but he can't leave because he is too small to reach the doorknob. Finally, when the class is over on June 7 and Larry leaves, he comments, "Goodby, ma'am. Whenever I think of you, I'll think of Gatsby and the green light at the end of Daisy's dock." Snoopy adds, in his thought balloon, "So long, old sport!"

Larry would reappear at Christmastime, still obsessed by his favorite book. On December 19, Sally asks the class if anyone knows why a star is placed on top of the Christmas tree. Larry responds, "Gatsby used to look across the street at the green star on top of Daisy's tree." Sally loses her cool again despite the seasonal spirit. What these sequences suggest is that in Larry's mind, anyway, the sacred and the secular have become confused. So influential is his respect for *Gatsby* as a classic work that he has moved the literary figure back into the great events of the biblical past and used him to explain the age-old traditions of society. So powerful was the force of a Jay Gatsby that he might have proved a Moses in another place and time.

Charles Schulz, *Peanuts,* June 3, 1991.

Copyright © United Feature Syndicate. Reprinted by permission of Charles M. Schulz.

Charles Schulz, *Peanuts,* June 7, 1991.

Copyright © United Feature Syndicate. Reprinted by permission of Charles M. Schulz.

A few years later, on June 26, 1995, we find Snoopy sitting beneath a tree with Woodstock and, as he often does in his philosophical moods, ruminating while contemplating the canine condition: "You're emotionally bankrupt . . . Scott Fitzgerald was emotionally bankrupt . . . we're all emotionally bankrupt." But this is not surprising coming from Snoopy, the great unread American writer, author of "It Was a Dark and Stormy Night" and other unpublished classics, who obviously feels an alliance with Fitzgerald, another misunderstood genius.

In a letter to me written February 27, 1996, Schulz reported that "Obviously *The Great Gatsby* is one of my favorite books, although it took about four readings before I understood it. I have certainly read almost everything Fitzgerald wrote except maybe a few short stories." The remainder of his letter, however, provides a cautionary tale for scholars too eager to make cultural connections where they may not

Charles Schulz, *Peanuts,* December 19, 1991.

Charles Schulz, *Peanuts,* June 26, 1995.

exist. As readers of *Peanuts* know, Sally often addresses the object of her affection, Schroeder, as "My sweet babboo," much to his annoyance. As scholars of Fitzgerald know, he inscribed a copy of *The Beautiful and Damned* to Zelda as "my dearest, sweetest baboo."[2] In my letter to Schulz, I noted that he must have borrowed the phrase from Fitzgerald. He was quick to correct me: "I did not get the phrase 'sweet babboo' from him, it's a phrase I heard my wife use now and then." Also, knowing that Fitzgerald scholar Matthew J. Bruccoli was a fan of *Peanuts* and had corresponded with Schulz, I thought that the character Larry looked a little like him, but I was wrong again: "Larry was not modeled after Matthew Bruccoli, I have never met Matthew so I don't know what he looks like." So much for seemingly obvious connections and influences.

Schulz is not the only cartoonist to express his admiration for Fitzgerald. John J. Liney spent most of his career writing and later drawing

Detail from Victoria Roberts, *My Day*

(London: Chatto & Windus/Hogarth Press, 1984), unpaged.
Copyright © Victoria Roberts. Reprinted by permission.

the comic strip *Henry,* originally created by Carl Anderson, one of the few strips in newspaper history to use no words and depend on the art of pantomime. Liney once noted: "All my life, I had been a voracious reader and devoured everything that F. Scott Fitzgerald ever penned. Fitzgerald once observed that a creative person had just so much talent in his make-up and when that was exhausted, he was finished. This intrigued me since every cartoonist is plagued with the fear that he will never top the excellent week's work he had just completed" (11). But one doesn't find any echoes of Fitzgerald in *Henry.* In this case, it is Fitzgerald as example and authority on creativity that has made the difference in Liney's career, although apparently the cartoonist never exhausted his share of talent. There is much to be said for the presence of the quotable Fitzgerald as source of wise and witty apothegms in American popular culture. I suspect most of us have lived by more than a few of his pungent observations.

Occasionally a Fitzgerald reference creeps into the comics when the focus is on a figure who was related to him in real life. *New Yorker* cartoonist Victoria Roberts once did a series called "My Day," each of which satirically depicts an average day of a major writer, artist, or political or cultural figure. In "My Day with Ernest Hemingway," Hemingway takes time in one panel to "phone Scott Fitzgerald and tell him how to write" (3). In another unlikely comic strip, called *Gertrude's Follies,* begun in May 1978 by Tom Hachtman for New York's *Soho News,*

Detail from Tom Hachtman, *Gertrude's Follies*

(New York: St. Martin's Press, 1980), unpaged.
Copyright © 1980 by T. Hachtman. Reprinted by permission.

Gertrude Stein and all her friends—especially Alice B. Toklas, Pablo Picasso, and Ernest Hemingway—participate in a series of comedy routines, sometimes in verse. A very uptight and heterosexual Hemingway often plays straight man (pun intended) to Gertrude and Alice in their lesbian antics, and Fitzgerald has been drawn into the comic repartee a time or two as well.

There have been no American comic book adaptations of *The Great Gatsby* in any of the classics comics series, despite its status as a major work of literature and a frequently assigned high school and college text. Primarily this has to do with copyright control. Most of the classics series have not used copyrighted materials to avoid permission fees, and probably the Scribner's firm would not have allowed it under any circumstances, given the general attitude that such adaptations are debasements of the originals.

It has happened indirectly, however. When a motion picture version of *The Great Gatsby* was released in late 1974, *Mad* magazine did one of its usual movie satires under the title "The Great Gasbag" in the January 1975 issue. Writer Stan Hart and artist Mort Drucker demonstrate more than a passing knowledge of the book, since they manage to incorporate many of the major scenes and conversations in their version—but with

Details from Stan Hart and Mort Drucker, "The Great Gasbag,"

Mad, no. 172 (January 1975): 4–10. Copyright © 1974 E. C. Publications, Inc.
All rights reserved. Used with permission of *MAD Magazine.*

a comic twist turned against the film. When *Mad*'s Nick Carrawayseed
says, "you can't repeat the past," Gasbag replies, "But we *did* repeat the
past! This is the *third time* Hollywood's made 'The Great Gasbag' . . .
and failed!!" (9). When Mr. Wolfshy says of Gasbag, "he's a fabulous
character, an amazing business genius, and a fine human being!," Nick
asks, "How do you know all this?" Wolfshy replies, "I read the book!"
(8). The implication is that one is not likely to get much from the less-

than-successful screen adaptation. Most of the satire is directed against Robert Redford's seeming indifference in playing the role and the slow pace of the film, so slow in fact that the eyes of "Dr. Yichleburg" finally doze off (10).

In the July 1976 issue of the comic book series *Tweety and Sylvester,* featuring the characters best known from the Warner Brothers animated cartoons first created by Bob Clampett, *The Great Gatsby* is adapted as a brief story entitled "The Great Catsby." In Sylvester's retelling, he plays the part of a dapper but poor soldier named Catsby who is pulled from the arms of his southern love, "Miss Nelly Belle," to fight in World War I. In his absence she marries another, and he returns heartbroken to roam the world until he strikes it rich, buys the White House, and moves it next door to her home in hopes she will attend one of his wild parties. When a meeting is finally arranged and she proves to be a rather large housewife with five kittens pulling at her, Catsby quickly escapes in horror. The basic plotlines of the novel are followed here, except for the reversal at the end, the intent of which is to bring an element of reality to a highly romantic situation. The world seldom lives up to one's romantic expectations, which is, of course, a basic theme of the novel too, so the different ending does not change the message. In fact, all of the Tweety and Sylvester animated films are invested with an ironic reversal of nature, in that the weak and defenseless canary always uses his intelligence to outwit the larger but dumber cat.

There is one other unacknowledged adaptation of a Fitzgerald story to the comic book format, and this in a very surprising place. The story is "The Diamond as Big as the Ritz," a popular and frequently reprinted example of an atypical Fitzgerald narrative that departs from his usual realistic fiction of Jazz Age society and manners for fantasy, horror, and tall-tale exaggeration. Written in 1922 with an eye on the popular magazine market, it incorporated several formulaic elements from pulp fiction: an isolated island or place where the normal rules of civilized society are suspended; the hero unexpectedly endangered from a seemingly benign quarter; the hunting down of humans as prey; the retention of slavery as a legal system; the self-destruction of a corrupt community; and the arrival of government forces just in time to save the hero. The story also serves, however, as a complex allegory of the settling of the United States, the importance of money and social status in creating the nation, and the corruption of the democratic system by human greed. It may be read as a parable of the youthful American who awakens to find the American dream a cruel and rapacious hoax.

Sometime late in 1955, two aspiring young writers decided to collaborate on a variety of projects. One was William F. Nolan, who would have a distinguished career as the author of numerous popular fictional and nonfictional works in several fields but would be best known for his series of science fiction novels beginning with *Logan's Run* in 1967, and the subsequent film and television adaptations. The other was Charles Beaumont, who would write stories of horror, suspense, and science fiction for *Playboy* and other magazines, as well as numerous screenplays, before his untimely death in 1967 (Smith 539–41, 43–44). Their collaborative project was the script for a story to appear in the *Mickey Mouse* comic book series published for Walt Disney by Dell Publishing Company.

Recalling Fitzgerald's "The Diamond as Big as the Ritz," the kind of fantasy either would have found attractive given their own interests in popular fiction, Nolan and Beaumont wrote "The Mystery of Diamond Mountain," illustrated by the prolific Disney studio artist Paul Murry and published in the April–May 1956 issue of *Mickey Mouse*. Mickey and his friend Goofy are found driving across a desert landscape headed for a fishing lake. They are sideswiped by a passing car, and when they pursue it to claim damages, it disappears into a mountainside. They discover a hydraulic lift that takes them to the mountaintop, where they find a huge mountain and an automobile made, they think at first, of glass. The owner, Gerald Fitz—a reversal of the original author's name, of course—arrives to inform them that the mountain and the car are diamonds and that as the proprietor of the legendary Diamond Mountain, he is "the richest man in the world."

Mickey and Goofy find themselves locked up with numerous airplane pilots who have discovered the mountain by flying over and who have been captured by a netting device. As in the short story, these unwilling guests are treated royally to good food and luxurious quarters but lose their liberty. Micky and Goofy escape, release the other prisoners, and try to capture Gerald Fitz. In response, he blows up the mountain and eludes his pursuers, until Mickey snatches him from an airplane cockpit with his fishing line, bringing his fishing trip to a successful conclusion of sorts.[3]

Detail from "The Mystery of Diamond Mountain,"

Walt Disney's Comics, no. 612 (series 2), May 1997, page 5.
© Disney Enterprises, Inc. Reprinted by permission.

Nolan and Beaumont have stripped the story of most of its characters, its social setting, and its cultural and political complexity in order to focus on basic formulaic elements of popular fiction, especially the imprisonment and escape of the heroes. But by maintaining the idea of a mountain-sized diamond owned by one individual willing to enslave human beings to protect his wealth, it does become a story about greed and how people are willing to bend the rules of civilized society on behalf of material power. The message is more direct, but both stories share the same ideology, that materialism corrupts, and ownership of a "diamond as big as the Ritz" corrupts absolutely.

Mickey remains the moral agent of mainstream American values, as opposed to material corruption, although it is interesting to note that he yields to its influence at one point. When Gerald Fitz offers him a $500,000 diamond in payment of a forty-dollar debt, Mickey plans to leave with it in hand and, we assume, keep the change. This makes Mickey like the rest of us and, like many of Fitzgerald's characters, aware of the difficulties of moral behavior in a less-than-perfect world.

One way to look at these various reflections and uses of Fitzgerald in the comics is to consider them as commentaries on his fiction and his importance in American culture. They are comments of praise in that they recognize the integral part Fitzgerald's work plays in our culture and the centrality of a book like *The Great Gatsby* to an understanding of our literary heritage. They are compliments to the reader because they assume a prior knowledge of some of the classic writing to be found in our literature. They are acknowledgments of Fitzgerald, not just as an icon of a period of time in our history, but as a continuing influential force on the products of the American imagination. And, as in the case of Mickey Mouse's borrowing, they suggest that a provocative idea or plot development can have many striking uses in other stories and genres of American popular culture.[4]

Notes

1. The 1996 catalog of the Circa company of St. Paul, Minnesota, offers a "Gatsby Dress" on page 4 for $159: "Daisy Buchanan (or Zelda Sayre) would have loved this dress—inspired by the Jazz Age, insouciant and breezy."

2. A photograph of the book with inscription appear in "F. Scott Fitzgerald & Zelda Sayre."

3. The earliest identification of the source of the story and Nolan as adapter was by Joe Torcivia in his *Mickey Mouse Checklist*. Nolan and Beaumont were confirmed as the scriptwriters, and Murry as the artist, in the credits for the 1990 reprint issued by Gladstone Publishing. Editor Geoffrey Blum adds this note inside the back cover: "The jewelled cell in which Mickey finds himself is clearly based on Fitzgerald's 'room that was like a platonic conception of the ultimate prison—ceiling, floor, and all, it was lined with an unbroken mass of

Diamonds.' But consulting Fitzgerald's own copy of his story, we find that the word intended for this passage was *prism*, not *prison;* so a key scene in Nolan and Beaumont's script hinges on a typographical error." Blum's information comes from a footnote to the story in Bruccoli's edition of *The Short Stories.*

4. This essay could not have been completed without the thoughtfulness and invaluable assistance of Disney expert Chris Barat; Randy Scott of the Michigan State University Comic Art Collection; Marvin Humphrey of Nostalgia Plus; John Miller and Michael Dean of *Comics Buyer's Guide;* and Charles M. Schulz.

14

The "Two Civil Wars" of F. Scott Fitzgerald

FREDERICK WEGENER

In February 1940, less than a year before his death, F. Scott Fitzgerald sent Edwin Knopf—head of the scenario department at MGM, where Knopf had arranged the novelist's third lucrative screenwriting job some time earlier—a letter in which he proposed to script a film adapting some of his own fiction set during the Civil War. As he expatiated on this idea, Fitzgerald shared some intriguing and provocative reflections never cited, to my knowledge,[1] in the voluminous body of scholarship on his career:

> There are two Civil Wars and there are two kinds of Civil War novels. So far, pictures have been made only from one of them— the romantic, chivalric, Sir Walter Scott story like *Gone with the Wind, The Birth of a Nation,* the books of Thomas Nelson Page and Mary Johnson. But there is also the realistic type modeled primarily on Stendhal's great picture of Waterloo in *La Chartreuse de Parme,* Stephen Crane's *The Red Badge of Courage,* and the stories of Ambrose Bierce. This way of looking at war gives great scope for comedy . . . because it shows how small the individual is in the face of great events, how comparatively little he *sees,* and how little he can do even to save himself. The Great War has been successfully treated like this . . . the Civil War never. (*Letters* 597)

Returning to his initial premise, Fitzgerald's letter concludes with the remark, "I would like to write this story, with any encouragement. What do you think?" (598).

One can only wonder what a studio official even as literate as Knopf (previously an editor in his brother Alfred A. Knopf's distinguished publishing firm) could have made of such a remarkable digression in a letter otherwise devoted to the screenwriter's mundane task of pitching a story line. Presumably unencouraged, Fitzgerald abandoned his notion for such a film, and he nowhere articulated further or enlarged upon the sharply posited dichotomy around which his synopsis revolves. Yet it is striking that Fitzgerald, at such a late point in his career, should have paused to consider so earnestly and decisively the treatment of the Civil War in fiction and film. In fact, his carefully pondered remarks to Knopf reflect not only an extensive knowledge of imaginative and cinematic depictions of the conflict but also a pervasive fascination with the Civil War itself, a fascination evidenced throughout Fitzgerald's letters, novels, short stories, dramatic writing, and critical prose. Although an interest in the Civil War is routinely noted by his biographers, the depth and extent of that interest have yet to be thoroughly or fully measured, perhaps eclipsed by the intervening, equally profound impact of the Great War or by Fitzgerald's other historical preoccupations. Complicating any attempt at such an appraisal, however, is the fact that there turn out to have been "two Civil Wars" for Fitzgerald in more ways than one, or more than one pair of Civil Wars: not only the Civil War of romance and of realism, but also the Civil War in the North and in the South, the Civil War as tragic or farcical, the Civil War in fact and in memory, and the Civil War as actuality and as represented or reconstituted in writing. Indeed, although it seldom explicitly appears as a setting in his fiction, one may argue that this lifelong engagement with the Civil War— governed by the arresting image of duality formulated in his letter to Knopf—came to perform an essential role in the development not only of Fitzgerald's historical awareness but also of his experience of the writer's life and of his aesthetic understanding as a whole.

In his film proposal, Fitzgerald conflated elements of two stories, "The Night of Chancellorsville" (1934), in which a northern train en route to Virginia is intercepted by the Confederate surprise attack of May 1863, and "The End of Hate," published later in 1939 and involving "a Confederate private" who "is identified as a Mosby guerilla [sic] . . . and hung up by his thumbs." Such an incident, he explained to Knopf, "actually happened to a cousin of my father's in the Civil War" (*Letters* 597) and was the subject of one of the various Civil War anecdotes with which Edward Fitzgerald had continually entertained his young son. "Much of my early childhood in Minnesota," the novelist recalled around the same time, "was spent in asking him . . . questions" about details like the maneuvers of "Early's column" or of "Jeb Stewart's [sic] cavalry," for "the impression of the fames and the domains, the vistas and the glories of Maryland followed many a young man West after the Civil War and my father was of that number" (Bruccoli and Bryer 158).[2] Indeed, his father—whose forebears included the wife of Roger Brooke Taney, the U.S. Supreme Court justice responsible for the infamous decision in the Dred Scott case, and Mary Surratt, hanged as an accomplice in Lincoln's assassination—virtually transmitted the Civil War itself as a part of Fitzgerald's patrimony or pedigree. One notes, for example, the meditation prompted by an aunt's death, only a couple of months before Fitzgerald's own, in a letter to his cousin Ceci: "With Father, Uncle John and Aunt Elise a generation goes. I wonder how deep the Civil War was in them—that odd childhood on the border between the states with Grandmother and old Mrs. Scott and the shadow of Mrs. Suratt [sic]. What a sense of honor and duty—almost eighteenth century rather than Victoria" (*Letters* 419). Returning to the United States in 1931 to attend his father's funeral, Fitzgerald had offered Bert Barr a terser, albeit somewhat maudlin, sense of these connections: "This is Virginia with names like Manassas and Culpepper full of the Civil War + I've been thinking about my father again + it makes me sad like the past always does" (Bruccoli and Duggan 261). Just how inveterately the two evoked each other in Fitzgerald's mind, and how much his own lasting interest in the Civil War owed to its association with his father, may be gleaned from the concluding passage of an unpublished eulogy in which the novelist conveys some idea of the appetite that he had developed, as a boy, for Edward Fitzgerald's repertoire of Civil War stories: "I'm so tired of them all that I can't make them interesting. But maybe they are because I used to ask father to repeat & repeat & repeat" (*The Apprentice Fiction* 68).[3]

As the northern-born son of a man described by C. Hugh Holman as "an ardent pro-Confederate advocate" (Bryer, *The Short Stories* 53), moreover, Fitzgerald would have inherited from his father's storytelling a peculiarly ambiguous and forked apprehension of the Civil War. A native of a Maryland town that was "Southern in sympathies but isolated behind the Union lines" (Le Vot 5), the young Edward Fitzgerald had escorted rebel spies across the Potomac and witnessed one of the last gasps of the secession, the gathering of troops in General Jubal Early's futile attempt to capture the city of Washington. So impassioned a Confederate enthusiast had he become that in 1865, "When he was twelve," Fitzgerald once claimed in an interview, his father "felt that life was finished for him" and consequently "went West, as far away from the scenes of the Civil War as possible" (Bruccoli and Bryer 296). Thus devastated by its outcome, he bequeathed his Confederate allegiances to his son, who "had a lifelong preference for the defeated South" as a result, who "attended the southerner's northern university" and "married a southern belle," and who once composed a jeu d'esprit privately printed to resemble a newspaper report, "The True Story of Appomattox" (1934), in which Grant is said to have surrendered to Lee (Way 7; Fitzgerald, *The Apprentice Fiction* 35; Bruccoli and Bryer 236–37). It is therefore not surprising that Amory Blaine, Fitzgerald's alter ego in his first novel, should declare at one point that he was "for the Southern Confederacy" (*This Side of Paradise* 31), or that a later protagonist with a name like Henry Clay Marston, in "The Swimmers" (1929), is described as "a Virginian of the kind who are prouder of being Virginians than of being Americans. That mighty word printed across a continent was less to him than the memory of his grandfather, who . . . fought from Manassas to Appomattox" (*The Short Stories* 498).

In a more celebrated extension of these sentiments, Sally Carrol Happer takes her northern fiancé, in "The Ice Palace" (1920), to "one of her favorite haunts, the cemetery," in Tarleton, Georgia—"a very thinly disguised Montgomery, Alabama," which "had been the capital," as Holman reminds us, "of the Confederacy" (Fitzgerald, *The Short Stories* 52; Bryer, *The Short Stories* 57). After "pointing to . . . a thousand grayish-white crosses stretching in endless, ordered rows like the stacked arms of a battalion" and representing "the Confederate dead," Sally attempts to explain "how real it is to me . . . that old time that I've tried to have live in me. These were just men, unimportant evidently or they wouldn't have been 'unknown'; but they died for the most beautiful thing in the world—the dead South" (*The Short Stories* 53–54). As Fitzgerald remarked to a friend, such an exchange originated in an early encounter

in which he and Zelda Sayre "wandered into a graveyard" in Montgomery: "She told me I could never understand how she felt about the
Confederate graves, and I told her I understood so well that I could put
it on paper" (Bruccoli and Duggan 61). It was a capability that may be
attributed to what the writer had learned as a boy, of course, from
Edward Fitzgerald's youthful wartime sagas. Indeed, that "his father's
Civil War stories . . . made him a strong Confederate sympathizer," as
Matthew J. Bruccoli observes (*Some Sort of Epic Grandeur* 20), had become discernible much earlier in his career, as far back as Fitzgerald's
prep-school writings. Already in his third short story, "The Room with
the Green Blinds" (1911), Fitzgerald radically, if improbably, rewrites the
aftermath of the Civil War along such lines, as the narrator inherits from
his grandfather ("a Southern sympathizer" [Fitzgerald, *The Apprentice
Fiction* 43]) a house in Georgia in which John Wilkes Booth has lived
in hiding for decades after Lincoln's assassination. An earlier tale, "A
Debt of Honor" (1910), concerns a formerly delinquent Confederate
private who redeems himself with an act of bravery, as does Captain
Jim Holworthy, who returns to Virginia "the last soldier of a lost cause"
and displays the medals awarded "for a flag I took at Chickamauga, and
. . . for saving [General Braxton] Bragg from being shot at Shiloh," in
Coward (1913), a two-act drama beginning in 1861 and ending on the
day of Lee's surrender at Appomattox (Fitzgerald, *Fitzgerald's St. Paul
Plays* 80).

Given such a pattern in his writing, one easily risks exaggerating the
gravitation of Fitzgerald's own spirit, however, to what he once sardonically called "the undissolved Confederacy" (*The Short Stories* 143), or
the degree to which "son like father was imbued with the romance of
the lost Southern cause" (Donaldson, "Scott Fitzgerald's Romance" 15).[4]
Few devotees of the slaveholding South, for one thing, would have
noted, as Fitzgerald once did, that "the American capitol [*sic*] not being
in New York was of enormous importance in our history" because "it
had saved the Union from the mobs in sixty-three" (*Notebooks* 195),
the year of the deadly, racially motivated draft riots in New York City.
Certainly, when he searches for an embodiment of "the man who
comes at the moment of colossal transition in American history," as
Richard D. Lehan remarks (*F. Scott Fitzgerald* 162), it is a northern figure
like Grant or Lincoln whom Fitzgerald tends to select in works like

Tender Is the Night and *The Last Tycoon*. In perhaps the most compelling of the numerous details that modify one's sense of his fidelity to the antebellum South, "The End of Hate" concludes with "the shocking news" of Lincoln's assassination: "The strongest man had taken the burden upon his great shoulders, given life its impetus again even in the accident of his death" (*The Price Was High* 751). Rather than a merely reflexive adherence to the Confederacy, what one detects in Fitzgerald's writing, in Robert Roulston's words, are "two distinct . . . attitudes toward the South," which "epitomizes for him glamour and romance" even as "it often also represents sloth, inertia, failure" (Bloom 158). More than that, however, it is an awareness that there were "two Civil Wars" in an experiential sense—the war from the perspective of the North and of the South—that Fitzgerald derived in a particularly immediate way from his father's enthralling anecdotage.

Whatever Edward Fitzgerald's partisanship, his tales had certainly made the Civil War "a sacred setting in Scott's reveries" (Le Vot 20) by the time he began to write fiction at the St. Paul Academy. It is a measure of how firm a hold the Civil War already exerted on his imagination that two youthful writings set in the Confederate South should have inaugurated in his work, according to Scott Donaldson, the "theme of failure and success, and the thin line between them," that "was to become an obsession in the mature Fitzgerald's treatment of such protagonists as Jay Gatsby and Dick Diver" ("Scott Fitzgerald's Romance" 16). As two of his first four stories, along with "the most ambitious of his juvenile plays" (Yates 25), explicitly share a Civil War setting with "The End of Hate"—the last of his tales, apart from the Pat Hobby stories, to be published in his lifetime—Fitzgerald's literary career as a whole was decidedly framed by this abiding interest in the Civil War.

Its appeal throughout his fiction is legible, for one thing, in the names of so many of Fitzgerald's characters: "the Stonewall Jackson Abrams of Georgia" (49) among the guests at Gatsby's house parties; or "Mr. Jubal Early Robbins and valet" on the "passenger list" (*The Price Was High* 324) of a cruise ship in "On Your Own" (written after the death of Fitzgerald's father); or director Earl Brady in *Tender Is the Night* (1934) and Pat Brady, the narrator's film-producing father in *The Last Tycoon* (1941), both reminiscent of Mathew Brady; or Lincoln Peters in "Babylon Revisited" (1931) and the Lincolnesque "Abe North" in *Ten-*

der Is the Night; or "Abe" Danzer, commemorated by the narrator of "I Didn't Get Over" (1936) as "twenty-one and commanding a battalion" in World War I, in which "he rode a horse at the head of it and probably pretended to himself that he was Stonewall Jackson" (*Afternoon of an Author* 172); or, finally, Basil Duke Lee, who is "got up like a Southern planter of the old persuasion" in the abortive plan to kidnap Hubert Blair in "The Scandal Detectives" (1928) and who "was off like a flash, tearing at his Confederate whiskers as he ran" (*Basil and Josephine* 28, 30), once Blair's father calls the police. In the latter protagonist's name, more-over, Robert E. Lee's merges, as one scholar observes, with that of Basil Duke, an officer in the Kentucky cavalry unit named after its leader, the legendary Confederate guerrilla John Hunt "Raider" Morgan, whose descendants included Zelda Sayre; even Hubert Blair and another of Basil's cronies, Ripley Buckner, "also bear the surnames of Civil War general officers," identified as "Union Major General Francis Preston Blair" and "Confederate Lieutenant General Simon Bolivar Buckner" (Tamke, "Basil Duke Lee" 231, 233).[5]

Such details, among others, indicate Fitzgerald's occasional willing-ness to handle not only his father's southern loyalties but Civil War lore itself with surprising irreverence and levity, reflecting the coexistence of the "sacred" Civil War forever enshrined in his imagination and a Civil War indecorously, often jocularly belittled. The habit emerges as early as "The Offshore Pirate" (1920), in Toby Moreland's remark upon noticing one of the lemons that Ardita Farnam has carelessly discarded on board her uncle's yacht: " 'Hm,' he said. 'Stonewall Jackson claimed that lemon-juice cleared his head. Your head feel pretty clear?' " (*The Short Stories* 76). (It is in "lemon-juice ink" that Basil and Ripley in-scribe the title page of "The Book of Scandal," the composition book in which they secretly "set down such deviations from rectitude on the part of their fellow citizens as had reached their ears," and which is later "discovered . . . beneath the trapdoor" by "a janitor" and "definitely entombed at last beneath a fair copy of Lincoln's Gettysburg Address" [*Basil and Josephine* 16, 17].) Another tale in the Basil and Josephine se-quence begins with a description of "the State Fair" in Minneapolis–St. Paul, "one of the most magnificent in America" and boasting, "as a compromise between the serious and the trivial, a grand exhibition of fireworks, culminating in a representation of the Battle of Gettysburg"

(*Basil and Josephine* 36–37). Indeed, the next evening, "A few Union troops were moving cannon about in preparation for the Battle of Gettysburg" just as Basil joins Gladys Van Schellinger in the grandstands after deserting his own companions, whom he then sees parading "along the now empty and brightly illuminated race track" in "a short but monstrous procession, a sort of Lilliputian burlesque of the wild gay life" incongruously juxtaposed to the Civil War reenactment under way on the fairgrounds (51, 52).

More than once, Fitzgerald stages a playful rapprochement of North and South or introduces a gimmick comically resolving the hostilities between them. "In a burst of glory, to the alternate strains of Dixie and the Star-Spangled Banner," just after "the procession" of Basil's friends passes by, for example, "the Battle of Gettysburg ended" as he returns to Gladys in the family limousine (*Basil and Josephine* 52–53). In "A Patriotic Short" (1940), Pat Hobby is "called in to the studio" that employs him as a screenwriter "to work upon an humble short . . . based on the career of General Fitzhugh Lee who fought for the Confederacy and later for the U.S.A. against Spain—so it would offend neither North nor South" (*Pat Hobby Stories* 116). As "Ben Brown, head of the shorts department," advises Hobby on the assignment, Fitzgerald derisively invokes the well-known, ideologically valuable role of the Spanish-American War in consolidating the post-Reconstruction reunion of the country: "We don't want any new angles, Pat. We've got a good story. Fitzhugh Lee was a dashing cavalry commander. He was a nephew of Robert E. Lee and we want to show him at Appomattox, pretty bitter and all that. And then show how he became reconciled—we'll have to be careful because Virginia is swarming with Lees—and how he finally accepts a U.S. commission from President McKinley" (117).

Of course it is in Fitzgerald's Hollywood fiction, more than anywhere else in his work, that the Civil War is shorn of its sacrosanct aura, as in the illustrative example cited by Monroe Stahr in defining "a routine" to his new screenwriter George Boxley: "It means an act. . . . Georgie Jessel talks about 'Lincoln's Gettysburg routine'" (*Love of the Last Tycoon* 33). At a more famous moment of *The Last Tycoon*, Fitzgerald turns again to the Civil War in order to capture, through another historically deflating image, "Hollywood's appropriation of the past for its entertainment purposes" (Sklar 336) as well as what Robert A. Mar-

tin calls "the shallowness of the Hollywood mentality" (Bryer, Margolies, and Prigozy 151). Observing the extras at rest over lunch in the
studio commissary, the Danish Prince Agge, touring the studio as a
guest of the producers, "saw Abraham Lincoln . . . sitting here, his legs
crossed, his kindly face fixed on a forty cent dinner, including dessert,
his shawl wrapped around him as if to protect himself from the erratic
air-cooling" (*Love of the Last Tycoon* 48). As the prince "stared" at the
costumed actor, in what becomes an instant of ironically epiphanic recognition, "Lincoln suddenly raised a triangle of pie and jammed it in
his mouth" (49). With this shrunken caricature of "the living presence
from the past of American history, the great and good Abraham Lincoln,
father of the new nation state," Prince Agge's "glimpse into the inner
meaning of things in this new society, this man-made nation, is shattered"; as Robert Giddings cogently argues, "In the United States . . .
the historic and the humdrum are one and the same" (Lee 91).

The sort of desecration epitomized by Prince Agge's vision, in an image
through which the most revered Civil War icon "is brought down to the
entertainment level of the movies" (Sklar 336),[6] serves Fitzgerald as a
particularly dispiriting sign of the extent of the nation's decline in the
time that had elapsed since the Civil War. Embodying a grievous division of the country into a pair of warring halves, and itself divided in
two even more variously than Fitzgerald suggests in his letter to Knopf,
the Civil War thus also had the effect of bisecting American history,
severing all that preceded from all that followed such a cataclysmic
event. "In my romantic days," as Fitzgerald would recall in 1927, "I tried
to conjure up the Princeton of Aaron Burr, Philip Freneau, James Madison and Light Horse Harry Lee, to tie on, so to speak, to the eighteenth
century, to the history of man. But the chain parted at the Civil War,
always the broken link in the continuity of American life" (*Afternoon of
an Author* 72).[7] It remained also the point of disconnection from which
one could trace a long national dwindling illustrated rather graphically
in a tale like "The Curious Case of Benjamin Button" (1922). Born in
1860, just before "the outbreak of the Civil War," of parents whose relations "entitled them to membership in that enormous peerage which
largely populated the Confederacy," Benjamin emerges from the womb
"an old man apparently about seventy years of age" (*The Short Stories*
166, 160, 162). Eerily inverting the normal human life span, his "aging"

parallels that of the nation in what becomes Fitzgerald's strange allegorical reading of its postbellum history—as if America itself had begun gradually but inexorably regressing to a kind of embryonic insentience over the decades that followed the Civil War.[8]

The gulf opened up by this emblem of national brokenness separates the present, thus diminished and fallen, from a historical past often mythically glorified by Fitzgerald's characters. In his hotel room back in Montgomery, Alabama, Charlie Clayhorne in "Diagnosis" (1932) mournfully registers his sense of the ensuing transformations in American life as he "looked from the window at a proud, white-pillared Acropolis that a hundred years ago had been the center of a plantation and now housed a row of stores," which "made him feel the profound waves of change that had already washed this country," including "the desperate war that had rendered the plantation house obsolete, the industrialization that had spoiled the easy-going life centering around the old courthouse" (*The Price Was High* 410). Elsewhere in Fitzgerald's fiction, that receding and superseded past is obscured even in the effort to preserve it. When Anthony Patch and Gloria Gilbert, in *The Beautiful and Damned* (1922), make "an ill-advised trip to General Lee's old home at Arlington" (165) while on their honeymoon, "a swarm of women and children" who "were leaving a trail of peanut-shells through the halls" (166) elicits from Gloria a response that becomes more than merely another nostalgic evocation of the "lost cause" of the Old South:

> "Do you think they've left a breath of 1860 here? This has become a thing of 1914. . . . It's just because I love the past that I want this house to look back on its glamourous moment of youth and beauty, and I want its stairs to creak as if to the footsteps of women with hoop skirts and men in boots and spurs. . . . I want it to smell of magnolias instead of peanuts and I want my shoes to crunch on the same gravel that Lee's boots crunched on. There's no beauty without poignancy and there's no poignancy without the feeling that it's going, men, names, books, houses—bound for dust—mortal. . . ." (166–67)

Through this "symbolic scene," as Robert Emmet Long remarks, Fitzgerald "comments upon the marriage of Anthony and Gloria at its outset, with the intimation that it, too, is doomed, that its glimpsed radiance will be cheapened in time, like the national monument that is strewn with tourists' garbage," and that it "forms a lengthy history of corruption by the world in which they had sought to keep alive their sense of romantic possibility" (*The Achieving of "The Great Gatsby"* 56). Theirs, however, is not the only such "history," for its setting in a Civil War landmark now reduced to a vulgar recreational attraction clearly widens the scope of Gloria's lament, in a measure of how far the nation had deteriorated and decayed between 1860 and 1914.

No better personification of this crucial historical shift can be found in Fitzgerald's work than the Virginian grandfather of John T. Unger's schoolmate in "The Diamond as Big as the Ritz" (1922), published in the same year as *The Beautiful and Damned,* and thus at a time when such vast transitions were apparently much on the novelist's mind. "At the close of the Civil War," according to his grandson's account, Fitz-Norman Culpeper Washington "was a twenty-five-year-old Colonel with a played-out plantation and about a thousand dollars in gold" (*The Short Stories* 192), which he invests in an expedition that leads to his discovery of the diamond mine out west. In a sinister version of the sort of reversal facetiously performed in "The True Story of Appomattox," Colonel Washington—having "selected two dozen of the most faithful blacks" from among his former slaves before departing for the frontier— "sent South for his younger brother" after reaching the diamond mine "and put him in charge of his colored following—darkies who had never realized that slavery was abolished. To make sure of this, he read them a proclamation that he had composed, which announced that General [Bedford] Forrest had reorganized the shattered Southern armies and defeated the North in one pitched battle" (192, 193). Such a ruse, insidious as it is, permits Fitz-Norman to disappear for two years while marketing his diamonds in Europe, from which "he returned to America in 1868" a vastly rich man. "From 1870 until his death in 1900," as a result, "the history of Fitz-Norman Washington," reflecting the "re-enslavement" of blacks after abolition (and overlapping the nation's own history following the Civil War), "was a long epic in gold" (194). Nor is such a trajectory limited in Fitzgerald's fiction to one or another enterprising Confederate veteran. Early in *The Beautiful and Damned,* Adam J. Patch, Anthony's grandfather—as if mirroring Fitz-Norman Washington's Gilded Age fortunes—"left his father's farm in

Tarrytown early in sixty-one to join a New York cavalry regiment," then "came home from the war a major, charged into Wall Street, and amid much fuss, fume, applause, and ill will . . . gathered to himself some seventy-five million dollars" by the time "he was fifty-seven years old" (4).

As these brisk foreshortenings of larger historical developments in the United States would indicate, Fitzgerald not only "believed that the turning point in America came after the Civil War," in Lehan's words, but also located "in the Civil War a destiny that was to end one order and to establish another—that of the commercial and industrial interests—the new financiers" (*F. Scott Fitzgerald* 137), dividing such a world from its predecessor just as the Civil War had divided the nation itself.[9] Yet the failure of such developments to obliterate the historical past entirely generates another recurrent bifurcation of the Civil War in Fitzgerald's writing. Having long since accumulated his wealth, Adam J. Patch "determined, after a severe attack of sclerosis, to consecrate the remainder of his life to the moral regeneration of the world," in "a campaign which went on through fifteen years" until it "had grown desultory; 1861 was creeping up slowly on 1895; his thoughts ran a great deal on the Civil War, somewhat on his dead wife and son, almost infinitesimally on his grandson Anthony" (*The Beautiful and Damned* 4–5). This resurfacing of the Civil War, corresponding psychologically to the regression undergone by Benjamin Button, has similar consequences in the case of Jerry Frost's eighty-eight-year-old father, Horatio, in one of Fitzgerald's next works, *The Vegetable* (1923). "*A Civil War pension has kept him quasi-independent,*" according to one of the stage directions, for although "*probably Jerry's superior in initiative,*" his father "*did not prosper, and during the past twenty years his mind has been steadily failing*" (18, 17–18), cluttered with recollections of the same period that preoccupies Adam Patch. Asked to speculate on who the nominee is likely to be in the upcoming presidential election, for example, Horatio replies, "I should say that Lincoln was our greatest President"; later, in an equally startling non sequitur, he informs his listeners, "I was twenty-seven years old when the war broke out," incoherently reverting to his participation in a long-ago conflict that randomly displaces his memory of far more recent events (19, 64).

The nation's great sectional clash thus also divided itself, in Fitzgerald's handling, into the Civil War as experienced and the Civil War as remembered, an often ineffaceably lingering Civil War that comes to occupy the foreground of even an elderly veteran's mind. The operation of "two Civil Wars" in this respect is clearly apparent even when the war itself can be recalled only vicariously, as in "Her Last Case" (1934), one of the more haunting of Fitzgerald's rarely studied later tales, inspired by several visits in the summer of 1934 to Welbourne, the antebellum mansion in Virginia tenanted by a cousin of Maxwell Perkins's.[10] Much as Josie Pilgrim "was going to be a nurse in a wartime hospital" before inadvertently straying behind Confederate lines in "The End of Hate" (and much as many other northern women had served as nurses during the Civil War), Bette Weaver journeys from Maryland to Virginia "in the capacity of trained nurse" to a southern lawyer suffering from the aftereffects of shell shock in World War I (*The Price Was High* 740, 572). As she awaits her patient's chauffeur after arriving at "an old town" with "an old church, an old courthouse, old frame or stone houses," Bette notices "over the main street . . . the usual iron sign," reminded that "there had been such signs all along the road" in Virginia: "HERE A SQUADRON OF STUART'S CAVALRY FOUGHT A FIERCE ENGAGEMENT WITH—" (571). Such memorials to the Civil War serve as an appropriate preparation for her experience in Ben Dagonet's home, which he introduces to Bette, during their first consultation, as "a quite historic house. Do you see that windowpane with the name scratched on it? Well, that was made by a diamond ring belonging to the Gallant Pelham—made on the morning of the day he was killed. You can see the year—1864. You know who the Gallant Pelham was? He commanded Stuart's horse artillery at twenty-three. He was my hero when I was a boy" (576).[11]

Summoning her after he indulges his tendency to walk about the house in the middle of the night, Dagonet reassures Bette, "Don't get afraid of me; these are just the perambulations of old stock—my father wandered and my grandfather wandered. He is the Confederate brigadier over your head. My grandfather used to wander around cursing [General James] Longstreet for not using his flanks at Gettysburg. I used to wonder why he wandered, but now I'm not surprised. I've been weeping a lot over a long time because they sent us up replacements, in 1918, that didn't know a trench mortar from a signal platoon" (577–78). Literally retracing his grandfather's footsteps on what he calls "my

nightly marches" (575), as if reincarnating a venerable Civil War fore-
bear, Dagonet implies that his experience of the conflict in which he
himself was wounded serves primarily to illuminate its overshadowing
predecessor. "After wars," he explains further to Bette, "everything goes
out of the men who fought them—everything except the war itself, but
that goes on and on forever. Don't you see this house is full of war?
Grandmother made it a hospital, and sometimes the Virginia women got
here to see their husbands, but the women from farther south usually
came too late, she used to say" (578).

In effect, Bette's presence—that of a nurse come to treat one victim
of later warfare—has returned the house to the role it assumed during
the Civil War, with which World War I is almost indistinguishably identified by Dagonet, who instructs Bette to listen as "the great front door
swung back slowly on its hinges and the hall was suddenly full of young
faces and voices" from the vanished past: "Can't you see it now? These
were my people, bred to the sword, perished by the sword! Can't you
hear?" (578). Later, Bette herself briefly appears to participate in her patient's hallucination under the influence of a Civil War text. "Back in
uniform" once she's bathed after being caught in a rainstorm while on
a ride with Dagonet, "Bette went out into the library adjoining, and
pulled a dusty volume of Pollard's *War Between the States* from the stacks
and sat down to read."[12] As the storm outside intensifies, "Perhaps the
very persistence of the thunder made Bette's hearing more acute in the
intervals—or perhaps the position of her chair was in line with some
strange acoustic of the house, for she began to be conscious of voices,
voices not far away" (583). Mistaken for those of her host's ancestors
in the war about which she is reading, the voices turn out to belong
to Dagonet's daughter and ex-wife, overheard in an encounter that
convinces Bette to remain there out of devotion to her patient. Not
coincidentally, it was in the middle of a Civil War vignette about his
grandfather ("back in '62"), during their ride before the rainstorm, that
Dagonet had expressed his love to Bette, who wonders in response, "Oh,
this is impossible. Am I falling in love with this man, this ruin of a
man?" (581).

What has "ruined" Ben Dagonet is a delusional resurrection, stimu-
lated or provoked by his experience in the Great War, of his own Confederate lineage. Perhaps nowhere else in his fiction does Fitzgerald en-

act more dramatically this branching of the Civil War into the event itself and the individual memory of that event, a spectral, obsessively recollected Civil War that "goes on and on forever," eventually overtaking World War I in the mind of someone like Dagonet, eternally "present" although more and more remote in time. In its tenacity, this vestigial Civil War induces in such characters, moreover, a condition aptly mimicking the nation's own self-polarization, which thus seems to have endured in Fitzgerald's imaginative life as a commanding prototype of certain irremediable inner fractures or emotional antagonisms. The instabilities that emerge help to form yet another of Fitzgerald's "two Civil Wars," the crisis itself and the strife within the minds of those characters either harmlessly or pathologically fixated on the Civil War, whether as an element of one's own life (as in the case of Adam J. Patch or Horatio Frost), or of one's ancestral heritage (as in that of Ben Dagonet), or even of American history as a whole. Here, surely, one finds a key to perhaps the best-known residue of the Civil War in Fitzgerald's work, associating Ulysses S. Grant with a figure like the psychiatrist Dick Diver, whose wife's schizophrenia ultimately functions as a counterpart to what might be called the devastating historical disorder that pitted North against South, a cleavage that had endowed America itself with a kind of split personality.[13]

Nor are these the most immediate or visceral ways in which the divisive internecine violence resulting from that breach recasts itself in Fitzgerald's work as a second "civil war," in the form of psychic turmoil or personal discord. Given what John Kuehl has called "his tendency to identify autobiographical and historical events" (Fitzgerald, *The Apprentice Fiction* 35), Fitzgerald appears, for example, to have experienced his increasingly combative marriage—uniting "the brilliant success of the North" and "the golden beauty of the South," as he once dubbed himself and Zelda Sayre—first as a kind of resolution, and then as a reenactment, of the conflict that had played since childhood such a formative role in shaping his consciousness. A similar transposition characterizes those tales that attempt to overcome the dissension of North and South by contriving the alliance of a northern protagonist and a woman through whom the Old South is revivified—not only Sally Carrol Happer in "The Ice Palace," but also the significantly named Ailie Calhoun from another of Fitzgerald's Tarleton stories, "The Last of the Belles"

(1929), in which her presence brings to mind "the suggested background of devoted fathers, brothers and admirers stretching back into the South's heroic age. . . . There were notes in her voice that ordered slaves around, that withered up Yankee captains" (*The Short Stories* 450). More than that, it may be said that Fitzgerald, who, C. Hugh Holman suggests, "saw himself as torn between the vigorous, successful, and aggrandizing North and an ancestral dignity, grace, and good manners associated with the South" (Bryer, *The Short Stories* 53), found a replica of the Civil War in the unending effort to balance or reconcile the northern and southern components of his own identity. "This sense of two selves clearly at war with each other," and embodying "the contrast of North and South," according to Holman (54, 55), stems from what might be termed Fitzgerald's internalization of the chasm that had sundered two different regions of the country. The inner rift resulting from such a process, and accentuated by the marital strife in which he later found himself embroiled, psychologically mirrored the effects of that great national fissure, in what John Kuehl has astutely called "a private conflict with consequences not unlike those Fitzgerald attributed to the Civil War" (Bryer, *The Short Stories* 170).

More than a conventionally defining benchmark in American history, the Civil War thus became on many other levels an essential reference point for Fitzgerald, animating his imagination as vigorously (if perhaps not as grandiloquently or programmatically) as that of, say, Faulkner or Glasgow among his literary contemporaries. "Of all wars," as Kuehl has observed, "the American Civil War exercised the most profound influence on him," becoming "even more important than Boom and Depression or, for that matter, other temporal obsessions like the American Revolution and World War I" (Fitzgerald, *The Apprentice Fiction* 34–35; Bryer, *The Short Stories* 169). One notes Charlie Clayhorne's encounter, in "Diagnosis," with "Mr. Chevril, the Confederate veteran who had lived at the hotel for fifty years," and who draws a defiant contrast between the impact of the Civil War and the human costs of the Great Depression up north: "I don't think you fellas know what hard times are. . . . When we got back here from Appomattox Court House in '65, I had a mule from the horse artillery, and Jim Mason had one plow that [Union general George] Stoneman hadn't smashed, and we had a crop planted before we dared think how we'd eat next winter. And we did a sight less hollerin' than you see in these Yankee newspapers" (*The Price Was High* 410). World War I similarly fades, in the beliefs of Fitzgerald's characters, by comparison to the Civil War. Having "thought how much easier patriotism had been to a homogeneous race, how much easier it would have been to fight . . . as the Confederacy fought," Amory Blaine eventually derides "the popular heroes of the war" in Europe like Pershing or Sergeant York after enlisting himself: "Even Foch hasn't half the significance of Stonewall Jackson" (*This Side of Paradise* 139, 199). Elsewhere in Fitzgerald's fiction, the Civil War is said to have exceeded in savagery the ravages of the Great War. Visiting the memorial on the site of a French battlefield at Thiepval with Rosemary Hoyt and Abe North, who remarks that "General Grant invented this kind of battle at Petersburg in sixty-five," Dick Diver denies such a campaign the romanticizing glamour that he attaches to World War I: "No, he didn't—he just invented mass butchery. This kind of battle . . . was a love battle—there was a century of middle-class love spent here. This was the last love battle" (*Tender Is the Night* 57).

Whatever its value as historical analysis, Dick's meditation concerning the nature of each calamity implies another "civil war," one that Fitzgerald recognized in the battle over the place to be assigned to the Civil War in history, and its status in the collective memory of the nation. As one might surmise from his letter to Knopf, Fitzgerald's work evinces an opinionated and carefully discriminating familiarity with a wide body of writing about the Civil War. Just how early he had begun to supplement his father's Civil War anecdotes with extensive and enthusiastic reading on the subject is clear from the "ledger" that Fitzgerald started compiling around 1920. According to entries dated January 1902 and March 1908, respectively, Fitzgerald "remembers Jack Butler who had two or three fascinating books about the Civil War" and notes "the thrill of . . . the 'Raiding with Morgan' series in their crisp tissue wrappers," referring to the popular narrative of Byron Archibald Dunn in which he first read of Zelda's ancestor, General Basil Duke (*Ledger* 156, 162; Tamke, "Basil Duke Lee" 232–33). As a sign of his ability to distinguish among such miscellaneous sources of information, one is reminded of the northern prostitute who narrates "The Night of Chancellorsville," in which she is "traveling . . . from Philadelphia to join

Hooker's Army—a dark side of the Civil War which did not find its way into the idealized history books so dear to the young Fitzgerald" (Petry 182). With such a grounding in the historical record, Fitzgerald evidently felt qualified, as an adult reader, to issue the sort of pronouncements that occur when he suggests a list of books to an old college friend and implores him, "For God's sake, order these right away and for good jazz I append . . . [A. H.] Burne's *Lee, Grant and Sherman,*" before indulging in some rather pungent commentary on "Hayes' [*sic*] book on Lincoln," denoting either *Lincoln and the Civil War in the Diaries and Letters of John Hay* or the biography that Hay coauthored with John Nicolay (*Letters* 581). It seems inevitable that Fitzgerald, late into his first night at Welbourne, should have found himself "reading an old account of Stuart's battles for an hour or so" (*Letters* 250), much as Bette Weaver, in the story based on such a visit, "sat down to read" a book like one of Pollard's volumes about the Civil War. Likewise, Englishman George Boxley, bristling under Monroe Stahr's demands, "knew he could sit . . . raging at Stahr, but he had been reading Lord Charnwood" (*Love of the Last Tycoon* 107), whose classic 1916 biography of Lincoln yields insights that place the film producer in a more sympathetic light.[14]

The wealth of material that Fitzgerald absorbed on such a convulsive historical trauma would have alerted him to another of the polarities around which his understanding of the Civil War revolves. Differentiating the series of events that transpired in the distant past from the recapitulation of those events by chroniclers and memoirists of the Civil War, this additional antithesis in fact underlies the distinction postulated in Fitzgerald's letter to Knopf. To the "two Civil Wars" may be correlated not only "two kinds of Civil War novels," as he would put it, but two modes of writing about the Civil War: the documentary or the "factual" on the one hand, and the "creative" or fictive on the other. That he saw the two as unavoidably entangled is conveyed in a letter in which Fitzgerald, only a year before presenting Knopf with his screenwriting proposal, described to his daughter Scottie his work on the film adaptation of *Gone with the Wind,* "a good novel" but "not very original, in fact leaning heavily on . . . all that has been written on the Civil War" (*Letters* 49–50).

Such an appraisal reflected a command on Fitzgerald's part not only of the historical and biographical literature but also of the sporadic imaginative response that the Civil War had continued to provoke up to his own time. By contrast to his remarks on *Gone with the Wind,* one notes the extravagance with which Fitzgerald welcomed a work like John Peale Bishop's stark, unjustly forgotten Civil War novella "The Cellar" (1931), "one of the best war things I've ever read—right up with the very best of Crane and Bierce—intelligent, beautifully organized and written—oh, it moved me and delighted me" (*Letters* 359). So impressive did Fitzgerald find the work that he amplified his comments in recommending it to Maxwell Perkins, declaring again that, "to my great astonishment, as a document of the Civil War, it's right up to Bierce and Stephen Crane—beautifully written, thrilling, and water tight as to construction and interest" (*Letters* 211). Although Perkins declined to publish "The Cellar," Fitzgerald later informed him, "I am sending you . . . a sister story of the novelette you refused, which together with the first one and three shorter ones will form [Bishop's] Civil-War-civilian-in-invaded-Virginia book [published as *Many Thousands Gone*], a simply grand idea and a new, rich field" (*Letters* 219).

Of the "two kinds of Civil War novels" that Fitzgerald would later describe to Knopf, Bishop's clearly belonged to "the realistic type" that his friend located in the work of writers like Bierce and Crane, a structurally and stylistically expert rendering worthy of *In the Midst of Life* or *The Red Badge of Courage* (a model for Fitzgerald, as for so many of his contemporaries, of fiction writing about not only the Civil War but warfare itself).[15] To be sure, even as he commends "The Cellar" in largely expressive terms, Fitzgerald cannot refrain from correcting Bishop on various inaccuracies, "which contrast sharply with your profound knowledge of the Civil War in story" (*Letters* 361). Yet his remark encapsulates a striking opposition in Fitzgerald's critical vocabulary, between the sort of knowledge exemplified in the work of historians or biographers and what might be called a knowledge of the Civil War uniquely derived from the imagination, knowledge recorded or embodied "in story": that is, in a distinct and autonomous form of narrative standing alongside the historical narratives on which a Civil War novelist initially relies.

Such judgments illustrate the manner in which the Civil War as an object of historical and imaginative representation constituted one of Fitzgerald's perennial concerns as a writer. If anything, he found the

Civil War practically duplicated in the sphere of representation, in an ongoing contest not only between the "two kinds of Civil War novels" that he defined to Knopf but between fictional as opposed to historical or reportorial incarnations of the war. It was with such nuances in mind that Fitzgerald, assailing the proletarian critic Kyle Crichton ("Robert Forsyte") for what he called "such condescension toward the creative life," specifically cited "his comments on fiction which would make any old 1864 copy of Leslie's [*Frank Leslie's Illustrated Newspaper,* renowned for its pictorial coverage of the Civil War] more humanly valuable than *The Red Badge of Courage*" (*Notebooks* 160). As Fitzgerald inserts himself into this "civil war" between competing representations, moreover, the very representability of the Civil War as an aesthetic question became closely intertwined with his sense of the writer's vocation. The degree to which the two became associated in his mind may be inferred from Fitzgerald's searching comments on Bishop's later novel, *Act of Darkness* (1935): "From the wildest fantasy . . . you went (and I was all for it) to the most complete realism, taking in passing the Civil War. The part taken in passing came closest to being your natural field. *You jumped over it too quickly*—I don't mean the war in particular—I mean the blend. *Because you're two people*—you are not yet your work as in a sense I am mine" (*Letters* 367). It is revealing that he should have expressed this inseparability of himself from his work while responding to another novelist's treatment of the Civil War, which composed in so many respects Fitzgerald's own "natural field," the "part taken in passing" again and again, often tangentially evoked and yet nonetheless ubiquitous, looming ineluctably in the background of his fiction.

Ultimately, to that extent, the challenge of imaginatively representing the Civil War typified in Fitzgerald's eyes the perils and ordeals of imaginative representation itself. When he attempts to convey the anguish and torment of the writing life, it is not coincidentally a figure of the Civil War whom Fitzgerald pairs with even the most celebrated of literary predecessors, as in a letter in which he describes to Scottie what he calls "the thing that lies behind all great careers, from Shakespeare's to Abraham Lincoln's, and as far back as there are books to read—the sense that life is essentially a cheat and its conditions are those of defeat, and that the redeeming things are not 'happiness and pleasure' but the deeper satisfactions that come out of struggle" (*Letters* 96). Shakespeare's career and Lincoln's, but presumably his own as well; for the struggle is not only that of experience but also, of course, that of writing, a struggle to which Fitzgerald finds a powerful equivalent in the historic struggle dominating the imaginations of figures like Lincoln and Grant.[16] Why else would he have declared to H. L. Mencken, regarding the differences between them as writers and individuals, that "there are times when it is nice to think that there are other wheel horses pulling the whole load of human grief + dispair [sic], + trying to the best of their ability to mould it into form—the thing that made Lincoln sit down in Jeff Davis' chair in Richmond and ask the guards to leave him alone there for a minute" (Bruccoli and Duggan 422)? It is this self-identification with an emblematic luminary of the Civil War that informs a familiar passage from Fitzgerald's last novel, in which George Boxley "recognized that Stahr like Lincoln was a leader carrying on a long war on many fronts; almost single-handed he had moved pictures sharply forward through a decade, to a point where the content of the 'A productions' was wider and richer than that of the stage. Stahr was an artist only as Mr. Lincoln was a general, perforce and as a layman" (*Love of the Last Tycoon* 107).

Boxley's perceptions here complete a pattern that emerges earlier in the novel, as the daily rushes viewed by Stahr in the projection room "were reports from the battle-line," forming one of the exercises that "made his work . . . hard to describe as the plans of a general—where the psychological factors become too tenuous and we end by merely adding up the successes and failures" (52, 28). Likening Stahr to Lincoln, artist to general (linked in role and vision), such passages also communicate Fitzgerald's sense of the artist *as* general, as combatant in the domain of representation, itself experienced as an arena of carnage, imaginative stratagems, and psychic bloodshed.[17] "To me," Fitzgerald once declared to a friend, "the conditions of an artistically creative life are so arduous that I can only compare to them the duties of a soldier in wartime" (*Letters* 435); and, on the basis of such a comparison, one observes throughout his writing a series of equally salient analogies by which Fitzgerald invariably ties himself, as writer and artist, to one or another Civil War personality (of both North and South). Referring to Douglass Southall Freeman's four-volume *Robert E. Lee* (1934–35), while offering Perkins minute specifications as to the arrangement of the abortive

Basil and Josephine volume, he acknowledges, "in the pressure of doing many things at once I am slipping into the old psychology that if I don't do it myself it will be all wrong. . . . This Lee biography is shooting me in that direction. Again and again his weakness in trusting others, when he carried only the main scheme in his head, is emphasized" (Kuehl and Bryer 212). The value and vitality that he attached to such parallels certainly seem to have been clear to Perkins, as one can tell from a letter of thanks that Fitzgerald sent him in 1936: "I enjoyed reading *General Grant's Last Stand* [by Horace Green], and was conscious of your particular reasons for sending it to me. It is needless to compare the difference in force of character between myself and General Grant, the number of words that he could write in a year, and the absolutely virgin field which he exploited with the experiences of a four-year life under the most dramatic of circumstances" (*Letters* 269). One notes here the aestheticizing language in which Fitzgerald discusses the Civil War, concerned as he is not so much with Grant the martial figure as with Grant the writer groping for a way to represent in prose an unprecedented catastrophe that provided him with uniquely valuable material.

A "general" in both senses of the term, having militarily participated in the war and then waged the very different (although not unrelated) battle of trying to write about it, Grant encompassed one of the binaries that always conditioned Fitzgerald's apprehension of the Civil War. And, even as he stressed the differences between them in writing to Perkins, one might do well to ponder the force of this underlying self-association on Fitzgerald's part with Grant the financially ruined former war hero, broken and gravely ill, and hastening throughout the last year of his life to complete a piece of writing that would represent his final triumph. It is perhaps in this sense that one may best appreciate the passages identifying such a figure with Dick Diver, whose emergence is synopsized in an account that "has the ring of a biography, without the satisfaction of knowing that the hero, like Grant, lolling in his general store in Galena"—the Illinois town where Grant worked for the year that preceded the outbreak of the Civil War—"is ready to be called to an intricate destiny" (*Tender Is the Night* 118). In this observation, Fitzgerald seems to be wistfully contemplating his own mission, and the triangular bond connecting him, through Diver, with Grant is strengthened in the novel's famous reference to the "last letter" that Nicole receives from her ex-husband, in which "he told her that he was practising in Geneva, New York. . . . Perhaps, so she liked to think, his career was biding its time, again like Grant's in Galena" (315).[18]

Significantly, Grant is again poignantly invoked in this context, along with two favorite icons of the Confederacy, in the later tale, "Afternoon of an Author" (1936). Having left his apartment after abandoning work on "a magazine story that had become so thin in the middle that it was about to blow away," the protagonist of this frankly autobiographical sketch "stood carefully on the street corner waiting for the light to change. . . . On the bus corner under the trees it was green and cool and he thought of Stonewall Jackson's last words: 'Let us cross over the river and rest under the shade of the trees.' Those Civil War leaders seemed to have realized very suddenly how tired they were—Lee shriveling into another man, Grant with his desperate memoir-writing at the end" (*Afternoon of an Author* 178, 179). Fitzgerald's own desperate final attempts at writing and his sense of fatigue and depletion toward the premature end of his career are vividly conjured in his unnamed alter ego's ruminations about three principal figures of the Civil War. It was the same sense of doubt and uncertainty that Fitzgerald had in mind in perhaps the grimmest of these confessions, as he asked Perkins, during the last year of his life, "Do you remember when I accused you of sending me the memoirs of General Grant because you thought I was a failure?" (Bruccoli and Duggan 577). In this respect, as Lehan aptly notes, "The story of U.S. Grant—the man who came back after a bitter defeat— seems to have touched Fitzgerald deeply" and "appealed to his romantic conviction that success, like the phoenix, can appear from the ashes of the past," to such a degree that the manuscript of *The Great Gatsby* (1925) contains a subsequently deleted passage in which "Jordan Baker asks about Gatsby's background and Nick mentions that nobodys often came 'from the lower east side of Galena, Illinois'" (Lehan, *F. Scott Fitzgerald* 137–38).

It is in its published form, however, that *The Great Gatsby* offers a more tantalizing, elliptical sign of the relationship that developed between Fitzgerald's immersion in Civil War lore—his knowledge of the Civil War historically and "in story"—and his endeavors as a literary craftsman. In its one overt reference to the conflict, conspicuously situated near the beginning of the novel, Nick describes the Carraways as "something of a clan" and remarks, "the actual founder of my line was my grandfather's brother, who came here in fifty-one, sent a substitute to the Civil War and started the wholesale hardware business that my father carries on today" (6). His father maintains, in other words, the business established by a great-uncle who had been secure enough to hire a replacement in the Civil War and from whom Nick sees himself as descending, in a novel much occupied with questions of descent, both individual and historical (whether Nick's or Gatsby's or that of the nation itself).

In the composition of the novel itself, however, another replacement obviously takes place with the narrating role of Nick Carraway, whom Fitzgerald may be said to have substituted for himself—sent out, in other words, as his own proxy onto the battlefield of literary representation. To that extent, it is not only "as the historical event from which an ancestor gave his family economic ballast," in John F. Callahan's words, that "Carraway has presented the Civil War" (50). Confirming the suggestive formal implications of Nick's seldom-noted reference to his great-uncle are an early Civil War tale like "The Room with the Green Blinds," only the second work in which Fitzgerald employs the "noteworthy device" of "the first person observer-narrator" (Higgins 4) that he perfected in *The Great Gatsby*, and the recurrence of such a device in "The Night of Chancellorsville," narrated by an onlooking prostitute who objects to the Civil War battle that rages offstage as a personal inconvenience. Fitzgerald's own authorial posture in such instances, along with the familiar Conradian strategy associated with his finest work, is thus also historically and imaginatively anchored in his incorporation of the Civil War, by which the technical command exhibited in *The Great Gatsby*, as well as his understanding of himself as a writer (and of writing itself), is covertly mediated. It seems no accident in this regard that Fitzgerald's synopsis of what would prove to be his final novel should have specified, however lightly, that Cecelia Brady, the last in this series of peripheral narrators—daughter of a film producer, and the celebrated Civil War photographer's namesake— "probably was born the day 'The Birth of a Nation' was previewed" (Bruccoli and Duggan 546).

Such a detail, of course, ironically associates not only Cecelia's birth but also her sober and observant account of Hollywood life with Hollywood's own classic renditions of the "romantic" or "chivalric" story included by Fitzgerald among the "two kinds of Civil War novels" that he would describe to Knopf only a few months later. Corresponding to this distinction between two conflicting sets of imaginative representations of the Civil War, the "two Civil Wars" of Fitzgerald's embattled consciousness thus served him as an elaborate conceit through which he metaphorized the national conflict that so engrossed him as a figure for the trials involved in the attempt to create imaginatively at all. That an assimilation of everything it represented to him should have become so integral even to his mastery of technique and form demonstrates just how thoroughly the Civil War permeated Fitzgerald's awareness as a writer. In its confrontation with such a phenomenon, and in the ways in which it extends (and incarnates) the cultural legacy of the Civil War, his work thus composes, if often obliquely or indirectly, a rich and neglected chapter in the reimagining of a war that has otherwise remained, in Daniel Aaron's eloquent phrase, so largely "unwritten."

Aaron himself refers only glancingly to "Fitzgerald's imaginative use of the War" (329), which goes unmentioned even by the novelist's old friend and literary custodian Edmund Wilson in his magisterial survey of Civil War writing, *Patriotic Gore* (1962).[19] If, as Robert A. Martin claims, it is "obvious . . . that Fitzgerald always had a sense of history" (Bryer, *The Short Stories* 143), and if "Scott's interest in history was initiated by his father's Civil War stories" (Bruccoli, *Some Sort of Epic Grandeur* 20), then a sharper appreciation of the central place that the Civil War came to occupy in the evolution of those interests, and in his development as a whole, will be necessary for Fitzgerald's historical imagination to achieve more of an acknowledgment in the growing scholarship on the relations of history and narrative in American literature.[20] That the Civil War in Fitzgerald's understanding fully matched World War I, say, as an event that set the United States distinctively and definitively apart is clear from a story like "The Swimmers," with its oracular concluding vision of an elusive nationhood: "France was a land, England was a people, but America, having about it still that quality of the idea, was harder to utter—it was the graves at Shiloh and the tired, drawn, nervous faces of its great men, and the country boys dying in the Argonne for a phrase that was empty before their bodies withered. It was a willingness of the heart" (*The Short Stories* 512). The reappearance of a couple of his short stories in recent volumes of Civil War fiction suggests that this dimension of Fitzgerald's work is beginning to be re-covered,[21] perhaps enabling us to decipher more precisely the impact of the nation's fundamentally traumatic episode on the sensibility of such a historically informed and engaged American novelist.

Notes

1. Bruccoli mentions Fitzgerald's film idea and identifies the letter to Knopf, but he passes over the central passage in question here (*Some Sort of Epic Grandeur* 484, 595n).

2. Some years earlier, Fitzgerald had lent such impressions to Dick Diver's father, from whom "Dick had learned the somewhat conscious good manners of the young Southerner coming North after the Civil War," and whose own stories are brought to mind as Dick observes a group of women widowed by World War I: "Momentarily, he sat again on his father's knee, riding with Moseby [*sic*] while the old loyalties and devotions fought on around him" (*Tender Is the Night* 164, 101). The allusion to John Singleton Mosby's notorious Confederate Rangers (who figure less agreeably, as Fitzgerald indicated to Knopf, in "The End of Hate") has occasioned some rather speculative, free-wheeling extrapolations in the critical scholarship (Sklar 273–74; Callahan 132–33, 157; Metzger 127–28).

3. An awareness of the influence of his father's Civil War annals and an-cestry is by now a standard part of the biographical record on Fitzgerald (see Turnbull 6; Piper 6–7; Bruccoli, *Some Kind of Epic Grandeur* 11–12, 15–17, 29, 409; Le Vot 5–6; and Donaldson, *Fool for Love* 5–6).

4. For one such overstatement, tracing Fitzgerald's demeanor in this regard on the basis of a narrowly biographical approach to the shifting images of the southern belle in his fiction, see Gammons.

5. For other brief considerations of Fitzgerald's Civil War "naming," see Tamke, "Abe North as Abe Lincoln," and Margolies, "Climbing 'Jacob's Lad-der'" (Bryer, *New Essays* 95–96).

6. A more subtle and disturbing reduction has been detected in *Tender Is the Night,* as Abe North drunkenly accuses an innocent black man of theft: "the arrested man's name is Freeman. To this the Great Emancipator has fallen" (Sklar 279). Compounding the offense is Abe's modification, in mock-defending himself, of his namesake's oft-quoted riposte about the drinking habits of the very Civil War figure soon linked with Dick Diver: "But remember what George the third said, that if Grant was drunk he wished he would bite the

other generals" (*Tender Is the Night* 108). On these nuances, see also Stern, *"Tender Is the Night"* 10–11. According to one biographer, incidentally, Fitzgerald "liked to compare himself to General Grant and recall Lincoln's famous remark about finding out what kind of whiskey Grant drank so he could send some of it to his less successful generals" (Donaldson, *Fool for Love* 169).

7. In an interview that same year, offering an even gloomier judgment of the hidden tensions and discontinuities of his nation's history ("There has never been an American tragedy. There have only been great failures"), Fitzgerald rather cryptically averred that "the story of . . . Jefferson Davis," among other such figures, "opens up things that we who accept the United States as an established unit hardly dare to think about" (Bruccoli and Bryer 276).

8. For a rare consideration of Benjamin Button, although without specific emphasis on the Civil War, as "the most dramatic example of an individual Fitzgerald character whose life encapsulates his era," see Petry 86–88.

9. In his treatment of "Dick Diver, historian once removed from Fitzgerald," Callahan argues even more ambitiously that *Tender Is the Night* advances "an elaborate recapitulation of America's elevation of property over humanity," a grand underlying historical narrative in which "the betrayal of freedom and the replacement of statesmen by magnates" that occurred in the period "between the Civil War and World War I" is dramatized (108, 110). If anything, one might extend yet further, as Stern does, the effect generated by the Civil War, "which for Fitzgerald was the real breaking point in American history, culminating in the emergent 'new' America following World War I" (*The Golden Moment* 370).

10. It was on one such visit, coincidentally, that Fitzgerald concocted "The True Story of Appomattox," informing Perkins, "I managed to have my joke about Grant and Lee taken down on paper" and later "had it faked up by the *Sun* here in Baltimore" (*Letters* 250).

11. According to Turnbull's correction, it was not Pelham's own but "Jeb Stuart's initials which Major John Pelham, Stuart's chief of artillery, had scratched on one of the window panes at 'Welbourne'" (*Letters,* 516n).

12. Fitzgerald presumably has in mind *Southern History of the War* (1865) or *The Lost Cause* (1866), the principal works of Edward A. Pollard, Confederate polemicist and historian whose subsequent transformation into a supporter of reunion perhaps makes his volumes an appropriate choice in the light of what develops between Bette and her patient. (It is unfortunate that the one substantial analysis of the tale dismisses both this scene and Dagonet's earlier homage to the "Gallant Pelham," thereby eliminating any sense of the crucial Civil War backdrop to the action; see George Monteiro, "Bette Weaver, R.N.: 'Her Last Case'" [Bryer, *New Essays* 238–39].)

13. "Like President Grant, Diver will put together in Nicole Warren the divided halves of America" (Callahan 76); such an insight, along with Alan Trachtenberg's equally valuable suggestion that "Dick is drawn to Nicole in part as Grant is drawn to the Civil War," insofar as "both destinies seem to be opportunities for the exercise of a traditional American ideal, a dedication to the healing of moral wounds" (Stern, *Critical Essays* 180), gains additional force when integrated into an analysis of the place of the novel in Fitzgerald's entire imaginative response to the Civil War.

14. Nor are Fitzgerald's characters always content with merely reading such material, as in a sportive moment from "The Curious Case of Benjamin Button," in which "even old General Montcrief" of the Confederacy "became reconciled to his son-in-law when Benjamin gave him the money to bring out his 'History of the Civil War' in twenty volumes" (*The Short Stories* 173).

15. Thomas Boyd's *Through the Wheat* (1923), for example, struck Fitzgerald as "not only the best combatant story of the great war, but also the best war book since 'The Red Badge of Courage,'" a compliment he had already extended in congratulating Boyd on Scribner's acceptance of the novel: "The more I see the book the more I'm convinced that its [*sic*] a perfectly superb piece of work. Quite as good as The Red Badge of Courage—which, by the way, you can now safely read" (Bruccoli and Bryer 144; Bruccoli and Duggan 122). Crane's novella was then safe to read, in Fitzgerald's estimation, because Boyd, having already completed his own work of war fiction, had succeeded in escaping the shadow of such a towering predecessor. Even beyond its value as the exemplary war narrative, however, Crane's work had become for Fitzgerald a touchstone in a more expansive way. As he declared in reviewing another work of fiction, "A novel interests me on one of two counts," the first of which is that "it is something entirely new and fresh and profoundly felt, as, for instance, 'The Red Badge of Courage'" (Bruccoli and Bryer 127).

16. The convergence emerges even when Fitzgerald expresses himself privately, as in his remarkable letter of condolence to Gerald and Sara Murphy on the death of yet another of their sons: "I can see the silence in which you hover now after this seven years of struggle and it would take words like Lincoln's in his letter to the mother who had lost four sons in the war to write you anything fitting at the moment" (*Letters* 426).

17. It is strange that the aesthetic value openly attached here to Stahr's role, and thus the implicit kinship between Fitzgerald and Lincoln, is typically overlooked in readings of *The Last Tycoon* (see Piper 268–69; Callahan 206–7; and Millgate [Bloom 85–86]). The larger historical parallel between Lincoln's achievements and Stahr's, on the other hand, has been firmly grasped (Sklar 337; Callahan 203).

18. Insofar as he was later implicated, as president, in the corruptions of Gilded Age America, the great northern general also came to signify, of course, the split between the nation before and the nation after the Civil War; and, to that extent, Dick Diver is badly compromised by "the very link to Grant, that notorious moral and political failure who . . . presided over the reformation of America in the image of Robber Baron" (Callahan 72). In underscoring the importance of Fitzgerald's image of Grant as a *writer,* my reading of such a "link" diverges sharply from what might be called the critical consensus on this motif of *Tender Is the Night* (see Sklar 272–73, 278; Stern, *The Golden Moment* 311–12, 318; Callahan 111, 197–98; and Metzger 147–48).

19. Fitzgerald is also not discussed in an earlier study, Robert A. Lively, *Fiction Fights the Civil War: An Unfinished Chapter in the Literary History of the American People* (1957). The absence of any consideration of his work from a recent critical anthology like *Classics of Civil War Fiction* (ed. David Madden and Peggy Bach [1991]), which includes an essay reviving, ironically enough, the Civil War short story cycle by John Peale Bishop that Fitzgerald so much admired, would appear to be further symptomatic of this blind spot in scholarship on the literature of the Civil War.

20. Even where his work is explored, a continuing emphasis in American literary study on forms of "romance" can result in an exclusive focus on *Gatsby* and an avoidance of Fitzgerald's concern with historical realities like the Civil War; see Budick 143–63. Other relevant scholarship in which Fitzgerald is overlooked altogether would include Harry B. Henderson's *Versions of the Past: The Historical Imagination in American Fiction* (1974) and Lois Hughson's *From Biography to History: The Historical Imagination and American Fiction, 1880–1940* (1988).

21. "A Debt of Honor" is reprinted in *Confederate Battle Stories,* ed. Martin H. Greenberg, Frank D. McSherry, Jr., and Charles G. Waugh (1992), while Shelby Foote includes "The Night of Chancellorsville" in *Chickamauga, and Other Civil War Stories* (1993), remarking that "even the incidental attention of writers like Fitzgerald . . . produces for us an insight we would otherwise lack" (x).

15

"A Writer for Myself"

F. Scott Fitzgerald and Haruki Murakami

TOSHIFUMI MIYAWAKI

A young Japanese woman writer who is now deceased once told a friend, "I wouldn't mind being forgotten forever, if I could shine like Fitzgerald for one moment."[1] As far as her works are concerned, I see very little evidence of Fitzgerald's influence. But she had an image of him as "shining and sparkling"—and she is not the only one who regards F. Scott Fitzgerald in this way.

This image of Fitzgerald as "shining and sparkling" remains quite strong in Japan, and these adjectives are commonly heard when his story is told. He and Zelda sometimes appear in Japanese women's fashion magazines and men's lifestyle magazines, and they are always crowned with these terms of brilliance. Charles Scribner III points out in his introduction to *Tender Is the Night* that "[Fitzgerald's] name still conjures up the magic of the Jazz Age and his immortality rests secure upon his literary masterpiece, *The Great Gatsby*" (ix). This is certainly the case in Japan. Students of English in Japan usually know about *The Great Gatsby,* but not much about the rest of Fitzgerald's works. For them, Fitzgerald is Gatsby and Gatsby is Fitzgerald. The formula has been established. This image of Fitzgerald is not totally wrong, but it requires considerable qualification, and of course "Gatsbyism" is not all there is to him. But the Japanese public knew him in this partial and superficial way until the early 1980s, when a young writer made his debut and, while writing his own novels, also began to introduce Fitzgerald and his works. This young writer, Haruki Murakami, helped change the stereotyped image of Fitzgerald and introduced a truer face.

Murakami is one of the most important contemporary writers in Japan, and many of his works—six novels and two collections of short stories—have been translated into English and published in the United States.[2] Some of his short stories have appeared in the *New Yorker.* He has received four major literary prizes in Japan so far. He is, besides being a novelist, also a translator of American writers, including Fitzgerald.[3]

Murakami calls Fitzgerald "a writer for myself." In the postscript to *Za sukotto fittsujerarudo bukku* (The Scott Fitzgerald Book), Murakami says, "As a novelist, I see Scott Fitzgerald as a standard or norm to measure where I stand. And sometimes I sigh, sometimes I brace myself up. Most novelists, more or less, I think, have 'a novelist for oneself' on their minds." He continues: "Of course there are many differences between Fitzgerald and me: first of all, he is more talented (both in quality and quantity); he had a different lifestyle; he lived in different times; he has a different style in writing, and so forth. It is almost impossible to find our similarities. But his novels and short stories fascinate me always, and I have been reading them over and over again" (281–82).

Za sukotto fittsujerarudo bukku contains several travel diaries, recording Murakami's visits to places connected with Fitzgerald such as New York; Hollywood; Rockville, Maryland; Montgomery, Alabama; and St. Paul, Minnesota. The book also contains translations of "On Your Own" and "The Rich Boy" and several essays by Murakami, including "On Two Versions of *Tender Is the Night*," "A Short Biography of Zelda Fitzgerald," and "A Comment on the Movie Version of *The Great Gatsby.*" Murakami has translated other Fitzgerald short stories, such as "The Lees of Happiness," "The Ice Palace," "Three Hours between Planes," "An Alcoholic Case," and "Lo, the Poor Peacock!" Together with his translation of "My Lost City," these stories are collected into a single volume under the title of *Mai losuto shitii* (My Lost City) (1981).[4]

In his preface to *Mai losuto shitii,* which is entitled "Fittsujerarudo taiken" (Getting to Know Fitzgerald), Murakami categorizes Fitzgerald as "the kind of writer who brings back readers after many months and many years, as if the readers had left their hearts there in his novels." He declares that Fitzgerald was that kind of novelist to him: "There was nobody else. He was the only one who caught me like that" (8). In this preface, Murakami also recalls reading one of Fitzgerald's short stories at the age of sixteen. That was his first encounter with the writer, but he doesn't remember what the story was. Then, at the age of eighteen, he read *The Great Gatsby.* At that time he was fascinated with Ernest Hemingway, and he took some interest in Fitzgerald because he was one of Hemingway's contemporaries. *The Great Gatsby* was not a boring novel to Murakami. He thought the style of the novel was excellent and found some of the scenes in it fascinating. He also thought that it was "an elaborately written novel with a lingering effect." But he could not help feeling that the style was rather old-fashioned compared with the "crispness" of Hemingway. To him, Fitzgerald was "a novelist of manners, first-rate but weathered by the passage of time." He says that Fitzgerald's "minutely out-of-focus style" was probably beyond his understanding at that time (8).

And then Murakami read *Tender Is the Night* for the first time, when he was a twenty-one-year-old college student. At a used bookstore he found a copy of the Japanese translation, which was already out of print at the time, and began to read it without much expectation. He wasn't moved much by it. He thought it was too long and had a poor structure, and soon he forgot about the novel.[5] After several months, however, "something inexplicable" (*Mai losuto shitii* 10) happened to him. He pulled out the Japanese translation of *Tender Is the Night* from the bookshelf and began to read it again. This time he devoured it and was deeply moved. He had never been moved like that before in his reading life. He felt a certain kind of passion in Fitzgerald's writing, which had seemed to him too prolix and chaotic before.

After this experience, Murakami began to read Fitzgerald's works one after another. He reread *The Great Gatsby* and read *This Side of Paradise, The Last Tycoon,* and many of the short stories. Above all, he read "Winter Dreams" and "Babylon Revisited" twenty times each, examining them closely to discover why he was so fascinated by them. He plunged into the reading only because he wanted to grasp the hidden charm of novels as a form of literature, not because he was going to be a novelist. He never had the nerve to think that he would write a novel himself someday after reading Fitzgerald. In this way, Fitzgerald had been for many years Murakami's one and only "teacher of literature, [his] college and literary companion" (*Mai losuto shitii* 11). As he put it, "Something in me seemed to have changed completely after several years of this 'experience of encountering Fitzgerald.' Generally speaking, in my twenties, Dostoyevsky, Balzac and Hemingway had gradually gone out of my mind. They were surely fine writers, but not the writers *for me* any more" (*Mai losuto shitii* 13).

Was Murakami's writing influenced by Fitzgerald? "The answer is yes and no," he says. He finds little of Fitzgerald's influence in his own writing in terms of style, theme, structure, and storytelling: "If he had given me anything, that might be something vaguer and greater. It could be something like an attitude toward the novel which one has to assume (either as a writer or a reader), which, in other words, is an understanding that the novel is eventually life itself" (*Mai losuto shitii* 13). He sensed Fitzgerald's human nature in his writing. Fitzgerald's sincere attitude toward life influenced this Japanese writer. Murakami gives a touching eulogy to Fitzgerald in his essay "Sukotto fittsujerarudo no gen'ei: Asshubiru, 1935" (The Illusion of Scott Fitzgerald: Asheville, 1935), in which he beautifully describes Fitzgerald's attitude toward life as a writer:

> The summer of 1935 was a sterile season for Scott. He produced nothing then. He could not write any good stories. He could not make anybody happy, nor could he make himself happy either. But the darkness without end and the deep despair he underwent during those days, and also the emptiness he felt on Chimney Rock, eventually bore good fruit in the form of the "The Crack-up" trilogy toward the end of the year. And the essays move us greatly. We can sense a sympathy-evoking sound there, as if in writing them he was carving them from his own flesh. Moreover, the style is firmly noble and each word that he picked is filled with a fine sadness. There is no longer the unmanly sound of a drunkard's self-pity there, nor is there any dramatic, immature philosophy. What is there are the pathetic, earnest eyes of a man who takes seriously the essential sadness and sorrow that the act of living involves and tries to live rightly with a positive view of life. There lies a profound despair that almost surpasses everything. However, we can see something in his writings that even surpasses the despair. Scott Fitzgerald was a man filled with contradictions and faults. That is for sure. But he could be the noblest man when he wrote. Once he took up his pen, he could sit up straight far better than anybody

else no matter how heavily he was beaten down. That is probably why he did not steer his life toward suicide. He always believed in writing no matter how deep his despair was, and it served as a talisman for him to the end of his life. He clung to the brilliance of the writing to the last moment of his life, no matter how unmanly he was said to be. He always believed that he could be redeemed someday as long as he kept writing. Hemingway, who looked like a winner, gave up his hope of ever writing again and killed himself after all. But Fitzgerald didn't.

It has been more than fifty years since Scott Fitzgerald was "resolved back into the elements." But people are still reading his works. (Fitzgerald, *Babiron ni Kaeru* 247–49)

Here, Murakami successfully depicts Fitzgerald's hidden charm, which few who knew him when he was alive could catch. This is a tribute from one who was touched by and truly appreciated Fitzgerald.

Murakami must have sensed this hidden charm in *Tender Is the Night* when he first read it, although it was still "inexplicable" to him when he was a college student. That is why he has affection even for the flaws in the novel.[6] It took Fitzgerald nine years to finish it, and naturally it contains his life. Murakami sensed something serious about Fitzgerald's attitude toward life, something profound and sincere, which a piece of biographical work usually cannot transmit to readers. It was Fitzgerald's life itself.

In an essay for a leading Japanese newspaper, Murakami refers again to Fitzgerald's redemption through writing ("Bunshou ni yoru"). What is this redemption through writing, and why does Murakami stress it? The answers are found in Fitzgerald's powerful will to survive whatever lies before him. Though he might have been seen as an unmanly and pessimistic person, deep in his heart he was strong. His attitude toward life is very similar to that of Jay Gatsby. Although Gatsby was killed just as he was becoming chillingly aware of the illusive quality of his ambition, he persistently had rowed his boat against the current of time toward his dream. To survive tragedy and adversity by writing was Fitzgerald's main preoccupation. The protagonists of Murakami's works also keep surviving despite whatever they have to face in the world around them.

But surviving in what place? The city. Cities like New York and Tokyo. What Murakami has been trying to write about is how to live in
a thriving, active, capitalist city like Tokyo. That is his main preoccupation, and he found in Fitzgerald the same kind of theme, though there
is a distance of half a century between the two writers. Murakami
found a parallel in Fitzgerald's works. Fitzgerald responded with excitement to the throb of the city. Living, surviving, and thriving in a big
city was a challenge for Americans who lived in the booming and burgeoning cities of the 1920s. It is also a central concern for contemporary
Japanese living in big cities today. Just like the young American writers
in the 1980s, who are often called minimalists, Haruki Murakami felt
a closeness with Fitzgerald. Both the minimalists and Murakami have
found a common theme in Fitzgerald's imaginative focus on the city.
An American writer of the 1980s could not become a Hemingway, because there were no more wars like World War I or the Spanish Civil
War. As Amory Blaine discovers in *This Side of Paradise,* all the wars have
been fought already. In place of war, the minimalists found the city as
the force to fight against and the subject to write about. Hemingway
dimmed in Murakami's interest and Fitzgerald became brighter because
Murakami began to face the same problem: big-city life. This theme of
young people living in the city in contemporary Japan is clearly seen in
Murakami's *Norwegian Wood* (1987). And in this novel we can see an
allusion to *The Great Gatsby* that is not accidental.

Since he is a very popular and well-known writer, with a wide and
large readership, Murakami's influence on the general readership is tremendous. When his readers found a passage referring to Fitzgerald and
The Great Gatsby in *Norwegian Wood,* they naturally came to develop an
interest in the writer and the novel:

> I was always reading, yet I wasn't your voracious reader. I read
> my favorites over and over again, which at the time included
> Truman Capote, Scott Fitzgerald, and Raymond Chandler. I never
> ran into another soul in my classes or at the dorm with my tastes
> in fiction. . . .
>
> To my eighteen-year-old tastes, John Updike's *The Centaur* had
> been the pinnacle of writing, yet after a few readings it began to

lose its original luster, making way for *The Great Gatsby* to ease into the number one slot. Whenever I felt like it, I'd take *Gatsby* down from the shelf, open it at random, and read a passage. It never once let me down. Never a boring page. Just amazing. Nonetheless, there wasn't another person around who'd read *Gatsby*, or anyone even conceivably a *Gatsby*-reader type. Even if no one campaigned against the reading of Fitzgerald, no one exactly recommended it either.

At the time there was but one other person who'd read *The Great Gatsby*, and that was how he fell in with me. A Tokyo University law student named Nagasawa, two years my senior. He lived in the same dorm, so I pretty much knew him by sight. When I was sitting soaking up the sun in a spot in the dining hall one day with my copy of *Gatsby*, he came up and sat beside me. He wanted to know what I was reading and I told him *Gatsby*. Interesting? he asked. Interesting enough for me to read it three times through and still feel tingles.

"Any guy who reads *The Great Gatsby* three times through has gotta be okay by me," he said, half to himself. And so we became friends. That was October. . . .

I can't even begin to touch the number of books he'd read, yet he made it a rule never to read anything by writers who'd been dead for less than thirty years. Can't trust them, he'd say.

"It's not that I don't trust contemporary literature. It's just that I don't want to waste my precious hours on something that hasn't stood the test of time. Life is short."

"So tell me, Nagasawa, what sort of writers do you like?" I asked.

"Balzac, Dante, Conrad, Dickens," he rattled off.

"Nobody very up-to-date, as writers go."

"That's why I read them. If I read what everybody else reads, I'd only wind up thinking like everybody else. That's for hicks, riff-raff. People with a decent head on their shoulders shouldn't stoop to that. Think about it, Watanabe. Do you know you and I are the only two halfway decent guys in this dorm? The rest are trash."

"What makes you think that?" I asked, taken aback.

"I just know, clear as if there was a mark on our foreheads. That and we're the only ones who've read *Gatsby*."

I did a quick calculation in my head. "But Scott Fitzgerald's only been dead twenty-eight years."

"Who's to quibble over two years?" he said. "Under par is fine for a writer as great as Fitzgerald." (*Norwegian Wood* [trans. Birnbaum] Part I, 58–61)

Murakami refers to *The Great Gatsby* in this novel, and not out of caprice. In doing so he suggests that the novel being narrated and *The Great Gatsby* have something in common. *Norwegian Wood* opens with Toru Watanabe, the thirty-seven-year-old protagonist, arriving at Hamburg airport by Boeing 747. But this plane is from nowhere; we are not told where it originated. Nor are we allowed to know why its destination was Hamburg. From the moment the airplane arrives, the readers are lured into the world of the protagonist's memories. We are brought back to the year 1968 and are informed that this is the story of the narrator, Toru Watanabe, and his girlfriend, Naoko. The story is told in flashback.

By chance Toru meets Naoko, whom he had known in high school, on the train right after he enters a university in Tokyo. She was a girlfriend of his friend Kizuki, who committed suicide when he was a high school student. Toru and Naoko begin to go out and, after a year, become lovers on her twentieth birthday. But she disappears right after that. After a while, he receives a letter from her and learns that she is mentally ill and in a sanitarium in the mountains of Kyōto.

Soon after he finds out about Naoko, Toru meets a girl named Midori on campus. She is young and fresh, full of life—exactly the opposite of Naoko. The love story continues with Toru wavering between these two girls. Toward the end of the story, Toru eventually fails to save Naoko from mental illness, and she kills herself in the deep forest. Overcome with grief, he tries to reach Midori but ends up in a telephone booth calling her name without knowing where he is. That is the end of the story.

We can catch a glimpse of Murakami's meaning.[7] Despite being deeply lost in the city, Murakami's protagonist puts up with it and tries to survive, fighting against the oppression of modern civilization. This attitude toward life reminds us of the final passage in *The Great Gatsby:*

> Gatsby believed in the green light, the orgastic future that year by year recedes before us. It eluded us then, but that's no matter—tomorrow we will run faster, stretch out our arms farther. . . . And one fine morning—
> So we beat on, boats against the current, borne back ceaselessly into the past. (141)

Here we can see a hopeful and expectant attitude toward life, surviving through the strong and swift currents in the city. Fitzgerald was caught by the city, and Murakami felt caught in the same way. Murakami sees no influence of Fitzgerald upon him in terms of theme, but when it comes to writing about living in the city, he is without doubt greatly influenced by Fitzgerald.

Norwegian Wood sold almost three million copies, so here also Murakami contributed greatly to the popularization of Fitzgerald and *The Great Gatsby,* especially among the younger generation. Murakami's gradual introduction of Fitzgerald, appearing serially in various publications, created a revival of books related to Fitzgerald. First, a reprint of the translation of *Tender Is the Night* came out in 1989. This translation had first appeared in 1960 and had been out of print for a long time. The text is Malcolm Cowley's 1951 revised edition. The reprint edition soon sold out, and its price at used bookstores tripled. It became a sort of collector's item.[8]

The translation of Sheilah Graham's *Beloved Infidel* also came back to life. The Japanese version of Nancy Milford's *Zelda* was piled side by side with Graham's book in the most conspicuous sections of bookstores. Several other publications also enjoyed the benefits of this Fitzgerald boom in Japan. It is noteworthy that an authoritative literary magazine in Japan called *Eureka* featured Fitzgerald in 1988, with the title of "Fittsujerarudo: Kirabiyaka de kanashii amerikan gurafitii" (F. Scott Fitzgerald: Brilliant but Sad American Graffiti).[9] This issue soon sold out too.

The Fitzgerald boom in the Japanese publishing business may be called the "Fitzgerald revival in Japan," but it is not a revival in the true sense. The Japanese version of *This Side of Paradise* is still out of print. *The Beautiful and Damned* has never been translated into Japanese. And there are many good short stories that remain untranslated.[10] Much remains to be done before Japan has a true revival of Fitzgerald and his works. In this sense, if we take his contemporaries as examples, Fitzgerald is still relatively handicapped compared to Hemingway and Faulkner, for most of their major works are available in translation. Fitzgerald cannot be rightly evaluated by the general readership until this handicap is overcome.

As Murakami's contribution as a writer continues, Japanese researchers should continue studying Fitzgerald from an academic viewpoint. In this way, the study of Fitzgerald can be carried forward from the two different angles, that of the contemporary writer and that of scholars, each giving stimulus to the other. The fact is that more and more students are becoming interested in Fitzgerald after being influenced by Murakami. As scholars of Fitzgerald, we should lead them, who are *our* lost generation, to further research and a better understanding of Fitzgerald. "So we beat on," as Fitzgerald himself might say, toward a truer appreciation of Fitzgerald in Japan.

Although a true revival of Fitzgerald is yet to come, Murakami has laid the basis for it and made a valuable contribution to the popularization of Fitzgerald among general readers in Japan. As long as Murakami keeps writing, he will refer to Fitzgerald in some way or other. Through him, people will not forget Fitzgerald. Murakami will continue to work on translating more of Fitzgerald's works into Japanese and to write essays on him. He has also expressed his strong intention of doing his own translation of *The Great Gatsby*. Although he has tried the project many times, he claims that he has always failed on the first page.[11] But he will do it someday, and no doubt his *Gatsby* will fascinate more and more readers. No matter what kind of stories Murakami writes, Fitzgerald will always be there on his mind.

F. Scott Fitzgerald was born in 1896 in St. Paul, Minnesota. Over one hundred years later, though he has been dead for more than half a century, his soul is still actively working on a writer across the Pacific Ocean, in Tokyo, Japan. Through Murakami, in Japan Fitzgerald is a more familiar name among the universal masters of literature, gaining new and ever wider readership.

Notes

1. The writer's name is Agata Hikari (1943–92). Her reference to F. Scott Fitzgerald is quoted from a memorial essay about her by Motoko Michiura. Unless otherwise indicated, all English translations are by the author.

2. *Wild Sheep Chase* (New York: Plume, 1990), *Hard-Boiled Wonderland and the End of the World* (New York: Vintage International, 1991), *Dance Dance Dance* (New York: Vintage International, 1995), *The Wind-Up Bird Chronicle* (New York: Vintage International, 1998), *South of the Border, West of the Sun* (New York: Knopf, 1999) and *Sputnik Sweetheart* (New York: Knopf, 2001) are novels; *Elephant Vanishes* (New York: Knopf, 1993) and *After the Quake* (New York: Knopf, 2002) are collections of short stories.

3. For example, he has translated C. D. B. Bryan's *The Great Dethriffe;* Truman Capote's *I Remember Grandpa: A Christmas Memory* and *One Christmas;* Tim O'Brien's *The Nuclear Age* and *The Things They Carried;* John Irving's *Setting Free the Bears;* Paul Theroux's *World's End and Other Stories;* and above all, the complete works of Raymond Carver. He has also introduced to Japan the picture books of Chris Van Allsburg and three cat stories of Ursula K. Le Guin.

4. There is another collection of Fitzgerald's short stories translated by Haruki Murakami, *Babiron ni kaeru: Za sukotto fittsujerarudo bukku 2* (Babylon Revisited: The Scott Fitzgerald Book 2). It includes translations of "The Jelly-Bean," "A New Leaf," "Babylon Revisited," "The Cut-Glass Bowl," and "The Bridal Party" and an essay entitled "Sukotto fittsujerarudo no gen'ei: Asshubiru, 1935" (The Illusion of Scott Fitzgerald: Asheville, 1935).

5. The Japanese version he read is the translation of Cowley's 1951 "final version."

6. From my interview with Haruki Murakami at Cambridge, Massachusetts, in 1995. He was at that time a visiting fellow at Tufts University after having spent two and half years at Princeton University as a visiting fellow.

7. In the postscript to *Noruwei no mori,* which is not included in the English version (*Norwegian Wood*), Murakami again refers to *The Great Gatsby:* "[Norwegian Wood] . . . is personal to me just like F. Scott Fitzgerald's *Tender Is the Night* and *The Great Gatsby* are personal novels for me. Probably this is a matter

of some sort of sentiment. . . . I just hope that . . . [*Norwegian Wood*] will survive alone, separated from me" (Part II, 259–60).

8. There is another out-of-print Japanese version of *Tender Is the Night* published by Arechi Publishing in 1957, and it is also from the 1951 Cowley edition.

9. This issue contains eight translations of short stories and essays by Scott and Zelda as well as ten essays on them. The titles of the translations are "The Bridal Party," "Tarquin of Cheapside," "Teamed with Genius," "The Freshest Boy," "Eulogy on the Flapper," "Looking Back Eight Years," "The Pampered Man," and "What Became of Our Flappers and Sheiks?" (Fitzgerald's part only).

10. *The Great Gatsby* is one of the most popular translations in Japan; currently there are five translations available.

11. From my interview with Haruki Murakami.

16

Pat Hobby and the Fictions of the Hollywood Writer

CHRISTOPHER AMES

Pat Hobby is a has-been, and even his reputedly glorious past is shady. But in one of those rare moments in the seventeen stories in which something positive is said about Pat Hobby, a producer recalls that "he used to be a good man for structure" (Fitzgerald, *Pat Hobby Stories* 30). By structure, Jack Berners means plot outline; for even in the days in which Hobby garnered thirty screen credits (twenty-nine more than his creator, by the way), he needed to be paired with "some man who wrote dialogue" (14). Fitzgerald indicates, in various subtle ways, that Hobby remains capable of inventing stories and plotlines. But the stories that Hobby struggles to invent comment on the stories within which he exists. The series thus becomes oddly self-referential: not only are these stories about a storywriter, tales of a screenwriter written on the weekends Fitzgerald had off from screenwriting, but they are stories in which Hobby's narrative failings transmute into personal humiliations. The plots of *The Pat Hobby Stories* mirror the plots Pat invents within them. Arnold Gingrich, editor of *Esquire* during the time the seventeen Pat Hobby stories appeared there between January 1940 and May 1941, dismisses the common critical response as an instance of the pathetic fallacy: "these stories are about a hack, *ergo* these stories are hack work" (*Pat Hobby Stories* xxiii). He is right to reject such a reduction of these clever tales, but the pathetic fallacy remains relevant. *The Pat Hobby Stories* comment ironically on hackneyed stories by making the hack the victim of the very plots he puts in motion. Throughout the series, the structure of the stories comically reflects the structure of Pat

Hobby's feeble attempts to generate ideas for screenplays. The intentionally clichéd and predictable plots of the stories satirize the hackneyed nature of Hollywood storytelling at its worst.

Pat Hobby's narrative skill, such as it is, is the story concept, the narrative germ of a scenario. In the degraded state in which the stories find him, he hunts for the easiest assemblage of plot notions that might get him a check or a brief salaried appointment. His art has become the art of "the pitch." "The pitch" is a brief oral summary of a plot for a motion picture, often couched in terms of genre. Screenwriter Jeff Silverman, discussing the story pitch in a 1992 *New York Times* article, defines it as "the verbal presentation of a story or idea in hopes of selling it before actually writing it" (1).[1] Narrative theorists might call it "content-based plot typologizing," a phrase from Seymour Chatman (88) that describes a practice going back to Aristotle of reducing narratives to plot essentials. That a film project may be given the green light based on an extraordinarily brief narrative précis (even perhaps an improvised one) is a central satirical target in depictions of moviemaking and in the memoirs of screenwriters. James M. Cain offers a hilarious account of a wholly improvised report he delivered at a Paramount story conference to cover not having made any progress on a screenwriting assignment (McGilligan 115–16). Similarly comic story pitches appear in a host of Hollywood novels and films about Hollywood that feature screenwriters. Some of the most notable include James Cagney and Pat O'Brien's dual inventions in the film *Boy Meets Girl* (1938) and the comic pitches that run through Robert Altman's film version of Michael Tolkin's *The Player* (1992).

Fitzgerald's Pat Hobby is one of the first to make creative use of this way of examining the conventions of Hollywood narrative. Indeed, these slight stories have a more seminal place in Hollywood fiction than is generally acknowledged. *The Pat Hobby Stories* prefigure elements of the most famous depiction of a screenwriter in Hollywood film and literature, *Sunset Boulevard:* in "The Homes of the Stars," Pat Hobby's car breaks down on Sunset Boulevard; in "Pat Hobby Does His Bit," Pat hustles all his studio colleagues for loans to keep his car from being repossessed. Identical events precipitate the fall of down–and–out screenwriter Joe Gillis in *Sunset Boulevard.* John Updike has noted echoes of Fitzgerald in one of the finest Hollywood novels of the 1990s, calling the main character in Bruce Wagner's *Force Majeure* "a post-modern heir of Scott Fitzgerald's downtrodden scribbler Pat Hobby" (74). *Force Majeure,* like *The Pat Hobby Stories,* uses story pitches as mini-narratives to examine the relationship between the character's fictions and the fictional character's life. The device of the alienated screenwriter whose story is told in part by the miniature stories he invents in his trade owes a lot to Fitzgerald's final fictions.

The comically presented pitch that recurs throughout Hollywood fiction is central to *The Pat Hobby Stories.* "A Man in the Way" is structured around two scenarios Pat pitches, one in which a writer mistakes a female writer for a stenographer, and another in which an aged painter watches as his works are crated up for safe storage during the war while he himself is ignored. That the first scenario is simply what happened to Pat that day and the second is stolen from the writer he mistakes for a stenographer merely demonstrates how little Hobby thinks he needs or needs to think to snag a contract. The stories abound in improvised story pitches. In "A Patriotic Short," Hobby's "high concept" involves inserting a Jewish angle into a Civil War picture; in "Mightier Than the Sword," he participates in telling the story of a popular composer as one who began as a plasterer's apprentice; in "Pat Hobby's College Days," he modifies a scene he witnesses in the office of a college dean into a pitch about a student who steals to support his younger brother, the star of the football team. All of Pat's pitches are weak and unsuccessful; they satirize through exaggeration the paucity of narrative material sufficient to qualify in Hollywood as a story idea. Indeed, in some of the stories Hobby's desperation reveals itself through his attempts to profit from something even slighter than a story idea. In "'Boil Some Water—Lots of It,'" he offers a single line. In "Teamed with Genius" and "No Harm Trying," he attempts to pass off stolen scripts. In "Pat Hobby's Secret," he repeats part of a pitch he has overheard. In "On the Trail of Pat Hobby," he tries to capitalize on a clever title idea.

"A Man in the Way" reveals the most about how Fitzgerald saw Hobby as a writer, and it prefigures how Hobby's writing skills would function structurally in the subsequent stories. It is the first story in order of composition and probably would have been the first published had not *Esquire* capitalized on a holiday tie-in with "Pat Hobby's Christmas Wish." As noted above, "A Man in the Way" is structured around two paltry story pitches Hobby uses to garner two weeks on salary. That Hobby steals one pitch wholesale and simply modifies his office faux pas into the other is part of the ironic point. But the two stories Pat pitches also reflect his character as "a man in the way," a characteristic underscored by the beginning of the story, which describes the difficulty Pat has even getting on the studio lot. The first pitch, about mistaking the writer for a stenographer, builds a scenario from Pat's own alienation on the lot: he walks into the office of someone who has "left Hollywood" (15) since Pat was last at the studio, and then he insultingly assumes that the female writer must be a secretary (this from the man who in the preceding story fires his secretary on Christmas Eve to avoid buying her a gift). The second pitch, about the forgotten artist who becomes "a man in the way," so clearly expresses Hobby's self-conception that he makes the connection explicitly in the pitch, as a plea for a higher salary: "'You make me feel like that old painter—' . . . 'Don't oversell it,' [Jack Berners replies]" (19). Indeed, as Berners's comment hints, both scenarios elevate the autobiographical figure to a once great artist who commands people's sympathy if not respect. Hobby clearly commands neither in this story. Twice he is bluntly told, "I can't put you on salary for that" (18, 14). The story also reveals that Hobby doesn't read the material he adapts (and then shows others laughing at him because of it). "A Man in the Way" exposes him as virtually incapable of putting an idea into writing: "[Berners] knew Pat couldn't write anything out" (14). The "whipped misery in Pat's eye" is thoroughly explained by his pathetic inadequacy (14). As an opening to the series, "A Man in the Way" announces a striking antihero whose failures as a writer are consistently tied to his personal and moral failures as a human being. Remarkably, Fitzgerald argued that this story should precede "Pat Hobby's Christmas Wish" because the Christmas story "characterize[d] him in a rather less sympathetic way" (*Pat Hobby Stories* xv).

Hobby's existence as a man in the way is also developed through this story's play on naming and authorship. In a business in which screen credits are often handed out arbitrarily (the theme of "Pat Hobby's Preview") and in which ideas, stories, lines, and even whole scripts can be stolen, the name of the author acquires special force. In "A Man in the Way," Hobby stumbles into the wrong office because the new scriptwriter hasn't been adequately identified: "they forgot to put up my name," she says (15). In their conversations, he suggests that she sell ideas to other studios under "another name" (16). When she sends him away, Hobby finds "an office with no name on it" and takes a nap (17). As in "Pat Hobby and Orson Welles," Pat's identity seems to disappear with his writing talent; he stumbles from nameless office to nameless office trying to find his place. His lack of authorship threatens to erase his name, though Fitzgerald deliberately includes his name in the titles of half of the stories. "A Man in the Way" prepares the reader for stories about a nonentity, a writer who no longer writes. It prefigures what is truly innovative and daring in these stories: the use of a failed writer as an embodiment of the seamy and unredeemed side of Hollywood.

Hobby's pathetic attempts to sell bits and pieces of narratives reveal his character, and *The Pat Hobby Stories* are generally thought of as character sketches. But the fragments of screenplay ideas tell us something about narrative construction in the Hollywood system, a system that oddly mixes the collaborative and the hierarchical. The making of popular mythology for profit involves recasting familiar narrative elements and patterns in a way that seems new but resonates with the archetypal stories of the culture and the genre. Producers act as narrative gatekeepers, deciding (often on the basis of story pitches) what narratives will be made into movies. Where do such stories come from? Mr. Banizon, a producer, wishes, in "Pat Hobby's Secret," that "writers could be dispensed with altogether. If only ideas could be plucked from the inexpensive air!" (60). Of course, the majority of film stories are literally recirculated—they come from novels or plays. Hobby has advice on how to adapt such material, advice that interestingly dispenses with reading it: "Give the book to four of your friends to read it. Get them to tell you what stuck in their minds. Write it down and you've got a picture" (16). At its best, the Hobby method turns the audience into co-writers, just as some believe the extensive use of test marketing has done. At its worst, the Hobby method adds the writer to the club of Hollywood's semi-literate. Traditionally, supposedly intellectual writers told stories in disbelief about producers who needed to have scripts read to them. But Hobby's method appealed to the screenwriter portrayed by Humphrey Bogart in the 1950 film *In a Lonely Place;* there Bogart, because he can't bear to read a sentimental romance, brings a hatcheck girl home to tell him the plot of a novel he needs to adapt. A producer reminds Bogart's character, however, that the hatcheck girl represents his audience and thus may be particularly suited to the task of narrative encapsulation.

Hobby has a method for "original" screenplays as well: in "No Harm Trying," he combs the daily newspapers and *Life* magazine for story ideas, just as the upstart producer Larry Levy does in the film of *The Player*. When Levy combs the newspapers for stories, however, it is part of his move to get rid of writers entirely, in the spirit of Fitzgerald's Mr. Banizon. Hobby does it to hang on. His machinations to find creative shortcuts satirize the absurdities of studio-era screenwriting, in which scripts were farmed out to multiple writers for treatments, rewrites, dialogue work, script doctoring, and so forth. Many writers and critics have commented on the frustrations and inefficiency of the way Hollywood handled writers. Fitzgerald's correspondence over his work on *Three Comrades* (1938) is full of passionate complaints about the role of producers and collaborators in the screenwriting process. To producer Joe Mankiewicz he raged: "I gave you a drawing and you simply took a box of chalk and touched it up" (Fitzgerald, *Screenplay for "Three Comrades"* 263). Ben Hecht wrote of "the pain of having to collaborate with such dullards" (476). In the famous article "Writers in Hollywood," Raymond Chandler described a system that renders the art of the screenplay impossible because "it is the essence of this system that it seeks to exploit a talent without permitting it the right to be a talent" (John Miller 72).

Fitzgerald, however, examines the weaknesses of the system from the perspective of a hack writer rather than from the more familiar perspective (in memoirs and articles) of the prominent writer outraged by the debasing demands of Hollywood screenwriting. Thus by using a bad writer as hero, Fitzgerald avoids the risk of pedantry and naïveté that can characterize the familiar laments of writers who went west.[2]

The story pitch also reminds us of how much screenwriting depends on audience familiarity with genres, on working within plot typologies, and on modifying already existing narratives to fit Hollywood formulas. But what of Hollywood fiction itself? Where does it stand in relation to the narrative methods it lampoons? We must not forget that *The Pat Hobby Stories* are stories about a writer, fictions about a fiction maker, and thus are inevitably self-referential and metafictional. So when we identify the narrative characteristics of these stories—their brevity, their clichéd plots, their predictable structures—we should get the ironic point: they satirize similar conventions in motion pictures and they satirize, by example, the degraded state of Pat Hobby's narrative imagination.

I do not refer here to the autobiographical elements that have achieved such notoriety: that Fitzgerald was churning out these short stories for *Esquire*'s low fees while writing of a screenwriter passing off fragmentary work for whatever the market would yield. Though Arnold Gingrich's introduction to the *Pat Hobby* volume practically reads like an eighteenth Pat Hobby story, the autobiographical elements are actually few, as many (including Gingrich) have pointed out: Hobby has far more screen credits than Fitzgerald, but he has no intellectual life at all and no other writing career outside the studios. Still, Gingrich's story of the composition of the series invites such comparisons. While he does provide detailed evidence of Fitzgerald's careful revision of the stories and concern with their quality and their order of publication (very un-Hobbylike traits), he also provides a comical chronicle of Fitzgerald's demands for rapid advance payments. In Gingrich's rendering, the composition of the stories themselves exists as a background to the correspondence about pay. Gingrich also relates Fitzgerald's proposals to use a pseudonym for some other stories *Esquire* held the rights to so that they could be published concurrently with the Hobby stories. In raising those issues, Fitzgerald playfully signs cables and letters with his proposed pseudonyms: the familiar "John Darcy" (xvii) and the more comical "John Blue" (xix). It is little surprise, then, that Fitzgerald signed one piece of correspondence about the stories "Pat Hobby Fitzgerald" (xv).

Gingrich himself identifies the enduring Fitzgerald theme prominent in these stories: "Failure always fascinated Fitzgerald." He continues to draw a biographical parallel: "[Fitzgerald] would have felt sardonic satisfaction in having created, in Pat, such a thoroughgoing failure that he couldn't even, so to speak, 'get on the lot' [i.e., get published in collected form] for more than twenty-one years" (Fitzgerald, *Pat Hobby Stories* xxi). In spite of his very warnings, Gingrich can't resist making the leap from the stories to their reception, suggesting that it is appropriate that stories about a failure fail.

Of course, we shouldn't exaggerate the biographical connections. Like most of Fitzgerald's memorable characters, Pat Hobby contains some elements of Fitzgerald's own character. In particular, he is an alcoholic struggling with the realization that he has not fulfilled his youthful promise (poignantly symbolized by the empty swimming pool in "A Patriotic Short"). But Hobby draws as well on Hollywood types whom Fitzgerald recognized and despised: self-important writers who held their craft in low esteem and exploited the idiocies of the Hollywood scene. After deploring the intervention of producers into the business of writing, Chandler acknowledges that most Hollywood writers have "never had an idea in their lives . . . have never written a photographable scene. . . . They are, to put it bluntly, a dreary lot of hacks, and most of them know it" (John Miller 72). Fitzgerald's most imaginative stroke in these stories is using just such a writer as the means of presenting a portrait of Hollywood, a strategy thoroughly in opposition to that employed in *The Last Tycoon*.

Ultimately, however, if we read Gingrich's introduction to the collection as a kind of metafictional Pat Hobby story, we discover, atypically, a twist in which the writer–hero benefits: the stories, now collected and available to readers and scholars, outlive their detractors. Beyond the temptations of biographical parallels, narrative self-referentiality still emerges in two interrelated ways: in how the sketches of Pat Hobby replay the very set narrative formulas characteristic of hackneyed film pitches, and in how the cinematic ideas proffered by Hobby always have an ironic origin in his life. That is, *The Pat Hobby Stories* exhibit the same kind of structure its eponymous hero is known for, and that becomes their ironic point.

Each story has a "hook," generally Pat Hobby cadging for money. (In one story he is hiding from a police investigation of a motel where he works as a clerk under a pseudonym; in another he is trying to talk his way out of a drunk driving charge. Otherwise, the stories are all structured as quests for money.) Pat then hits upon a feeble stratagem that succeeds more dramatically than he would have hoped. In predictable and O. Henry–like twists, his good fortune turns to bad and he is revealed as a fraud of one kind or another. The pattern of a hook that leads into a character-revealing quest and concludes with a plot twist could characterize many a literary plot and many a cinematic one, especially comedies. But, in spite of their comic structure (and comic elements like faulty disguises and unbelievable coincidences), the Hobby stories almost all end unhappily, and the character revealed is consistently unadmirable and largely unsympathetic. Fitzgerald discouraged an attempt to dramatize the stories by arguing that the "bitter humor" would not work dramatically and that only "the fact that Pat is a figure almost incapable of real tragedy or damage saves [the sequence] from downright unpleasantness" (Bruccoli, *Some Sort of Epic Grandeur* 473). Hard enough to imagine on the stage, the stories are unthinkable for the screen: the endings are too consistently dark and the character too unheroic and frankly unlikable. But the structure of the stories of Pat Hobby, "structure man," is pure Hollywood, or at least a parody of pure Hollywood.

Pat's schemes are undone by a variety of wrong turns: in "Pat Hobby's Christmas Wish," "A Man in the Way," "No Harm Trying," and "Teamed with Genius," Pat conspires with the wrong people (in three of them he unwittingly conspires with the lover of the person he is trying to dupe). When he nervously steals a hat in the commissary (in "On the Trail of Pat Hobby"), it turns out to be the property of the studio head. In "Pat Hobby, Putative Father" and "Pat Hobby Does His Bit," he accidentally stumbles on camera during shooting. In "The Homes of the Stars," "Pat Hobby's Preview," and "Fun in an Artist's Studio," he exaggerates his status and ends up revealed as a fraud in front of the person he hoped to impress; in the latter story he is literally stripped naked for her amusement. The figure of Pat Hobby anticipates the schlemiel hero and the literature of embarrassment exemplified by Stanley Elkin. Hobby is hapless like Chaplin's tramp but without the lovable quality. In "Pat Hobby and Orson Welles," Fitzgerald even invokes an old Chaplin number in which a crowded streetcar ejects one passenger for each new one taken on; Pat is inevitably the one ejected. While these plot twists are commonly taken as evidence of the stories' mediocrity, I think they are better seen as an intentional comic pattern by which the maker of hackneyed narratives becomes their victim.

That interrelation is made clearer in the way in which the predictable plot twists mingle the "real" and "cinematic" worlds within the stories. Two simple examples illustrate this principle with a single line. In " 'Boil Some Water—Lots of It,' " the title recounts the one line Hobby contributes to a medical screenplay on the day in question. Later, in the midst of a comic crisis in the studio commissary, Pat beans an upstart with a tray, only to discover he is a senior writer engaging in a friendly gag. Furious and bewildered, Pat hears a doctor order: "Boil some water, lots of it!" As in his script, "he did not think he could go on from there" (28). His single hackneyed invention springs upon him in the real world, and his writers' block in the scriptwriting process translates into general befuddlement and paralysis in the studio commissary.

In "Pat Hobby's Secret," he conspires with a producer to discover the end of a scenario the producer was told by another writer. The writer is holding out for a longer contract in return for explaining the plot resolution. Pat gets drunk with the writer and wheedles the conclusion from him, but the writer realizes he has been tricked and fights with Pat. A bystander intervenes and kills the other writer. At the trial, Pat feigns amnesia rather than implicate the frightening bystander: "Everything went white!" (58) he proudly invents on the stand. When the time comes for the payoff with the producer, proud Pat can only recall his courtroom line, not the ending the dead writer gave him in the bar. "Everything's white," he repeats (59). The simple doubling of a particular line in these two stories highlights the narrative structure: Pat's trite inventions (which he believes will serve him in good stead in the scriptwriting world) fail him or haunt him in the real world. His inability to develop a script magnifies into his commissary blunder; his courtroom lie neutralizes the deception from which he had hoped to profit. In both cases, "what comes next" is Pat's humiliation, the "pat" endings of virtually all the stories.

A blatant pattern of doubling fictions structures "Two Old-Timers," in which a literal automobile collision represents the collision of Hollywood dream and reality. Pat Hobby collides with an actor who fails to recognize him. Worse for Pat, the police sergeant admires the actor's realistic and heroic portrayal of a soldier in a war movie. But as Pat tries to jog the actor's memory of him, he relates the sordid details of how the director trapped the actor in a dirt hole and reduced him to tears in order to get the emotion he wanted. The higher-ranking police captain seems to believe Hobby's story and, surprisingly, the actor is held in jail while Hobby is given a ride home. The story is neatly structured as two tales told by Hollywood old-timers. Uncharacteristically, Hobby gains ascendancy over the clearly more successful actor. The competitive storytelling plays to what was once Hobby's strength—instant narrative.[3]

"Two Old-Timers" is one of several stories in which Hobby's real narrative gifts emerge in ways other than actual screenwriting. In one story, Pat composes a fake letter informing his collaborator that his brothers have been killed in the war; in another, we learn that Pat had coauthored a "sucker-trap" guide to writing pictures; in still another, Pat lies about why his salary is so low and the narrator comments that the lie was "his best piece of imaginative fiction in a decade" (144). Writing in the cells of the writers' block becomes a con game in which as much fiction-making is devoted to office intrigue as it is to creative narrative. Similarly, the very practice of "the pitch" rewards improvisatory narrative performance over written production.

Fitzgerald's stories about Pat Hobby depend on their simplistic structure. In spite of Gingrich's complaint that, in response to *The Pat Hobby Stories,* "the scholars began falling, with singular uniformity, into the pathetic fallacy" (Fitzgerald, *Pat Hobby Stories* xxiii), a version of the pathetic fallacy is very much the point. Hobby's status as a narrative hack is reflected comically and intentionally in the structure of the stories, particularly in their manipulation of the "real" and the "cinematic." Fitzgerald uses his vantage point as a writer struggling in the studio system to explicate the narrative limitations of Hollywood screenwriting in a disarmingly self-referential way. Hobby's consistent, well-developed, and thoroughly unpleasant character is explicated through the predictable plot devices. Hobby becomes a fictional character who is victimized by the very fictions he invents, a writer trapped in the clichéd twists of his own plots. Pat Hobby's survival as a structure man testifies to the durability of the banal, while the structure of the stories emphasizes the fragmentary and petty environment out of which emerged the century's new narrative form—which Fitzgerald, in "Pasting It Together," famously prophesied would "make even the best selling novelist as archaic as silent pictures" (Wilson, *The Crack-up* 78).

Notes

1. In spite of Silverman's definition, there is ample evidence that pitches can be used to sell screenplays that are already written, because those with the

power to acquire them often aren't interested in reading them. Silverman also asserts that "the pitch" is essentially a part of Hollywood after the studio system, but *The Pat Hobby Stories* (as well as other Hollywood novels and films of the thirties, forties, and fifties) provides ample evidence that the pitch has a long history in Hollywood.

2. The best study of how established novelists, playwrights, and journalists responded to the particular demands of writing for the film industry is Fine's *Hollywood and the Profession of Authorship, 1928–1940.*

3. Metcalf reads this story as an attack on Hemingway's promotion of himself as a war hero through the movie *The Spanish Earth,* which Hemingway narrated. Here the biographical parallel may explain the atypical twist in which Hobby is victorious rather than humiliated.

17

Tune in Next Month

Fitzgerald's Pat Hobby and the Popular Series

TIM PRCHAL

A curious consistency is found in critical appraisals of F. Scott Fitzgerald's Pat Hobby stories. Richard D. Lehan describes them as "very slight" (*F. Scott Fitzgerald* 164); John A. Higgins tells us they are weak due to their "slightness" (177); Wheeler Winston Dixon contends that they "are slight pieces far below Fitzgerald's normal standards" (11); and Gene D. Phillips feels that the stories "are too slight to be placed among Fitzgerald's finest short fiction" (147). The repetition of the adjective "slight" in these commentaries reinforces the firm agreement among certain prominent critics that this series belongs toward the bottom of Fitzgerald's oeuvre. Indeed, the Hobby stories *become* slight when placed beside—and judged upon criteria befitting—the author's other writing, be it his other short pieces or his novels.

Herein lies a problem, however. Standard literary criteria may not apply to these stories in that they are not designed to adhere to standard literary conventions. Pat Hobby is a series character unlike, for example, the title character of "Bernice Bobs Her Hair." Furthermore, Hobby does not evolve psychologically, morally, or in virtually any other way, unlike Fitzgerald's series characters Basil and Josephine. Susan Garland Mann places the Basil and Josephine stories—as well as other critically respected series such as Sherwood Anderson's *Winesburg, Ohio*, and Ernest Hemingway's *In Our Time*—into the bildungsroman tradition (9, 71), a type of narrative that definitely excludes the Hobby series because Pat decidedly does not mature. In fact, Fitzgerald mentions that

Pat is forty-nine years old in just about every other story, reminding readers that Pat grows neither older nor, by association, wiser.

Such evolution would violate one of the foundations of the narrative genre in which Fitzgerald has cast Hobby. This genre has no convenient name, but it features series characters who are "flat" (as opposed to "round" or designed to change in some way). It appears to be more often found in media other than the paper and ink of literary fiction, and some critics liken the Hobby stories to material found in these other media. Ellen Moers tells us that Pat's "dialogue, his gestures, the plot of his existence are made of celluloid. Fitzgerald did a witty job of blending movie with fiction: at his funniest, Pat Hobby is himself a silent movie comic" (528). Higgins adds that the stories exhibit "something of a comic-strip quality" (173). In Fitzgerald's era, radio was yet another medium in which characters lived episodic lives with virtually no growth, ranging from soap opera's Mary Noble, Backstage Wife, to situation comedy's Fibber McGee and Molly. Still, the closest analogy to Pat Hobby found in traditional prose might be the hard-boiled detective stories that were popular in the twenties and thirties. In some ways, Pat Hobby is a hard-boiled scriptwriter, having a temperament every bit as cynical, streetwise, and alcoholic as a Sam Spade or a Philip Marlowe. As such, the genre Fitzgerald chose for this series is one common to several media, from film to comic strips, from radio to prose.

Generally, these series have been created for popular audiences, monetary gain being a significant part of the artist's inspiration. This seems to be the case with Fitzgerald and Pat Hobby, and it likely contributes to the disdain that many highbrow critics express for the Hobby series. The series was written about the time Fitzgerald was working on *The Last Tycoon,* a novel that, along with Pat Hobby, clearly appears to stem from the author's unhappy experiences working in Hollywood. This has led some critics to put the Hobby stories into a subservient relationship to *The Last Tycoon.* Robert Sklar says that the series served a "primary purpose as a source of income" for Fitzgerald, but it also "drained off his small vindictiveness and petty piques, leaving his mind clear and objective for the large task at hand, a new novel" (328). Matthew J. Bruccoli shares the view that the Hobby stories "purged the bitterness that might otherwise have found its way into the novel." He also emphasizes the financial benefits, stating, "The most important contribution of the

Hobby stories to the novel is that they earned $4,500 worth of writing time" (*Some Sort of Epic Grandeur* 473). Dixon ignores any psychological concerns and describes the stories as "commercial pieces" that "paid the bills" while Fitzgerald wrote his novel (19). Cast in this light, the Hobby stories become devalued as "commercial" or a "commodity" while *The Last Tycoon* is implicitly relegated to the realm of "art," presumably above the taint of commercial considerations.

The critical notion that fiction can be categorized as either "commodity" or "art" began during the eighteenth-century rise of mass-reading audiences, when capitalism supplanted patronage as a means to finance literary production. However, whether any piece of literature written after this shift can be placed exclusively in one or the other of these categories is questioned by Christopher Pawling. He writes: "Whilst one is not denying that the emergence of a market economy has profound implications for the relationship between author and reader, it seems naive to claim that literature as 'art' is somehow immune from this process" (10). While the premise that the Hobby stories facilitated the writing of *The Last Tycoon* financially or psychologically may be valid, it does not logically lead to the conclusion that the novel is unaffected by commercial considerations or, more to the point, that the Hobby stories are without their own artistic merit.

With this in mind, one can begin to see that Fitzgerald has not simply created a flat character and placed him within a type of series made popular in mass media. Rather, he has cast Hobby in this narrative genre to portray the incapacity for growth suffered by a character immersed in mass-market fiction. The Hollywood fantasy factory that surrounds and sustains Hobby also permeates and romanticizes his self-image. The deceptions Hobby creates continually turn back on him, hoodwinking him instead of others until his own identity becomes unstable. Without a sound identity, he has no grounding upon which to grow. Hobby is comic because he cannot learn from his mistakes, but this inability also reveals a tragic insight into human psychology. By keeping Hobby a "flat" character, Fitzgerald follows the conventions of the popular series while investing it with literary depth.

However, this rich characterization is revealed through plots that very likely might distract and disappoint some critics. When considering these plots, we first must remember that the tales were designed to appear as monthly episodes in *Esquire* magazine, and this complicates reading them in a single collection as one might read the chapters of a novel. (Presumably, most readers—critics included—have read the stories in just such a manner ever since they were published as a book in 1962.) Milton R. Stern explains: "If they are read as a book, the stories suffer badly from too much repetition in too brief a space. . . . In the inescapable need to reintroduce Pat Hobby with each new story, according to the demands of that story as a freestanding individual entity in a monthly magazine that the reader might not have seen before and might not see again, Fitzgerald had to repeat many basic details." Stern speculates that Fitzgerald would have amended such repetitions had he had the chance to revise the series for a single book. Without those changes, though, Stern concedes, critics' complaints of "stiffness and tiresomeness in the prose" are justified (Bryer, *New Essays* 316). A mass audience might be as justified in losing its love for almost any popular series if several of its episodes were experienced back-to-back in quick succession.

In addition to repeating basic details, though, Fitzgerald repeats a basic plot structure, and this especially helps to explain why critics have so readily dismissed the Hobby series. "A Man in the Way," the first Hobby story Fitzgerald wrote, provides a basic portrait of the central character, one to which Fitzgerald would add complexities as the series progressed. At the same time, this tale's plot sets a pattern that recurs throughout the series. Here, Hobby attempts to sell Jack Berners, a studio executive, an idea stolen from another scriptwriter, Priscilla Smith. His act of plagiarism (along with his having the audacity to call Smith for a date afterward) sets up Hobby for a retributive downfall. The downfall results from his ignorance of the close relationship between Berners and Smith. As in most of the stories, Hobby returns to his original "sad sack" condition through his own incompetent conniving or some stroke of bad luck.

Such a plot structure might make the piece entertaining, but it fails to evoke the sense of beauty, authenticity, or defamiliarization that traditionally grants literature the status of art. Rather, since it relies upon contrived occurrences and coincidence to work, such a plot structure might be dubbed "hackneyed." Hobby's happening into Smith's office, Smith being a female scriptwriter in the 1930s (something that catches

Hobby off guard), and her being involved with Berners outside the office all add to the sense that Fitzgerald neglects probability in order to make his story end with the main character back in his original place, ready to go through essentially the same process in the next month's episode.

Contrived plots and routine resolutions are often reasons to complain about popular narrative. Regarding predictable endings, we know justice will be served in the vast majority of detective stories. Would it not be more honest to the uncertain, often unfair, predicament of modern humanity to let crime occasionally pay? Would not a more unique, more inventive flourish impress the reader were the detective shot dead just prior to divulging the murderer's identity? The basic plot structure involving an upsetting and rebalancing of the scales of justice that occurs in detective stories and the Pat Hobby series, in which crimes such as plagiarism are committed, brand these works as formulaic. Certainly, they become so when the critic commenting on them focuses primarily on plot. Plot, though, is a rather unusual element of fiction for a critic to use as a criterion for assessing a literary work's aesthetic appeal. Instead, such criticism traditionally is more attentive to a work's fertile symbolic motifs, its penetrating characterizations, its profound and enlightening themes, and other such elements.

The same approach also reveals the best attributes of the Pat Hobby stories. In "A Man in the Way," the story idea that Hobby steals involves an old painter whose artworks are far more cherished than is the artist himself. This is a symbolic parallel, not to Hobby, but to Hobby's romanticized self-image. Much as the painter has grown lamentably unappreciated, the self-pitying Hobby sees himself as having earned better treatment. For this reason, upon describing the painter to Berners, Hobby "warmed to his conception of himself" (*Pat Hobby Stories* 18). It is doubtful that he has truly earned better treatment, however. While we learn that Hobby was once financially well off, we are given several other indications that taking shortcuts, such as stealing story ideas, was as much a part of his past as it is of his present. Fitzgerald reveals that, in "the good old days," Pat relied upon plots, gags, and dialogue created by other people (13–14). Another shortcut is revealed when Hobby explains his tried-and-true method to avoid the trouble of reading novels assigned for film adaptation. He tells Smith, "Give the book to four of your friends to read it. Get them to tell you what stuck in their minds. Write it down and you've got a picture—see?" (16). Taking the easy route appears to have been a lifelong practice for Hobby, but it no longer pays off as it had in previous years.

Nevertheless, Pat uses his past successes to bolster his image in the present. He reminds Berners, "I've got a list of credits second to none" (14). Hobby conveniently forgets that these credits are most likely ill-deserved, and in his mind they become legitimate grounds for better treatment from the studio. This is an early indication of his romanticization of his past, something that becomes more prominent in subsequent stories.

In "Pat Hobby's Christmas Wish," Hobby devises a plan to blackmail producer Harry Gooddorf with a letter that the screenwriter takes to be a signed admission of murder. After Hobby quizzes Gooddorf on his whereabouts on the day of the murder, Gooddorf asks why Hobby thinks it is his business. "It's the business of every decent man," replies Hobby, and after Gooddorf asks when Hobby has ever been a decent man, Pat says, "All my life" (9). This is said in the middle of—and despite—Hobby's blackmailing scheme, revealing the contrast between his grimy actions and his well-laundered image of his past.

Hobby's distortions of his past play a central role in "A Patriotic Short," and they are paralleled to Hollywood's distortions of history. Here, a swimming pool that Hobby once had symbolizes his sparkling past; however, Fitzgerald introduces the pool by saying that "it was entirely cement, unless you should count the cracks where the water stubbornly sought its own level through the mud." The image of the pool—presumably with the cracks erased—emerges in Hobby's mind when he is faced by a low-paying assignment. Fitzgerald says that "all the insolence of office could not take that memory away" (115). Remembering that he once owned a pool sustains Hobby while he does menial rewrite work on the script of a historical biography.

Readers also are prompted to be on guard concerning the veracity of this biography. First, its subject is General Fitzhugh Lee, a national hero who "fought for the Confederacy and later for the U.S.A. against Spain—so it would offend neither North nor South" (116). Concerned with mass appeal and nationwide ticket sales, the film producers take a very selective attitude toward a film's subject matter, even when it concerns American history. We also learn that the script needs to be revised because the "guy that wrote it was a Red and he's got all the Spanish officers with ants in their pants" (117). Again, rather than risk presenting a version of history that would be controversial, if not downright unpopular, by displaying Communist sympathies, Hollywood turns to a writer who can offer a far more palatable story to the audience. In this sense, Pat Hobby is the perfect man for the job.

However, Hobby turns out to be *too* adept at romanticizing the past. Wanting to make this chapter of history even more appealing to the audience, he alludes to the sympathy that can be evoked by Nazi atrocities when he tells Berners that "it might be a good thing if we could give [the movie] a Jewish touch" because of "the way things are and all." Hobby's plan to give the Civil War hero a Jewish love interest is abruptly dismissed by Berners (116). Berners's rejection of this absurd form of revisionist history reveals that at least a few decision makers in Hollywood have limits when it comes to falsification.

Hobby's own limits are not as clearly set, though. He finds comfort in remembering his swimming pool, his chauffeured arrivals at the studio, the bows he received at the gate, and "his ascent to that long lost office which had a room for the secretary and was really a director's office" (116–17). By placing these lush images of the past immediately after Hobby's laughable mangling of American history, Fitzgerald prompts readers to be suspicious of Hobby's recollections. The tale continues to sway between Hobby's glorified memories and the groundless embellishments he adds to the biography. When we finally read about Hobby's memory of none other than the president of the United States telling him that he must "get lots of inspiration sitting by the side of that fine pool" (119), we know that what we have been told about Hobby's past is probably little more than aggrandized personal history and self-delusion. His memory retains truthful images as poorly as his cracked pool held water.

Not only do Hobby and Hollywood invent versions of the past to give it more appeal; both let fiction supplant reality in the present as well. Hobby often crosses between fiction and reality, either deliberately, as when posing as a tour guide in "Homes of the Stars," or accidentally, as when he lands an unwanted acting role in "Pat Hobby Does His Bit." Breaches between fiction and reality also intrude upon Hobby's life. In

"'Boil Some Water—Lots of It,'" Hobby writes the line that gives the story its title, then goes in search of some believable reason why the movie's doctor character might say it. Eventually, he assaults another writer who has crossed from reality to fiction when, as a gag, he disguised himself as a costumed extra. Fiction then turns to reality when the doctor attending him calls, "Boil some water! Lots of it!" (28). Hobby himself becomes an expression of Hollywood's penchant to blur the line between reality and pretense.

Fitzgerald was able to use this theme to comment not only on Hollywood but on the difficulty of maintaining a personal identity when engulfed by such surroundings. With "Pat Hobby and Orson Welles," Fitzgerald satirizes the milieu in which he found himself while writing the series. Simultaneously, he explores the predicament facing a character whose distortions of the past and ruses of the present overtake his ability to trust his own sense of self.

Its title already combining a fictional character with a real person, "Pat Hobby and Orson Welles" places the authentic event of Welles's arrival in Hollywood into the center of Hobby's fictional world. Hobby impugns the lucrative contract that lured the theater and radio sensation to direct films while a colleague mocks his beard. The coveted contract and the beard were both matters that drew much attention when the real Welles went to Hollywood (see Callow 457–58). Welles serves as an apt symbol of crossing the borders of fact and fiction because he had gained renown from his 1939 *War of the Worlds* radio broadcast that panicked thousands by effectively passing off wild fantasy as trustworthy news.

As the tale goes on, people start to notice a resemblance between Hobby and Welles, and Hobby is sometimes addressed as "Orson." Fitzgerald writes: "Now to lose one's identity is a careless thing in any case. But to lose it to an enemy, or at least to one who has become scapegoat for our misfortunes—that is a hardship. Pat was *not* Orson" (47–48). Finally, to raise a few dollars, Hobby allows a makeup artist to apply a fake beard to his face. After the usual foiling of his scheme to secure a writing job, Hobby finds himself in a bar, where he merges into the "corporate whiskers" of bit actors also wearing false beards (51). In the end, Hobby has lost any sense of his individual identity. Even more terrifying, he also has lost his ability to maintain even a shaky sense of self-hood by assuming a false identity.

Ascertaining Hobby's true identity via art is explored in one of the most intriguing of the stories, "Fun in an Artist's Studio." Here, a painter sees Hobby and decides "to make art out of him" (127). The artist goes by the title Princess Dignanni, a dubious appellation that highlights the theme of obscured identity. Hobby sees posing for her as an opportunity for seduction. Of course, his scheme is thwarted, but in a particularly ironic way. The princess calls a cop and, under his authoritative eye, Hobby must undress and pose in nothing but a turkish towel. Even so, Hobby fails "to realize that the Princess was not interested in his shattered frame but in his face" (135). Once Hobby is adequately foiled and frustrated, powerless and stupid, and most tellingly, *exposed,* the artist is able see "the exact expression that had wooed her" (135) into painting Hobby as a portrait representative of "Hollywood and Vine," her title for the work. In this way, Fitzgerald makes Hobby's unveiled self a symbol of the sorry reality underlying his place on the map, Hollywood.

Certainly, Hollywood's reach spreads throughout the country and the world. Facades have an appeal for us all, as shown either by our attraction to the fantasies filmed in Hollywood or by those we ourselves create to find success and erase failure in our own lives. Hobby is not alone in distorting the past and the present to make living easier. As a self-deluding con man in Hollywood, though, he is more prone to become engulfed by facades, and his stories remind us of the dangers of losing ourselves to falsified lives. The core theme of the Pat Hobby stories, then, is hardly "slight." Hobby's psychology is fairly complex, too, especially for a static character. Finally, meaningful symbols also appear, as when a leaky pool parallels Hobby's leaky memory or when Orson Welles's beard becomes an emblem of obscured identity.

Curiously, John A. Higgins says that "a flaw of the Hobby series" is that each story "does not stand too well on its own but gains its full effect only as part of the whole" (177). Exactly why this is a "flaw" is unclear; the Hobby stories, after all, were intentionally designed by Fitzgerald to be an interconnected *series.* Such a rebuff seems based on criteria suitable to typical, independent short stories. However, like the chapters of a Victorian novel appearing in monthly magazine install-ments, the Hobby stories would be appreciated on a more artistic level by their original *Esquire* readers as the series progressed. Such episodic series, featuring characters who never evolve, are still prominent today on television and in other media. When read with this type of narrative in mind, the Pat Hobby stories' literary merit becomes apparent.

18

Fitzgerald

The Authority of Failure

MORRIS DICKSTEIN

It felt strange indeed in the fall of 1996 to mark the centennial of the birth of F. Scott Fitzgerald, a writer whose work still feels so fresh, who died young and seems perpetually young, like Keats, the poet he most loved. Fitzgerald scholars and enthusiasts met at Princeton to celebrate his life and work, and on his actual birthday I found myself speaking about him at the Great Neck Public Library on Long Island, in the very town where he conceived *The Great Gatsby* and began writing it in 1922 and 1923. Great Neck was then a fashionable new suburb much beloved by show business types like Eddie Cantor. But it was also the place Fitzgerald and his wife threw themselves into the wild, sad, drunken parties portrayed with satiric gusto yet also a tragic edge in *Gatsby,* parties that meant as little to Gatsby as to the guests who sponged off him.

Fitzgerald's Great Neck years were not the happiest time of his life, though he seemed, like Gatsby, to be sitting on top of the world. He had only one writer friend there, Ring Lardner, who drank even more than he did. Fitzgerald himself tended to go off on benders for two or three days in New York. It was there he wrote his only play, a political fantasy called *The Vegetable,* which he hoped would make his fortune, but it died in Atlantic City in November 1923, on its way to a Broadway staging that never took place. This was a taste of failure he never forgot. "I worked hard as hell last winter," he later wrote, "but it was all trash and it nearly broke my heart as well as my iron constitution" (Turnbull 141). He was only twenty-seven years old.

Many people would have been surprised at the sad note of waste and decline that creeps into this comment—partly because his best work was still before him, but also since Fitzgerald and his young wife, Zelda, were just then the very embodiments of youthful energy and style for much of fashionable America. But our continuing sense of Fitzgerald as a poet of lyrical longing and dreamy aspiration can easily obscure the darker, more somber side of his work. Like his friend Hemingway, Fitzgerald was not simply a writer but a figure, a cultural icon who would always remain linked in the popular mind with the fizz and exuberance of what he himself named the Jazz Age.

A key element of the Fitzgerald myth, especially that sense of his perpetual high spirits, began with his connection to Princeton. Much to his embarrassment, he never graduated, but in a sense he graduated posthumously when the university became the much-visited haven for his voluminous papers. When Fitzgerald arrived in 1913, Princeton was in many ways far from a serious university, though it had become more serious under its most recent president, Woodrow Wilson, who had gone on to become governor of New Jersey and, earlier that year, president of the United States. It was a very white, very male university, hardly expensive by today's standards but accessible mainly to the children of the rich, those from "good" families who had gone to elite boarding schools. While Fitzgerald's friend and classmate Edmund Wilson, later America's leading literary critic, managed to get a splendid education there, for many others the gentleman's C was a way of life, and there was a long tradition behind it. You could get by quite well without cracking a book. Most Ivy League colleges were so frivolous that the more thoughtful undergraduates, Fitzgerald included, later believed they got their education only after they left school.

As a midwestern boy, Fitzgerald felt like an outsider, not one to the manor born. But *as* an outsider he came to love everything about the school: the dating rituals, the drunken sprees, the football games he never managed to compete in, and the Triangle shows he helped write with his friend Wilson, which became the high points of his college career. A few years later, in the spring of 1920, he published *This Side of Paradise,* a thinly disguised version of his college experiences; to everyone's surprise, it became an overnight sensation. Like Lord Byron in 1812, he awoke and found himself famous. His commercial and literary

careers were launched. A few days later, in a grand ceremony in St. Patrick's Cathedral, he married the belle of Montgomery, Alabama, Zelda
Sayre, a daffy and beautiful young woman who had once broken off her
engagement to him because his financial prospects looked so dim.

With the wild success of the book and the brilliance of their marriage, Scott and Zelda embarked on a decade-long odyssey as the shining young couple whose beauty, charm, and sense of fun embodied the
devil-may-care spirit of the new postwar generation. Whether they
were living among theater people in Great Neck, swimming with other
expatriate Americans along the Riviera, or writing amusing little stories
and articles about each other for stylish popular magazines, Scott and
Zelda came to personify the new youth culture of the Jazz Age, when
life seemed like a drunken lark and a good part of privileged young
America went on a big hedonistic spree.

Living in the public eye, always furnishing good copy, Scott and
Zelda helped write the script that cast them as legends. This was the
beginning of the media age, with its emphasis on personality, novelty,
showmanship, and style. The best one can say about Fitzgerald's role as a
celebrity was that, unlike Hemingway, he never believed his own clippings, and always kept a good deal of himself in reserve, a sense of being
answerable to posterity rather than to the newspapers.

Part of Fitzgerald's problem came later, during the Depression, when
his name remained associated with his portraits of the rich; this in turn
was mistaken for admiration, approval, and envy of their fashionable
lives. But Fitzgerald, though fascinated by the manners and morals of
the rich and intrigued by the freedom that came with their money,
nourished a burning ambition to be a serious writer, someone whose
work would matter to people fifty years later. Among the rich he never
forgot that he was an outsider, but Fitzgerald also proved to be a wick-
edly percipient yet empathetic observer. He took note of how much
and yet how little their money could do for them—how much freedom
and style it gave them, but how little protection it furnished against disappointment and unhappiness, as he himself would later discover.

Fame is famously fickle. Soon after the Crash, everything from the
1920s seemed like ancient history, a tale of sound, fury, and innocence
before the fall; and Fitzgerald's shallow celebrity was no exception.
Within a few short years, F. Scott Fitzgerald would become an icon of a

different kind: once a byword for youth, elegance, and exuberance, he would become an emblem of failure, a back number. Once again, with a vengeance, the icon would obscure the writer and come close to obliterating him. This remains the lesser-known Fitzgerald, the gifted but chastened Fitzgerald of the 1930s. The legend of his decline, which he helped broadcast—everyone who met him during his last years in Hollywood heard it—continues to haunt his reputation today.

Perhaps the worst moment in this unhappy story comes in the fall of 1936. Fitzgerald is about to turn forty, no easy transition for someone whose life was so identified with the passion and promise of youth. Things had long since begun to sour for him. In 1930, Zelda, increasingly desperate to find herself as a writer, a dancer, or simply someone who had a life in her own right, had suffered a nervous breakdown, and since then she had been in and out of hospitals. Scott himself had had a critical success in 1925 with *The Great Gatsby,* a book admired by writers as different as Edith Wharton and T. S. Eliot, but its sales proved disappointing compared to those of his apprentice novels and widely read short fiction. His effort to storm Broadway had failed. Once he had had an almost golden facility; his prose had a spontaneous poetry all its own, but he had struggled for nine years to finish his next novel, *Tender Is the Night,* which got a mixed reaction from critics and the public when it finally appeared in 1934. Reviewers were puzzled and ambivalent; sales again fell short of expectations. Fitzgerald had become a chronic alcoholic, and the failure of his most ambitious book sent him over the edge. But Fitzgerald did more than abuse his health and break down: in the spring of 1936, in a shocking series of articles for *Esquire,* he wrote about his problems in a harsh, unsparing, confessional vein— something familiar to us today from memoirs and talk shows, in which dysfunction has gone public, but completely unheard-of in those more reticent and buttoned-up times.

In these articles Fitzgerald hardly came clean about either his marital problems or his drinking, but he described in surprising detail his loss of confidence and vitality, his failure to take care of his talent, his waste of energy on simply being a celebrity—on his need to be liked, to be charming and personable, to be all things to everyone he knew. This was not yet a therapeutic culture, though Dale Carnegie was just then making his auspicious debut. Hemingway, his friend and cruel rival, who would spend a lifetime burnishing his own myth, was aghast that he would expose himself in this way. Their mutual editor, the legendary Maxwell Perkins of Scribner's, a man of infinite discretion, was saddened and disapproving. Another friend, John Dos Passos, couldn't imagine how anyone could waste his energy on merely personal problems when the whole world was coming apart. But these poignantly written articles brought Fitzgerald's name before the public again, as it had not been for a long time.

Into this picture came a reporter for the *New York Post,* perhaps not so different then from the Murdoch-driven paper it is today, a reporter with the ominous name of Michel Mok, to interview Scott for his fortieth birthday. There was a scent of blood in the water. Fitzgerald was under a nurse's care at an inn in Asheville, North Carolina, but he was still drinking, and the reporter described in wretched detail how he kept popping up for a thimbleful of gin from the makeshift bar, how his face twitched and hands shook as he described his life and made the usual drunkard's rationalizations.

The front page of the *Post* the next day told the whole story: "The Other Side of Paradise / F. Scott Fitzgerald, 40, / Engulfed in Despair / Broken in Health He Spends Birthday Re-/ gretting That He Has Lost Faith in His Star" (Bruccoli, *Some Sort of Epic Grandeur* 413). What had been eloquent if not wholly frank in Fitzgerald's own articles became pathetic in the tabloid version. *Time* picked up the story and gave it much wider currency. The effect on Fitzgerald was catastrophic. He thought he was ruined and took an overdose of morphine, but luckily vomited it up. He felt that his credibility as a writer and a serious man was gone. The *Post* interview was perhaps the lowest point he reached in the decade, but it fixed his image as a washed-up, self-pitying writer, a miserable caretaker of his talent, the relic of a distant and unlamented era. (Even nine years later, when reviewers like Lionel Trilling wrote about *The Crack-up,* Edmund Wilson's collection of his late friend's articles and letters, they would still point to the effects of the *Post* story on Fitzgerald's waning reputation.)

In a limited sense this image endures even today. No one, of course, thinks of Fitzgerald as a pathetic drunk—a "rummy," as Hemingway called him. In fact, Fitzgerald's reputation bounced back amazingly after the war, and *The Great Gatsby* is secure as one of the most widely taught of twentieth-century American classics. But most people still think of his life in the 1930s as the melancholy aftermath of his brilliant decade, a period of decline and failure as vividly portrayed by the man himself. There is no doubt how much he really did suffer during this period, when his golden marriage was all but over, when drink and disappointment often made him behave strangely, when his stories were no longer welcome in magazines that had provided most of his income, when even Hollywood could find no real use for his talents. In the popular mind today, he remains the chronicler of the Jazz Age, the flapper era, the frivolous youth culture, and the more flagrant excesses of the American dream.

To the socially minded critics of the Depression years he was simply irrelevant. This view has curiously been resurrected among some scholars today, who have repeatedly drawn attention to neglected black, proletarian, or women writers of the period. It would be an exaggeration to say that an interest in Zora Neale Hurston, Langston Hughes, or the Harlem Renaissance has been purchased at the expense of, say, *The Great Gatsby, The Sun Also Rises,* or *As I Lay Dying.* Making space for the rediscovered books of Hurston or Nella Larsen doesn't undercut Faulkner and Fitzgerald: the literary canon isn't a zero-sum game, even if the syllabus may be limited. But to many professors Fitzgerald has simply become one of the dead white males, more a burden than a revelation.

Overall, Fitzgerald's work has weathered the politics of multiculturalism reasonably well. Students today still respond passionately to his books, especially *The Great Gatsby,* even if their teachers have gotten bored with connecting it to the American dream, and perhaps have passed some of this boredom on to their charges. There are scholars today who feel that Fitzgerald deals with much too narrow a class of privileged Americans. This echoes the widespread disapproval of his work that was heard during the Marxist 1930s, when proletarian critics grew tired of reading about the Lost Generation and the emotional entanglements of wealthy expatriates on the Riviera in the 1920s. As the young critic Philip Rahv wrote in the Communist *Daily Worker,* reviewing *Tender Is the Night* when it appeared in 1934, "Dear Mr. Fitzgerald, you can't hide from a hurricane under a beach umbrella" (Bryer, *Fitzgerald: The Critical Reception* 317). The hurricane, of course, was the Depression, which exposed the failure of capitalism and drew attention to the class antagonisms that Americans had usually tried to soften and blur.

To his credit, Rahv understood that Fitzgerald's most complex novel, with its assortment of wealthy and idle characters, was a fierce yet subtle indictment of the rich, not a sycophantic tribute to them. But the interests of readers and critics alike had turned elsewhere; the language of fiction, partly under Hemingway's influence, had grown simpler and more plebeian, and Rahv felt that Fitzgerald's celebrated style obscured his harsh theme, "transforming it into a mere opportunity for endless psychologizing" (Bryer, *Fitzgerald: The Critical Reception* 317). Marxists of the 1930s generally saw psychology as self-indulgence, for it drew attention to personal problems—a bourgeois luxury—rather than the social structures of exploitation and injustice. The *New Masses* reviewer of Henry Roth's *Call It Sleep,* published the same year, had mocked the young protagonist as a "six-year-old Proust" and lamented that "so many young writers drawn from the proletariat can make no better use of their working class experience than as material for introspective and febrile novels" (Rideout 189). The same buzzword, "introspective," appears in Rahv's review of Fitzgerald when he complains about the novel's "delicate introspective wording . . . its tortuous style that varnishes rather than reveals the essential facts" (Bryer, *Fitzgerald: The Critical Reception* 316).

It's certainly no news that Marxist critics of the 1930s were none too fond of introspection or stylistic elaboration. They thought they already knew all "the essential facts" about our society, and they preferred a more hard-boiled manner to lay bare the unvarnished truth as they saw it. Ironically, Fitzgerald's own style did become more spare and direct as his life went downhill after 1929 and 1930. The content of his work changed as well, for he was struck by the eerie parallels between his own change of fortunes and the fate of Americans at large. He had prospered in the 1920s when he was at the peak of his fame, then had broken down just as Zelda had her first nervous breakdown in 1930, and suffered deeply as he himself came apart after the relative failure of *Tender Is the Night.* "My recent experience parallels the wave of despair that swept the nation when the Boom was over," he wrote in the last *Esquire* piece (Wilson, *The Crack-up* 84). Fitzgerald felt he had experienced the Crash in personal terms.

In short, it was an already wounded man who was mocked in the *Post* in 1936, but, oddly, someone who had become more of a Depression writer than his critics realized, a writer whose own reverses made him more sympathetic to the failure and misery of others. There is irony here: like another great figure from the 1920s, the seemingly mandarin poet Wallace Stevens, he was attacked by the camp which, in his own fashion, he was actually trying to join. Still, as Fitzgerald began to see himself not as the favored child of fortune, the young prince in the fairy tale, but as a representative man, his work became *more* introspective, not less. In the 1930s, taking stock of his own problems, trying to salvage something out of his losses, Fitzgerald virtually invented the confessional mode in American writing. Later works like Mailer's *Advertisements for Myself* or Robert Lowell's *Life Studies* (both published in 1959) would have been impossible or quite different without the much-maligned example of the "Crack-up" essays. This suggests that it may not be the lyrical, romantic Fitzgerald of the 1920s who most claims our attention today, but the shattered, disillusioned Fitzgerald of the 1930s— not the poet of early success, romantic possibility, and nostalgic regret, but the hard-edged analyst of personal failure and irretrievable loss, the man who redeemed in his work what was slipping away from his life, who achieved a hard-won maturity even as he described himself as a failure, an exhausted man, a spent force.

This is the final irony—that the dark image of Fitzgerald in the 1930s came from Fitzgerald himself, not from the malicious pen of Mr. Mok and the *Post* headline writers. Starting with stories he wrote in 1929 and 1930, long before the "Crack-up" articles, Fitzgerald gave an unsparing account of what was going wrong in his life. More than that, he made creative use of it to take his work in a daring new direction. As in the 1920s, *he* was the source of the myths that circulated around him, but unlike Hemingway, he saved them for his own work, not simply for the gossip columns. This points to the great difference between a writer who breaks down and cannot work and one who uses his frustrations and disappointments as new material, producing work that shows a quantum leap in human understanding.

In one sense, Fitzgerald's writing after 1929 or 1930 became the opposite of everything that preceded it. He became the poet of failure and decline rather than youthful, romantic inspiration. With each revision of the book that became *Tender Is the Night,* the expatriate life of Gerald and Sara Murphy gave way to the troubled history of Scott and Zelda, including her breakdown and his sense of creative blockage and diminishing promise. Yet in other ways this was a clear development from his earlier writings. In an essay on "Early Success," written in 1937 when such success was long behind him, he recalled how everything seemed to go awry for his young heroes: "All the stories that came into my head had a touch of disaster in them—the lovely young creatures in my novels went to ruins, the diamond mountains of my short stories blew up, my millionaires were as beautiful and damned as Thomas Hardy's peasants" (Wilson, *The Crack-up* 87). Fitzgerald came to realize that there was in his fiction always a kernel of tragedy, a dose of melancholy, a backdrop of dark clouds that he had not yet experienced in his own life. But it was all bathed in a romantic glow, a poignant sense of thwarted possibility, loss, and regret.

One of my favorite examples is "Winter Dreams" (1922). Fitzgerald himself said it was an early sketch for *The Great Gatsby.* The very title embodies the story's contradictory moods of hope and frustration, dream and denial. The young hero, with the slightly foolish name of Dexter Green, has invested *his* winter dreams in a young woman with an even more banal name, Judy Jones—a forerunner of Gatsby's great flame, Daisy Buchanan. By the end, after she has toyed with him for years, he finds that Judy Jones has married a man who mistreats her and, worse still, that she has lost her looks, has become commonplace—a shattered dream rather than one that was simply unfulfilled: "The dream was gone. Something had been taken from him." He thinks of

> her mouth damp to his kisses and her eyes plaintive with melancholy and her freshness like new fine linen in the morning. Why, these things were no longer in the world! They had existed and they existed no longer.
>
> For the first time in years the tears were streaming down his face. But they were for himself now. He did not care about mouth and eyes and moving hands. He wanted to care, and he could not

care. For he had gone away and he could never go back any more.
(*The Short Stories* 235)

No one can fail to be moved by the tender simplicity of these lines, which combine a plangent feeling of loss with a hard-nosed sense of inevitability: these things once seemed possible, but now they are not to be. In his early work Fitzgerald was a dreamer but not someone who believed that dreams could be realized. Already in the 1920s, his work had a tragic and elegiac cast, yet he still valued his heroes, like Gatsby, for their generous illusions, for the glow of possibility that surrounded them. *The Great Gatsby* is a novel about a self-made man, about the grandeur and failure of our dreams, but it is also about all that distinguishes them from reality. Think of Nick Carraway's harsh judgment of Daisy Buchanan and the illusions Gatsby has fabricated around her. But think also of Nick's surprisingly warm farewell to Gatsby himself, to whom he alone remains faithful. With his impetuous faith in people, Gatsby is the kind of creature Emily Dickinson had in mind when she wrote, "I dwell in Possibility— / A fairer House than Prose."

This poetic glow of possibility was precisely what diminished into prose for Fitzgerald after 1929 or 1930, starting with some harsh stories about the disintegration of a marriage—"The Rough Crossing" (1929) and "One Trip Abroad" (1930)—stories he never reprinted because they were too close to the material he was developing for *Tender Is the Night*. Both stories, like the novel, are about Americans abroad; both use travel and even bad weather as metaphors for what distracts people from each other, wears them out, and shows up the fault lines in their marriages; both make disillusion and disappointment their central theme. While "The Rough Crossing" centers on a single bad trip, "One Trip Abroad" follows a couple through years of aimless wandering as they move from one hollow niche of "Society" to another. Now broken in health, they have finally landed in a sanitarium in Switzerland, "a country where very few things begin, but many things end" (*The Short Stories* 594). There they see another couple and, in a melodramatic flash of lightning, realize that the pair are their younger selves as we saw them at the beginning of the story, not yet tired, ill, decadent, and out of tune with each other. Despite its unusual gothic touches, "One Trip Abroad" is a schematic miniature of *Tender Is the Night*—its heroine is even called

Nicole—in much the same way "Winter Dreams" contains the seed of *The Great Gatsby.*

But "One Trip Abroad" also connects directly with Fitzgerald's next important piece of fiction and one of his most resonant and enduring stories, "Babylon Revisited" (1931), probably the only Fitzgerald work as widely taught as *The Great Gatsby.* "Babylon" also has its nonfiction parallel in an oft-quoted essay written around the same time, "Echoes of the Jazz Age." Always a staple for historians writing about the 1920s, the essay debunks the very period with which Fitzgerald's name is associated; by 1931, less than two years after the stock market crashed, the 1920s already felt like ancient history—"Only Yesterday," as Frederick Lewis Allen put it in the title of his famous social history, also published in 1931. Fitzgerald sees the period somewhat nostalgically, with mock horror, as his own and the culture's "wasted youth," a "flimsy structure" built on "borrowed time" that came tumbling down when the players lost all their confidence (Wilson, *The Crack-up* 21, 22). But whatever elegiac glow could be found in the essay was ruthlessly excised from the story, where there is almost nothing of value to redeem the old way of life.

Charlie Wales returns to Paris, the scene of many a debauch in the 1920s, to reclaim his daughter from the fierce sister-in-law to whom he had been forced to surrender custody. His wife had died under circumstances for which he bore some responsibility, and his own health had broken under the weight of his drinking, but now, like Fitzgerald himself in "The Crack-up," he has somehow managed to paste it all together. Sober and serious for the first time in years, he wants his daughter back before her childhood has completely passed him by, before she no longer really knows him. Much of the story is taken up with his reflections on his former life: "he suddenly realized the meaning of the word 'dissipate' [a word that had also figured significantly in "One Trip Abroad"]—to dissipate into thin air; to make nothing out of something. . . . He remembered thousand-franc notes given to an orchestra for playing a single number, hundred-franc notes tossed to a doorman for calling a cab" (620). This had once seemed insouciant, carefree, impulsive; but "In retrospect it was a nightmare" (629).

His high-strung sister-in-law blames him unfairly for her sister's death, but much as she dislikes him, she is beginning to relent. She can see that he's a changed man, a man who desperately wants his daughter, his future, restored to him. But into this volatile mix comes a blundering, drunken, intrusive couple from his earlier life—"sudden ghosts out of the past" (622), revenants like the couple in "One Trip Abroad"—the worn remnants of a time when they all lived for pleasure, for the moment. After one particularly jarring intrusion, Charlie's sister-in-law pulls back, refuses even to see him. By reminding everyone of how he used to live, the doppelgänger couple has done him in, ruined him all over again. Once Fitzgerald had focused lovingly on characters who dreamed a life for themselves, imagined an idyllic or romantic future. Now he writes about people who have learned that the past cannot easily be set aside: our actions have consequences, and the ghosts of our earlier selves will continue to haunt us, without a trace of their old romantic gleam.

Elements of Fitzgerald's new hard-edged, almost tragic outlook can be found in virtually every significant piece of writing he did in the 1930s—in stories like "Babylon Revisited" and "Crazy Sunday"; in the essays, letters, and journals collected in Edmund Wilson's landmark edition of *The Crack-up* (1945), the book that did so much to restore Fitzgerald's reputation after the war; in novels like *Tender Is the Night* and the unfinished *The Last Tycoon;* and even in commercial formula fiction like the seventeen Pat Hobby stories he wrote for *Esquire* in the last year of his life, stories that continued to appear month after month even after Fitzgerald's death in December 1940.

These terse and brutally satiric sketches, written mainly for money, give us Hollywood through the eyes of a hack writer, not Fitzgerald himself but the kind of facile mediocrity who drove him crazy when he was trying to learn screenwriting as a serious craft. As his name suggests, Pat Hobby is the sort of talentless fellow who knows all the little tricks (tricks so old they don't even work anymore), who steals ideas and schemes for screen credit but would hardly dream of reading the books he's supposed to adapt. According to the formula Fitzgerald evolved, Pat Hobby gets his well-deserved comeuppance in every story.

But Fitzgerald could never write about people entirely from the outside, without insinuating something of himself into them, seeking some authentic core of emotion in their character. The mildly despicable Pat Hobby is washed up, an ineffectual remnant of the silent film days, hanging on by a thread. So Fitzgerald invests some of his own sense of failure in Hobby, just as he had invested it, much more subtly, in the inexorable decline of his real alter ego, Dick Diver, in the second half of *Tender Is the Night*. Hobby has always been a hack, even when the little tricks still came off, but Diver was once a serious, promising, brilliant man, a psychiatrist who made an unfortunate marriage to one of his former patients and, though he was acutely aware of the risk of being bought, gradually allowed himself to be taken over by her wealthy family as a private nursemaid. But this is only one of many reasons that his life went awry. Diver's decline has no single, definite cause; it has too many causes. Fitzgerald may have modeled it on the vague disintegration of the ambitious and idealistic young minister in one of his favorite novels, Harold Frederic's *The Damnation of Theron Ware* (1896). Diver's fate rivals the precipitous descent of Hurstwood in *Sister Carrie* as the greatest failure story in American literature. Like the gifted but flawed protagonist of Santayana's 1936 novel *The Last Puritan,* Diver is a man who simply "peters out."

This focus on failure is what makes the last phase of Fitzgerald's career resonate so strongly with the Depression for us in ways that contemporary readers failed to register. The critics who attacked him for still writing about the rich were as misguided as the friends who accused him of wallowing in self-pity. Fitzgerald had always worked not simply by investing himself in his characters but by mythologizing himself, heightening his dreams and disappointments into representative moments, carrying much of the culture on his back. Now, as the world tried to forget him, to relegate him to the past, he turned the miseries of his life into confessional fables, becoming again a symbol of the age, but this time an unwelcome one, a reminder of how much America had lost. Comparing himself as usual to Hemingway, he wrote in his notebooks: "I talk with the authority of failure—Ernest with the authority of success" (Wilson, *The Crack-up* 181). The operative word here is "authority," not simply "failure": *Something broke in me, but I speak with the force of experience. I am a different animal, someone who has gained a hard-won maturity.* In Whitman's famous words from "Song of Myself," "I am the man, I suffer'd, I was there" (225). He lived it, but rather than buckling under its weight, he also wrote it, transforming it into a story he'd never told before.

Eventually, *Tender Is the Night* grew on readers who had disliked or misunderstood it when it first appeared. Hemingway, though he later came grudgingly to admire the book, at first objected fiercely to the touches of tragedy in it. His own view was more stoical, fatalistic. "We are all bitched from the start," he wrote to Fitzgerald. "You see Bo, you're not a tragic character. Neither am I" (Hemingway, *Selected Letters* 408). A few years later Fitzgerald was determined to write a tragic novel about Hollywood at exactly the moment he was satirizing it in his stories. The source was not self-pity, as Hemingway mistakenly imagined, but something richer, harsher, deeper—a sense of deprivation and loss that alters one's outlook, a distilled clarity that comes through in every line of "The Crack-up," *Tender Is the Night,* and the unfinished text of *The Last Tycoon.*

My emblem for this last phase of Fitzgerald's work is a little-noted passage in his 1932 essay "My Lost City," one of the greatest tributes ever written to New York. Near the end, Fitzgerald does what many New Yorkers did that year, just as the Depression is approaching its darkest point: he goes up to the top of the Empire State Building, then newly built, and finds that instead of scaling the heavens, as he might have hoped to do, he gets a better perspective on the terrestrial world below:

> Full of vaunting pride the New Yorker had climbed here and seen with dismay what he had never suspected, that the city was not the endless succession of canyons that he had supposed but that *it had limits*—from the tallest structure he saw for the first time that it faded out into the country on all sides, into an expanse of green and blue that alone was limitless. And with the awful realization that New York was a city after all and not a universe, the whole shining edifice that he had reared in his imagination came crashing to the ground. (Wilson, *The Crack-up* 32; emphasis in original)

On one level this passage is a little joke on the provinciality of New Yorkers, much like Saul Steinberg's celebrated cartoon of the contracted world west of the Hudson as seen from Manhattan. But something more serious is happening here as well. The "country on all sides," the "expanse of green and blue that alone was limitless," is clearly an allusion to the great climax of *The Great Gatsby* when, before the narrator's very eyes, "the inessential houses began to melt away until gradually I became aware of the old island here that flowered once for Dutch sailors' eyes—a fresh, green breast of the new world." There, in Fitzgerald's grandiose leap of imagination, man had come "face to face for the last time in history with something commensurate to his capacity for wonder" (140). Here, in "My Lost City," that dreamy Utopian capacity for wonder, the whole imagined sense of possibility, crumbles before a new sense of limits.

The *Gatsby* passage, though hedged with subtle qualifications, speaks for the poetic, expansive Fitzgerald of the 1920s; this new version, with its tone of mockery and humility, speaks for the chastened Fitzgerald of the 1930s, a writer who accords far better with our own painfully acquired sense of limits. What was the watchword of social policy and political frustration in post-1960s America if not a sense of dashed hopes and more limited goals? This is the clear-eyed, un-self-pitying mood that underlies every Fitzgerald text of the Depression decade, most patently in "The Crack-up," which his contemporaries misread and undervalued, though it should have been as congenial to hard times as it is to our own post-utopian era.

This was the mood of the great romantic crisis poems, which formed Fitzgerald's sensibility long before he fully understood them, before he actually experienced their peculiar mixture of elation and regret, loss and renewal, crisis and resolution. This was the disintoxicated mood of the last stanza of Keats's Nightingale Ode, a poem Fitzgerald could never read aloud without tears. On the surface it appears that Fitzgerald goes from being a pie-eyed romantic in the 1920s to a disillusioned realist in the 1930s, except that this very disintoxication is a crucial moment of the romantic imagination. It's the moment of clarity when the dreamer, the visionary, is humanized by loss, by suffering, by fellow feeling, when the mental traveler, no longer adrift in "faery lands forlorn," turns homeward, in Keats's words, in "Ode to a Nightingale," to the "sole self," the self without romantic illusions (371–72).

All these poems proceed from a sense of visionary possibility, through a maelstrom of inner crisis and loss, and finally to a more modest rededication to new beginnings, exactly as Fitzgerald does in the "Crack-up" essays. This was the thrust of both "Tintern Abbey" and the Intimations

Ode, but perhaps Wordsworth put it best in his "Elegiac Stanzas" about Peele Castle written in 1805, after his beloved brother John was lost at sea. He gazes at the turbulent seascape painted by a friend and thinks how he would once have added some calming touch, a romantic glow— in Wordsworth's famous phrase, "the gleam, / The light that never was, on sea or land." (How much like the way Fitzgerald himself had provided a shimmer of iridescence at every turn in his early stories, even the sad ones.) But Wordsworth tells us he can do this no longer. His whole sense of reality has been altered by his brother's unexpected death. Nature now appears anything but benign:

> So once it would have been,—'tis so no more;
> I have submitted to a new control:
> A power is gone, which nothing can restore;
> A deep distress hath humanised my soul. (*Selected Poems* 373–74)

These troubled but grimly hopeful lines, stark yet consoling, could serve as a motto for all the neglected writing of F. Scott Fitzgerald's last decade, when the lyrical dreamer gave way to the disillusioned realist with his chastened sense of maturity. This may be the work of Fitzgerald's that makes the deepest claim on us today. Even Hemingway, ever competitive, came around in the end. "Scott's writing got better and better, but no one realized it, not even Scott," he told his son Gregory. "The stuff he was writing at the end was the best of all. Poor bastard!" (Gregory Hemingway 103).

19

The Last Tycoon and Fitzgerald's Last Style

MILTON R. STERN

As Fitzgerald matured in his novelistic development, he steadily hard-ened his presentations of the actual—the daily circumstances and fac-ticity and events of his protagonists' lives and livelihoods. Concurrently, his style became more sinewy as he incorporated his early attempts at gorgeousness into narrative progress and objectifications of theme. The direction of Fitzgerald's stylistic development as a novelist is signaled by the extent to which his conception of his protagonists' worlds of work becomes progressively enlarged, specified, and scenically objectified from book to book. The development of Fitzgerald's materials and the development of his style are corollaries of each other. One could say the same of his style and his life.

As Edmund Wilson states flatly in the brief introduction to his 1941 edition of *The Last Tycoon,* it is not only the clearly conceived and mas-terfully understood internality of Monroe Stahr's character but also the external circumstantial concreteness, the close-range observation of Stahr's "proper place in a larger scheme of things[,] . . . [t]he moving-picture business in America . . . studied with a careful attention," that for Wilson marked this novel as "Fitzgerald's most mature piece of work" (*The Last Tycoon* 6).[1]

Whatever the statistical relative increase in details of the workaday world, Fitzgerald's fragment is rich in suggestions that thematically, at least, the author was going to do what he always had been most com-pelled to do with his specific details: he was going to write another magically haunting tale about the moral significances of American history. This time Hollywood would be the central metaphor for the trajectory of that history out of the past and into the present-day omens for the future.

As *The Last Tycoon* promises a return to the poignantly evocative imagery and to the historical and moral dimensions of motifs and themes characteristic of a Fitzgerald masterwork, it also indicates a further step in—not a departure from—the development of Fitzgerald's style. Alas and of course, the imagery, theme, and motifs were never fully worked out in Fitzgerald's lovely fragment. But though we can glimpse them only in part, what we can see clearly is their direction and probability. And we do have a full view, in drafts and revisions, of what already had happened to Fitzgerald's style. Although I question Wilson's blanket edict that *The Last Tycoon* is "Fitzgerald's most mature piece of work," his observation about objective facticity offers an expanding hint about style.

Fitzgerald always had two loves in the stylistic directions of his art. One was that of the lyricist, the other that of the scenarist. As *This Side of Paradise* gave notice in almost every paragraph, he experienced an early lyrical intoxication with what he would later come to identify in Keats's poetry, which he defined for his daughter as "the richest most sensuous imagery" at its "most utter value for evocation, persuasion or charm" (*Letters* 88). But Fitzgerald also experienced an early childhood excitement with backyard skits and, when he was fourteen and fifteen, with the Elizabethan Drama Club's presentations of his plays *The Captured Shadow* (1910) and *Coward* (1911). The failure of his play *The Vegetable* (1923) when he was twenty-seven did not deter him from trying his hand again and again with the scenario's demand for the spoken word and the communicative power of concrete objectification—ideas and emotions shown rather than described in "the richest most sensuous imagery." Furthermore, from George Lorimer's *Saturday Evening Post* audience of the 1920s to Arnold Gingrich's *Esquire* audience of the 1930s, Fitzgerald's financial dependence on the short story made him necessarily concerned with the demands of the magazine marketplace for a clear, straight story line. Most especially, his continuing labors with movie scripts kept him at constant practice in techniques designed for meaning through action, through concrete, compacted scenes rather than richly or sensuously expanded expressions of his own and other people's inner selves.

The development of Fitzgerald's style in his novels reflected his continuing practice as a professional commercial writer. It is true that the Pat Hobby stories and movie scripts—amidst the exigencies of his life— were among what he considered the junk necessities of his craft and his being. But their intrusions and interruptions while he was working on *The Last Tycoon*—which he was trying to model after *The Great Gatsby,* a book he considered the high art of his craft and being—were not detrimental only (or completely) when we consider the direction in which his style was developing.[2] In short, the effects of Fitzgerald's necessary emphasis on commercial work should not be dismissed, for they were positive in many ways. If indeed, and to the extent that, "*The Last Tycoon* is . . . even in its imperfect state, Fitzgerald's most mature piece of work," it is in any case fair to say that the development of style in Fitzgerald's novels was a progress from lyrical celebration toward what Eliot long ago called the objective correlative—that is, toward the combination of thematic idea and associational evocation in a unifying objectification within the concretely actualized scene. That is, again, from the lyricist to the scenarist. And from the very birth of Fitzgerald's identity as novelist, the scenarist was beginning to emerge from the lyricist, eventually to become a coequal and, finally, the senior partner.

At the beginning, in *This Side of Paradise,* except for the first chapter, we learn much more of Amory Blaine's internal lyrical sentience than we actually see of the concrete specifics of his daily existence within the context of his studies, his family, his income, and their exigencies. To say this is not to kick cows because they are not horses: *This Side of Paradise* is wholly itself, a bildungsroman, and is also wholly entitled to its own characteristics. The point is that despite the book's many promissory moments of Fitzgerald's genius with externalities, it is fair to note that his early sense of serious writing was the lush expression of internalities, the young man's excited sensibilities, feeling and response, mood for its own sake and for the luxurious literary showing off it afforded. Yet, even in this earliest book Fitzgerald vented the scenarist's impulse, inserting a thirty-one-page three-act playlet about "The Debutante," interspersed with only four pages of prose narrative. But even more important than the physical form of presentation was the scenarist's early presence in the visual specificity of such items as those that objectified the distance between the identity that Amory pretends and the actualities of the fourteen-year-old little boy: the dirty moccasins born yellow but turned greenish brown, the gray plaid mackinaw, the red toboggan cap, and the gray one that pulled down over his face.

In *The Beautiful and Damned,* Fitzgerald moved from extended romantic description and singing himself toward his genius with composite characters and concentrated description of objective circumstance. If his first novel was the necessary outlet of his youthful, great lyrical urge, his second was the necessary learning of narrative craft. Here, only nine pages into the book, the scenarist is given a six-page playlet, "The Three Men," which is separated by three pages of narrative prose from a three-page playlet called "A Flashback in Paradise." But if the pages of playscript are fewer, it is only to have them give way to an increased facticity of visualized event outside the protagonist. The subjectivity of the lyricist begins to give way to the objectivity of the storyteller who sees the autonomy and significance of circumstance.

In his second novel, Fitzgerald made a large step toward the primacy of narrative. In the process, the density of his social and moral observation increased as he paid closer attention to subsidiary materials that were objectifications of the moral dimensions of the narrative, and not just means toward rich imagery or his protagonist's inner song. Richard Caramel and Joseph Bloeckman, who do the daily work and who earn the money that Anthony does not, and the Patch family, with its households, history, and money, all become important narrative ingredients of Anthony's and Gloria's contexts, and Fitzgerald approached them with greater specificity than he had provided for his presentation of the Blaine money.

As *The Beautiful and Damned* made a long step from lush rhetoric toward narrative objectification, *The Great Gatsby* made a gigantic step in the merger of the two. Yet even here, in a book profoundly concerned with money, we see Gatsby at work only for a moment as we eavesdrop while he's on the telephone, and only for a hint while he's at lunch with Meyer Wolfshiem and Nick. Otherwise he remains completely a luftmensch, which, of course, is at the center of the novel's purpose. But we retain a vision of Nick heading every morning down Manhattan's canyons toward the financial district where he works, and we see the red and gold set of Nick's unused books on banking and investments; we breathe the gray dust of Wilson's bleak garage and we smell the gas-pump; and we know how Carraway and Wilson earn their income. Nick's (and thus the book's) rich and sensual imagery serves to convey the lyrical dimension of Gatsby's romantic dream of self, but the context is the destructive facticity—the hard *thereness*—of American society, manners, history, economics, and popular culture. Holding the dream's demand for lyric in marvelous tension with the circumambient hardness of the external world, Fitzgerald distanced dreaming Gatsby even from his own dense actualities: "'The dance?' He dismissed all the dances he had given with a snap of his fingers. 'Old sport, the dance is unimportant'" (85).

The enormous advance of Fitzgerald's marvelous third novel is marked by what he had learned from following *This Side of Paradise* with *The Beautiful and Damned:* his evocative mastery in combining lyric and scenario. Yet, as set pieces like the famous paragraph about the "fresh, green breast of the new world" indicate, Fitzgerald's descriptions could still abound with lyrical feeling couched in romantic abstraction. In fact, that paragraph and the last three paragraphs, the most widely quoted and familiar paragraphs of the entire book, though essentially styled by brilliantly evocative scenic objectifications, retain a surprising amount of lyric feeling presented in abstract terms like "the last and greatest of all human dreams," "a transitory enchanted moment," "an aesthetic contemplation [man] neither understood nor desired," "something commensurate to [man's] capacity for wonder" (140), and "the orgastic future that year by year recedes before us" (141). In the context of stylistic relationship between the juvenilia of *This Side of Paradise* and the magnificence of *The Great Gatsby,* I am struck by how much of these closing four paragraphs is abstract lyricism cast in "words [at] their most utter value for evocation, persuasion or charm."

But by now the lyrical abstractions are enclosed within and resonate against the thematic recapitulation made by the closing seven paragraphs, which scenically objectify and hold the richness of feeling—the final car arriving too late for any gala; the obscene word scrawled with a bit of brick on the white step, rasped out by Nick's shoe in the moonlight; the shadowy, moving glow of a ferryboat across the sound; the green light; the blue lawn. At this point in Fitzgerald's stylistic development, lyrical evocation, persuasion, and charm—what Fitzgerald referred to as "elaborate and overlapping blankets of prose" in *The Great Gatsby* (*Letters* 480)—had been thoroughly buttressed, buffered, and contextualized by objective specificity and visualization that exists not only for the sake of mood, but also, and brilliantly, for a functional recapitulation of thematic strains. The emotionally evocative creation of feeling, the expression of lyrical urge, no longer arises merely as an extended cry *de profundis pueri*. It arises from the functional scene *seen*.

The magical, ironic place that *The Great Gatsby* occupies in the development of Fitzgerald's style lies in the consideration that the thousand objective details Gatsby dismisses with a snap of his fingers are now Fitzgerald's scenic building blocks of connections between myth and facticity, between moral theme and social observation, between evocation and history—between lyric and scenario.

Intensifying and expanding the scrutiny of his building blocks of facticity, social observation, history, and scenario through almost nine years of delay and revision, Fitzgerald brings us to what is arguably his richest novel, *Tender Is the Night*. Here, although for the first forty-two chapters[3] Fitzgerald gives us Dick's life and self from the inside, we see much more of Diver at work as he makes his rounds in the clinic and as he extravagantly plies his trade as host and protector. We *see* him in his profession, and we know about his earnings and the cost of his clinic and the source of the money to meet its purchase price. And by the time Fitzgerald arrived at the seventeenth draft of *Tender Is the Night,* even the "overlapping blankets of prose" are just about all gone. (That's equivocal: here and there are a few brief moments, like the description of the view looking down from the funicular at Montreux, but even such bits, like the overlapping blankets of prose in *Gatsby,* have their ideational use.) It is the direction of Fitzgerald's stylistic development that accounts for general impressions of the books: we tend to remember *The Great Gatsby* in terms of compellingly moving rhetorical set pieces, and to remember *Tender Is the Night* in terms of compellingly moving scenes. In the latter, all descriptions—like our tour of Nicole's garden, or the evening of Dick's magical garden party, or the beach when Dick makes his final farewell—are, like the description of one of Gatsby's typical parties, thematically functional scenes filled with highly charged ions of language, specific particles of character and object, but all impelled with the forward energy of narrative event.

At the premature close of his life, by the time Fitzgerald wrote his way into *The Last Tycoon* he left in this unfinished novel not one single passage of description extended in Keatsian overtones. The advent of a Tennessee dawn is presented through Cecilia's mildly sardonic voice: "There was an eager to-do in the eastern sky" (19). Period.[4]

And in *The Last Tycoon,* in chapters 3 and 4 of Edmund Wilson's version, which are episodes 7 through 12 in Bruccoli's,[5] we are brought factually, visually, and dramatically to the details of the hero's working day—to the very heart of it, both inside and outside the hero himself.

As is well known, for Fitzgerald the requirements of the scenarist did not stop in 1923 with the failure of *The Vegetable.* After tentative attempts to be a Hollywood screenwriter in 1927 and 1931, he returned to the West Coast in 1937 to spend the last four years of his life working on scenarios for the studios, on short stories—and on *The Last Tycoon.*

We like to insist on one-half of Fitzgerald's caveat, that the short stories and the movies were bread-and-butter work of the moment, junk work for money, and that the novels were his serious works of art. If only he had stuck to the "line" he discovered in *Gatsby,* he lamented.[6] Very true. But not entirely. For we also know Fitzgerald's other caveat that only the ignorant think you can write short stories on the bottle. Those who thought so didn't know George Horace Lorimer or the pains that Fitzgerald took with vision, revision, and re-revision. We must take account of two salient facts. First, Fitzgerald made it clear that *The Last Tycoon* was in the *Gatsby* "line" of serious high art, a "line" he so heartbreakingly rediscovered while up to his eyes in short stories and scriptwriting. Second, in *The Last Tycoon* he forcefully gave superiority to his scenario-savvy central character in a confrontation between the serious scenarist and the serious novelist of ideas: between Monroe Stahr and George Boxley, stand-ins for two seriously gifted people, Irving Thalberg and Aldous Huxley. The confrontation leaves no doubt that Fitzgerald as novelist retained an artist's deep professional respect for the scenaristic talents and sensibilities that were able to create story and idea by arranging narrative relationships and forward momentum visually and objectively. The scene is so clearly at the heart of what Fitzgerald was doing stylistically that it is worth reproducing at length.

George Boxley, the novelist who is very aware of himself as a man of fine and high writing (the *Gatsby* "line"), is frustrated in his attempt to write with assigned collaborators—typical studio hacks—the screenplay for which he was hired. Contemptuous of the very idea of scenario, he is so angry in his interview with Monroe Stahr that he remains in his seat only as if held there by invisible attendants.

"I can't get what I write on paper," broke out Boxley. "You've all been very decent, but it's a sort of conspiracy. Those two hacks you've teamed me with listen to what I say, but they spoil it—they seem to have a vocabulary of about a hundred words."

"Why don't you write it yourself?" asked Stahr.

"I have. I sent you some."

"But it was just talk, back and forth," said Stahr mildly. "Interesting talk, but nothing more."

Now it was all the two ghostly attendants could do to hold Boxley in the deep chair. He struggled to get up; he uttered a single quiet bark which had some relation to laughter but none to amusement, and said:

"I don't think you people read things. The men are duelling when the conversation takes place. At the end one of them falls into a well and has to be hauled up in a bucket."

He barked again and subsided.

"Would you write that in a book of your own, Mr. Boxley?"

"What? Naturally not."

"You'd consider it too cheap."

"Movie standards are different," said Boxley, hedging.

"Do you ever go to them?"

"No—almost never."

"Isn't it because people are always duelling and falling down wells?"

"Yes—and wearing strained facial expressions and talking incredible and unnatural dialogue."

"Skip the dialogue for a minute," said Stahr. "Granted your dialogue is more graceful than what these hacks can write—that's why we brought you out here. But let's imagine something that isn't either bad dialogue or jumping down a well. Has your office got a stove in it that lights with a match?"

"I think it has," said Boxley stiffly, "—but I never use it."

"Suppose you're in your office. You've been fighting duels or writing all day and you're too tired to fight or write any more. You're sitting there staring—dull, like we all get sometimes. A pretty stenographer that you've seen before comes into the room and you watch her—idly. She doesn't see you, though you're very close to her. She takes off her gloves, opens her purse and dumps it out on a table—"

Stahr stood up, tossing his key-ring on the desk.

"She has two dimes and a nickel—and a cardboard match box. She leaves the nickel on the desk, puts the two dimes back into her purse and takes the black gloves to the stove, opens it and puts them inside. There is one match in the matchbox and she starts to light it kneeling by the stove. You notice that there's a stiff wind blowing in the window—but just then your telephone rings. The girl picks it up, says hello—listens—and says deliberately into the phone, 'I've never owned a pair of black gloves in my life.' She hangs up, kneels by the stove again, and just as she lights the match, you glance around very suddenly and see that there's another man in the office, watching every move the girl makes—"

Stahr paused. He picked up his keys and put them in his pocket.

"Go on," said Boxley smiling. "What happens?"

"I don't know," said Stahr. "I was just making pictures."

Boxley felt he was being put in the wrong.

"It's just melodrama," he said.

"Not necessarily," said Stahr. "In any case, nobody has moved violently or talked cheap dialogue or had any facial expression at all. There was only one bad line, and a writer like you could improve it. But you were interested."

"What was the nickel for?" asked Boxley evasively.

"I don't know," said Stahr. Suddenly he laughed. "Oh, yes—the nickel was for the movies."

The two invisible attendants seemed to release Boxley. He relaxed, leaned back in his chair and laughed.

"What in hell do you pay me for?" he demanded. "I don't understand the damn stuff."

"You will," said Stahr grinning, "or you wouldn't have asked about the nickel." (41–44)

As for the studio hacks, the short stories that occupied Fitzgerald while he was writing *The Last Tycoon* were the Pat Hobby stories for *Esquire*. Though certainly not in the *Gatsby* "line," these hurried commercial pieces have much more than Hollywood material in common with the high art of *The Last Tycoon*. They share a stylistic context.

In the modernist merger of realist and romantic that characterized experimental artistic newness in the first quarter of the twentieth century, these otherwise opposing parties of metonymy and metaphor met, especially in the disillusioning effects of World War I, in an insistence on style as truth—dialogue, event, sentence structure, and characterization stripped down to and symbolic of the essentials of experience. The experiential, outer facticity, the scenaristic, was rendered to develop the path that had been blazed by the impressionists—the lyrical, the inner impression of the experiential externality, the "internal difference, where the meanings are," as Emily Dickinson put it in "A Certain Slant of Light."

In American fiction the two great postwar leaders in the advance of symbolic experiential style and purpose over conventional narrative style and purpose were Mark Twain, post–Civil War, and Ernest Hemingway, post–World War I. The modernist conquest was completed in the 1920s, and by 1939, the year Fitzgerald began composing the Pat Hobby stories and *The Last Tycoon, Esquire* revealed the extent to which the effects of the modernist revolution had established the mode of the popular literary marketplace. Not only because of its marketing attempt at male sophistication but also because of its marketing attempt at modern sophistication, *Esquire* cultivated a macho savoir faire, a cosmopolitan, ironic style whose terseness and metonymic surface bespoke both marketing attempts at once. With the visual, ironic, stripped, macho metonymics in his fiction creating the unstated, deep internals, Hemingway became the prize horse in *Esquire*'s stable, and his influence on Fitzgerald should be reckoned as part of the magazine's demands in the dynamics of the development of Fitzgerald's style.

The Pat Hobby stories are characterized by irony, compression, swift efficiency, objective visualization, and a hint of the hard–boiled wise–guy perspective that carry all the tonal implications Fitzgerald needed in his narration of character, ambience, and plot for *Esquire*. The drunken Irish hack, Pat Hobby, was part of Fitzgerald's revulsed vision of one possible aspect of himself, just as the exhausted creative Jew, Monroe Stahr, was Fitzgerald's tragic vision of another. But Pat Hobby and Monroe Stahr are also composite with aspects of other people, and like all of Fitzgerald's protagonists (except, possibly, for Amory Blaine), they are not auto-biographical self-portraits. We need note the hint of autobiographical flavor only to point out that whatever the concurrently created short stories and uncompleted novel tell us about Fitzgerald's psychological wholeness or acuity, they tell us more about his rhetorical directions, and are more important for a grasp of the development of Fitzgerald's style than for a grasp of his biography. Although the Pat Hobby stories do not belong among Fitzgerald's best, they carry an important merger into the style of *The Last Tycoon.* It was a merger of the development of style in late-nineteenth-century and early-twentieth-century American prose fiction with the parallel development of style in Fitzgerald's prose fiction from his first novel onward.

To glance at an overview of the stylistic development I am suggesting, consider this description of a moonlit night, back at the very beginnings of Fitzgerald's career as a novelist, in *This Side of Paradise:* "The great tapestries of trees had darkened to ghosts back at the last edge of twilight. The early moon had drenched the arches with pale blue and weaving over the night, in and out of the gossamer rifts of moon, swept a song, a song with more than a hint of sadness, infinitely transient, infinitely regretful" (46). We can glimpse here a promise of the Fitzgerald to be, but the gorgeous language is there for its own lyrical sake, satisfying the author's pride and pleasure in showing off a passage of mood in language that is there only for its "most utter value for evocation, persuasion or charm."

Now jump ahead, through the stylistic hints of reportorial development in *The Beautiful and Damned,* through the alembic of the great merger of lyric and scenario in *The Great Gatsby,* through the increased visualization of the world of work and the decrease of lyric in *Tender Is the Night,* through the compression, visualization, and initiate irony of the Pat Hobby stories, and the circumambient context of Fitzgerald the Hollywood scenarist, and see where the moon is now. In *The Last Tycoon,* when we fly down at last with Cecilia into the lights of the Glendale airport, "The California moon was out, huge and orange over the Pacific" (28). That's all we are told about the moon. And Fitzgerald leaves the picture hanging, preferring that his terseness should emphasize the evocative power of the words. Within the metaphoric context of the westering airplane flight (New York to the Hermitage, the Hermitage to Hollywood), the associations of the historical westwarding with Hollywood hype are all summed up in the modifier—a California moon. The evocative association of hype and West are intensified in "huge and orange over the Pacific." The single adjective preceding "moon" and the simple descriptive phrase following it are perfect for the associations Fitzgerald wishes to create: the staginess and tropical social weather of the Hollywood that the West had become—a production item . . . yet somehow also gorgeous.

Similarly, the compression and tone become functionally apt for the theme as Stahr stands alone on the lot, waiting to meet a woman who will turn out to be only a mistaken illusion of the person he seeks: "There was a moon down at the end of the boulevard, and it was a good illusion that it was a different moon every evening, every year" (77). *A* moon. Period. In the context of Stahr's ironic perception at the moment, that indefinite article, *a,* tells us sardonically that it was another, same, gorgeous, illusionally varied California moon and also provides an implicit but full evocation of Stahr's lonely, cynically operational state of being and seeing. Or, when the weather is changing in Stahr's relationship with Kathleen, as the pair drives to his beach house in progress: "Out here a moon showed behind the clouds. There was still a shifting light over the sea" (105). And that's all. But the context develops the terseness: for Stahr perhaps there's romantic light showing promise again behind the gloom of his loneliness. Fitzgerald shows moons in contexts and presents them in understated facticity. When we see Hollywood itself as phantasmagoria, "under the moon the back lot was thirty acres of fairyland" (34), and the last time that Stahr ever sees Kathleen again "it was a dark night with no moon" (134). Sparse as they are, in their context these passages are wonderfully functional and evocative. And almost all of them could have been directions in a scenario script. Most tellingly, when Fitzgerald presents a moon through a reversion to his earlier use of lush metaphor for its own sake, because, presumably, it sounded good to him at the moment—something he did fleetingly only two or three times in *The Last Tycoon*—it is so out of plumb with what Fitzgerald's style had become that it is excruciatingly noticeable, and we wince:

Stahr is waiting for a theme to play itself out within himself. "It would come in some such guise as the auto horns from the technicolor boulevards below, or be barely audible, a tattoo on the muffled drum of the moon" (114). The auditory and visual trope of auto horns and technicolor boulevards works with beautiful efficiency in this *scenaristically* evocative style, which makes us acutely aware that a reversion to the fancy showiness of the subjectively inspired tropes of *This Side of Paradise* does not. "A tattoo on the muffled drum of the moon" indeed!

None of this is to say that the more Fitzgerald's style might become like Raymond Chandler's and less like Keats's the better it would be. That would be as absolutely nonsensical as saying that at his best Fitzgerald was merely an imitator of Hemingway. Fitzgerald was completely and exquisitely his own genius. He managed—magically, given his circumstances in the 1930s—to retain his signature power of compelling evocation even as his style moved closer to the *Esquire* aspect of modernism that characterized the circumambient current of his times. A reading of *The Great Gatsby* followed immediately by a reading of *The Last Tycoon* will make clear to almost any reader what direction Fitzgerald's style had taken in his great major novels. What is revealed in the continuing stylistic development through the course of all his novels is that Fitzgerald's genius lay not in the repudiation of the lyricist but in the wedding of the lyrical imagist and the evocative scenarist—with the scenarist emerging toward the end of his life as the larger figure.

The dawn taxi ride to the Hermitage at the beginning of *The Last Tycoon* exemplifies the descriptive component created by its double function of providing actualizing visual specifics for a scene in motion and providing an evocative objective correlative for a theme:

> We drove for a long time over a bright level countryside, just a road and a tree and a shack and a tree, and then suddenly along a winding twist of woodland. I could feel even in the darkness that the trees of the woodland were green—that it was all different from the dusty olive-tint of California. Somewhere we passed a Negro driving three cows ahead of him, and they mooed as he scatted them to the side of the road. They were real cows, with warm, fresh, silky flanks, and the Negro grew gradually real out of the darkness with his big brown eyes staring at us close to the car,

as Wylie gave him a quarter. He said, "*Thank* you—thank you," and stood there, and the cows mooed again into the night as we drove off. (16)

The scenaristic quality of this passage is the result of Fitzgerald's steady development toward evocative concentration that, at its most spare, characterizes all of what we have of *The Last Tycoon*. We cannot say that in final form *The Last Tycoon* would have been the least lyrical of all of Fitzgerald's novels. And we should not say that it would have been a good thing if it had been. But we can say that we could have trusted the incorporation of lyric feeling into the scenario style that Fitzgerald had forged. It would have been entirely composed of the kind of pungent facticity that created the evocative power of the specific names on Nick Carraway's old train schedule.

Fitzgerald had shaped his genius and trimmed his talent by smelting and testing them in the smithy of adversity, forming his style from his screenwriting, his late short stories, the demands of his marketplace, the directions of literary history, and a gift that yet remained merged with what was left of the lyrical heart's evocations. On the West Coast he was in new time and territory, bringing with him some tricks of the heart from his old home. Like Monroe Stahr, in his *Last Tycoon* and what turned out to be his last style, F. Scott Fitzgerald had been westering to a new dawn of his old brilliance, which was cut off by death before it could run the course of its own bright day.

Notes

1. Because I have reservations about Matthew J. Bruccoli's Cambridge edition, questionably titled *The Love of the Last Tycoon: A Western* (1993), and because Edmund Wilson's 1941 edition is hard to come by, for the reader's convenience I use the more available 1970 reprint of Wilson's edition. All quotations from the text are cited from this edition.

2. "I am deep in [*The Last Tycoon*]," Scott wrote to Zelda on October 23, 1940, "living in it, and it makes me happy. It is a *constructed* novel like *Gatsby*, with passages of poetic prose when it fits the action, but no ruminations or side-shows like *Tender*. Everything must contribute to the dramatic movement"

(*Letters* 128). Fitzgerald's apparent denigration of *Tender Is the Night* is not to be taken at face value, for at times he had thought of *Tender* as his best book, his "testament of faith," and he kept trying to revise it for republication, which queasy publishers and then death prevented. But he consistently used *Gatsby* as his benchmark for excellence, proud of its fine construction. His many references to *Tycoon* as *Gatsby* may be found, among fugitive items in other works, in Turnbull, in Bruccoli and Duggan, and in Bruccoli's introduction to *The Love of the Last Tycoon*. The point is that Fitzgerald returned to *Gatsby* for the artistry of its *structure*. The rhetorical *style* that culminated in *The Last Tycoon* had long since moved toward that of the despised studio scenarios and Pat Hobby stories, and by the late 1930s Fitzgerald was able to identify at least the nature of that style with the serious high art he associated with *The Great Gatsby* and *Tender Is The Night*.

3. I refer to the chapters as given in the 1951 edition, "With the Author's Final Revisions," which in turn is reprinted in *Three Novels of F. Scott Fitzgerald* (1953). This is Fitzgerald's "final" version—an uncompleted eighteenth draft of the novel—as he would have liked it could he have found a willing publisher. This version is out of print and hard to find, but it reveals much more clearly than the first-edition version the shift in Fitzgerald's use of point of view concerning our seeing Dick Diver from the inside or from the outside. There are several more compelling reasons to claim Fitzgerald's revised version as the better of the two, but it is unlikely that we shall see it in print, anew and definitively edited, in the near future.

4. It might be objected that the voice here is Cecelia Brady's, not Fitzgerald's. But all through the manuscript, in parts that Fitzgerald had not yet worked out as being part of Cecelia's knowledge, the voice, necessarily Fitzgerald's, remains the same. It is terse and presents its story in scenaristic chunks of action.

5. I prefer to remain with Edmund Wilson's edition. In the 1,691 paragraphs of the manuscript proper, with only three exceptions there are only minor differences between Wilson and Bruccoli. One of the exceptions is a change of names from Jane Meloney to Rose Meloney. Another comprises the deletion of Mr. Marcus's phone call (paragraphs 470–79) and the insertion of part of a sentence in paragraph 503, both instances part of the Prince Agge episode. The third is the deletion of three and one-half sentences and the addition of one in the middle of the second paragraph of Wilson's chapter 4 (paragraph 542). Markings on the manuscript make Bruccoli's changes equivocal. Especially equivocal is the marking on the manuscript page on which Bruccoli bases his change of the title from *The Last Tycoon* to *The Love of the Last Tycoon: A Western*. Except for the ambiguous intent of the marking, there is nothing

else on which to base the title change. Sheilah Graham disagreed with the change, insisting that the shorter title was the one Fitzgerald always used and the one that was reminiscent of the cadence of the title *The Great Gatsby.* She also said that *The Last Tycoon* was Fitzgerald's title, not something imposed by Edmund Wilson. Frances Kroll Ring, who was Fitzgerald's secretary at the time he was writing *The Last Tycoon,* remembers that she and Fitzgerald always referred to the title as either *Stahr* or *The Last Tycoon* and that he never indicated any but an amused sense of the title as *The Love of the Last Tycoon: A Western* (see *Love of the Last Tycoon* xc–xci, and also my "On Editing Dead Modern Authors" [15n]). Bruccoli's choice of title and his questionable deletions make Wilson's the preferable version. However, Bruccoli's edition is useful for its introduction and for the several places in which Bruccoli cleaned up details of accidence and a few minor substantives. But, overall, as in his doing away with Wilson's chapter numbers and divisions and replacing them with "Episodes," it is important to recognize that Bruccoli prepared what is essentially a researcher's presentation of the manuscript rather than a reader's edition. As such, it occupies a problematical place as a volume in the Cambridge University Press "definitive" edition of *The Works of F. Scott Fitzgerald.*

6. "What little I've accomplished has been by the most laborious and uphill work," Fitzgerald wrote to his daughter six months before his death, "and I wish now I'd *never* relaxed or looked back—but said at the end of *The Great Gatsby:* 'I've found my line—from now on this comes first. This is my immediate duty—without this I am nothing'" (*Letters* 79).

WORKS CITED

Aaron, Daniel. *The Unwritten War: American Writers and the Civil War.* Oxford, UK: Oxford UP, 1975.

Acland, Charles. *Youth, Murder, Spectacle: The Cultural Politics of "Youth in Crisis."* Boulder, CO: Westview, 1995.

Aldridge, John W. *After the Lost Generation.* New York: McGraw-Hill, 1951.

Allen, Joan M. *Candles and Carnival Lights: The Catholic Sensibility of F. Scott Fitzgerald.* New York: New York UP, 1978.

Alpers, Paul. *What Is Pastoral?* Chicago: U of Chicago P, 1996.

Aristotle. *The Rhetoric.* Trans. Lane Cooper. Englewood Cliffs, NJ: Prentice-Hall, 1960.

Bakan, David. "Adolescence in America: From Idea to Social Fact." *Daedalus* 100 (1971): 979–95.

Bargainnier, Earl F. "The Myth of Moonlight and Magnolias." *Louisiana Studies* 15 (1976): 5–20.

Baudrillard, Jean. *The System of Objects.* Trans. James Benedict. London: Verso, 1996.

Berman, Ronald. *"The Great Gatsby" and Fitzgerald's World of Ideas.* Tuscaloosa: U of Alabama P, 1997.

———. *"The Great Gatsby" and Modern Times.* Urbana: U of Illinois P, 1994.

Bewley, Marius. "Scott Fitzgerald's Criticism of America." *Sewanee Review* 62 (1954): 223–46.

Bier, Jesse. *The Rise and Fall of American Humor.* New York: Henry Holt, 1968.

Bloom, Harold, ed. *Modern Critical Views: F. Scott Fitzgerald.* New York: Chelsea House, 1985.

Booth, Wayne C. *The Company We Keep: An Ethics of Fiction.* Berkeley: U of California P, 1988.

————. *The Rhetoric of Fiction.* Chicago: U of Chicago P, 1961.

Breit, Harvey. "Talk with James Thurber." *New York Times Book Review* June 29, 1952: 19.

Brooke, Rupert. *The Collected Poems of Rupert Brooke.* New York: Dodd, Mead, 1927.

Brooks, Cleanth. "The American 'Innocence' in James, Faulkner, and Fitzgerald. *Shenandoah* 16.1 (1964): 21–37.

Bruccoli, Matthew J. *Fitzgerald and Hemingway: A Dangerous Friendship.* New York: Carroll and Graf, 1994.

————. "'An Instance of Apparent Plagiarism': F. Scott Fitzgerald, Willa Cather, and the First *Gatsby Manuscript." Princeton University Library Chronicle* 39 (1978): 171–78.

————, ed. *New Essays on "The Great Gatsby."* Cambridge, UK: Cambridge UP, 1985.

————. *Some Sort of Epic Grandeur: The Life of F. Scott Fitzgerald.* New York: Harcourt Brace Jovanovich, 1981.

Bruccoli, Matthew J., ed., with the assistance of Jennifer McCabe Atkinson. *As Ever, Scott Fitz—: Letters between F. Scott Fitzgerald and His Literary Agent Harold Ober, 1919–1940.* Philadelphia: J. B. Lippincott, 1972.

Bruccoli, Matthew J., with Judith S. Baughman. *Reader's Companion to F. Scott Fitzgerald's "Tender Is the Night."* Columbia: U of South Carolina P, 1996.

Bruccoli, Matthew J., and Jackson R. Bryer, eds. *F. Scott Fitzgerald in His Own Time: A Miscellany.* Kent, OH: Kent State UP, 1971.

Bruccoli, Matthew J., and Margaret M. Duggan, eds., with the assistance of Susan Walker. *Correspondence of F. Scott Fitzgerald.* New York: Random House, 1980.

Bryer, Jackson R., ed. *F. Scott Fitzgerald: The Critical Reception.* New York: Burt Franklin, 1978.

————. *New Essays on F. Scott Fitzgerald's Neglected Stories.* Columbia: U of Missouri P, 1996.

————. *The Short Stories of F. Scott Fitzgerald: New Approaches in Criticism.* Madison: U of Wisconsin P, 1982.

Bryer, Jackson R., Alan Margolies, and Ruth Prigozy, eds. *F. Scott Fitzgerald: New Perspectives.* Athens: U of Georgia P, 2000.

Budick, Emily Miller. *Fiction and Historical Consciousness: The American Romance Tradition.* New Haven: Yale UP, 1989.

Burhans, Clinton S., Jr. "Structure and Theme in *This Side of Paradise." JEGP* 68 (1969): 605–24.

Calinescu, Matei. *Five Faces of Modernity: Modernism, Avant-Garde, Decadence, Kitsch, Postmodernism.* Durham, NC: Duke UP, 1987.

Callahan, John F. *The Illusions of a Nation: Myth and History in the Novels of F. Scott Fitzgerald.* Urbana: U of Illinois P, 1972.

Callow, Simon. *Orson Welles: The Road to Xanadu.* London: Jonathan Cape, 1995.

Cantor, Norman. *Twentieth-Century Culture: Modernism to Deconstruction.* New York: Peter Lang, 1988.

Capp, Al. *Li'l Abner Dailies: Vol. 17 (1951).* Northampton, MA: Kitchen Sink P, 1993.

———. *Li'l Abner Dailies: Vol. 18 (1952).* Northampton, MA: Kitchen Sink P, 1993.

Cash, W. J. *The Mind of the South.* 1941. New York: Vintage, 1981.

Cather, Willa. *A Lost Lady.* 1923. New York: Vintage, 1990.

———. *Not Under Forty.* New York: Knopf, 1936.

Chase, Richard. *The American Novel and Its Tradition.* Baltimore: Johns Hopkins UP, 1957.

Chatman, Seymour. *Story and Discourse: Narrative Structure in Fiction and Film.* Ithaca, NY: Cornell UP, 1978.

Cole, Thomas. *The Journey of Life: A Cultural History of Aging.* New York: Cambridge UP, 1991.

Crim, Lottie R., and Neal B. Houston. "The Catalogue of Names in *The Great Gatsby.*" *Research Studies* 36 (1968): 113–30.

Crosland, Andrew T. *A Concordance to F. Scott Fitzgerald's "The Great Gatsby."* Detroit: Bruccoli Clark/Gale, 1975.

Cross, K. G. W. *F. Scott Fitzgerald.* New York: Grove P, 1964.

de Beauvoir, Simone. *The Second Sex.* 1949. Ed. and trans. H. M. Parshley. New York: Vintage, 1974.

Delbanco, Andrew. *The Death of Satan: How Americans Have Lost the Sense of Evil.* New York: Farrar, Straus and Giroux, 1995.

Dijkstra, Bram. *Evil Sisters: The Threat of Female Sexuality and the Cult of Manhood.* New York: Knopf, 1996.

Dixon, Wheeler Winston. *The Cinematic Vision of F. Scott Fitzgerald.* Ann Arbor: UMI Research P, 1986.

Donaldson, Scott, ed. *Critical Essays on F. Scott Fitzgerald's "The Great Gatsby."* Boston: G. K. Hall, 1984.

———. *Fool for Love: F. Scott Fitzgerald.* New York: Congdon & Weed, 1983.

———. "Scott Fitzgerald's Romance with the South." *Southern Literary Journal* 5.2 (1973): 3–17.

Douglas, Mary, and Baron Isherwood. *The World of Goods.* New York: Basic Books, 1979.

Drake, Constance. "Josephine and Emotional Bankruptcy." *Fitzgerald/Hemingway Annual* 1 (1969): 5–13.

Dupee, F. W., ed. *The Question of Henry James: A Collection of Critical Essays.* New York: Henry Holt, 1945.

Eble, Kenneth. *F. Scott Fitzgerald.* Boston: G. K. Hall, 1977.

———, ed. *F. Scott Fitzgerald: A Collection of Criticism.* New York: McGraw-Hill, 1973.

Eliot, T. S. *Collected Poems, 1909–1962.* New York: Harcourt Brace Jovanovich, 1963.

———. *The Sacred Wood: Essays on Poetry and Criticism.* London: Methuen, 1920.

Ewen, Stuart. *All Consuming Images: The Politics of Style in Contemporary Culture.* New York: Basic Books, 1989.

Fass, Paula S. *The Damned and the Beautiful: American Youth in the 1920's.* New York: Oxford UP, 1977.

Faulkner, William. *Absalom, Absalom!* 1936. New York: Vintage, 1990.

———. *The Sound and the Fury.* 1929. New York: Random House, 1984.

Ferguson, Robert A. "The Grotesque in the Novels of F. Scott Fitzgerald." *South Atlantic Quarterly* 78 (1979): 460–77.

Fine, Richard. *Hollywood and the Profession of Authorship, 1928–1940.* Ann Arbor: UMI Research P, 1985.

"The Fitzgerald Flap." *Friends of the Princeton University Library Newsletter* 3 (1988): 1–3.

Fitzgerald, F. Scott. *Afternoon of an Author: A Selection of Uncollected Stories and Essays.* New York: Scribner's, 1958.

———. *The Apprentice Fiction of F. Scott Fitzgerald: 1909–1917.* Ed. John Kuehl. New Brunswick, NJ: Rutgers UP, 1965.

———. *Babiron ni kaeru: Za sukotto fittujerarudo bukku 2* (Babylon Revisited: The Scott Fitzgerald Book 2). Trans. Haruki Murakami. Tokyo: Chuokoron-sha, 1996.

———. *Babylon Revisited and Other Stories.* New York: Scribner's, 1971.

———. *The Basil and Josephine Stories.* Ed. Jackson R. Bryer and John Kuehl. New York: Scribner's, 1973.

———. *The Beautiful and Damned.* New York: Scribner's, 1922.

———. *Flappers and Philosophers.* Ed. James L. W. West III. Cambridge, UK: Cambridge UP, 2000.

———. *F. Scott Fitzgerald: Manuscripts.* Ed. Matthew J. Bruccoli. 6 vols. New York and London: Garland, 1990–91.

———. *F. Scott Fitzgerald on Authorship.* Ed. Matthew J. Bruccoli with Judith S. Baughman. Columbia: U of South Carolina P, 1996.

———. F. Scott Fitzgerald Papers, Firestone Library, Princeton University.

———. *F. Scott Fitzgerald's Ledger: A Facsimile.* Washington, DC: NCR/Microcard Editions, 1972.

———. *F. Scott Fitzgerald's St. Paul Plays, 1911–1914*. Ed. Alan Margolies. Princeton, NJ: Princeton University Library, 1978.

———. *F. Scott Fitzgerald's Screenplay for "Three Comrades" by Erich Maria Remarque*. Ed. Matthew J. Bruccoli. Carbondale: Southern Illinois UP, 1978.

———. "A Full Life." *Princeton University Library Chronicle* 49 (1988): 167–72.

———. *The Great Gatsby*. 1925. Ed. Matthew J. Bruccoli. New York: Macmillan/ Scribner's, 1992.

———. *The Great Gatsby: A Facsimile of the Manuscript*. Ed. Matthew J. Bruccoli. Washington, DC: Microcard Editions, 1973.

———. *The Last Tycoon*. 1941. New York: Scribner's, 1970.

———. *The Letters of F. Scott Fitzgerald*. Ed. Andrew Turnbull. New York: Scribner's, 1963.

———. *A Life In Letters*. Ed. Matthew J. Bruccoli, with the assistance of Judith S. Baughman. New York: Scribner's, 1994.

———. *The Love of the Last Tycoon*. Ed. Matthew J. Bruccoli. Cambridge, UK: Cambridge UP, 1993.

———. *Mai losuto shitii* (My Lost City). Trans. Haruki Murakami. Tokyo: Chuokoron-sha, 1981.

———. "A Note on My Generation." F. Scott Fitzgerald Papers, Firestone Library, Princeton University.

———. *The Notebooks of F. Scott Fitzgerald*. Ed. Matthew J. Bruccoli. New York: Harcourt Brace Jovanovich/Bruccoli Clark, 1978.

———. *Novels and Stories, 1920–1922*. Ed. Jackson R. Bryer. New York: Library of America, 2000.

———. *The Pat Hobby Stories*. New York: Scribner's, 1962.

———. *Poems, 1911–1940*. Ed. Matthew J. Bruccoli. Bloomfield Hills, MI: Bruccoli Clark, 1981.

———. *The Price Was High: The Last Uncollected Stories of F. Scott Fitzgerald*. Ed. Matthew J. Bruccoli. New York: Harcourt Brace Jovanovich/Bruccoli Clark, 1979.

———. *The Short Stories of F. Scott Fitzgerald: A New Collection*. Ed. Matthew J. Bruccoli. New York: Scribner's, 1989.

———. *Six Tales of the Jazz Age and Other Stories*. New York: Scribner's, 1960.

———. *The Stories of F. Scott Fitzgerald*. New York: Scribner's, 1951.

———. *Tender Is the Night*. 1934. New York: Scribner's, 1962.

———. *This Side of Paradise*. 1920. Ed. James L. W. West III. Cambridge, UK: Cambridge UP, 1995.

———. *Three Novels of F. Scott Fitzgerald*. New York: Scribner's, 1953.

———. *The Vegetable; or, From President to Postman*. New York: Scribner's, 1923.

Fitzgerald, F. Scott, et al. *Safety First*. Cincinnati: John Church, 1916.

Fitzgerald, Zelda. *The Collected Writings*. Ed. Matthew J. Bruccoli. New York: Scribner's, 1991.

Flusche, Michael. "Thomas Nelson Page: The Quandary of a Literary Gentleman." *Virginia Magazine of History and Biography* 84 (1976): 464–85.

Foote, Shelby, ed. *Chickamauga, and Other Civil War Stories*. New York: Delta, 1993.

Freeman, Donald C., ed. *Essays on Modern Stylistics*. New York: Methuen, 1981.

Frye, Northrop. *Anatomy of Criticism*. Princeton, NJ: Princeton UP, 1957.

Fryer, Sarah Beebe. *Fitzgerald's New Women: Harbingers of Change*. Ann Arbor: UMI Research P, 1988.

"F. Scott Fitzgerald & Zelda Sayre." *People* February 12, 1996: 163–64.

Gallop, Jane. *Reading Lacan*. Ithaca, NY: Cornell UP, 1985.

Gammons, P. Keith. "The South of the Mind: The Changing Myth of the Lost Cause in the Life and Work of F. Scott Fitzgerald." *Southern Quarterly* 36.4 (1998): 106–12.

Gavin, William Joseph. *William James and the Reinstatement of the Vague*. Philadelphia: Temple UP, 1992.

Gervais, Ronald J. "Gatsby's Extra Gardener: Pastoral Order in the Jazz Age." *Illinois Quarterly* 43.3 (1981): 38–47.

Gilman, Charlotte Perkins. *Women and Economics*. 1898. New York: Harper, 1966.

Giltrow, Janet, and David Stouck. "Style as Politics in *The Great Gatsby*." *Studies in the Novel* 29 (1997): 476–90.

Goldhurst, William. *F. Scott Fitzgerald and His Contemporaries*. Cleveland: World, 1963.

Goldman, Emma. *Anarchism and Other Essays*. 1910. Port Washington, NY: Kennikat P, 1969.

"The Great Catsby." *Tweety and Sylvester*, no. 59 (1976): 25–31.

Greeley, Andrew. *The Catholic Myth: The Behavior and Beliefs of American Catholics*. New York: Scribner's, 1990.

Green, Harvey. *The Uncertainty of Everyday Life, 1915–1945*. Fayetteville: U of Arkansas P, 1992.

Griffith, Bill. *Zippy*. Comic strip. *Washington Post* April 20, 1991.

Gross, Barry. "Back West: Time and Place in *The Great Gatsby*." *Western American Literature* 8 (1973): 3–13.

Gross, Theodore. *Thomas Nelson Page*. New York: Twayne, 1967.

Grossberg, Lawrence. *We Gotta Get Out of This Place: Popular Conservatism and Postmodern Culture*. New York: Routledge, 1992.

Guiles, Fred Lawrence. *Marion Davies: A Biography*. New York: McGraw-Hill, 1972.

Hachtman, Tom. *Gertrude's Follies.* New York: St. Martin's P, 1980.

Hall, G. Stanley. *Adolescence and Its Psychology and Its Relations to Physiology, Anthropology, Sociology, Sex, Crime, Religion, and Education.* 2 vols. New York: Appleton, 1904.

Hall, Stuart, and Tony Jefferson, eds. *Resistance through Rituals: Youth Subcultures in Post-War Britain.* London: Hutchinson, 1976.

Halliday, M. A. K., and Ruqaiwa Hasan. *Cohesion in English.* London: Longman, 1976.

Harper, Ralph. *Nostalgia.* Cleveland: P of Western Reserve U, 1966.

Hart, Jeffrey. "'Great Gatsby' Offers Insight into Watergate Affair." *Richmond (VA) Times-Dispatch* May 8, 1973: 16.

Hart, Stan, and Mort Drucker. "The Great Gasbag." *Mad,* no. 172 (1975): 4–10.

Hebdige, Dick. *Hiding in the Light: On Images and Things.* New York: Comedia, 1988.

Hecht, Ben. *A Child of the Century.* New York: Simon and Schuster, 1954.

Hemingway, Ernest. *Selected Letters, 1917–1961.* Ed. Carlos Baker. New York: Scribner's, 1981.

———. *The Sun Also Rises.* 1926. New York: Scribner's, 1986.

Hemingway, Gregory H. *Papa: A Personal Memoir.* Boston: Houghton Mifflin, 1976.

Hendriksen, Jack. *"This Side of Paradise" as a Bildungsroman.* New York: Peter Lang, 1993.

Higgins, John A. *F. Scott Fitzgerald: A Study of the Stories.* Jamaica, NY: St. John's UP, 1971.

Holman, Harriet R. "Magazine Editors and the Stories of Thomas Nelson Page's Late Flowering." *Essays Mostly on Periodical Publishing in America.* Ed. James Woodress. Durham, NC: Duke UP, 1973. 148–61.

Inge, M. Thomas. *Comics as Culture.* Jackson: UP of Mississippi, 1990.

James, William. *Writings, 1902–1910.* Ed. Bruce Kuklick. New York: Library of America, 1987.

Kazin, Alfred, ed. *F. Scott Fitzgerald: The Man and His Work.* Cleveland: World, 1951.

Keats, John. *The Poems of John Keats.* Ed. Jack Stillinger. Cambridge, MA: Harvard UP, 1978.

Kehl, D. G. "Varieties of Risible Experience: Grades of Laughter in Modern American Literature." *Humor: International Journal of Humor Research* 13 (2000): 379–93.

Kennedy, Elizabeth Lapovsky. "Lesbianism." *The Reader's Companion to U.S. Women's History.* Ed. Wilma Mankiller et al. Boston: Houghton Mifflin, 1998. 327–29.

Kerr, Frances. "Feeling 'Half Feminine': Modernism and the Politics of Emotion in *The Great Gatsby.*" *American Literature* 68 (1996): 405–31.

Kett, Joseph F. *Rites of Passage: Adolescence in America 1790 to the Present.* New York: Basic Books, 1973.

Kierkegaard, Søren. *Stages on Life's Way.* 1845. Trans. Walter Lowrie. Princeton, NJ: Princeton UP, 1940.

Kristeva, Julia. *Desire in Language: A Semiotic Approach to Literature and Art.* Trans. Leon S. Roudiez, Alice Jardine, and Thomas Gora. New York: Columbia UP, 1984.

Kruse, Horst H. *Schlüsselmotive der amerikanischen Literatur.* Düsseldorf: Francke, 1979.

———. "Teaching Fitzgerald's *Tender Is the Night:* The Opening and Closing Chapters of a Great Novel." *Literatur in Wissenschaft und Unterricht* 31 (1998): 251–67.

Kuehl, John, and Jackson R. Bryer, eds. *Dear Scott/Dear Max: The Fitzgerald-Perkins Correspondence.* New York: Scribner's, 1971.

Kuhnle, John H. "*The Great Gatsby* as Pastoral Elegy." *Fitzgerald/Hemingway Annual* 10 (1978): 141–54.

Labrie, Ross. *The Catholic Imagination in American Literature.* Columbia: U of Missouri P, 1997.

Lacan, Jacques. *Écrits: A Selection.* Trans. Alan Sheridan. New York: Norton, 1977.

Lacan, Jacques, and the *école freudienne. Feminine Sexuality.* Ed. Juliet Mitchell and Jacqueline Rose. Trans. Jacqueline Rose. New York: Norton, 1982.

Lasky, David. *Minit Classics Presents: Joyce's "Ulysses."* Falls Church, VA: D. Lasky, 1991.

Lears, Jackson. *Fables of Abundance: A Cultural History of Advertising in America.* New York: Basic Books, 1994.

Lee, A. Robert, ed. *Scott Fitzgerald: The Promises of Life.* New York: St. Martin's P, 1989.

Lehan, Richard D. *F. Scott Fitzgerald and the Craft of Fiction.* Carbondale: Southern Illinois UP, 1966.

———. *"The Great Gatsby": The Limits of Wonder.* Boston: Twayne, 1990.

Lerner, Gerda. *The Creation of Patriarchy.* New York: Oxford UP, 1986.

Le Vot, André. *F. Scott Fitzgerald: A Biography.* Trans. William Byron. Garden City, NY: Doubleday, 1983.

Liney, John J. "Henry." *Cartoonist Profiles,* no. 31 (1976): 11–16.

Long, Robert Emmet. *The Achieving of "The Great Gatsby": F. Scott Fitzgerald, 1920–1925.* Lewisburg, PA: Bucknell UP, 1979.

———. "The Vogue of Gatsby's Guest List." *Fitzgerald/Hemingway Annual* 1 (1969): 23–25.

MacKethan, Lucinda H. "Plantation Fiction: 1865–1900." *The History of Southern Literature*. Ed. Louis J. Rubin, Jr., et al. Baton Rouge: Louisiana State UP, 1981. 209–18.

Mangum, Bryant. *A Fortune Yet: Money in the Art of F. Scott Fitzgerald's Short Stories*. New York: Garland, 1991.

Mann, Susan Garland. *The Short Story Cycle: A Genre Companion and Reference Guide*. New York: Greenwood P, 1989.

Marx, Leo. *The Machine in the Garden: Technology and the Pastoral Ideal in America*. New York: Oxford UP, 1964.

McGilligan, Pat, ed. *Backstory: Interviews with Screenwriters of Hollywood's Golden Age*. Berkeley: U of California P, 1986.

Mencken, H. L. *In Defense of Women*. Rev. ed. New York: Knopf, 1922.

———. *The Philosophy of Friedrich Nietzsche*. 1913. 3rd ed. Port Washington, NY: Kennikat P, 1967.

———. *Prejudices: Second Series*. New York: Knopf, 1920.

Metcalf, Greg. "A Source for 'Two Old Timers.'" Unpublished paper delivered at the F. Scott Fitzgerald Centennial Conference, September 1996, Princeton University, Princeton, NJ.

Metzger, Charles R. *F. Scott Fitzgerald's Psychiatric Novel: Nicole's Case, Dick's Case*. New York: Peter Lang, 1989.

Michiura, Motoko. "Shisen: Itamu, Hikari Agata san" (Her Eyes: In Memory of Agata Hikari). *Subaru Monthly* November 1992: 300–302.

Milford, Nancy. *Zelda: A Biography*. New York: Harper & Row, 1970.

Miller, James E. *F. Scott Fitzgerald: His Art and His Technique*. New York: New York UP, 1964.

Miller, John, ed. *Los Angeles Stories: Great Writers on the City*. San Francisco: Chronicle Books, 1991.

Mizener, Arthur. *The Far Side of Paradise: A Biography of F. Scott Fitzgerald*. 1951. New York: Vintage, 1959.

———, ed. *F. Scott Fitzgerald: Twentieth Century Views*. Englewood Cliffs, NJ: Prentice-Hall, 1963.

Moers, Ellen. "F. Scott Fitzgerald: Reveille at Taps." *Commentary* 34 (1962): 526–30.

Monk, Craig. "The Political F. Scott Fitzgerald: Liberal Illusion and Disillusion in *This Side of Paradise* and *The Beautiful and Damned*." *American Studies International* 33 (1995): 60–70.

Monk, Donald. "Fitzgerald: The Tissue of Style." *Journal of American Studies* 17 (1983): 77–94.

Montrelay, Michèle. "Inquiry into Femininity." *French Feminist Thought: A Reader*. Ed. Toril Moi. Oxford, UK: Basil Blackwell, 1987. 227–49.

Moore, Benita A. *Escape into a Labyrinth: F. Scott Fitzgerald, Catholic Sensibility, and the American Way.* New York: Garland, 1988.

Moore, Marianne. *The Complete Poems of Marianne Moore.* New York: Macmillan/Penguin Books, 1982.

Moreland, Kim. *The Medievalist Impulse in American Literature: Twain, Adams, Fitzgerald and Hemingway.* Charlottesville: UP of Virginia, 1996.

Morris, Wright. *The Territory Ahead.* New York: Harcourt, Brace, 1957.

Murakami, Haruki. "Bunshou ni yoru kyuusai o shinjite: Sukotto fittujera-rudo" (Believing in Redemption by Writing: Scott Fitzgerald). *Asahi Shinbun* (morning ed.) June 21, 1996: 23.

———. *Noruwei no mori* (Norwegian Wood). Tokyo: Kodansha, 1987.

———. *Norwegian Wood.* 1987. Trans. Alfred Birnbaum. Tokyo: Kodansha International, 1989.

———. *Za sukotto fittsujerarudo bukku* (The Scott Fitzgerald Book). Tokyo: TBS Buritanika, 1988.

"News of the Screen: News from Hollywood." *New York Times* June 16, 1937: 27.

Nietzsche, Friedrich. *The Genealogy of Morals.* Trans. Horace B. Samuel. New York: Boni & Liveright, 1921.

———. *The Philosophy of Friedrich Nietzsche.* New York: Modern Library, 1940.

Nolan, William F., and Charles Beaumont. "The Mystery of Diamond Mountain." *Mickey Mouse,* no. 47 (1956): 1–15. Reprinted in *Walt Disney's Comics and Stories,* no. 547 (1990): 47–63, and no. 612 (1997): 41–55.

O'Connor, Flannery. *The Habit of Being: Letters of Flannery O'Connor.* Ed. Sally Fitzgerald. New York: Farrar, Straus and Giroux, 1979.

O'Hara, John. *Assembly.* New York: Random House, 1961.

Ornstein, Robert. "Scott Fitzgerald's Fable of East and West." *College English* 18 (1956): 139–43.

Page, Thomas Nelson. "Marse Chan." 1884. *The Literary South.* Ed. Louis J. Rubin, Jr. Baton Rouge: Louisiana State UP, 1981. 342–60.

Parker, Dorothy. "Professional Youth." *Saturday Evening Post* April 28, 1923: 14, 156–57.

Pater, Walter. *The Renaissance: Studies in Art and Poetry.* London: Macmillan, 1910.

Pawling, Christopher, ed. *Popular Fiction and Social Change.* New York: St. Martin's P, 1984.

Percy, Walker. *Love in the Ruins.* 1971. New York: Avon, 1981.

Petry, Alice Hall. *Fitzgerald's Craft of Short Fiction: The Collected Stories, 1920–1935.* Ann Arbor: UMI Research P, 1989.

Phillips, Gene D. *Fiction, Film and F. Scott Fitzgerald.* Chicago: Loyola UP, 1986.

Piper, Henry Dan. *F. Scott Fitzgerald: A Critical Portrait.* New York: Holt, Rinehart and Winston, 1965.

Potts, Stephen W. *The Price of Paradise: The Magazine Career of F. Scott Fitzgerald.* San Bernardino, CA: Borgo, 1993.

Prigozy, Ruth. "Gatsby's Guest List and Fitzgerald's Technique of Naming." *Fitzgerald/Hemingway Annual* 4 (1972): 99–112.

——. "The Unpublished Stories: Fitzgerald in His Final Stage." *Twentieth Century Literature* 20 (1974): 69–90.

Quirk, Tom. "Fitzgerald and Cather: *The Great Gatsby.*" *American Literature* 54 (1982): 576–91.

Reiter, Rayna R., ed. *Toward an Anthropology of Women.* New York: Monthly Review P, 1975.

Rideout, Walter B. *The Radical Novel in the United States.* 1956. New York: Hill and Wang, 1966.

Riviere, Joan. "Womanliness as a Masquerade." 1929. *Formations of Fantasy.* Ed. Victor Burgin, James Donald, and Cora Kaplan. London: Methuen, 1986. 15–44.

Roberts, Victoria. *My Day.* London: Chatto & Windus/Hogarth P, 1984.

Rodewald, F. A. "Faulkner's Possible Use of *The Great Gatsby.*" *Fitzgerald/Hemingway Annual* 7 (1975): 97–101.

Roethke, Theodore. *Straw for the Fire: The Notebooks of Theodore Roethke, 1943–63.* Ed. David Wagoner. Garden City: Anchor, 1974.

Roulston, Robert. "Whistling 'Dixie' in Encino: *The Last Tycoon* and F. Scott Fitzgerald's Two Souths." *South Atlantic Quarterly* 79 (1980): 355–63.

Roulston, Robert, and Helen H. Roulston. *The Winding Road to West Egg: The Artistic Development of F. Scott Fitzgerald.* Lewisburg, PA: Bucknell UP, 1995.

Rubin, Louis D., Jr. *The Comic Imagination in American Literature.* New Brunswick, NJ: Rutgers UP, 1983.

Scholes, Robert E. "The Modern American Novel and the Mason-Dixon Line." *Georgia Review* 14 (1960): 193–204.

Schopenhauer, Arthur. *Essays and Aphorisms.* Trans. R. J. Hollingdale. Baltimore: Penguin, 1970.

Schulz, Charles M. Letter to M. Thomas Inge. February 27, 1996.

——. *Peanuts.* Comic strip. *Washington Post* May 31, June 3, June 7, December 19, 1991; June 26, 1995.

Scott, Walter. "Personality Parade." *Parade* May 13, 1973: 2.

"Screen News in Brief." *New York Times* June 5, 1937: 10: 4.

Siegfried, Charlene Haddock. *William James's Radical Reconstruction of Philosophy.* Albany: State U of New York P, 1990.

Silverman, Jeff. "To Make a Hit, You Need a Pitch." *New York Times* May 3, 1992: 2: 1, 20–21.

Simms, L. Moody, Jr. "Corra Harris on the Declining Influence of Thomas Nelson Page." *Mississippi Quarterly* 28 (1975): 505–9.

Simpson, Lewis P. "Garden Myth." *Encyclopedia of Southern Culture.* Ed. Charles Reagan Wilson and William Ferris. Chapel Hill: U of North Carolina P, 1989. 1108–9.

Sklar, Robert. *F. Scott Fitzgerald: The Last Laocoön.* New York: Oxford UP, 1967.

Smith, Curtis C., ed. *Twentieth-Century Science Fiction Writers.* 2nd ed. Chicago: St. James P, 1986.

Smith-Rosenberg, Carroll. "The New Woman." *The Reader's Companion to U.S. Women's History.* Ed. Wilma Mankiller et al. Boston: Houghton Mifflin, 1998. 430.

Spacks, Patricia Meyer. *The Adolescent Idea: Myths of Youth and the Adult Imagination.* New York: Basic Books, 1978.

Stallman, R. W. *The Houses that James Built and Other Literary Studies.* East Lansing: Michigan State UP, 1961.

Stavola, Thomas J. *F. Scott Fitzgerald: Crisis in an American Identity.* New York: Barnes & Noble, 1979.

Stern, Milton R., ed. *Critical Essays on F. Scott Fitzgerald's "Tender is the Night."* Boston: G. K. Hall, 1986.

——. *The Golden Moment: The Novels of F. Scott Fitzgerald.* Urbana: U of Illinois P, 1970.

——. "On Editing Dead Modern Authors: Fitzgerald and Trimalchio." *F. Scott Fitzgerald Society Newsletter* 10 (2000): 9–18.

——. *"Tender Is the Night": The Broken Universe.* New York: Twayne, 1994.

Stone, Edward. "More About Gatsby's Guest List." *Fitzgerald/Hemingway Annual* 4 (1972): 315–16.

Suckiel, Ellen Kappy. *The Pragmatic Philosophy of William James.* Notre Dame, IN: U of Notre Dame P, 1982.

Tamke, Alexander R. "Abe North as Abe Lincoln in *Tender Is the Night.*" *Fitzgerald Newsletter,* no. 36 (1967): 6–7.

——. "Basil Duke Lee: The Confederate F. Scott Fitzgerald." *Mississippi Quarterly* 20 (1967): 231–33.

Thompson, Anne. "Late Author Connects Jazz Age to Generation X." *Montgomery (AL) Advertiser* September 23, 1996: D2.

Toklas, Alice B. "They Who Came to Paris to Write: Impressions, Observations and Asides by Gertrude Stein's Closest Companion." *New York Times Book Review* August 6, 1950: 1, 25.

Torcivia, Joe. *Mickey Mouse Checklist.* Los Angeles: The Duckburg Times, 1983.

Tracy, David. *The Analogical Imagination.* New York: Crossroad, 1981.

Trilling, Lionel. *The Last Decade: Essays and Reviews, 1965–75.* New York: Harcourt Brace Jovanovich, 1977.

———. *The Liberal Imagination.* 1950. New York: Harcourt Brace Jovanovich, 1977.

Turnbull, Andrew. *Scott Fitzgerald.* New York: Scribner's, 1962.

Updike, John. "Tummy Trouble in Tinseltown." *New Yorker* August 5, 1996: 74–75.

Wagner-Martin, Linda. *The Modern American Novel, 1914–1945.* Boston: Twayne, 1990.

Way, Brian. *F. Scott Fitzgerald and the Art of Social Fiction.* New York: St. Martin's P, 1980.

West, James L. W., III. "Fitzgerald Explodes His Heroine." *Princeton University Library Chronicle* 49 (1988): 159–65.

———. *The Making of "This Side of Paradise."* Philadelphia: U of Pennsylvania P, 1983.

White, E. B. *Essays of E. B. White.* New York: Harper, 1977.

Whitman, Walt. *Complete Poetry and Collected Prose.* Ed. Justin Kaplan. New York: Library of America, 1982.

Wilson, Earl. "Kindness Brings Actress Tears." *Richmond (VA) Times-Dispatch* June 10, 1973: H-2.

Wilson, Edmund, ed. *The Crack-up.* New York: New Directions, 1945.

———. *Patriotic Gore: Studies in the Literature of the American Civil War.* New York: Oxford UP, 1962.

Witham, W. Tasker. *The Adolescent in the American Novel, 1920–1960.* New York: Frederick Ungar, 1964.

Woodward, Kenneth. "Do We Need Satan?" *Newsweek* November 13, 1995: 63–68.

Wordsworth, William. *The Prelude: 1799, 1805, 1850.* Ed. Jonathan Wordsworth, M. H. Abrams, and Stephen Gill. New York: Norton, 1979.

———. *Selected Poems and Prefaces.* Ed. Jack Stillinger. Boston: Houghton Mifflin, 1965.

Yates, Donald A. "The Road to 'Paradise': Fitzgerald's Literary Apprenticeship." *Modern Fiction Studies* 7 (1961): 19–31.

Yongue, Patricia L. "*A Lost Lady:* The End of the First Cycle." *Western American Literature* 7 (1972): 3–12.

Zabel, Morton D. *Craft and Character.* New York: Viking P, 1957.

Žižek, Slavoj. *The Metastases of Enjoyment.* London: Verso, 1994.

CONTRIBUTORS

CHRISTOPHER AMES is provost at Oglethorpe University. He is the author of *Movies about the Movies: Hollywood Reflected* and *The Life of the Party: Festive Vision and Modern Fiction,* which includes a chapter on parties in Fitzgerald's work. He teaches twentieth-century literature and film; his current research is on Hollywood fiction.

MARY MCALEER BALKUN is associate professor of English at Seton Hall University. She has published essays on William Faulkner, Walt Whitman, and Phillis Wheatley. She is working on a book-length study of the intersections of authenticity, identity, and material culture in American literature between 1880 and 1930.

STANLEY BRODWIN was emeritus professor of English at Hofstra University. He was the editor of *The Old and New World Romanticism of Washington Irving* and the coeditor of *William Cullen Bryant and His America* and *The Harlem Renaissance: An Appraisal.* His essays on, among other subjects, Melville, Emerson, Hawthorne, Twain, Steinbeck, and the Broadway theater, appeared in such journals as *PMLA, Journal of the History of Ideas, American Literature, Philological Quarterly,* and *Criticism.* He was a sponsored Fellow of the Jewish Theological Seminary.

JACKSON R. BRYER is professor of English at the University of Maryland. He is co-founder and president of the F. Scott Fitzgerald Society and author of *The Critical Reputation of F. Scott Fitzgerald;* editor of *F. Scott Fitzgerald: The Critical Reception, The Short Stories of F. Scott Fitzgerald: New Approaches in Criticism,* and *New Essays on F. Scott Fitzgerald's Neglected Stories;* and coeditor of *F. Scott Fitz-*

gerald in His Own Time: A Miscellany, Dear Scott/Dear Max: The Fitzgerald-Perkins Correspondence, The Basil and Josephine Stories, French Connections: Hemingway and Fitzgerald Abroad, F. Scott Fitzgerald: New Perspectives, and *Dear Scott, Dearest Zelda: The Love Letters of F. Scott Fitzgerald and Zelda Fitzgerald.*

KIRK CURNUTT is associate professor of English at Troy State University in Montgomery, Alabama, where he serves on the board of the F. Scott and Zelda Fitzgerald Museum, located in the home which the Fitzgeralds rented in 1931–32. He is the author of *Wise Economics: Brevity and Storytelling in American Short Stories, Ernest Hemingway and the Expatriate Modernist Movement,* and *Alienated-Youth Fiction,* and the editor of *The Critical Response to Gertrude Stein.* He is currently editing "An Historical Guide to F. Scott Fitzgerald."

ANNE MARGARET DANIEL has taught at Princeton University, Georgetown University, the University of Richmond, the New School University, and the Yeats International Summer School in Sligo, Ireland. She is completing a book about cultural and literary representations of redheads; her future plans include a biography of Vanessa Bell.

MORRIS DICKSTEIN is distinguished professor of English at the Graduate Center of the City University of New York. He is the author of *Keats and His Poetry, Gates of Eden, Double Agent: The Critic and Society,* and *Leopards in the Temple: The Transformation of American Fiction, 1945–1970.* He is a senior fellow and founder of CUNY's Center for the Humanities.

EDWARD GILLIN is associate professor of English at the State University College of New York in Geneseo. He is the author of numerous essays and book reviews on Fitzgerald and has published articles on Melville, Thomas Wolfe, Lillian Hellman, and several Irish playwrights.

JANET GILTROW is associate professor of English at the University of British Columbia, where she teaches in the language and rhetoric program. She is the author of *Academic Writing: Writing and Reading in the Disciplines* (currently in its 3rd edition), editor of *Academic Reading: Reading and Writing in the Disciplines* (currently in its 2nd edition), and author of numerous articles and book chapters on literary and non-literary stylistics, travel narrative, rhetorical theories of genre, and ideologies of language.

M. THOMAS INGE is the Robert Emory Blackwell professor of English and Humanities at Randolph-Macon College, where he teaches American studies, interdisciplinary humanities, and Asian literature. Among his recent books are *Conversations with William Faulkner*, *Charles M. Schulz: Conversations*, and the 4-volume *Greenwood Guide to American Popular Culture*. His current projects include books on William Faulkner, American humor, Walt Disney, and comics and American literature.

D. G. KEHL is professor of English at Arizona State University, where he teaches courses in American literary humor, contemporary Southern fiction, American literature and the Holocaust, Fitzgerald, Flannery O'Connor, and Eudora Welty. He has published articles on modernist and post-modernist American writers and three books, including *Poetry and the Visual Arts*.

HORST H. KRUSE is professor emeritus of English and American literature and former head of American Studies at the University of Munster in Germany. He is the author of *Mark Twain and "Life on the Mississippi"* and of numerous essays on Fitzgerald.

VERONICA MAKOWSKY is associate dean of the College of Liberal Arts and Sciences at the University of Connecticut, where she is also professor of English and Women's Studies. She is the editor of *MELUS* and has published books and articles on Susan Glaspell, Caroline Gordon, Margaret Atwood, and Walker Percy, among others.

TOSHIFUMI MIYAWAKI is professor of American literature at Seikei University, Tokyo, Japan. He is the co-editor of *Lamentations of America: Puritanism in American Literary History* and author of essays on Fitzgerald, Hemingway, and Haruki Murakami. He has also translated Janet Flanner's *Paris Was Yesterday: 1925–1939* into Japanese.

MICHAEL NOWLIN teaches American literature at the University of Victoria in Canada. He has published articles on Fitzgerald, Edith Wharton, Toni Morrison, and Lionel Trilling and has edited Wharton's *The Age of Innocence*. Currently, he is writing a study of Fitzgerald, race, and American popular culture.

TIM PRCHAL is visiting assistant professor of English at Oklahoma State University, where his specialties include nineteenth- and early-twentieth-century American literature, comparative ethnic literature (especially immigration literature), and popular genres of fiction. He is currently writing a book on how American realism offered its original readers games of make-believe that helped them adapt to profound cultural changes.

RUTH PRIGOZY is professor and former chair of the English Department at Hofstra University. She is the author of *F. Scott Fitzgerald: An Illustrated Life;* editor of *The Cambridge Companion to F. Scott Fitzgerald, The Great Gatsby, This Side of Paradise;* and coeditor of *F. Scott Fitzgerald: New Perspectives, Theory and Practice of Classic Detective Fiction, The Detective in American Fiction, Film, and Television,* and *Frank Sinatra and Popular Culture.* She is co-founder and executive director of the F. Scott Fitzgerald Society.

WALTER RAUBICHECK is professor of English at Pace University. He has co-edited a book on the films of Alfred Hitchcock and has published articles on American writers such as Whitman and Eliot. He also specializes in the study of detective fiction.

MILTON R. STERN is Alumni Association Distinguished Professor Emeritus at the University of Connecticut. His books include *The Fine Hammered Steel of Herman Melville, The Golden Moment: The Novels of F. Scott Fitzgerald, Contexts for Hawthorne,* and *Fitzgerald's "Tender Is the Night": The Broken Universe.* He is one of the founders of the Connecticut Humanities Council.

DAVID STOUCK is professor of English at Simon Fraser University in British Columbia, where he teaches American and Canadian literature. He is the author of *Willa Cather's Imagination* and *Major Canadian Authors* and editor of numerous books, including the scholarly edition of Cather's *O Pioneers!* In collaboration with Janet Giltrow, he has written essays on mode and language in the work of Hawthorne, Cather, and Michael Ondaatje.

STEPHEN L. TANNER is Ralph A. Britsch Humanities professor at Brigham Young University. He is the author of four books and numerous articles on American literature. He is a four-time Senior Fulbright Lecturer and recipient of the Lionel Trilling Award for distinguished literary criticism.

FREDERICK WEGENER is associate professor of English and director of the program in American Studies at California State University, Long Beach. He is the editor of *Edith Wharton: The Uncollected Critical Writings.* His essays have appeared in *American Literature, Texas Studies in Literature and Language, Tulsa Studies in Women's Literature,* and other journals.

INDEX